The Middle East in Turmoil Series

Iraq: Forward, Backward or Nowhere?

THE MIDDLE EAST IN TURMOIL SERIES

**The Middle East in Turmoil
Volume 1**
*John Canfeld
(Editor)*
2001. ISBN: 1-59033-160-5

Stabilizing and Rebuilding Iraq
*Russell E. Hargrove
(Editor)*
2009. ISBN: 978-1-60692-366-5

**Public Opinion and Solution Prospects
For Israeli-Palestinian Peace**
Jacob Shamir and Jim Zanotti
2010. ISBN: 978-1-60876-060-2

**Public Opinion and Solution Prospects
For Israeli-Palestinian Peace**
Jacob Shamir and Jim Zanotti
2010. ISBN: 978-1-60876-060-2
(Online Book)

**Nuclear Ambitions and Issues
in the Middle East**
*Nathan E. Cohen
(Editor)*
2010. ISBN: 978-1-61668-353-5

**Nuclear Ambitions and Issues
in the Middle East**
*Nathan E. Cohen
(Editor)*
2010. ISBN: 978-1-61668-389-4
(Online Book)

Israel vs. Hamas
*Nejc Kardelj
(Editor)*
2010. ISBN: 978-1-60741-518-3

**Iraqi Refugees:
A Humanitarian Crisis?**
*Agustin Sánchez
(Editor)*
2010. ISBN: 978-1-60876-131-9

**Regional Spillover
Effects from Iraq's Upheaval**
*Borje Ostergard
(Editor)*
2010. ISBN: 978-1-60741-520-6

**Palestinian History,
Politics and International Relations**
*George D. Hayes and Marcus P. Cooper
(Editors)*
2010. ISBN: 978-1-61668-809-7

**Palestinian History,
Politics and International Relations**
*George D. Hayes and Marcus P. Cooper
(Editors)*
2010. ISBN: 978-1-61668-877-6
(Online Book)

**Iraq: Forward,
Backward or Nowhere?**
*Frederick M. Golenberg
(Editor)*
2010. ISBN: 978-1-60741-018-8

THE MIDDLE EAST IN TURMOIL SERIES

IRAQ: FORWARD, BACKWARD OR NOWHERE?

FREDERICK M. GOLENBERG
EDITOR

Nova Science Publishers, Inc.

New York

Copyright © 2010 by Nova Science Publishers, Inc.

All rights reserved. No part of this book may be reproduced, stored in a retrieval system or transmitted in any form or by any means: electronic, electrostatic, magnetic, tape, mechanical photocopying, recording or otherwise without the written permission of the Publisher.

For permission to use material from this book please contact us:
Telephone 631-231-7269; Fax 631-231-8175
Web Site: http://www.novapublishers.com

NOTICE TO THE READER

The Publisher has taken reasonable care in the preparation of this book, but makes no expressed or implied warranty of any kind and assumes no responsibility for any errors or omissions. No liability is assumed for incidental or consequential damages in connection with or arising out of information contained in this book. The Publisher shall not be liable for any special, consequential, or exemplary damages resulting, in whole or in part, from the readers' use of, or reliance upon, this material. Any parts of this book based on government reports are so indicated and copyright is claimed for those parts to the extent applicable to compilations of such works.

Independent verification should be sought for any data, advice or recommendations contained in this book. In addition, no responsibility is assumed by the publisher for any injury and/or damage to persons or property arising from any methods, products, instructions, ideas or otherwise contained in this publication.

This publication is designed to provide accurate and authoritative information with regard to the subject matter covered herein. It is sold with the clear understanding that the Publisher is not engaged in rendering legal or any other professional services. If legal or any other expert assistance is required, the services of a competent person should be sought. FROM A DECLARATION OF PARTICIPANTS JOINTLY ADOPTED BY A COMMITTEE OF THE AMERICAN BAR ASSOCIATION AND A COMMITTEE OF PUBLISHERS.

LIBRARY OF CONGRESS CATALOGING-IN-PUBLICATION DATA

ISBN : 978-1-60741-018-8

Available Upon Request

Published by Nova Science Publishers, Inc. ✦ *New York*

CONTENTS

Preface		vii
Chapter 1	Iraq: Politics, Elections, and Benchmarks *Kenneth Katzman*	1
Chapter 2	Iraq: Key Issues for Congressional Oversight *Government Accountability Office*	17
Chapter 3	Measuring Stability and Security in Iraq *Department of Defense Supplemental Appropriations*	69
Chapter 4	Operation Iraqi Freedom: Strategies, Approaches, Results and Issues for Congress *Catherine Dale*	141
Chapter Sources		277
Index		279

PREFACE

The United States seeks an Iraq that is sovereign, stable, and self-reliant; an Iraqi Government that is just, representative, and accountable; neither a safe haven for, nor sponsor of, terrorism; integrated into the global economy; and a long-term partner contributing to regional peace and security. The United States is pursuing this goal along political, security, economic, diplomatic, and rule of law lines of operation. In 2009, the war in Iraq appears to be winding down, as security gains made since the height of the insurgency in 2006 and 2007 continue to be sustained, and as Iraqis increasingly seek management of their own affairs. A new U.S.-Iraqi Security Agreement that went into effect on January 1, which confirmed the Iraqi's responsibility for their own security, introduced a new era in Operation Iraqi Freedom, and in U.S.-Iraqi bilateral relations. This book measures the stability and security in Iraq today, and looks at the strategies, approaches, results and "winding down" of military involvement of Operation Iraqi Freedom.This book consists of public documents which have been located, gathered, combined, reformatted, and enhanced with a subject index, selectively edited and bound to provide easy access.

Chapter 1 - Iraq's political system, the result of a U.S.-supported election process, is increasingly exhibiting peaceful competition but continues to be riven by sectarianism and ethnic and factional infighting. As 2009 began, there was renewed maneuvering by opponents of Prime Minister Nurial-Maliki who view him as authoritarian and might try to replace him, particularly if his party had fared poorly in the January 31, 2009 provincial elections. However, campaigning for the provincial elections, held in all provinces except Kirkuk and the Kurdish-controlled provinces, was relatively peaceful and enthusiastic and there was a more diverse array of party slates than those that characterized the January 2005 provincial elections. The elections appear to have strengthened Maliki and others who believe that power should remain centralized in Baghdad.

Internal dissension within Iraq aside, the Bush Administration was optimistic that the passage of key laws in 2008, coupled with the provincial elections, would sustain recent reductions in violence. President Obama praised the orderliness and relative absence of violence of the elections—an outcome that appears to have reaffirmed the Obama Administration's belief that a reduction of the U.S. troop presence in Iraq can proceed without inordinate risk to Iraqi stability. The elections appear to also have reduced U.S. concerns about Iran's influence in Iraq, in part because pro-Iranian parties—particularly those that maintain militias armed by Iran—fared poorly in the elections. See CRS Report RL3 1339, *Iraq: Post-Saddam Governance and Security*, by Kenneth Katzman.

Chapter 2 - To assist the 111th Congress, we have enclosed a series of issue papers for consideration in developing congressional oversight agendas and determining the way forward in securing and stabilizing Iraq. These papers are based on the continuing work of the U.S. Government Accountability Office (GAO) and the more than 130 Iraq-related products we have issued since May 2003.

Since fiscal year 2001, Congress has provided about $808 billion to the Department of Defense (DOD) for military efforts primarily in support of the Global War on Terrorism.[1] The majority of this amount has been for military operations in support of Operation Iraqi Freedom. Moreover, since fiscal year 2003, about $49 billion[2] has been provided to U.S. agencies for stabilization and reconstruction efforts in Iraq, including developing Iraq's security forces, enhancing Iraq's capacity to govern, and rebuilding Iraq's oil, electricity, and water sectors, among other activities. This report expands on issues discussed on GAO's transition Web site, http://www.gao.gov/media/video/gao-09-294sp.

In January 2007, President Bush announced *The New Way Forward* in Iraq to stem violence and enable the Iraqi government to foster national reconciliation. This strategy established goals and objectives through July 2008 and reasserted the long-term goal or end state for Iraq: a unified, democratic, federal Iraq that can govern, defend, and sustain itself and is an ally in the war on terror. To support the strategy, the United States increased its military presence through a surge of brigade combat teams and associated forces. In June 2008, we reported that the United States had made some progress in reducing overall violence in Iraq and working with the Iraqi government to pass legislation promoting national reconciliation. However, many unmet goals and challenges remained, including building capacity in Iraq's ministries, helping the government execute its capital investment budgets, and providing essential services to the Iraqi people.[3]

With the completion of *The New Way Forward* and the end of the military surge in July 2008, we recommended that the Administration develop an updated strategy that clearly articulates U.S. goals, objectives, roles and responsibilities, and the military and civilian resources needed to build on security and legislative gains. Furthermore, in a second report,[4] we recommended revisions to the Joint Campaign Plan for Iraq—an operational plan for U.S. military and civilian activities in Iraq developed by the Multinational Force-Iraq (MNF-I) and the U.S. Embassy Baghdad— that would help Congress assess progress in achieving the conditions that would allow for the continued drawdown of U.S. forces in Iraq. Specifically, we recommended that DOD and the Department of State (State) identify and prioritize the conditions that must be achieved in each phase of the campaign to enable a drawdown; report the number of U.S. combat brigade teams and other forces required for each campaign phase; and estimate the time needed to reach the desired end state and end the military portion of the campaign. The strategic level actions we called for in our first report would guide revisions to the Joint Campaign Plan.[5]

In February 2009, President Obama described a new strategy for Iraq consisting of three parts: (1) the responsible removal of combat brigades, (2) sustained diplomacy on behalf of a more peaceful and prosperous Iraq, and (3) comprehensive U.S. engagement across the region. According to DOD, the United States plans to reduce the number of combat troops from about 140,000 projected in March 2009 to about 128,000 by September 2009—a difference of 12,000 troops representing two brigades and their support units. Under the schedule announced by the President, U.S. force levels would decline further by August 31, 2010, to no more than 50,000 troops. Under the November 2008 bilateral security agreement[6] between the United States and Iraq, the United States must remove all of its remaining forces by December 31, 2011.

The issues discussed in the enclosures to this report should be considered in further defining the new strategy and its supporting operational plans. Key issues include:

- The security agreement establishes dates for repositioning U.S. forces in Iraq and removing them from the country—a significant change from the United States' prior, conditions-based strategy for Iraq. A responsible drawdown in Iraq will need to balance the timetable established in the security agreement, military doctrine that calls for the delineation of conditions that must exist before military operations can end, and the wishes of the Iraqi government.
- If the United States adheres to the timetable contained in the security agreement, DOD will need to remove about 140,000 troops by the end of 2011. The redeployment of these forces and the removal of their equipment and material will be a massive and expensive effort.
- The large U.S. military presence has provided vital support to civilian operations and has undertaken many traditionally civilian tasks. In moving forward, the United States will need to consider how to transition from a predominantly military presence to a civilian one as U.S. forces draw down.
- As U.S reconstruction efforts end, Iraq will need to develop the capacity to spend its resources, particularly on investment that will further economic development and deliver essential services to its people. GAO estimates that the Iraqi government had a cumulative budget surplus of $47 billion at the end of 2008.

We obtained information from agency documents and interviews with U.S. officials in Iraq and Washington, D.C., including DOD, State, and the Departments of Energy and the Treasury; the U.S. Agency for International Development (USAID); the Army Corps of Engineers; MNF-I; and the Defense Intelligence Agency. We conducted this performance audit in accordance with generally accepted government auditing standards. Those standards require that we plan and perform the audit to obtain sufficient, appropriate evidence to provide a reasonable basis for our findings and conclusions based on our audit objectives. We believe that the evidence obtained provides a reasonable basis for our findings and conclusions based on our audit objectives. Appendix I contains additional details about our scope and methodology. Appendix II provides updated information on the levels of violence in Iraq, as measured by the number of enemy-initiated attacks, and on the number of U.S. troops in Iraq. Appendix IV contains a list of GAO products directly related to this letter and each of the enclosures.

The Department of the Treasury provided written comments on a draft of this report, which are reprinted in appendix III. Treasury agreed that although Iraq's end-2008 cumulative surplus fell short of GAO's earlier projection, Iraq's budget surpluses will sufficiently cover its projected 2009 budget deficit. Treasury also agreed that Iraq's inability to fully execute its budgets hampers the government's efforts to further reconstruction and economic growth. Treasury, DOD, State, and USAID also provided technical comments, which we have incorporated as appropriate.

We are sending copies of this report to the congressional committees listed below. In addition, we are sending copies of this report to the President and Vice President of the

United States, and executive branch agencies. The report also is available at no charge on the GAO Web site at http://www.gao.gov. If you have any questions, please contact Joseph A. Christoff at (202) 512-8979 or christoffj@gao.gov, or the individual(s) listed at the end of each enclosure. Contact points for our Offices of Congressional Relations and Public Affairs can be found on the last page of this report. For press inquiries, please contact Chuck Young at (202) 512-4800. Key contributors to this report are included in appendix V.

Chapter 3 - This report to Congress, Measuring Stability and Security in Iraq, is submitted pursuant to Section 9204 of the Supplemental Appropriations Act for 2008, Public Law 110-252. This report is also submitted pursuant to Section 1508(c) of the Department of Defense Authorization Act for 2009, Public Law 110-417. The report includes specific performance indicators and measures of progress toward political, economic, and security stability in Iraq, as directed by legislation. This is the fifteenth report in this series of quarterly reports. The most recent report was submitted in January 2009. The report complements other reports and information about Iraq provided to Congress and is not intended as a single source of all information about the combined efforts or the future strategy of the United States, its Coalition partners, or Iraq.

The United States seeks an Iraq that is sovereign, stable, and self-reliant; an Iraqi Government that is just, representative, and accountable; neither a safe haven for, nor sponsor of, terrorism; integrated into the global economy; and a long-term partner contributing to regional peace and security. The United States is pursuing this goal along political, security, economic, diplomatic, and rule of law lines of operation. This report indicates progress along these lines from December 2008 through February 2009 and highlights the challenges in achieving both Coalition and Iraqi objectives.

With the entry into force and implementation of the Strategic Framework Agreement (SFA) and Security Agreement (SA), this reporting period witnessed a historic transition in the nature of the relationship between the United States and Iraq. A comprehensive agreement, the SFA begins to normalize U.S.-Iraq relations through economic, diplomatic, cultural, and security ties, and it will serve as a foundation for a longterm bilateral relationship based on common goals and interests. The SA governs U.S. forces' presence in Iraq, provides Iraqi authority for combat operations and detention activities, and provided the time frame for withdrawal from Iraq. The successful transfer of security authority from Coalition forces to the Government of Iraq (GoI), conducted on January 1, 2009, marked an important milestone in the development of this relationship. There have been no major issues to date in the coordination of detention operations. Multi-National Forces-Iraq (MNF-I) continues to release security detainees captured prior to December 31, 2008, in a safe and orderly manner in consultation with the GoI.

On February 27, 2009, the President of the United States announced a plan to commence a phased drawdown of U.S. combat brigades from Iraq by August 31, 2010. By this time, U.S. forces will have completed the transition from combat and counterinsurgency activities to a more limited mission set that focuses on training and assisting the Iraqi Security Forces (ISF), providing force protection for U.S. military and civilian personnel and facilities, conducting targeted counter-terrorism operations, and supporting civilian agencies and international organizations in their capacity-building efforts. Further drawdowns will occur in accordance with the U.S.-Iraq SA. The pace of the drawdown takes into consideration Iraq's improved, yet fragile, security gains and provides U.S. commanders sufficient flexibility to assist the Iraqis with emerging challenges. As combat brigades are responsibly redeployed, the United States will also continue to pursue other aspects of its strategy, including sustained diplomacy with a more peaceful and prosperous Iraq.

Iraq continues to make progress, as Iraqis increasingly choose the political process over violence. On January 31, 2009, the people of Iraq demonstrated their confidence in both the political process and the improved security environment through active participation in provincial elections. Although the first provincial elections in 2005 marked an important step in Iraq's transition to democracy and representative governance, this year's provincial elections were the first to draw broad-based participation by all religious and ethnic groups. The Independent High Electoral Commission (IHEC), with significant support from the United Nations Assistance Mission for Iraq (UNAMI), organized, conducted, and monitored the process. The elections were deemed credible and legitimate by international monitors and observers, taking place with minimal violence or complaints of voter fraud or intimidation. The process of forming governing provincial coalitions is underway.

Despite these positive developments, national reconciliation and accommodation continue to be hindered by the pursuit of ethno-sectarian agendas and disagreements over the distribution of power and resources at all levels. This is underscored by significant distrust between partisan national leaders. Arab-Kurd tensions continue to grow, surrounding the debate over the centralization versus decentralization of power, the resolution of disputed internal boundaries, property rights and restitution, the status of the Kurdistan Regional Government's (KRG) Peshmerga, the status of Kirkuk, and the resolution of hydrocarbon policy. Tensions between the Iraqi Army (IA) and the Peshmerga in and around disputed territories continue to be a flashpoint for potential violence. In addition, longstanding Sunni-Shi'a discord remains, with some Sunnis suspicious of the extent of the Shi'a political parties' ties to Iran and doubtful of the GoI's long-term commitment to the Sons of Iraq (SoI) transition program and the implementation of the Amnesty and Accountability and Justice Laws. Intrasectarian political tensions also continue, as evidenced by the defection of some members of Tawafuq to other same-sect parties competing for voter support during the provincial elections. Furthermore, there is growing opposition between those favoring a strong central government versus a highly decentralized government. The GoI will also have to address the issue of resettling refugees and internally displaced persons. These issues will require Iraq's political blocs to overcome their fears and build coalitions that reach across ethnic lines to compromise on sensitive political issues. Additional efforts toward dispute resolution will be required for the development of a secure and stable Iraq.

The overall security situation continues to slowly improve, with security incidents remaining at the same low levels as experienced in early 2004. In much of the country, a sense of normalcy is returning to everyday life, and citizens are increasingly focused on economic issues and the delivery of essential services. With more Iraqis now describing their neighborhoods as calm, the environment is slowly growing more conducive to economic and infrastructure development. Numerous factors have contributed to improved security, including effective Coalition and Iraqi counter-terror operations, increasing capabilities of the ISF, and the rejection of violence and extremism by the Iraqi people. Insurgent- initiated attacks have decreased from an average of 22 per day during the previous reporting period to 12 per day during this reporting period, but insurgents still have the capacity to conduct high-profile attacks. Although these security achievements are increasingly positive, they remain fragile in some places, most notably in Ninewa and Diyala Provinces, as well as in some parts of Baghdad.

Several threat groups remain dangerous and require continued focus to prevent their resurgence. The long-term threat remains Iranian-sponsored Shi'a militant groups, Asa'ib Al-Haq (AAH), Ketaib Hezbollah (KH), and unaligned Shi'a extremists, including the newly-formed Promised Day Brigade. In addition, violent Sunni insurgent groups and Al Qaeda in Iraq (AQI) are still a major security concern.

Iran continues to pose a significant challenge to Iraq's long-term stability and political independence. Despite repeated promises to the contrary, Iran attempted to derail the negotiation of a security agreement between the United States and the GoI, but ultimately achieved little success in affecting the SFA or the SA. Iran continues to host, train, fund, arm, and guide militant groups that seek to bleed the U.S. in Iraq, and Tehran remains opposed to a long-term partnership between the GoI and the United States. Tehran's overarching policy goal for Iraq is to prevent the emergence of a threat to Iran from Iraqi territory, either from the GoI or the United States. Iran seeks a Shi'a-led government in which Tehran's Shi'a allies—such as the Islamic Supreme Council in Iraq (ISCI) and the Da'wa party—hold the majority of political, economic, and security power. Tehran would prefer the GoI remain stable but relatively weak, providing Iran with opportunities to exert political and economic influence in Iraq and preventing the emergence of a regional competitor. Tehran remains determined to build influence in Iraq as part of a strategy to attain a preeminent role in the region, but Iraqi nationalism may act as a check on Iran's ambitions.

Despite these challenges, Iraqi forces continue to steadily improve their ability to provide basic security to the Iraqi people and, with Coalition support, extend security toward Iraq's borders. During this reporting period, the number of ISF battalions capable of taking the lead in counterinsurgency (COIN) operations has increased, and ISF leadership has improved its ability to command and control multiple brigade-sized elements from both the Iraqi Army and the National Police. With decreased Coalition support, Iraqi forces are beginning to take the lead in eliminating terrorist safe havens and reducing the flow of foreign fighters into Iraq. Tactical successes in ongoing joint Coalition and ISF operations against AAH, KH, Special Groups (SG), and AQI in Baghdad, Basrah, Diyala, Maysan, and Ninewa Provinces have demonstrated ISF's slow, but steady, improvement in their capability to combat extremists. A good demonstration of this continued progress was the planning and execution of a well-crafted security plan in support of the provincial elections held in late January 2009 with limited Coalition assistance. The ISF continues to gain the trust, confidence, and support of the Iraqi populace.

While making significant gains, the ISF continue to rely on the Coalition for logistics, fire support, close air support, communications, planning assistance, and intelligence, surveillance, and reconnaissance capabilities, particularly in northern Iraq. The leadership of the Ministries of Defense (MoD) and Interior (MoI) are making improvements in these areas and have prioritized efforts to expand infrastructure and improve budget execution. However, the global economic downturn and steep drop in oil prices could curtail the rate at which Iraqi forces can become fully modernized, self sufficient, and COIN capable, particularly in the near term. Finally, the Coalition remains a moderating force in the sometimes tense areas near disputed internal boundaries.

In addition to the SFA and SA, the GoI has negotiated Memoranda of Understanding with the United Kingdom, Australia, and Romania for military forces from those countries to continue supporting operations in Iraq through July 31, 2009. The size of the U.S. and Coalition footprint in Iraq continues to be steadily reduced and reshaped. Since January 1, 2009, five U.S. military units have redeployed from Iraq without replacement to include military police, engineers, logistics, and explosive ordnance disposal units, varying in size from detachment to battalion headquarters. Similarly, Coalition forces from Albania, Armenia, Azerbaijan, Bosnia, Bulgaria, Czech Republic, Denmark, El Salvador, Estonia, Georgia, Japan, Kazakhstan, Korea, Latvia, Lithuania, Macedonia, Moldova, Mongolia, Poland, Tonga, and Ukraine successfully completed their missions and departed Iraq since the last report. The GoI and NATO have negotiated an arrangement to enable the NATO Training Mission – Iraq (NTM-I) to continue specified missions until July 2009; follow-on negotiations to extend this training program beyond July 2009 are ongoing.

Turnover of the SoI program to the GoI has proceeded smoothly thus far. On October 1, 2008, the GoI assumed responsibility for nearly 51,000 SoI in the Baghdad area. Since then, the GoI has taken control of SoI programs in Diyala, Babil, Wasit, Qadisiyah, and Anbar Provinces, marking an important step toward national reconciliation. As of January 31, 2009, 77% of Iraq's SoI members have been transferred to GoI responsibility, and by April 1, 2009, SoI from Ninewa, Salah ad Din, and Tamim Provinces are scheduled to be transferred. Of the 94,000 SoI members remaining as of October 1, 2008, the GoI has pledged that 20% will be transitioned to the ISF, with the rest to be vetted for other civil servant positions or provided training or other support for transitioning into private-sector employment. Since October 2008, more than 5,000 of these have transitioned to the ISF, other ministries, or other non-security education, training, and support jobs programs. Long-term plans include increased education, training, and private sector employment opportunities. Although these steps have been encouraging, successfully transitioning SoI to permanent employment remains a long-term challenge for the GoI, particularly in light of recent budget concerns.

The decline in world oil prices has presented a number of challenges forcing the GoI to adopt a more conservative fiscal approach and seek additional efficiencies. Revenue from oil production comprises over 90% of the GoI's revenues, making the economy highly vulnerable to changes in the market price of oil. This situation has alerted Iraqi leaders of the need to heavily invest in oil infrastructure capacity to ensure stable production levels in the short term and to increase non-oil sector growth in the long term. The GoI currently faces a budget deficit of $20 billion in 2009 based on a price of $50 per barrel and an export rate of 2.0 million barrels per day. Current oil prices and export levels fall short of these estimates and will increase the budget deficit if the price of oil remains at its current levels. These shortfalls forced several revisions of the 2009 Iraqi Budget, passed by the Council of Representatives (CoR) on March 5, 2009. Core inflation remains persistent, although the Central Bank of Iraq continues to appreciate its exchange rate gradually to quell inflationary pressures and stimulate employment.

The GoI continues to show improvement in managing and executing its operations budget and capital projects, though significant challenges remain. From January through the end of November 2008, the GoI had spent a total of $41.2 billion, significantly more the $23 billion spent over the same period in 2007. The Ministry of Finance's (MoF) special report on capital funds indicates that through the end of September 2008, a total of $7.6 billion had been spent or committed. GoI ministries and provinces spent or committed $1.5 billion in September 2008 alone, a 20% share of the 2008 total. Additionally, Iraq continues to reduce its external debt burden. Following three years of satisfactory performance under

International Monetary Fund Stand-By Arrangements, the GoI received its final tranche of Paris Club debt relief.

Improvement continues, albeit slowly, in the provision of essential services. Recent electricity production has reached record highs, and although the overall average generation for 2008 was 14% higher than 2007, demand for electricity continues to increase and exceed supply. Similarly, many Iraqis continue to have limited access to clean water, and challenges continue with respect to sewage services and water treatment plant operations, maintenance, and sustainment. Also, the Ministry of Health (MoH) continues to face a severe shortage of healthcare professionals, though the much improved security environment and concerted efforts by the MoH have resulted in more than 1,000 Iraqi physicians being repatriated and returned to serve in Iraq during 2008.

The GoI continues to strengthen its bilateral diplomatic relationships with regional partners and the international community. Iraqi Ambassadors have been dispatched to Syria, Lebanon, Turkey, and Qatar; and in recent months, the Arab League, Bahrain, Jordan, Kuwait, Syria, and the United Arab Emirates appointed ambassadors to Iraq. Also, Egypt has pledged to re-establish its diplomatic mission. In addition, trilateral talks with Turkey and the United States are encouraging and are a positive step toward improving security conditions in northern Iraq. UNAMI and NTM-I are engaged in a broad range of ongoing efforts and are committing their support for Iraq. Iraq's diplomatic relations with its regional neighbors will become increasingly important for security and stability as the GoI and the United States transition to a long-term strategic relationship.

Establishing a foundation for the rule of law in Iraq continues to face a number of challenges, and helping the GoI to bolster programs for judicial security has become one of the highest priorities. To counter intimidation of judicial officials, the Higher Judicial Council currently provides transportation for judges who try cases away from their home districts as a temporary measure. Until the GoI can provide adequate security to allow the full-time posting of judges within all judicial districts, the exercise of a fair criminal justice system in Iraq remains at risk. Additionally, the court system faces severe capacity challenges, leaving courts that handle the most serious violent crimes overwhelmed. Despite these challenges, Iraq's judicial security and rule of law capacity continues to mature with the assistance of the U.S. Embassy and Provincial Reconstruction Teams throughout Iraq.

In summary, the political, security, economic, diplomatic, and rule of law trends in Iraq remain generally positive, though key challenges remain. With the conclusion and the implementation of the SFA and SA, this reporting period witnessed significant steps toward the development of a U.S.-Iraq strategic relationship, setting the stage for long-term cooperative efforts as Iraq continues to develop as a stable partner in the region. At the same time, continued reductions in violence have afforded Iraqis an environment in which political and economic development can occur, and the peaceful conduct of provincial elections in January 2009 was an indicator of progress. In accordance with the SA, the ISF have assumed primary security responsibility for Iraq and continue to improve their operational and tactical capabilities, although still relying on U.S. combat support enablers.

Despite the continued progress, these gains remain fragile and uneven throughout the country, and their durability has not been seriously tested. Iraq remains fragile, primarily because the underlying sources of instability have yet to be resolved—the nation's major power brokers do not share a unified national vision, they disagree on the nature of the state, and they are reluctant to share power and resources. As security has improved, underlying political disputes have risen to the forefront, and political tension remains a problem. The world witnessed issue-based provincial elections in Iraq in January 2009, signaling the emergence of unresolved problems, such as delivery of essential services and infrastructure improvement, as important to the Iraqi people. To institutionalize and sustain its sovereignty and stability, the GoI must build its legitimacy through the provision of basic services and improved security for the Iraqi people, as well as the continued resolution of political, ethnic, and sectarian divisions.

Chapter 4 - Operation Iraqi Freedom (OIF), the U.S.-led coalition military operation in Iraq, was launched on March 20, 2003, with the immediate stated goal of removing Saddam Hussein's regime and destroying its ability to use weapons of mass destruction or to make them available to terrorists. Over time, the focus of OIF shifted from regime removal to the more open-ended mission of helping the Government of Iraq (GoI) improve security, establish a system of governance, and foster economic development.

In 2009, the war in Iraq appears to be winding down, as security gains made since the height of the insurgency in 2006 and 2007 continue to be sustained, and as Iraqis increasingly seek management of their own affairs. A new U.S.-Iraqi security agreement that went into effect on January 1, 2009, which confirmed the Iraqis' responsibility for their own security, introduced a new era in OIF and in US-Iraqi bilateral relations. Secretary of Defense Robert Gates called the agreement a "watershed, a firm indication that American military involvement in Iraq is winding down." U.S. military commanders on the ground have indicated that in most parts of Iraq, the focus of U.S. military efforts has shifted from counterinsurgency (COIN) to stability operations, including advising the Iraqi Security Forces (ISF), and supporting security, economic, and governance capacity-building. On February 27, 2009, at Camp Lejeune in North Carolina, President Obama delivered a speech addressing "how the war in Iraq will end," in which he announced the drawdown of U.S. combat forces by August 2010 and the transition of the rest of the military mission to training and advising Iraq security forces, conducting counter-terrorism operations, and providing force protection for U.S. personnel.

The United States begins this transition from a position of significant commitment – including some 140,000 U.S. troops deployed in Iraq, in addition to civilian experts and U.S. contractors, who provide substantial support to their Iraqi counterparts in the fields of security, governance, and development. Senior U.S. officials, including outgoing U.S. Ambassador to Iraq Ryan Crocker, and Secretary Gates, have suggested that lasting change in Iraq will require substantially more time, and that while the U.S. military presence will diminish, U.S. engagement with Iraq is likely to continue. The Government of Iraq (GoI), for its part, still faces challenges at the operational level, in countering the lingering strands of the insurgency; and at the strategic level, in achieving a single, shared vision of the Iraqi state, and in improving its capacity to provide good governance, ensure security, and foster economic development for the Iraqi people.

Key policy issues the Obama Administration may choose to address, with oversight from the 111th Congress, include identifying how U.S. national interests and strategic objectives, in Iraq and the region, should guide further U.S. engagement; monitoring and evaluating the impact of the changes in the U.S. presence and role in Iraq; and laying the groundwork for a future, more traditional bilateral relationship.

In: Iraq: Forward, Backward or Nowhere?
Editor: Frederick M. Golenberg

ISBN: 978-1-60741-018-8
© 2010 Nova Science Publishers, Inc.

Chapter 1

IRAQ: POLITICS, ELECTIONS AND BENCHMARKS

Kenneth Katzman

SUMMARY

Iraq's political system, the result of a U.S.-supported election process, is increasingly exhibiting peaceful competition but continues to be riven by sectarianism and ethnic and factional infighting. As 2009 began, there was renewed maneuvering by opponents of Prime Minister Nurial-Maliki who view him as authoritarian and might try to replace him, particularly if his party had fared poorly in the January 31, 2009 provincial elections. However, campaigning for the provincial elections, held in all provinces except Kirkuk and the Kurdish-controlled provinces, was relatively peaceful and enthusiastic and there was a more diverse array of party slates than those that characterized the January 2005 provincial elections. The elections appear to have strengthened Maliki and others who believe that power should remain centralized in Baghdad.

Internal dissension within Iraq aside, the Bush Administration was optimistic that the passage of key laws in 2008, coupled with the provincial elections, would sustain recent reductions in violence. President Obama praised the orderliness and relative absence of violence of the elections—an outcome that appears to have reaffirmed the Obama Administration's belief that a reduction of the U.S. troop presence in Iraq can proceed without inordinate risk to Iraqi stability. The elections appear to also have reduced U.S. concerns about Iran's influence in Iraq, in part because pro-Iranian parties—particularly those that maintain militias armed by Iran—fared poorly in the elections. See CRS Report RL3 1339, *Iraq: Post-Saddam Governance and Security*, by Kenneth Katzman.

OVERVIEW OF THE POLITICAL TRANSITION

After the fall of Saddam Hussein's regime in April 2003, the United States set up an occupation structure, reportedly based on concerns that immediate sovereignty would favor major factions and not produce democracy. In May 2003, President Bush, reportedly seeking strong leadership in Iraq, named Ambassador L. Paul Bremer to head a "Coalition Provisional Authority" (CPA), which was recognized by the United Nations as an occupation authority. Bremer discontinued a tentative political transition process and instead appointed (July 13, 2003) a non-sovereign Iraqi advisory body: the 25-member "Iraq Governing Council" (IGC). After about one year of occupation, the United States handed sovereignty to an appointed Iraqi interim government on June 28, 2004. It was headed by a Prime Minister, Iyad al-Allawi, leader of the Iraq National Accord, a secular, non-sectarian faction. Allawi himself is a Shiite but many INA leaders were Sunnis, and some of them were formerly members of the Baath Party. The president of this interim government was Ghazi al-Yawar, a Sunni tribal figure who spent many years in exile in Saudi Arabia. A series of elections in 2005 produced the full term government that is in power today.

January 2005 National Assembly and Provincial Elections

In line with a March 8, 2004, "Transitional Administrative Law" (TAL, interim constitution), the first post-Saddam election was held on January 30, 2005, for a 275-seat transitional National Assembly (which formed an executive), four-year term provincial councils in all 18 provinces and a Kurdistan regional assembly (111 seats). The election system was proportional representation/closed list: voters chose among "political entities" (a party, a coalition of parties, or persons); 111 entities were on the national ballot, of which nine were multi-party coalitions. Sunni Arabs (20% of the overall population) boycotted, winning only 17 Assembly seats, and only one seat on the 51 seat Baghdad provincial council. That council was dominated (28 seats) by representatives of the Islamic Supreme Council of Iraq (ISCI), led by Abd al-Aziz al-Hakim. Radical Shiite cleric Moqtada Al Sadr, then at odds with U.S. forces, also boycotted, leaving his faction relatively under-represented on provincial councils in the Shiite south and in Baghdad. The resulting transitional government placed Shiites and Kurds in the most senior positions— Patriotic Union of Kurdistan (PUK) leader Jalal Talabani was President and Da'wa (Shiite party) leader Ibrahim al-Jafari was Prime Minister. Sunnis were Assembly speaker, deputy president, a deputy prime minister, and six ministers, including defense.

Permanent Constitution

The elected Assembly was to draft a constitution by August 15, 2005, to be put to a referendum by October 15, 2005, subject to veto by a two-thirds majority of voters in any three provinces. On May 10, 2005, a 55-member drafting committee was appointed, but with only two Sunni Arabs (15 Sunnis were later added as full members and 10 as advisors). In August 2005, the talks produced a draft, providing for: a December 31, 2007, deadline to hold a referendum on whether Kirkuk (Tamim province) will join the Kurdish region (Article 140); designation of Islam "a main source" of legislation;[1] a 25% electoral goal for women (Article 47); families choosing which courts to use for family issues (Article 41); making only primary education mandatory (Article 34); and having Islamic law experts and civil law judges on the federal supreme court (Article 89). Many women opposed the two latter provisions as giving too much discretion to male family members. It made all orders of the U.S.-led occupation authority (Coalition Provisional Authority, CPA) applicable until amended (Article 126), and established a "Federation Council" (Article 62), a second chamber with its size and powers to be determined by subsequent law (not adopted to date).

The major disputes—still unresolved—centered on regional versus centralized power. The draft permitted two or more provinces together to form new autonomous "regions"— reaffirmed in passage of an October 2006 law on formation of regions. Article 117 allows "regions" to organize internal security forces, legitimizing the fielding the Kurds' *peshmerga* militia (allowed by the TAL). Article 109 requires the central government to distribute oil and gas revenues from "current fields" in proportion to population, and gave regions a role in allocating revenues from new energy discoveries. Disputes over these concepts continue to hold up passage of national hydrocarbons legislation—Sunnis dominated areas of Iraq have few proven oil or gas deposits, and favor centralized control of oil revenues. The Kurds want to maintain maximum control of their own burgeoning oil sector.

With contentious provisions unresolved, Sunnis registered in large numbers (70%-85%) to try to defeat the constitution, prompting a U.S.-mediated agreement (October 11, 2005) providing for a panel to propose amendments within four months after a post-December 15 election government took office (Article 137), to be voted on within another two months (under the same rules as the October 15 referendum.) The Sunni provinces of Anbar and Salahuddin had a 97% and 82% "no" vote, respectively, but the constitution was adopted because Nineveh province only voted 55% "no," missing the threshold for a "no" vote by a two-thirds majority in three provinces.

December 15, 2005 Elections

In the December 15, 2005 elections for a four-year national government (in line with the schedule laid out in the TAL), each province contributed a predetermined number of seats to a "Council of Representatives" (COR)— a formula adopted to attract Sunni participation. Of the 275-seat body, 230 seats were allocated this way, with 45 "compensatory" seats for entities that would have won additional seats had the constituency been the whole nation. There were 361 political "entities," including 19 multi-party coalitions, competing. As shown in the table, voters chose lists representing their sects and regions, and the Shiites and Kurds again emerged dominant. The COR was inaugurated on March 16, 2006, but political infighting caused the Shiite bloc "United Iraqi Alliance" to replace Jafari with another Da'wa figure, Nuri Kamal al-Maliki, as Prime Minister. On April 22, the COR approved Talabani to continue as president. His two deputies are Adel Abd al-Mahdi (incumbent) of the Islamic Supreme Council of Iraq (ISCI) and Tariq alHashimi, leader of the Sunni-based Accord Front ("Tawafuq"—within which Hashimi leads the Iraqi Islamic Party). Another Accord figure, the hardline Mahmoud Mashhadani (National Dialogue Council party), became COR speaker.

Maliki won a COR vote for a 37-member cabinet (including himself and two deputy prime ministers) on May 20, 2006. Three key slots (Defense, Interior, and National Security) were not filled permanently until June 2006, due to infighting. Of the 37 posts, there were 19 Shiites; 9 Sunnis; 8 Kurds; and 1 Christian. Four were women.

BENCHMARKS, RECONCILIATION, AND PROVINCIAL ELECTIONS

The 2005 elections were considered successful by the Bush Administration but—possibly because they took place in the context of ongoing insurgency and sectarian conflict—the elections did not resolve the grievances in Iraq's communities over their new positions in the post-Saddam power structure. In August 2006, the Administration and Iraq agreed on a series of "benchmarks" that, if adopted and implemented, might achieve political reconciliation. Under Section 1314 of a FY2007 supplemental appropriation (P.L. 110-28), "progress" on eighteen political and security benchmarks—as assessed in Administration reports due by July 15, 2007 and then September 15, 2007—were required for the United States to provide $1.5 billion in Economic Support Funds (ESF) to Iraq. The President used the waiver provision. The law also mandated an assessment by the GAO, by September 1, 2007, of the degree to which the benchmarks have been met, as well as an outside assessment of the Iraqi security forces (ISF).

As 2008 progressed, citing the achievement of almost all of the major legislative benchmarks— and the dramatic drop in sectarian-motivate violence attributed to the U.S. "troop surge"—the Bush Administration asserted that political reconciliation was well under way. However, U.S. officials continue to maintain that the extent and durability of reconciliation will largely depend on the degree of implementation of the adopted laws and on further compromises on intercommunal differences and disputes. A June 2008 study by the Government Accountability Office (GAO-08-837) said the legislative moves until that time have had limited effect in healing the rifts in Iraqi politics. Iraq's performance on the "benchmarks" is in the table below.

The Strengthening of the Iraqi Government during 2008

The passage of key legislation in 2008 and the continued calming of the security situation enhanced Maliki's political position. This represented a reversal from 2007, when Maliki appeared weakened substantially by the pullout of the Accord Front, the Sadr faction, and the bloc of former Prime Minister Iyad al-Allawi from the cabinet, leaving it with 13 vacant seats out of a 37 seat cabinet. A March 2008 offensive ordered by Maliki against the Sadr faction and other militants in Basra and environs ultimately pacified the city, weakened Sadr politically, and caused some Sunnis and Kurds to see Maliki as more even-handed and non-sectarian than previously thought. This contributed to a decision by the Accord Front to return to the cabinet in July 2008. Other cabinet vacancies were filled, mostly by independents, to the point where the cabinet now only has one vacancy (ministry of Justice).

Maliki's growing strength caused concern even among Maliki's erstwhile political allies. The Kurds, who had been a key source of support for him, are increasing at odds with his leadership because of his formation of government-run "tribal support councils" in northern Iraq, which the Kurds see as an effort to prevent them from gaining control of disputed territories. ISCI, the longstanding main ally of Maliki's Da'wa Party, competed with the Da'wa for provincial council seats, as discussed below, and has accused him of surrounding himself with Da'wa veterans to the exclusion of other decision-makers. The competition prompted reports in late 2008 that several major factions were considering attempting to bring about a "no-confidence" vote against Maliki. The late December 2008 resignation, under pressure, of Sunni COR Speaker Mahmoud al-Mashhadani, who was perceived as blocking a no confidence motion, could be one outward indicator of the dissension. (Several attempts to replace him, most recently on February 19, 2009, have failed to achieve the 138 vote majority needed to confirm a successor.)

Throughout 2008, U.S. officials grew concerned that Maliki's increasing independence from the United States could lead to reversals, for example by creating restiveness among the Sunni "Sons of Iraq" fighters who Maliki has refused to fully integrate wholesale into the Iraqi Security Forces. The 100,000 fighters nationwide cooperate with U.S. forces against Al Qaeda in Iraq and other militants. Still, the assumption of the payments of about half of the Sons by the Iraqi government in November 2008 went relatively without incident, calming U.S. fears to some extent. The remainder will transition to the Iraqi government payroll by April 2009. Emboldened by his political strength but also attentive to pressure by Iran, Maliki insisted on substantial U.S. concessions in the U.S.-Iraq "status of forces agreement" (SOFA) that passed the COR on November 27, 2008 over Sadrist opposition, and notwithstanding Sunni efforts to obtain assurances of their future security. The pact took effect January 1, 2009, limiting the prerogatives of U.S. troops to operate in Iraq and setting a timetable of December 31, 2011 for a U.S. withdrawal.

January 31, 2009 Provincial Elections

The Obama Administration, as did the Bush Administration, looked to the January 31, 2009 provincial elections to consolidate the reconciliation process. Under a 2008 law, provincial councils in Iraq choose the governor and provincial governing administrations in each province, making them powerful bodies that provide ample opportunity to distribute patronage and guide provincial politics. The elections had been planned for October 1, 2008, but were delayed when Kurdish restiveness over integrating Kirkuk and other disputed territories into the KRG caused a presidential veto of the July 22, 2008 election law needed to hold these elections. The draft law provided for equal division of power in Kirkuk (between Kurds, Arabs, and Turkomans) until its status is finally resolved, prompting Kurdish opposition to any weakening of their dominance in Kirkuk. Following the summer COR recess, the major political blocs agreed to put aside the Kirkuk dispute and passed a revised provincial election law on September 24, 2008, providing for the elections by January 31, 2009. The revised law stripped out provisions in the vetoed version to allot 13 total reserved seats (spanning six provinces) to minorities. However, in October 2008, the COR adopted a new law restoring six reserved seats for minorities: Christian seats in Baghdad, Nineveh, and Basra; one seat for Yazidis in Nineveh; one seat for Shabaks in Nineveh; and one seat for the Sabean sect in Baghdad.

In the elections, in which there was virtually no violence on election day, about 14,500 candidates vied for the 440 provincial council seats in the 14 Arab-dominated provinces of Iraq. About 4,000 of the candidates were women. The average number of council seats per province is about 30,[2] down from a set number of 41 seats per province (except Baghdad) in the 2005-2009 councils. The new Baghdad provincial council has 57 seats. This yielded an average of more than 30 candidates per council seat, which some see as enthusiasm for democracy in Iraq. However, the reduction in number of seats in most provinces also meant that many incumbents would not win re-election. Voters were able to vote only for a party slate, or for an individual candidate (although they must also vote for that candidate's slate as well)—a procedure that encourages voting for slates, not individuals. As a consequence, the political parties are generally able to choose who on their slate will occupy seats allotted for that party. This election system was widely assessed to favor larger, well organized parties, because smaller parties might not meet the vote threshold to obtain any seats on the council in their province.[3] This was seen as likely to set back the hopes of some Iraqis that the elections would weaken the Islamist parties, both Sunni and Shiite, that have dominated post-Saddam politics.

About 17 million Iraqis were eligible to vote. Any Iraqi 18 years of age or older was eligible. The vote was run by the Iraqi Higher Election Commission (IHEC). Pre- election-related violence was minimal, although five candidates and several election/political workers were killed. There were virtually no major violent incidents on election day. The Iraqi Security Forces (ISF) took the lead in defending polling places, with U.S. forces as back-up if needed. Turnout was about 51%, somewhat lower than some expected, and some voters complained of being turned away at polling places because their names were not on file. Other voters had been displaced by sectarian violence in prior years and were unable to vote in their new areas of habitation.

The vote totals were finalized on February 19, 2009. Within fifteen days of that (by March 6, 2009) the provincial council are to convene under the auspices of the incumbent provincial governor, and to elect a provincial council chairperson and deputy chairperson. Within another 30 days after that (by April 5, 2009), the provincial councils are to elect (by absolute majority) a provincial governor and deputy governors. The term of the provincial councils is four years from the date of first convention.

Outcomes and Implications

Some of the primary outcomes of the elections appear to be evident based on the results for the the two main Shiite parties, which have been allies but were rivals in the provincial elections. In the mostly Shiite southern provinces, ISCI (Shahid Mihrab list) and Maliki's Da'wa "State of Law Coalition" offered competing lists. Maliki's post-election political position apparently has been enhanced by the strong showing of this list. Any discussions of a possible vote of no confidence against Maliki are likely derailed, based on the election results, although some Sunni deputies did introduce such a motion in the COR in late February 2009. With 28 out of the 57 total seats, the Maliki slate will likely end up in effective control of Baghdad province, displacing ISCI, and in control of or very politically strong in most of the Shiite provinces of the south, including Basra. (State of Law won an outright majority of 20 out of 35 total seats in Basra.) Maliki's slate also fended off a challenge from former Prime Minister Ibrahim al-Jafari's slate, which is considered strong among some Islamist Shiites, although Jafari had been in political eclipse for two years and his showing was stronger than expected. Still, in most provinces in the Shiite south, Maliki's candidates will need to form coalitions, perhaps even with the Sadrists, to gain control of the provincial administration in that province. Results are in the chart below.

The apparent big loser in the elections was ISCI, which had been favored because it is well organized and well funded. ISCI favors more power for the provinces and less for the central government; centralization is perceived as Maliki's preferred power structure. ISCI did not even fare well in Najaf province, which it previously dominated and which because of Najaf's revered status in Shiism is considered a center of political gravity in southern Iraq. ISCI won only 3 seats on the Baghdad province council, down from the 28 it held previously, and only five in Basra. It did win an equal number of seats to the Maliki slate (seven seats each) in the key southern province of Najaf. ISCI's ally, the Badr Organization (political front for the Badr Brigades militia run by ISCI) also fielded candidates. Some observers believe that the poor showing for ISCI was a product not only of its call for devolving power out of Baghdad, but also because of its perceived close ties to Iran, which some Iraqis believe is exercising undue influence on Iraqi politics.

The unexpected strength of secular parties such as that of former Prime Minister Iyad al-Allawi, appeared to show that voters favored slates committed to strong central government and "rule of law," as well as to the concept of Iraqi nationalism. This trend was also reflected in the strong showing of a single candidate in Karbala province. The figure, Yusuf al-Habbubi, is well thought of in the province for even-handedness and his boasts of close ties to Saddam's elder son Uday (killed in Operation Iraqi Freedom in 2003) did not hurt him politically, even though most Karbala residents are Shiites repressed by Saddam's government. Still, because al-Habbubi is a single candidate, he only won his own seat on the Karbala provincial council. He is however allied with another slate in the province, called "Hope of Mesopotamia," which won 8 seats there.

Other results the trend toward strong central government were the relatively poor showings of the Fadhila (Islamic Virtue) Party. Fadhila previously dominated the Basra provincial council and administration, a platform from which it launched a move by file a petition, under the 2006 regions law, to form a new region consisting only of Basra province. This effort did not attract the needed 10% of provincial residents' signatures to trigger a referendum by the time of the provincial elections. It is likely that Fadhila's relatively poor showing and the broader trend of support for strong central government will derail the Basra region movement for the near future.

U.S. officials had hoped that the elections would bring Sunni Muslims ever further into the political structure. Sunnis boycotted the January 2005 provincial elections and have been poorly represented in some mixed provinces, such as Diyala and Nineveh. It was also hoped that the elections would help incorporate into the political structure the tribal leaders ("Awakening Councils") who recruited the Sons of Iraq fighters. These Sunni tribalists offered election slates and were expected to show strength at the expense of the established Sunni parties, particularly the Iraqi Islamic Party (IIP).

The established, mostly urban Sunni parties, led by the IIP, had been struggling in 2008 as the broader Accord Front (Tawafuq) fragmented. In the provincial elections, one of its component parties—the National Dialogue Council—ran on slates that competed with the IIP in several provinces. That competing slate came in first in the almost entirely Sunni province of Al Anbar, and it also finished ahead of the several lists fielded by the tribes of the Awakening movement. The tribal leaders accused their rivals of manipulating the vote and there were some reports of violence—or threatened violence—in response to the perceived misfeasance. However, subsequent talks with government and other mediators calmed Anbar and it appears that most factions are now likely to refrain from further violent challenges to the results.

Another expected outcome of the election was that Sunni Arabs would wrest control of the Nineveh provincial council from the Kurds, who won control of that council in the 2005 election because of the broad Sunni Arab boycott of that election. That appears to have occurred, with a Sunni list (al-Hadba'a) winning a clear plurality of the Nineveh vote. That slate is composed of Sunnis who openly oppose Kurdish encroachment in the province and who are committed to the "Arab and Islamic identity" of the province. Nineveh contains numerous territories inhabited by Kurds and which have been a source of growing tension between the Kurdistan Regional Government (KRG) and the central government in Baghdad.

Another mixed province, Diyala, was hotly contested between Shiite and Sunni Arab and Kurdish slates, reflecting the character of the province as another front line between the Kurds and the central government. As noted in the elections results chart below, the provincial version of the Accord Front narrowly beat out the Kurds for first place. Some Shiite slates, including Maliki's list, the list loyal to former Prime Minister Ibrahim al-Jafari, and the pro-Sadr slate, also won significant votes. There continues to be substantial friction between Sunni and Shiite Arabs in that province, in part because Sunni militants drove out many Shiites from the province at the height of the civil conflict during 2005-2007.

Other U.S. officials saw the elections as key opportunity to move Moqtada al-Sadr's faction firmly away from armed conflict against the mainstream Shiite parties. That conflict surged in the March 2008 Basra offensive discussed above. Sadr announced in October 2008 that he would not field a separate list in the provincial elections but support Sadrists on other lists. Sadr's faction, represented mainly in the "Independent Liberals Trend" list, filed candidate slates in several provinces mostly in the south. The slate fared well enough in several southern provinces to be a potential coalition partner, but not well enough to control any provinces outright. The failure of Sadrists to win control of any councils could reflect voter disillusionment with parties that continue to field militias—which many Iraqis blame for much of the violence that has plagued Iraq since the fall of Saddam Hussein.

Elections Going Forward

Some observers maintain that the success of the provincial elections could be determined by subsequent contests. By July 31, 2009, district and sub-district elections are to take place. On May 19, 2009, there will be elections for the Kurdistan National Assembly and the presidency of the KRG. There is also a planned referendum by June 30, 2009 on the U.S.-Iraq status of forces agreement, although some believe this referendum might not be held at all if there is no popular agitation to hold them. Moreover, Iraq is supposed to hold new national elections in December 2009—upon the expiration of the term of the existing Council of

Representatives. This election, according to some observers, might slip until March 2010. This election would determine Iraq's national leadership for the subsequent four years.

Several other possible elections in Iraq are as yet unscheduled. For example, there are to be provincial elections in the three Kurdish controlled provinces and the disputed province of Kirkuk, subsequent to a settlement of the Kirkuk dispute. Depending on political outcomes, there could be further elections. Among them would be a referendum on whether Basra province could form a new "region;" a referendum on any agreed settlement on Kirkuk; and a vote on amendments to Iraq's 2005 constitution.

Table 1. January 31, 2009 Provincial Election Results (Major Slates)

Baghdad - 55 regular seats, plus one Sabean and one Christian set-aside seat	State of Law (Maliki) – 38% (28 seats); Independent Liberals Trend (pro-Sadr) – 9% (5 seats); Accord Front (Sunni mainstream) – 9% (9 seats); Iraq National (Allawi) – 8.6%; Shahid Mihrab and Independent Forces (ISCI) – 5.4% (3 seats) ; National Reform list (of former P.M. Ibrahim al-Jafari) – 4.3% (3 seats)
Basra – 34 regular seats, plus one Christian seat	State of Law – 37% (20); ISCI – 11.6% (5); Sadr – 5% (2); Fadhila (previously dominant in Basra) – 3.2% (0); Allawi – 3.2% (0); Jafari list – 2.5% (0)
Nineveh – 34 regular seats, plus one set aside for each of: Shabaks, Yazidis, and Christians	Hadbaa – 48.4%; Fraternal Nineveh – 25.5%; IIP – 6.7%;
Najaf – 28 seats	State of Law – 16.2% (7); ISCI – 14.8% (7); Sadr – 12.2% (6); Jafari – 7% (2); Allawi – 1.8% (0); Fadhila – 1.6% (0)
Babil – 30 seats	State of Law – 12.5% (8); ISCI- 8.2% (5); Sadr – 6.2% (3); Jafari – 4.4% (3); Allawi – 3.4%; Accord Front – 2.3% (3); Fadhila – 1.3%
Diyala – 29 seats	Accord Front list – 21.1%; Kurdistan Alliance – 17.2%; Allawi – 9.5%; State of Law – 6 %
Muthanna– 26 seats	State of Law – 10.9% (5); ISCI – 9.3% (5); Jafari – 6.3% (3); Sadr – 5.5% (2); Fadhila – 3.7%
Anbar – 29 seats	National Iraqi Project Gathering (established Sunni parties, excluding IIP) – 17.6%; Iraq Awakening (Sahawa – Sunni tribals) – 17.1%; Allawi – 6.6%; Tribes of Iraq – 4.5%;.
Maysan – 27 seats	State of Law – 17.7% (8); ISCI – 14.6% (8); Sadr – 7; Jafari – 8.7% (4); Fadhila – 3.2%; Allawi – 2.3%
Dhi Qar – 31 seats	State of Law – 23.1% (13); pro-Sadr – 14.1% (7); ISCI – 11.1% (5); Jafari – 7.6% (4); Fadhila – 6.1%; Allawi – 2.8%
Karbala – 27 seats	List of Maj. Gen. Yusuf al-Habbubi (Saddam era local official) – 13.3% (1 seat); State of Law – 8.5% (9); Sadr – 6.8% (4); ISCI – 6.4% (4); Jafari – 2.5% ; Fadhila – 2.5%
Salah Ad Din – 28 seats	IIP-led list – 14.5%; Allawi - 13.9%; Sunni list without IIP – 8.7%; State of Law – 3.5%; ISCI – 2.9%
Qadissiyah – 28 seats	State of Law – 23.1% (11); ISCI 6.7% (2); Fadhila – 4.1% – 11.7% (5); Jafari – 8.2% (3); Allawi – 8%; Sadr
Wasit – 28 seats	State of Law – 15.3% (13); ISCI 2.7% – 10% (6); Sadr – 6% (3); Allawi – 4.6%; Fadhila –

Source: UNAMI translation of results issued February 2, 2009 by the Independent Higher Election Commission of Iraq; Vissar, Reidar. The Provincial Elections: The Seat Allocation Is Official and the Coalition-Forming Process Begins. February 19, 2009.

Table 2. Election Results (January and December 2005)

Bloc/Party	Seats (Jan. 05)	Seats (Dec. 05)
United Iraqi Alliance (UIA, Shiite Islamist). Now 85 seats after departure of Fadilah (15 seats) and Sadr faction (28 seats) in 2007. Islamic Supreme Council of Iraq of Abd al-Aziz al-Hakim has 30; Da'wa Party (25 total: Maliki faction, 12, and Anizi faction, 13); independents (30).	140	128
Kurdistan Alliance - KDP (24); PUK (22); independents (7)	75	53
Iraqis List (secular, Allawi); added Communist and other mostly Sunni parties for Dec. vote.	40	25
Iraq Accord Front. Main Sunni bloc; not in Jan. vote. Consists of Iraqi Islamic Party (IIP, Tariq al-Hashimi, 26 seats); National Dialogue Council of Khalaf Ulayyan (7); General People's Congress of Adnan al-Dulaymi (7); independents (4).	—	44
National Iraqi Dialogue Front (Sunni, led by former Baathist Saleh al-Mutlak) Not in Jan. 2005 vote.	—	11
Kurdistan Islamic Group (Islamist Kurd) (votes with Kurdistan Alliance)	2	5
Iraqi National Congress (Chalabi). Was part of UIA list in Jan. 05 vote	—	0
Iraqis Party (Yawar, Sunni); Part of Allawi list in Dec. vote	5	—
Iraqi Turkomen Front (Turkomen, Kirkuk-based, pro-Turkey)	3	1
National Independent and Elites (Jan)/Risalyun (Message, Dec) pro-Sadr	3	2
People's Union (Communist, non-sectarian); on Allawi list in Dec. vote	2	—
Islamic Action (Shiite Islamist, Karbala)	2	0
National Democratic Alliance (non-sectarian, secular)	1	—
Rafidain National List (Assyrian Christian)	1	1
Liberation and Reconciliation Gathering (Umar al-Jabburi, Sunni, secular)	1	3
Ummah (Nation) Party. (Secular, Mithal al-Alusi, former INC activist)	0	1
Yazidi list (small Kurdish, heterodox religious minority in northern Iraq)	—	1

Notes: Number of polling places: January: 5,200; December: 6,200; Eligible voters: 14 million in January election; 15 million in October referendum and December; Turnout: January: 58% (8.5 million votes)/ October: 66% (10 million)/ December: 75% (12 million).

Table 3. Assessments of the Benchmarks

Benchmark	July 12, 2007 Admin. Report	GAO (Sept. 07)	Sept. 14, 2007 Admin. Report	Subsequent Actions and Assessments - May 2008 Administration report, June 2008 GAO report, International Compact with Iraq Review in June 2008, and U.S. Embassy Weekly Status Reports (and various press sources)
1. Forming Constitutional Review Committee (CRC) and completing review	(S) satisfactory	unmet	S	CRC continues debating 50 amendments regarding federal vs. regional powers and presidential powers; Kurds want Kirkuk issue settled before finalizing amendments. Sunnis want presidential council to have enhanced powers relative to prime minister. Some progress on technical, judicial issues. Deadlines for final recommendations repeatedly extended.
2. Enacting and implementing laws on De-Baathification	(U) unsatisfact.	unmet		"Justice and Accountability Law" passed Jan. 12, 2008. Allows about 30,000 fourth ranking Baathists to regain their jobs, and 3,500 Baathists in top three party ranks would receive pensions. But, could allow for judicial prosecution of all ex-Baathists and to firing of about 7,000 e services, and bars ex-Saddam security personnel from regaining jobs. Some reports suggest some De-Baathification officials using the new law to purge political enemies or settle scores.
3. Enacting and implementing oil laws that ensure equitable distribution of resources	U	unmet	U	Framework and three implementing laws stalled over KRG-central government disputes; only framework law has reached COR to date. Revenue being distributed equitably, and 2008 budget adopted February 13, 2008 maintains 17% revenue for KRG. Some reports in December 2008 suggested KRG-Baghdad compromise is close on framework and revenue sharing implementing law.
4. Enacting and implementing laws to form semi-autonomous regions	S	partly met	S	Regions law passed October 2006, with relatively low threshold (petition by 33% of provincial council members) to start process to form new regions, but main blocs agreed that law would take effect April 2008. November 2008: petition by 2% of Basra residents submitted to IHEC (another way to start forming a region) to convert Basra province into a single province "region. Signatures of 8% more were required by mid-January 2009 to trigger refere reshhold was not achieved.

Table 3. (Continued)

Benchmark	July 12, 2007 Admin. Report	GAO (Sept. 07)	Sept. 14, 2007 Admin. Report	Subsequent Actions and Assessments - May 2008 Administration report, June 2008 GAO report, International Compact with Iraq Review in June 2008, and U.S. Embassy Weekly Status Reports (and various press sources)
5. Enacting and implementing: (a) a law to establish a higher electoral commission, (b) provincial elections law; (c) a law to specify authorities of provincial bodies, and (d) set a date for provincial elections	S on (a) and U on the others	overall unmet; (a) met	S on (a) and (c)	Draft law stipulating powers of provincial governments adopted February 13, 2008, took effect April 2008. Required implementing election law adopted September 24, 2008: (1) Provides for provincial elections by January 31, 2009; (2) postpones elections in Kirkuk and the three KRG provinces; (3) shunts broader issue of status of Kirkuk and disputed territories to a parliamentary committee to report by March 31, 2009; (4) provides open list/proportional representation voting, which allows voting for individual candidates; (5) stipulates 25% quota for women (although vaguely worded); (6) bans religious symbols on ballots. Under amending law, some seats now set aside for Christian, Yazidi, Shabak, and Sabean minorities.
6. Enacting and implementing legislation addressing amnesty for former insurgents	no rating	unmet	Same as July	Law to amnesty "non-terrorists" among 25,000 Iraq-held detainees passed February 13, 2008. Of 17,000 approved for release (mostly Sunnis and Sadrist Shiites), only a few hundred released to date. 19,000 detainees affected, but will be transferred to Iraqi control under SOFA which took effect January 1, 2009.
7. Enacting and implementing laws on militia disarmament	no rating	unmet	Same as July	Basra operation, discussed above, viewed by Bush Administration as move against militias. On April 9, 2008, Maliki demanded all militias disband as condition for their parties to participate in provincial elections. Law on militia demobilization stalled.
8. Establishing political, media, economic, and services committee to support U.S. "surge"	S	met	met	No change. "Executive Steering Committee" works with U.S.-led forces.
9. Providing three trained and ready brigades to support U.S. surge	S	partly met	S	No change. Eight brigades assigned to assist the surge. Surge now ended.

Table 3. (Continued)

Benchmark	July 12, 2007 Admin. Report	GAO (Sept. 07)	Sept. 14, 2007 Admin. Report	Subsequent Actions and Assessments - May 2008 Administration report, June 2008 GAO report, International Compact with Iraq Review in June 2008, and U.S. Embassy Weekly Status Reports (and various press sources)
10. Providing Iraqi commanders with authorities to make decisions, without political intervention, to pursue all extremists, including Sunni insurgents and Shiite militias	U	unmet	S to pursue extremists U on political interference	No significant change. Still some U.S. concern over the Office of the Commander in Chief (part of Maliki's office) control over appointments to the ISF - favoring Shiites. Still, some politically-motivated leaders remain in ISF. But, National Police said to include more Sunnis in command jobs and rank and file than one year ago.
11. Ensuring Iraqi Security Forces (ISF) providing even-handed enforcement of law	U	unmet	S on military, U on police	Administration interpreted Basra operation as effort by Maliki to enforce law even-handedly, but acknowledges continued militia influence and infiltration in some units.
12. Ensuring that the surge plan in Baghdad will not provide a safe haven for any outlaw, no matter the sect	S	partly met	S	No change. Ethno-sectarian violence has fallen sharply in Baghdad.
13. (a) Reducing sectarian violence and (b) eliminating militia control of local security	Mixed. S on (a); U on (b)	unmet	same as July 12	Sectarian violence continues to drop, but Shiite militias still hold arms. 100,000 Sunni "Sons of Iraq," still distrusted as potential Sunni militiamen. Iraq government assumed payment of 54,000 Sons as of November 10, but opposes integrating more than about 20% into the ISF.
14. Establishing Baghdad joint security stations	S	met	S	Over 50 joint security stations operating at the height of U.S. troop surge.
15. Increasing ISF units capable of operating independently	U	unmet	U	Continuing but slow progress training ISF. U.S. officials say ISF likely unable to secure Iraq internally until 2009-2012; and against external threats not for several years thereafter. Basra operation initially exposed factionali leadership in ISF, but also ability to rapidly deploy.

Table 3. (Continued)

Benchmark	July 12, 2007 Admin. Report	GAO (Sept. 07)	Sept. 14, 2007 Admin. Report	Subsequent Actions and Assessments - May 2008 Administration report, June 2008 GAO report, International Compact with Iraq Review in June 2008, and U.S. Embassy Weekly Status Reports (and various press sources)
16. Ensuring protection of minority parties in COR	S	met	S	No change. Rights of minority parties protected by Article 37 of constitution.
17. Allocating and spending $10 billion in 2007 capital budget for reconstruction.	S	partly met	S	About 63% of the $10 billion 2007 allocation for capital projects was spent.
18. Ensuring that Iraqi authorities not making false accusations against ISF members	U	unmet	U	Some governmental recriminations against some ISF officers still observed.

Source: Compiled by CRS

Author Contact Information

Kenneth Katzman
Specialist in Middle Eastern Affairs
kkatzman@crs.loc.gov, 7-7612

End Notes

[1] http://www.washingtonpost.com/wpdyn/content/article/2005/10/12/AR2005101201450.html.
[2] Each province is to have 25 seats plus one seat per each 200,000 residents over 500,000.
[3] The threshhold for winning a seat is: the total number of valid votes divided by the number of seats up for election.

In: Iraq: Forward, Backward or Nowhere?
Editor: Frederick M. Golenberg

ISBN: 978-1-60741-018-8
© 2010 Nova Science Publishers, Inc.

Chapter 2

IRAQ: KEY ISSUES FOR CONGRESSIONAL OVERSIGHT

Government Accountability Office

> This is a work of the U.S. government and is not subject to copyright protection in the United States. The published product may be reproduced and distributed in its entirety without further permission from GAO. However, because this work may contain copyrighted images or other material, permission from the copyright holder may be necessary if you wish to reproduce this material separately.

March 24, 2009

Congressional Committees

To assist the 111th Congress, we have enclosed a series of issue papers for consideration in developing congressional oversight agendas and determining the way forward in securing and stabilizing Iraq. These papers are based on the continuing work of the U.S. Government Accountability Office (GAO) and the more than 130 Iraq-related products we have issued since May 2003.

Since fiscal year 2001, Congress has provided about $808 billion to the Department of Defense (DOD) for military efforts primarily in support of the Global War on Terrorism.[1] The majority of this amount has been for military operations in support of Operation Iraqi Freedom. Moreover, since fiscal year 2003, about $49 billion[2] has been provided to U.S. agencies for stabilization and reconstruction efforts in Iraq, including developing Iraq's security forces, enhancing Iraq's capacity to govern, and rebuilding Iraq's oil, electricity, and water sectors, among other activities. This report expands on issues discussed on GAO's transition Web site, http://www.gao.gov/media/video/gao-09-294sp.

In January 2007, President Bush announced *The New Way Forward* in Iraq to stem violence and enable the Iraqi government to foster national reconciliation. This strategy established goals and objectives through July 2008 and reasserted the long-term goal or end state for Iraq: a unified, democratic, federal Iraq that can govern, defend, and sustain itself and is an ally in the war on terror. To support the strategy, the United States increased its military presence through a surge of brigade combat teams and associated forces. In June 2008, we reported that the United States had made some progress in reducing overall violence in Iraq and working with the Iraqi government to pass legislation promoting national reconciliation. However, many unmet goals and challenges remained, including building capacity in Iraq's ministries, helping the government execute its capital investment budgets, and providing essential services to the Iraqi people.[3]

With the completion of *The New Way Forward* and the end of the military surge in July 2008, we recommended that the Administration develop an updated strategy that clearly articulates U.S. goals, objectives, roles and responsibilities, and the military and civilian resources needed to build on security and legislative gains. Furthermore, in a second report,[4] we recommended revisions to the Joint Campaign Plan for Iraq—an operational plan for U.S. military and civilian activities in Iraq developed by the Multinational Force-Iraq (MNF-I) and the U.S. Embassy Baghdad— that would help Congress assess progress in achieving the conditions that would allow for the continued drawdown of U.S. forces in Iraq. Specifically, we recommended that DOD and the Department of State (State) identify and prioritize the conditions that must be achieved in each phase of the campaign to enable a drawdown; report the number of U.S. combat brigade teams and other forces required for each campaign phase; and estimate the time needed to reach the desired end state and end the military portion of the campaign. The strategic level actions we called for in our first report would guide revisions to the Joint Campaign Plan.[5]

In February 2009, President Obama described a new strategy for Iraq consisting of three parts: (1) the responsible removal of combat brigades, (2) sustained diplomacy on behalf of a more peaceful and prosperous Iraq, and (3) comprehensive U.S. engagement across the region. According to DOD, the United States plans to reduce the number of combat troops from about 140,000 projected in March 2009 to about 128,000 by September 2009—a difference of 12,000 troops representing two brigades and their support units. Under the schedule announced by the President, U.S. force levels would decline further by August 31, 2010, to no more than 50,000 troops. Under the November 2008 bilateral security agreement[6] between the United States and Iraq, the United States must remove all of its remaining forces by December 31, 2011.

The issues discussed in the enclosures to this report should be considered in further defining the new strategy and its supporting operational plans. Key issues include:

- The security agreement establishes dates for repositioning U.S. forces in Iraq and removing them from the country—a significant change from the United States' prior, conditions-based strategy for Iraq.[7] A responsible drawdown in Iraq will need to balance the timetable established in the security agreement, military doctrine that calls for the delineation of conditions that must exist before military operations can end, and the wishes of the Iraqi government.
- If the United States adheres to the timetable contained in the security agreement, DOD will need to remove about 140,000 troops by the end of 2011. The redeployment of these forces and the removal of their equipment and material will be a massive and expensive effort.
- The large U.S. military presence has provided vital support to civilian operations and has undertaken many traditionally civilian tasks. In moving forward, the United

States will need to consider how to transition from a predominantly military presence to a civilian one as U.S. forces draw down.
- As U.S reconstruction efforts end, Iraq will need to develop the capacity to spend its resources, particularly on investment that will further economic development and deliver essential services to its people. GAO estimates that the Iraqi government had a cumulative budget surplus of $47 billion at the end of 2008.

We obtained information from agency documents and interviews with U.S. officials in Iraq and Washington, D.C., including DOD, State, and the Departments of Energy and the Treasury; the U.S. Agency for International Development (USAID); the Army Corps of Engineers; MNF-I; and the Defense Intelligence Agency. We conducted this performance audit in accordance with generally accepted government auditing standards. Those standards require that we plan and perform the audit to obtain sufficient, appropriate evidence to provide a reasonable basis for our findings and conclusions based on our audit objectives. We believe that the evidence obtained provides a reasonable basis for our findings and conclusions based on our audit objectives. Appendix I contains additional details about our scope and methodology. Appendix II provides updated information on the levels of violence in Iraq, as measured by the number of enemy-initiated attacks, and on the number of U.S. troops in Iraq. Appendix IV contains a list of GAO products directly related to this letter and each of the enclosures.

The Department of the Treasury provided written comments on a draft of this report, which are reprinted in appendix III. Treasury agreed that although Iraq's end-2008 cumulative surplus fell short of GAO's earlier projection, Iraq's budget surpluses will sufficiently cover its projected 2009 budget deficit. Treasury also agreed that Iraq's inability to fully execute its budgets hampers the government's efforts to further reconstruction and economic growth. Treasury, DOD, State, and USAID also provided technical comments, which we have incorporated as appropriate.

We are sending copies of this report to the congressional committees listed below. In addition, we are sending copies of this report to the President and Vice President of the United States, and executive branch agencies. The report also is available at no charge on the GAO Web site at http://www.gao.gov. If you have any questions, please contact Joseph A. Christoff at (202) 512-8979 or christoffj@gao.gov, or the individual(s) listed at the end of each enclosure. Contact points for our Offices of Congressional Relations and Public Affairs can be found on the last page of this report. For press inquiries, please contact Chuck Young at (202) 512-4800. Key contributors to this report are included in appendix V.

Gene L. Dodaro
Acting Comptroller General of the United States

List of Congressional Committees

The Honorable Carl Levin
Chair
The Honorable John McCain
Ranking Member
Committee on Armed Services
United States Senate

The Honorable John F. Kerry
Chair
The Honorable Richard G. Lugar
Ranking Member
Committee on Foreign Relations
United States Senate

The Honorable Joseph I. Lieberman
Chair
The Honorable Susan M. Collins
Ranking Member
Committee on Homeland Security and Governmental Affairs
United States Senate

The Honorable Daniel K. Inouye
Chair
The Honorable Thad Cochran
Vice Chairman
Subcommittee on Defense
Committee on Appropriations
United States Senate

The Honorable Patrick J. Leahy
Chair
The Honorable Judd Gregg
Ranking Member
Subco mmittee on State, Foreign Operations, and Related Programs
Committee on Appropriations
United States Senate

The Honorable Ike Skelton
Chair
The Honorable John M. McHugh
Ranking Member
Committee on Armed Services
House of Representatives

The Honorable Howard L. Berman
Chair
The Honorable Ileana Ros-Lehtinen
Ranking Member
Committee on Foreign Affairs
House of Representatives

The Honorable Edolphus Towns
Chair
The Honorable Darrell E. Issa
Ranking Member
Committee on Oversight and Government Reform
House of Representatives

The Honorable John P. Murtha
Chair
The Honorable C.W. Bill Young
Ranking Member
Subcommittee on Defense
Committee on Appropriations
House of Representatives

The Honorable Gary L. Ackerman
Chair
The Honorable Dan Burton
Ranking Member
Subcommittee on the Middle East and South Asia
Committee on Foreign Affairs
House of Representatives

The Honorable Nita M. Lowey
Chair
The Honorable Kay Granger
Ranking Member
Subcommittee on State, Foreign Operations, and Related Programs
Committee on Appropriations
House of Representatives

ENCLOSURE I:
DETERMINING WHAT CONDITIONS NEED TO BE MET TO UNDERTAKE A RESPONSIBLE DRAWDOWN OF U.S. FORCES

Background

In November 2008, the United States and Iraq signed a bilateral security agreement, which governs the operations of U.S. forces in Iraq. The security agreement entered into force on January 1, 2009.

Issue

The security agreement between the United States and Iraq establishes a timetable—but no conditions—for drawing down U.S. forces from Iraq by the end of 2011. Adopting a drawdown timetable marks a major change from the prior U.S. approach of drawing down forces based on security and other conditions in Iraq. Military doctrine states that effective campaign planning cannot occur without a clear understanding of the conditions that must exist to draw down forces. In February 2009, the President described a new strategy in Iraq, calling for a responsible drawdown of U.S. forces. In further defining this strategy and revising the Joint Campaign Plan for Iraq, the administration will need to clarify what conditions need to be met to undertake this drawdown responsibly.

Key Findings

Before signing the security agreement with Iraq, the prior administration had linked the drawdown of U.S. forces to the achievement of security, political, economic, and diplomatic conditions. Meeting these conditions would enable the United States to achieve its strategic goal for Iraq: a unified, democratic, and federal Iraq that could govern, defend, and sustain itself and become an ally in the war on terror. Some conditions the United States sought to achieve in Iraq included an improved security situation; more capable Iraqi security forces; improved essential services such as access to clean water and reliable electricity; and the passage of legislation promoting national reconciliation, such as laws governing the distribution of oil revenues and amnesty for former insurgents.

Under Prior Administration, Conditions-based Strategy Shifted to a Time-based Approach for Drawing Down U.S. Forces

As GAO has previously reported, progress toward achieving these conditions has been mixed. For example, while the security situation remains tenuous, violence has decreased significantly over the past 2 years: enemy-initiated attacks decreased from a peak of almost 180 per day in June 2007 to about 27 per day in January 2009 (see app. II). Further, the number of Iraqi army and police forces nearly doubled from about 320,000 in January 2007 to just over 600,000 in October 2008. However, according to the Department of Defense (DOD), over the same period, the number of Iraqi army units capable of conducting operations independently remained at about 10 percent of total units.

The November 2008 security agreement marked a major shift from a conditions-based strategy to a time-based approach for drawing down U.S. forces. The security agreement sets a two-phase timetable—but with no security, political, economic, or other conditions—for removing U.S. forces from Iraq over a 3-year period, primarily because the Iraqi government did not agree to include conditions, according to DOD and State officials:

- **June 30, 2009:** U.S. combat forces must withdraw from Iraqi cities, villages, and localities. According to DOD officials, U.S. combat forces would continue to conduct combined operations in these areas from bases located outside Iraqi cities, villages, and localities. Further, some U.S. forces who train Iraqi forces may be co-located with Iraqi units in these areas.

- **December 31, 2011:** All U.S. forces must leave Iraq. According to DOD and Department of State (State) officials, the agreement does not envision any U.S. forces remaining in Iraq after that date.

Either government can unilaterally terminate the security agreement by providing 12 months advance notice. Without a security agreement or other mandate, U.S. forces would lack the authority to continue operating in Iraq and would have to leave. For example, if Iraqis reject the security agreement in a referendum that may be held in July 2009, the Iraqi government has said it would abide by the results of this referendum. Thus, Iraq would likely terminate the security agreement, and U.S. forces would have to leave Iraq by as early as July 2010.

Iraq and the United States Could Move Forward or Extend the Drawdown Time Frame

In addition, DOD and State officials noted that the U.S. and Iraqi governments can amend the security agreement by mutual agreement. Such amendments could include an extension of the drawdown timetable or an authorization of a residual U.S. force to continue training Iraqi security forces after 2011. However, according to officials at State and DOD, the Iraqi government did not agree to include conditions-based provisions in the security agreement due to political pressure against a continued U.S. presence.

The new administration has emphasized the importance of a responsible drawdown of U.S. forces but has not yet defined this term. In February 2009, the President announced a significant drawdown of U.S. forces by August 31, 2010 and, consistent with the security agreement, the removal of all U.S. forces by the end of 2011. According to DOD and Multinational Force-Iraq (MNF-I) officials, the United States plans to reduce the U.S. force level from about 140,000 projected in March 2009 to about 128,000 by September 2009, where it would remain through Iraq's national election scheduled at the end of 2009. Based on conditions in Iraq, the MNF-I Commanding General may recommend further reductions prior to the election. A few months after the election, the United States plans to reduce forces to no more than 50,000 troops by August 2010 (see app. II).

The Administration Should Further Define What Conditions Must Be Achieved to Allow a Responsible Drawdown of U.S. Forces

Military doctrine states that effective planning cannot occur without a clear understanding of the end state for U.S. operations and the conditions that must exist to end military operations and draw down forces. According to doctrine, military operations generally should be driven by conditions rather than time requirements. However, DOD officials stated they are well aware that a 3-year timetable now exists for removing all U.S. forces from Iraq.

In further defining a new U.S. strategy and revising the Joint Campaign Plan for Iraq, the administration must establish the parameters of a responsible drawdown, including clarifying the end state for U.S. military operations and prioritizing the conditions that would allow U.S. troops to draw down. It should also consider how the United States would respond if it does not achieve the conditions necessary for a responsible drawdown within the security agreement timetable. The administration must work with the Iraqi government in further defining the new strategy for Iraq.

Oversight Questions

1. How does the administration define a responsible drawdown from Iraq?
2. What is the current strategic goal for Iraq and how does it differ from the prior goal of a unified, democratic, and federal Iraq that can govern, defend, and sustain itself and become an ally in the war on terror?
3. To what extent will the administration's plans for removing U.S. forces be based on achieving specified conditions in Iraq?
4. To what extent will the United States attempt to renegotiate provisions of the security agreement if security conditions deteriorate or other conditions are deemed insufficient to draw down responsibly?
5. What are the U.S. contingency plans in the event that Iraqis vote against the security agreement in July 2009?

Point of Contact

Joseph A. Christoff, 202-512-8979, christoffj@gao.gov

ENCLOSURE II:
IMPLEMENTING KEY OPERATIONAL REQUIREMENTS OF THE U.S.-IRAQ SECURITY AGREEMENT

Background

The U.S.-Iraq security agreement provides the basis for a U.S. military presence in Iraq, which previously was authorized by United Nations (UN) Security Council resolutions. It also defines legal jurisdiction over U.S. servicemembers and DOD civilians and contractors in Iraq, which previously were covered by a Coalition Provisional Authority (CPA) order.

Issue

In addition to setting a timetable for drawing down U.S. forces, the security agreement governs the operations of U.S. forces supporting Iraqi efforts to maintain security and stability. It requires Iraqi agreement for U.S. military operations; defines U.S. and Iraqi legal jurisdiction over individual members of U.S. forces, Department of Defense (DOD) civilian employees, and U.S. forces' contractors in Iraq; and generally requires all U.S.-held detainees to be released or transferred to Iraqi custody. However, many implementing details remain to be resolved. In further defining the U.S. strategy and Joint Campaign Plan for Iraq, the administration will need to accommodate the substantial changes in U.S. operational authority in Iraq.

Key Findings

The security agreement marks a change in the nature and authority of the U.S. military presence in Iraq; its implementation will require a shift in how U.S. forces plan, coordinate, and execute operations in the country. From 2003 through 2008, the UN Security Council authorized the U.S.-led multinational force to take all necessary measures to maintain security and stability in Iraq. Acting under this mandate, U.S. forces were able to conduct combat operations against violent groups, search for and secure weapons, and detain Iraqis and others considered to be a threat to Iraq's security and stability.

Iraqi Goverment Must Agree to All U.S. Military Operations in Iraq

Under the security agreement, all U.S. military operations in Iraq must be conducted with the Iraqi government's concurrence and fully coordinated with Iraqi authorities through a new Joint Military Operations Coordinating Committee. For example, U.S. forces must obtain Iraqi warrants or other legal authorization to detain individuals and search homes, except during combat operations undertaken with Iraqi concurrence. U.S. forces retain the right of self-defense in Iraq, as defined in international law.

According to DOD and Department of State (State) officials, many implementing details in the security agreement must be resolved. For example, it is unclear whether U.S. forces will have a "blanket" authorization to conduct certain types of operations, such as medical evacuations or routine joint patrols. As of mid-January 2009, the new joint coordinating committee had held two initial meetings to develop details on implementing the security agreement's requirements for U.S. military operations in Iraq.

The security agreement covers individual U.S. military service members, DOD civilian employees, and U.S. contractors and subcontractors, as well as their employees in Iraq that supply goods, services, and security to or on behalf of U.S. forces under a contract with or for those forces. Before the security agreement, CPA Order 17 granted immunity from the Iraqi legal process to U.S. military personnel under the multinational force and to U.S. contractors operating in Iraq for acts performed pursuant to the terms and conditions of their contracts.

Security Agreement Defines U.S. and Iraqi Legal Jurisdiction over U.S. Military Servicemembers and DOD Civilians and Contractors

Under the security agreement, Iraq has the primary right to exercise jurisdiction over members of U.S. forces and the civilian component for asyet-unspecified, grave premeditated felonies, when such crimes are committed outside agreed facilities and duty status. The United States has jurisdiction over all other crimes. The security agreement requires Iraqi authorities to notify U.S. authorities immediately if they detain U.S. service members or DOD civilians and transfer them to U.S. custody within 24 hours.

Under the security agreement, Iraq has the primary right to exercise jurisdiction over U.S. forces' contractors, subcontractors, and their employees in Iraq. In addition, Iraqi authorities have recently suspended CPA Order 17, making all U.S. and foreign contractors and their employees in Iraq subject to Iraqi law, according to U.S. officials. According to State, a joint U.S.-Iraqi committee is working to establish procedures and guidelines for exercising Iraqi jurisdiction for private contractors operating in Iraq, including those covered by the security agreement.

DOD, UN, and human rights reports have identified significant shortcomings in Iraq's judicial system. A December 2008 Human Rights Watch report, for example, concluded Iraq's central criminal court "seriously" failed to meet international standards of due process and fair trials. Some of these reports raise concerns that detainees in Iraqi custody may be tortured or mistreated because Iraqi officials often rely on coerced confessions instead of physical evidence, particularly in criminal cases. Whether contractors could renegotiate their contracts given the changes in circumstances would depend on the terms of their contracts, according to DOD officials. These officials said that U.S. contractors and their employees are subject to host government jurisdiction in other countries where U.S. forces operate under a status of forces agreement. Moreover, they note that many U.S. contractor employees are Iraqi nationals and, as such, would be subject to Iraqi jurisdiction.

Reports Raise Concerns about Iraqi Judicial System

The security agreement requires the release or transfer to Iraqi authorities of all detainees held by U.S. forces in Iraq unless otherwise requested by the Iraqi government. Acting under UN mandate, U.S. forces detained thousands of Iraqis and others considered a threat to Iraq's security and stability. As of January 2009, more than 15,000 detainees remained in U.S. custody, according to State and DOD. DOD officials plan to release or transfer to Iraqi custody about 1,200 to 1,500 detainees per month based on their assessment of Iraqi authorities' ability to process and absorb these transfers. Under the security agreement, U.S. forces are to provide available information about all detainees in their custody to Iraqi authorities, who will then obtain arrest warrants for persons wanted by those authorities. U.S. forces are to transfer custody of those detainees subject to an arrest warrant and release the remaining detainees unless otherwise requested by the Iraqi government. According to DOD and State, many implementing details for this process must be resolved.

Security Agreement Requires U.S. Forces to Release or Transfer Detainees

Oversight Questions

1. To what extent will the change in authority for the U.S. military operations affect U.S. planning efforts in Iraq?
2. To what extent will the security agreement's provisions granting Iraq primary legal jurisdiction over U.S. contractors and their employees in Iraq affect the availability and cost of contractors to support U.S. forces?
3. What kinds of legal protection, if any, could the United States provide to contractors in Iraq given the current state of the Iraqi judicial system?
4. To what extent have Iraqi and U.S. officials identified appropriate legal authority and developed options for detaining individuals that pose continuing security threats to Iraqi or U.S. forces?
5. What possible amendments to the security agreement, if any, should the United States seek to negotiate with Iraq?

Point of Contact

Joseph A. Christoff, 202-512-8979, christoffj@gao.gov

ENCLOSURE III:
MANAGING THE REDEPLOYMENT OF U.S. FORCES AND EQUIPMENT FROM IRAQ

Background

Department of Defense (DOD) guidance emphasizes the importance of early planning for redeploying U.S. forces and equipment

Issue

The exact pace for redeploying U.S. forces from Iraq has yet to be determined. If the United States adheres to the timeline contained in the security agreement, DOD will need to remove about 140,000 troops by the end of 2011. In addition, the redeployment of U.S. forces and the removal of their equipment and material will be a massive and expensive effort. As of March 2008, the United States had in place about 170,000 pieces of equipment worth about $16.5 billion that would need to be removed from Iraq.

Key Findings

It is unclear how the timeline in the security agreement and operations in Afghanistan will affect DOD plans for redeploying U.S. forces and equipment from Iraq. As of September 2008, DOD's redeployment plans for Iraq were based on three key assumptions that may no longer be applicable:

- Any redeployment will be based on Multinational Force-Iraq (MNF-I) and Department of State assessments of security and other conditions in Iraq.
- There will be sufficient lead time to refine redeployment plans once an order with a specific timetable and force posture in Iraq is issued.
- The redeployment of forces will be deliberate and gradual, predicated on a 180-day process for units leaving Iraq and an estimated flow of no more than 2.5 brigades' worth of equipment and materiel out of Iraq through Kuwait each month.

DOD's Initial Plans for Redeploying U.S. Forces from Iraq Focused on Three Key Assumptions

DOD Should Consider Key Issues in Developing a Comprehensive Plan for Redeploying U.S. Forces from Iraq

Based on discussions with DOD officials and an analysis of planning efforts, GAO found that the effectiveness and efficiency of DOD's redeployment efforts will depend on the extent to which it develops plans that address several issues. For example:

- *Roles and responsibilities for managing and executing the return of materiel and equipment.* Although the U.S. Central Command has designated an executive agent to coordinate the redeployment of U.S. forces from the Iraqi theater, no unified structure exists to coordinate the teams and units engaged in efforts to manage and execute the return of materiel and equipment. This results in confusion on the ways in which those teams should be utilized. Joint doctrine states that an unambiguous chain of command and clear responsibilities and authorities are necessary for any such effort. In September 2008, GAO recommended that DOD take steps to clarify a unified or coordinated chain of command over logistical operations. In commenting on our draft report, DOD indicated it was taking steps to implement this recommendation.

- *Time and cost estimates for base closures.* Closing or handing over U.S. installations in Iraq will be time consuming and costly. As of November 2008, there were 283 U.S. installations in Iraq that will need to be closed or turned over to Iraqi forces. According to U.S. Army officials, experience has shown that it takes 1 to 2 months to close the smallest platoon- or company-size installations, which contain between 16 and 200 combat soldiers or marines. However, MNF-I has never closed large, complex installations—such as Balad Air Force Base, which contains about 24,000 inhabitants and has matured over 5 years. U.S. Army officials estimate it could take longer than 18 months to close a base of that size.

- *Uncertainties regarding redeployment of contractors.* Maintaining accountability for and managing the disposition of U.S. government property under the control of contractors may present challenges to redeploying U.S. forces from Iraq. According to Defense Contract Management Agency officials, there is at least $3.5 billion worth of contractor-managed government-owned property in Iraq. From late 2007 through July 2008, planning for the redeployment of U.S. forces did not include a theater-wide plan for redeploying contractors.

- *Use of facilities in Kuwait and other neighboring countries.* The pace at which units can be redeployed and U.S. equipment returned would be governed by the capacity of facilities in neighboring countries, and restrictions on their use. According to DOD, Kuwait is the main point of exit for all personnel, equipment, and materiel in Iraq. There are nine installations that the United States uses to support operations in Iraq, and the U.S.-Kuwait Defense Cooperation Agreement governs their use. Any redeployment must consider the terms of this agreement, particularly given Kuwait's desire to limit the U.S. footprint in Kuwait, according to DOD.

- *Availability of transportation and security assets and route restrictions.* The availability in theater of military owned and operated heavy equipment transports and convoy security assets, combined with limits on the primary supply route, could inhibit the flow of materiel out of Iraq. According to DOD, two types of heavy equipment transports support U.S. forces in the Iraqi theater of operations: commercially contracted unarmored transports and armored military transports. Any increase in the number of civilian transports without a corresponding increase in military transports to facilitate control and security increases the risk of accidents. However, DOD officials have reported shortages of military transports in theater.

Oversight Questions

1. To what extent has planning begun for the drawdown of U.S. forces from Iraq in accordance with the security agreement?
2. What are the plans and processes by which U.S. installations in Iraq will be turned over to the Iraqis?
3. What are the plans and processes for determining the disposition of contractor-managed, U.S.-government-owned property in Iraq?
4. To what extent will neighboring countries be able to support the drawdown of U.S. forces from Iraq in accordance with timelines outlined in the security agreement?
5. What effect, if any, will the expansion of operations in Afghanistan have on the drawdown of U.S. forces from Iraq?

Point of Contact

William Solis, 202-512-8365, solisw@gao.gov

Enclosure IV:

Managing and Overseeing U.S. Government Contractors in Iraq during a Drawdown

Background

The Departments of Defense (DOD) and State (State) have relied heavily on contractors in Iraq to support troops, civilian personnel, and reconstruction efforts. As of October 2008, DOD estimated it had more than 163,000 contractors under its contracts. Contractors have provided security services, life support, and facilities maintenance, among other things.

Issue

Over the past 6 years, contractors have played a key role in U.S. efforts to stabilize and rebuild Iraq. As the U.S. and Iraqi governments implement the November 2008 security agreement that governs the presence, activities, and drawdown of U.S. forces from Iraq, DOD and State will need to assess the type and level of contractor support needed during the drawdown of U.S. forces. At the same time, both departments will need to overcome challenges in providing a sufficient number of trained personnel to effectively manage and oversee contractor performance. As the administration further defines its plans for Iraq, it will need to consider the implications of the changing nature of contractor support, as well as ways to enhance DOD's and State's management capacity.

Key Findings

Both DOD's and State's ability to effectively manage their contractors in Iraq has been hindered by several challenges. The challenges experienced by one or both of these agencies include a failure to adequately plan for the use of contractors and clearly define their requirements, a lack of acquisition and trained contract management and oversight personnel with experience working in contingency operations, and a lack of policies and procedures. Further, both DOD and State have had difficulties identifying the number of contractor personnel in Iraq. The lack of visibility makes it difficult for commanders and other senior leaders to make informed decisions on the food, housing, and security needed for contractors who reside on U.S. facilities. In July 2008, DOD and State entered into an agreement to use a common database to track contractor personnel in Iraq; however, DOD officials have acknowledged that there are weaknesses in the systems designed to track contractor personnel in theater.

DOD and State Have Had Difficulties Managing and Overseeing Contractors in Iraq

DOD's and State's Capacity to Provide Personnel to Oversee Contractors Remains Uncertain

The lack of a sufficient number of trained acquisition and contractor oversight personnel continues to present a considerable challenge to both DOD and State. This has contributed to higher costs and schedule delays and has hindered operations. For example,

- In September 2008, GAO reported that the lack of qualified personnel to oversee contracts, including those providing linguistic services and maintaining the military equipment used in Iraq, hindered efforts to oversee and, as necessary, correct poor contractor performance in a timely manner. For example, in many cases, the contractor presented military equipment that failed government inspection and had to be repaired again at additional expense and time to the government. DOD personnel indicated they lacked the resources to perform data analyses, identify trends in contractor performance, and improve quality processes.

- In July 2008, GAO raised concerns about whether DOD could sustain increased levels of oversight on its private security contractors. GAO found, for example, that the Defense Contract Management Agency (DCMA), which had been recently tasked to provide contract administration over private security contracts, increased the number of its personnel in Iraq by shifting personnel from other locations and had no strategy for sustaining this increase.

- In January 2009, State's Office of the Inspector General reported that the department's Bureau of Diplomatic Security did not have a strong control environment to ensure its primary security service contract in Iraq is effectively managed due, in part, to frequent changes in management personnel and understaffing combined with a drastic increase in workload. In response, State noted that it planned to increase the number of contract oversight personnel in Iraq for its private security contract and develop additional policy and guidance to better manage these contractors.

As the drawdown of U.S. military forces occurs, DOD will need to assess the proper mix, roles, and responsibilities of military, civilian, and contractor personnel during this transitional period. Our prior work has shown that the nature and relative degree of contractor support can change as the military's mission changes. For example, in Bosnia and Kosovo, contractors assumed responsibility for certain support functions that had been previously performed by military personnel. Moreover, State's reliance on contractors may increase as the department currently depends on DOD to provide some services. The U.S.-Iraq security agreement complicates this assessment because it changes the conditions under which contractors operate. For example, the agreement includes several provisions that affect U.S. contractors working for DOD, such as providing the Iraqi government the primary right to exercise jurisdiction over U.S. contractors in the enforcement of criminal and civil laws. Similar agreements could also affect U.S. contractors working for DOD, particularly State's security contractors.

Level and Nature of Future Contractor Support Needs to Be Assessed

Oversight Questions

1. To what extent are DOD and State taking actions to improve their ability to track and identify contractor personnel in Iraq? To what extent do the departments know the functions these contractors are performing?
2. What are the desired mix, roles, and responsibilities of military, civilian, and contractor personnel in light of the planned drawdown of U.S. forces? What actions are needed to achieve this desired mix?
3. What process is DOD using to assess the impact of the November 2008 security agreement and its implementation on DOD's use of U.S. contractors to support deployed forces or other key functions? What plans has DOD developed in the event that contractors providing essential services withdraw their employees?
4. Is DCMA's workforce sufficient in terms of size and skill level to support contingency operations without degrading its ability to oversee contractor performance in the United States and elsewhere?
5. Have DOD and State (1) assessed whether the drawdown of U.S. forces in Iraq will increase its reliance on contractors and (2) taken action to ensure they have sufficient numbers of contract oversight personnel?
6. What action is State's Bureau of Diplomatic Security taking to ensure the effective oversight of its security contractors?

Points of Contact

William Solis, 202-512-8365, solisw@gao.gov
John Hutton, 202-512-7773, huttonj@gao.gov

ENCLOSURE V:
DETERMINING THE DEPARTMENT OF DEFENSE'S FUTURE COSTS FOR IRAQ

Background

Since 2001, Congress has provided about $808 billion to the Department of Defense (DOD) for military efforts in support of the Global War on Terrorism (GWOT). The majority of this amount has gone to military operations in support of Operation Iraqi Freedom.

Issue

DOD has reported substantial costs for Iraq and can expect to incur significant costs in the foreseeable future, even as the United States develops plans to scale back its presence in Iraq. GAO has found problems with DOD processes for cost reporting and estimating—processes that will be of critical importance to making sound decisions about the defense budget. In addition to the need for better cost information, moving funding that is currently outside the annual budget process into DOD's base budget would enable decision makers to better weigh priorities and assess trade-offs.

Key Findings

U.S. military commitments in Iraq, and their associated costs, will continue to be substantial, particularly in the near term. These types of costs include procurement of new and replacement equipment and operation and maintenance costs, which include items such as housing, food, and services; the repair of equipment; and transportation to move people, supplies, and equipment. The magnitude of DOD costs will depend on several factors and, in some cases, assumptions and decisions that have not been made. For example, these costs will likely be affected by:

- implementation of the U.S.-Iraq security agreement and associated troop redeployment plans;
- the nature and extent of continued U.S. military and civilian presence in Iraq;
- types of facilities needed to support troops remaining in and around Iraq and costs associated with turning facilities over to Iraq;
- availability of transportation and security assets to remove materiel from Iraq; and
- the amount of equipment to be repaired or replaced.

Near-term Costs for Iraq Are Likely to Be Considerable

Although reducing troops would appear to lower costs, GAO has seen from previous operations in the Balkans and Kosovo that costs could rise in the near term. For example, as

GAO reported in February 2008, the U.S. Army estimated it would cost $12 billion to $13 billion a year for at least 2 years after the operation ends to repair, replace, and rebuild the equipment used in Iraq. Moreover, as GAO reported in September 2008, the cost of closing the large number of installations in Iraq will likely be significant, according to U.S. Army officials. However, these costs are difficult to estimate due to uncertainties related to the management of hazardous materials and waste, as well as the transfer of personal property. Finally, after deployed units return home, DOD will need to invest in training and equipment to return these units to levels capable of performing "full spectrum operations"—all of which could increase war-related costs.

As of September 2008, DOD has reported about $508 billion in obligations for operations in and around Iraq as part of Operation Iraqi Freedom. However, our prior work has shown that the data in DOD's monthly report of GWOT obligations are of questionable reliability. GAO was unable to ensure that DOD's reported obligations for GWOT were complete and accurate. Therefore, these reported obligations, including obligations for specific operations, should be considered approximations. For example, GAO found numerous problems with DOD's processes for recording and reporting its war- related costs, including long-standing deficiencies in DOD's financial management systems and business processes, the use of estimates instead of actual cost data, and the lack of adequate supporting documentation. DOD has taken some steps to address these issues, but problems remain. Meanwhile, DOD uses these reported obligations to develop funding estimates for many types of costs associated with Operation Iraqi Freedom, such as procurement and some types of equipment reset. Without transparent and accurate cost information, Congress and DOD will not have reliable information on how much the war is costing, sufficent details on how appropriated funds are spent, or the reliable historical data needed to develop and provide oversight of future funding needs.

Reliable Cost Reporting and Cost Estimating Processes Are Critical for Sound Defense Funding and Budgetary Decision Making

Funding for operations in support of GWOT, including Operation Iraqi Freedom, has been provided through annual appropriations, as well as supplemental appropriations that are outside the annual budget process. With U.S. commitments in Iraq continuing for the foreseeable future, requiring decision makers to make difficult decisions, GAO has recommended that DOD consider moving recurring costs into the baseline budget, as it has done with other operations. As costs for an operation reach a known level of effort and costs become more predictable, additional funding should be built into the baseline budget to provide decision makers with more transparent information. GAO has made recommendations to improve transparency and fiscal responsibility related to funding the war on terrorism and to help Congress and the administration establish priorities and make trade-offs among those priorities in defense funding. DOD has taken steps to address several of GAO's recommendations in order to improve the reliability and transparency of its reported cost information and some progress has been made. However, until all DOD efforts are more fully implemented, it is too soon to know the extent to which these changes will improve the reliability of DOD's cost reporting.

Oversight Questions

1. To what extent has DOD estimated the future costs of any continued military involvement in Iraq?
2. How will the redeployment of U.S. forces and equipment from Iraq affect funding needs and requirements?
3. What steps is DOD taking to move recurring GWOT costs into its baseline budgets?
4. What steps is DOD taking to accurately report costs by operation?
5. How will DOD balance funding requirements for Iraq with funding needs to support other military operations, such as in Afghanistan?
6. What, if any, steady state funding will be required to support DOD activities in Iraq following the eventual drawdown of U.S. combat forces?

Point of Contact

Sharon Pickup, 202-512-9619, pickups@gao.gov

Enclosure VI:
Transitioning from a Predominantly Military to a Civilian Presence in Iraq

Background

A May 2004 presidential directive affirmed, upon the termination of the Coalition Provisional Authority, that the Chief of Mission would assume responsibility for all U.S. employees, policies, and activities in Iraq, except those under an area military commander. It also gave the U.S. Central Command responsibility for U.S. security and military operations in Iraq, and U.S. efforts to develop Iraqi security forces.

Issue

The United States had a projected 140,000 military personnel deployed in Iraq in March 2009 (see app. II). In addition, there are about 1,300 authorized U.S. personnel assigned to the U.S. embassy in Baghdad—one of the largest in the world—including about 450 civilian personnel at 28 Provincial Reconstruction Teams (PRT) at the provincial and neighborhood levels. The large U.S. military presence has provided vital support to civilian operations and has undertaken many traditionally civilian tasks. In further defining its strategy for Iraq, the administration needs consider how to transition from a predominantly military presence to a civilian one as U.S. forces draw down.

Key Findings

The projected 140,000 U.S. military personnel in Iraq are part of the Multinational Force-Iraq (MNF-I). This U.S.-led force operates under the U.S. Central Command and consists of three major units—the Multinational Security Transition Command-Iraq (MNSTC-I), which is responsible for organizing Iraqi security forces; the Multinational Corps-Iraq (MNC-I), the tactical unit responsible for command and control of operations throughout Iraq; and the Gulf Region Division, U.S. Army Corps of Engineers, which provides engineering, program, and project management support for civil and military construction throughout Iraq (see Figure 1).

U.S. Military Has an Extensive Organizational and Basing Footprint in Iraq

MNF-I has an extensive basing footprint in Iraq. According to a DOD report, as of March 2009, MNF-I had a total of 51 larger bases—known as contingency operation bases and sites—throughout the country. Contingency operating bases are usually occupied by an element larger than a brigade combat team, typically serve as a hub for command and control or logistics, and may include an airfield that can accomodate C-130 aircraft. MNF-I also has about 232 smaller bases, known as contingency operation locations, that are usually occupied by a battalion-size element capable of quick response to operations, security, civic assistance, and humanitarian assistance relief.

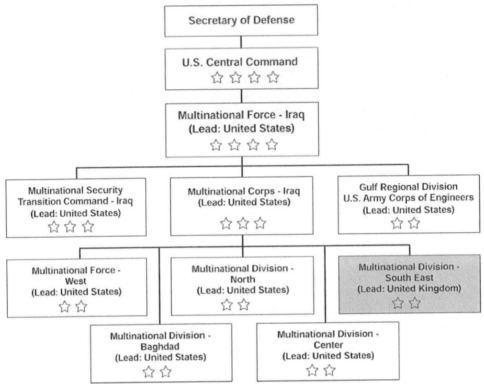

Source: GAO analysis of DOD and Multinational Force-Iraq documents.

Figure 1. Organization of Multinational Force-Iraq.

Large Military Presence Has Supported U.S. Civilian Operations and Has Undertaken Many Civilian Tasks

In addition to conducting counterinsurgency operations, U.S. military personnel under MNF-I and its subordinate commands have performed a wide range of activities in Iraq, including supporting U.S. civilian operations, rebuilding Iraq's infrastructure, and training and equipping Iraqi security forces. For example:

- U.S. military forces provide PRTs—most of which are located on U.S. military bases—with extensive security, food, housing, medical evacuation, and other support. The military commander has authority over the security and movement of embedded PRTs. Many others provide security for PRTs that are collocated with U.S. military units. As U.S. forces draw down, the Department of State (State) will have to play a larger role in providing security and other support for U.S. civilians.
- The U.S. Army Corps of Engineers, Gulf Region Division, and MNC-I have played key roles in reconstructing Iraq. As of January 2009, the Gulf Region Division had overseen nearly $7 billion in reconstruction projects in such areas as electricity, oil,

water, hospitals, and schools. Further, from fiscal years 2004 through 2008, DOD obligated about $3.3 billion in Commander's Emergency Response Program funds for projects that are intended to respond to urgent humanitarian relief and reconstruction requirements at the brigade and battalion levels. This program has funded about 34,400 education, electricity, sanitation, and other projects. In comparison, the U.S. Agency for International Development (USAID)—the primary U.S. foreign assistance agency—has obligated $7.2 billion on reconstruction projects in several areas in Iraq from fiscal year 2003 through the end of December 2008. It is unclear what assistance USAID will provide after U.S. forces leave Iraq.
- Two MNF-I subordinate commands support the development of capable Iraqi security forces. MNSTC-I is responsible for organizing, training, equipping, and mentoring Iraqi military and police, as well as advising Iraq's Ministry of Interior and Ministry of Defense. Brigades under MNC-I partner with Iraqi army units during operations. This arrangement differs from other countries where a DOD security cooperation organization manages security assistance programs for the military and State manages and funds police training under the direction and supervision of the Chief of Mission.

Oversight Questions

1. How does the U.S. government plan to provide security, housing, medical evacuation, and life support for its civilian personnel in Iraq as U.S. forces draw down and eventually leave Iraq?
2. What additional resources, if any, would State, USAID, or other civilian agencies require to compensate for the loss of military support to civilian government operations and tasks?
3. What is DOD and State's plan for transitioning assistance to Iraqi security forces from MNF-I to a traditional security cooperation organization and police training program under Chief of Mission authority?

Points of Contact

Joseph A. Christoff, 202-512-8979, christoffj@gao.gov

ENCLOSURE VII:

RIGHTSIZING THE U.S. CIVILIAN PRESENCE IN IRAQ

Background

The U.S. Embassy in Baghdad is one of the largest U.S. embassies in the world. As of March 2009, it had about 1,300 authorized U.S. civilian positions.

Issue

The U.S. Embassy in Baghdad was established under extraordinary circumstances in a war zone environment. Normalizing embassy operations, including determining appropriate staffing levels, will be a challenge. Security vulnerabilities and escalating costs have led to calls to evaluate and realign—or rightsize—the number and location of staff at U.S. embassies and consulates worldwide. A clearly defined strategy for U.S. efforts in Iraq will be critical for the rightsizing exercise at Embassy Baghdad.

Key Findings

In 2002, GAO developed a framework that provides a systematic approach for assessing overseas civilian government workforce size and identifying options for rightsizing. The framework links staffing levels to the mission's priorities and requirements, physical security, and operational costs. The rightsizing framework encourages consideration of a range of options for meeting workload requirements after an analysis of mission, security, and cost tradeoffs. Decision makers are then able to determine whether to add, reduce, or change the staff mix at an embassy. The Office of Management and Budget and Department of State (State) have adopted this framework. State has used it as the basis for rightsizing reviews at more than 120 embassies.

State Has Adopted GAO's Rightsizing Framework

Embassy Baghdad Is Scheduled to Conduct a Rightsizing Review in 2009

Embassy Baghdad is scheduled to conduct a rightsizing review in the fall of 2009 to link its long-term staffing needs to key mission goals. The embassy should consider the following as part of this review:

- *Assessing mission priorities and requirements.* The placement and composition of staff overseas must reflect the highest priority goals of U.S. foreign policy, both in terms of worldwide presence, and within a specific post. The 2009 rightsizing review will require a long-term, strategic assessment of Embassy Baghdad priorities and allow State and other agencies to determine their workload requirements.

- *Determining the appropriate mix of staff.* As of March 2009, Embassy Baghdad had about 1,300 authorized U.S. civilian positions and a mix of contractors, third country nationals, and locally hired Iraqis. Unlike most other posts, State has faced challenges in hiring and retaining Iraqi employees, as association with the U.S. government continues to place Iraqi embassy staff at risk. Thus, State has had to rely more extensively on U.S. direct-hire civilians and contractors than is customary at other U.S. embassies—a more costly approach than hiring local Iraqis.

- *Determining the future role of temporary U.S. civilian entities in Iraq.* The number of U.S. civilians in Iraq has been, in part, driven by the need to staff temporary entities in Iraq. For example, as of March 2009, the U.S. government had about 450 personnel deployed to U.S.- led Provincial Reconstruction Teams (PRT) in Iraq, which aim to increase Iraq's capacity to govern and deliver public services.
- According to State, PRTs will eventually draw down, but there is currently no determination as to what residual form, if any, the PRTs will take. Furthermore, in 2007, State established the temporary Iraq Transition Assistance Office (ITAO) to help maintain an effective diplomatic presence in Iraq. ITAO was tasked with supporting U.S. agencies in Iraq in their implementation of U.S. foreign assistance, including hiring temporary U.S. employees. At Embassy Baghdad, according to State, there are about 100 such positions. It is unclear what role, if any, temporary entities such as PRTs and ITAO will play in the future.

- *Providing security for U.S. civilian personnel during and after the U.S. military transition.* According to State, Embassy Baghdad has more security requirements than other U.S. embassies. Keeping staff secure, yet productive, remains one of the largest challenges for State's diplomatic security agents, who are responsible for securing the embassy's personnel, facilities, and information. According to State, in addition to diplomatic security agents, the department obligated about $1.1 billion from fiscal years 2006 through 2008 to fund approximately 1,400 security contractors in Iraq. To secure the embassy personnel and safeguard embassy information, State also has relied on support from the U.S. military. As the U.S. military transitions out of Iraq, State's workload—and thus its resource requirements—will increase.

- *Assessing the costs of Embassy Baghdad operations.* State has called for the consolidation of as many administrative and programmatic activities at overseas posts as possible to contain costs and expose fewer employees to security risks. The International Consolidated Administrative Support Services (ICASS) system offers a standard method of sharing administrative costs such as motor pool, utilities, and information technology services. According to State, ICASS is not operational in Iraq due to the mission's security needs. Some agencies may need to reassess their staffing levels in Iraq once they are required to pay their share of administrative costs.

Oversight Questions

1. What type of diplomatic mission does the administration envision in Iraq and how does it plan to provide for the security of its personnel, facilities, and information?
2. To what extent does State have contingency plans in place if Embassy Baghdad is unable to decrease its reliance on U.S. civiliangovernment personnel over the next 5 years?
3. To what extent does State have plans in place to balance priorities for temporary entities in Iraq, such as PRTs, and any future consulates in Iraq against the security requirements and costs of operations?
4. When should non-State agencies at Embassy Baghdad be expected to contribute to the full-cost recovery of administrative support services?

Points of Contact

Joseph A. Christoff, 202-512-8979, christoffj@gao.gov
Jess Ford, 202-512-4268, fordj@gao.gov

ENCLOSURE VIII:

CONSIDERING THE LEVEL OF ENGAGEMENT OF THE INTERNATIONAL COMMUNITY

Background

Since 2003, 38 countries have participated in the coalition to help secure Iraq. In addition, 42 nations and international organizations have provided direct financial assistance in the form of grants or loans for reconstruction efforts. Several nations have also forgiven some of Iraq's outstanding debt to help Iraq finance its reconstruction.

Issue

The international community is an important partner in Iraq's reconstruction and economic development efforts, providing varying levels of military and financial assistance since 2003. Since January 2004, the United States' 38 coalition partners have collectively contributed as many as 25,600 troops to help stabilize the security situation. International organizations and several countries also pledged substantial financial assistance for reconstruction efforts, offering Iraq almost $12 billion in loans and providing $5.6 billion in grants. The Paris Club and commercial creditors have forgiven most of Iraq's Saddam Hussein regime debt, as Iraq seeks relief from its high debt burden. As the United States further defines its assistance strategy for Iraq, it must coordinate its efforts with those of the international community.

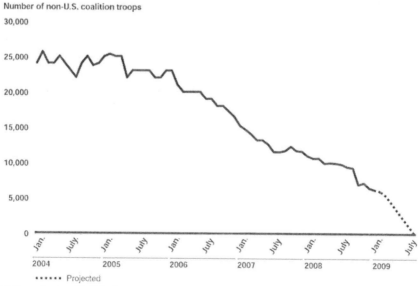

Source: GAO analysis of DOD data.

Figure 1. Non-U.S. Coalition Troops in Iraq.

Key Findings

By December 2003, the multinational force in Iraq included 34 nations and almost 151,000 troops—about 24,000 of which were provided by coalition partners.[8] As the security situation has improved and the United Nations (UN) mandate for the multinational force expired, most coalition partners have removed their troops. As of March 2009, only three coalition partners remain in Iraq—Australia, Romania, and the United Kingdom. These coalition partners have an agreement with Iraq to remove their troops by July 2009 (see figure 1). At that time, the United States will be the sole remaining nation with troops stationed in Iraq.

Non-U.S. Coalition Troops Expected to Leave Iraq by July 2009

To support reconstruction of Iraq's infrastructure and essential services, international donors have offered Iraq almost $12 billion in loans and provided about $5.6 billion in grants. As of January 2009, the Iraqi government had entered into agreements to borrow more than $3.7 billion from Italy, Iran, Japan, the International Monetary Fund (IMF), and the World Bank, according to the Department of State (State). Of the $5.6 billion given in grants, almost one-third—or $1.8 billion—has been deposited in the International Reconstruction Fund Facility for Iraq, which is composed of two trust funds, one run by the UN Development Group and the other by the World Bank. Almost all of these funds have been committed to almost 160 projects that will be completed by 2010. In February 2009, the UN and World Bank presented plans to commit the remaining funds and close out the trust funds by 2013. Both organizations plan to fund any additional assistance to Iraq through other funding streams, according to State.

The International Community Has Provided Reconstruction Funding

As the security situation has improved, international organizations have increased their assistance and re-examined their strategies. In August 2008, the UN released its Iraq Assistance Strategy for Iraq 2008-2010 that defines how the UN will support Iraq's reconstruction in various sectors, including governance, education, and economic reform through projects and technical assistance. In the last year, the UN also has added staff and is considering opening offices in Kirkuk, Najaf, Ramadi, and Mosul to support its increased assistance activities. Similarly, the World Bank is developing an updated assistance strategy to replace its current strategy from August 2005.

Some of Iraq's Creditors Have Supported Reconstruction through Debt Relief

To help attract investment needed to finance its economic reconstruction, Iraq has sought debt forgiveness for loans taken under the Saddam Hussein regime. At the end of 2004, Iraq owed about $120 billion to foreign creditors— an amount almost five times the size of its economy at the time. Of that external debt, Iraq owed about $36 billion to members of the Paris Club,[9] who committed to forgive 80 percent of that debt if Iraq agreed to follow an IMF reform program. Iraq received the final tranche of Paris Club debt relief in late 2008. Nevertheless, Department of the Treasury officials estimate that Iraq owes between $49 and

$77 billion in bilateral debt. In addition to these debts, Iraq owes $29 billion in compensation claims for damages and losses resulting from Iraq's invasion and occupation of Kuwait in 1990.[10] Iraq's oil revenues are currently immune from garnishment, liens, and other judgments that would compel Iraq to pay these debts and claims, but this immunity will expire in December 2009 absent further UN Security Council action.

Oversight Questions

1. What efforts are under way to help Iraq coordinate any future bilateral assistance, including the United States, for meeting its reconstruction and development needs?
2. How will U.S. strategic planning reflect the efforts of the UN and other international organizations in such areas as elections assistance, resolution of disputed internal boundaries, and electricity production?
3. How is the United States helping Iraq in its efforts to secure relief from its remaining Saddam Hussein regime debts?

Point of Contact

Joseph A. Christoff, 202-512-8979, christoffj@gao.gov

ENCLOSURE IX:

BUILDING IRAQ'S CAPACITY TO ASSUME A GREATER COST SHARE OF ITS SECURITY, RECONSTRUCTION, AND ECONOMIC NEEDS

Background

Oil export revenues are critical to Iraq's economy, accounting for over half of the country's gross domestic product and over 90 percent of revenues. From 2005 through 2008, Iraq generated an estimated $152 billion in revenues from crude oil export sales.

Issue

From 2005 through 2007, Iraq had an estimated cumulative budget surplus of $29 billion, in part due to limited spending of its investment budgets. The need for Iraq to spend its own resources has become increasingly critical as U.S. agencies have obligated nearly 90 percent of the $49 billion in U.S. appropriations since fiscal year 2003 for reconstruction and stabilization efforts in Iraq. Agencies have disbursed nearly 80 percent of these appropriations, as of December 2008. Iraq's substantial oil reserves and current budgetary resources offer the government of Iraq the potential to better finance more of the costs of its own security, reconstruction, and economic needs.

Key Findings

As of June 2008, the Iraqi government had accumulated financial deposits of $39.6 billion (a 33 percent increase from December 2007), held in the Development Fund for Iraq (DFI) at the New York Federal Reserve Bank and central government deposits at the Central Bank of Iraq (CBI) and Iraq's commercial banks. This balance is the result, in part, of an estimated cumulative budget surplus from 2005 through 2008.

Table 1. Iraqi Revenues, Expenditures, and Surpluses, 2005-2008.

(Billions of U.S. dollars)	2005	2006	2007	Total 2005-2007	2008	Total 2005-2008
Total revenues	$24.1	$32	$39.9	$96.0	$67.8	$163.7
MoF expenditures	17.6	22.8	26.6	67.0	49.5	116.5
Surplus	6.5	9.2	13.3	29.0	18.3	47.3

Source: GAO analysis of CBI and IMF data and Iraqi Ministry of Finance Budget (MoF).
Note: Total revenues for 2008 are based on actual crude oil export receipts and IMF projections for other revenues, such as taxes and domestic oil sales. Sums may differ from totals due to rounding.

This amount does not include funds in Iraq's foreign exchange reserves, funds held at the New York Federal Reserve Bank intended for Foreign Military Sales purchases, or funds disbursed from the DFI to J.P. Morgan Chase and Citibank for payment on letters of credit.

Iraqi Government Accumulated Surpluses from 2005 through 2008

For 2008, the Iraqi government generated an estimated $68 billion in total revenues, of which crude oil export sales accounted for about $62 billion. As displayed in table 1, Iraq ended 2005 through 2007 with a cumulative budget surplus of $29 billion. GAO estimates that Iraq ended 2008 with another budget surplus of $18.3 billion. As a result, the Iraqi government had a cumulative budget surplus of about $47.3 billion at the end of 2008. This is less than GAO's prior projection of a cumulative surplus of between $67 billion and $79 billion and reflects declining oil prices and an increase in Iraqi spending. In the preliminary 2009 Iraqi budget, the Iraqi government projects a budget deficit of $16 billion, which would indicate that it plans to spend a portion of the accumulated surpluses from prior years.

Iraq's inability to spend its resources, particularly on investment activities, limits the government's efforts to further economic development and deliver essential services to the Iraqi people. From 2005 through 2007, the Iraqi government spent an estimated $67 billion on operating and investment activities. Ninety percent was spent on operating expenses, such as salaries and goods and services, and the remaining 10 percent on investments, such as structures and vehicles. While total expenditures grew from 2005 through 2007, Iraq was unable to spend all of its budgeted funds. For example, in 2007, Iraq spent 80 percent of its $29 billion total operating budget and 28 percent of its $12 billion total investment budget. However, the central government ministries[11] responsible for providing essential services to the Iraqi people spent a smaller share, 11 percent, of their $8 billion investment budgets. In 2008, Iraq's investment expenditures have increased as compared to 2007. Iraq spent 39 percent of its $24 billion investment budget, while the central government ministries have spent 23 percent of their $16 billion investment budget. According to U.S. government, coalition, and international officials, a number of factors continue to affect the Iraqi government's ability to spend more of its revenues on capital investments and effectively manage resources. These factors include the shortage of trained staff, weak procurement and budgeting systems, and violence and sectarian strife.

Iraqi Government Has Been Unable to Spend All of Its Investment Budget

Since 2005, multiple U.S. agencies have led individual efforts to improve the capacity of Iraq's ministries without having an overall integrated strategy. In 2007, *The New Way Forward* emphasized the need to build capacity in Iraq's ministries and help the government execute its capital investment budgets. In response, U.S. capacity development efforts shifted their emphasis from longterm institution-building projects to an immediate effort to help Iraqi ministries overcome their inability to spend their capital investment budgets.

U.S. Has Funded Capacity Building Activities Since 2005 but Lacks Integrated Strategy

In October 2007, GAO recommended that Congress consider conditioning future appropriations on the completion of an integrated strategy for U.S. capacity development efforts. In June 2008, State and Treasury created a new Public Financial Management Action Group to help integrate and coordinate U.S. government assistance to improve budget execution. In addition, in September 2008, State hired a contractor to draft a strategic planning document for ministry capacity development. As of March 2009, State is reviewing the contractor's proposals.

Oversight Questions

1. How do U.S. capacity-building efforts and future foreign assistance programs in Iraq address the government of Iraq's ability to spend its resources on investment and maintenance activities?
2. What strategy does the United States have for transferring remaining defense and reconstruction costs to the government of Iraq as current U.S. appropriations for these rebuilding activities ends?
3. What budgetary resources can the government of Iraq provide to increase its support for security, economic, and reconstruction efforts in the country?

Point of Contact

Joseph A. Christoff, 202-512-8979, christoffj@gao.gov

Enclosure X:

Building Iraq's Capacity to Improve Critical Service Sectors

Background

Following the 2003 invasion, U.S. and Iraqi authorities inherited an infrastructure that had deteriorated due to the previous regime's neglect, international sanctions, and years of conflict, leaving many Iraqis with limited or no access to essential services.

Issue

The Iraqi government's efforts to increase its legitimacy and counter the insurgent threat depend, in large part, on its ability to expand its oil exports and provide essential services such as electricity and clean water to all Iraqi communities. Given that appropriated U.S. funds for rebuilding these sectors have largely been expended, continued reconstruction and sustainability will be dependent on an Iraqi government that can resolve the challenges it faces in delivering essential services. As the administration further defines its plans for Iraq, it will need to consider how best to support the Iraqi government's efforts and address these challenges.

Key Findings

Oil production and exports account for about 90 percent of Iraq's revenue. The Iraqi government's ability to fund reconstruction efforts and provide for its citizens depends, in part, on increasing oil production and exports. Iraqi and U.S. government investments in the oil sector have increased production and exports since 2003, but U.S. officials have stated that insufficient focus on security limited the impact of the initial U.S. investment. Iraq's oil production increased from an annual average of 1.3 million barrels per day (mbpd) in 2003 to 2.36 mbpd as of March 2009. According to the Departments of Defense and State (State), investment in Iraq's oil sector is below the minimum required to sustain current production; additional foreign and private investments are needed. The Ministry of Oil has indicated that investments between $25 billion and $75 billion are needed to achieve its production target of 6 mbpd. In 2008, the Ministry of Oil spent $421 million, or 19 percent of its investment budget for that year.

Oil Production and Exports Have Increased but More Investment Is Needed

Restoring the electrical infrastructure is critical to reviving the Iraqi economy and ensuring productivity of the oil sector; however, demand has grown subtantially and continues to outstrip capacity. For 2008, supply met around 52 percent of demand, even with increased generation. As a result, Iraq continues to experience electrical shutdowns despite billions of dollars invested. According to State, at the end of November 2005, average hours of power per day were 8.7 hours in Baghdad and 12.6 hours nationwide; by the end of November 2008, Baghdad averaged 15.4 hours and the rest of the country averaged 14.6 hours. The Iraqi Ministry of Electricity estimated in its 2006-2015 plan that it would need $27 billion over the next 6 to 10 years to provide reliable electricity across Iraq by 2015. However, U.S. government officials working with the ministry estimate twice that amount will be needed for power generation, transmission, distribution, and other infrastructure. Based on U.S. and United Nations reporting, inadequate operating and maintenance practices, as well as the lack of skilled technicians, inhibit an effective electrical infrastructure.

Electricity Production Has Increased, but Demand Continues to Outstrip Capacity

In the water sector, as of July 2008, U.S.-funded projects had the capacity to provide an additional 8.1 million Iraqis with potable water, short of the goal of 8.5 million. Even with the additional capacity, many Iraqis are without water or have access to water that puts them at risk of diseases such as cholera and dysentery, as evidenced by outbreaks in 2007 and 2008. According to the United Nations, only 40 percent of children have reliable access to safe drinking water; with water treatment plants operating at only 17 percent capacity, large volumes of untreated waste are discharged into Iraq's waterways. The health risks associated with a lack of access to potable water and proper sewage treatment are compounded by the shortage of medical professionals in Iraq's health care system. The World Bank has estimated $14.4 billion is needed to rebuild the Iraqi public works and water system.

Even with Additional Capacity, Many Iraqis Remain without Potable Water

Table 1. Comparison of U.S. and Iraqi Allocations and Spending for Selected Sectors (in billions of U.S. dollars)

Sectors	U.S. Government Fiscal years 2003–2008 Allocated	U.S. Government Fiscal years 2003–June 2008 Spent[a]	Government of Iraq 2005–2008 Allocated	Government of Iraq 2005–2008 Spent[a]
Oil	$2.7	$2.5	$10.8	$0.7
Electricity	5.3	4.8	5.2	0.8
Water resources	2.9	2.2	1.3	0.6
Total	$10.9	$9.5	$17.2	$2.0

Source: GAO analysis of Iraq Ministry of Finance budgets and expenditures, and Departments of State, Defense, and Treasury and U.S. Agency for International Development data.

Note: The Iraqi figures refer to investment expenses which include capital goods and capital projects. The sums may differ from totals due to rounding.

[a] This refers to funds disbursed by U.S. agencies and funds spent by the respective Iraqi ministries.

Iraqi Government Has Spent Little on Improving Essential Services and Faces Challenges in Sustaining Existing Projects

Iraq has not followed through on commitments to spend more of its own money on reconstruction efforts and faces challenges sustaining U.S.-funded projects. As table 1 indicates, U.S. agencies have spent 87 percent, or about $9.5 billion, of the $10.9 billion allocated since fiscal year 2003 for reconstruction activities in the oil, electricity, and water sectors. In contrast, Iraq has spent about 12 percent, or about $2.0 billion of the $17.2 billion allocated for investment activities in these sectors. In addition, Iraq has faced difficulties in sustaining U.S.-funded reconstruction projects. According to U.S. officials, Iraqi managers lack the skill level and authority to create plans and buy the materials necessary to sustain projects in the energy and water sectors. Moreover, poor security has prevented the successful implementation of long-term training programs to create the local capacity needed to operate and maintain U.S.-funded projects.

Oversight Questions

1. What activities are under way to strengthen the Iraqi government's ability to operate and maintain its essential services infrastructure, particularly for those efforts funded by the U.S. government?
2. How much additional investment in Iraq's oil infrastructure is needed to ensure sustained production and export levels? What actions is Iraq taking to encourage foreign investment?
3. While the capacity for providing potable water has increased, what steps are being taken to ensure both sustainable delivery and quality of water throughout Iraq?

Point of Contact

Joseph A. Christoff, 202-512-8979, christoffj@gao.gov

ENCLOSURE XI:

ENACTING IRAQI LEGISLATION TO PROMOTE NATIONAL RECONCILIATION

Background

In 2007, *The New Way Forward* identified Iraqi political compromise as crucial to promoting national reconciliation and stabilizing the country. The U.S. and Iraqi governments stated that passage of legislation to address core Sunni, Shi'a, and Kurd grievances and to share hydrocarbon resources equitably was essential.

Issue

Since 2007, the Iraqi government has passed legislation allowing some former members of the Ba'ath party to work for the government, granted amnesty to Iraqis accused of or in prison for certain crimes, defined provincial powers, and passed and implemented a provincial elections law. These actions could address grievances by Sunnis and others, namely that they have been removed from government, unfairly arrested, and underrepresented in provincial councils. However, Iraq has not fully implemented some of these laws, passed hydrocarbon legislation, or a law to demobilize militias. Finally, Iraq has not completed the constitutional review or the constitutionally mandated process to deal with claims over disputed areas, especially Kirkuk. In further defining the U.S. strategy for Iraq, the administration should consider how to support Iraq's reconciliation efforts.

Key Findings

Figure 1 shows the steps Iraq has taken as of February 2009 to enact key laws intended to promote national reconciliation.

Despite Sectarian Differences, the Iraqi Government Has Passed Key Legislation

Although Iraq has enacted laws on de-Ba'athification, amnesty, and provincial powers, it has been slow to fully implement them. For example, the Iraqi government passed de-Ba'athification reform in February 2008, but as of January 2009, the Council of Ministers had not nominated individuals to head the new commission to implement the law. The amnesty law provides for the release of Iraqis sentenced to prison and those under investigation or trial, provided they are not involved in certain crimes such as kidnapping or murder. According to the Department of State (State), Iraqi courts have granted amnesty to many, but releases are slow. Also, the Iraqi and U.S. governments are working to transfer detainees held by U.S. forces to Iraqi facilities, as required by this law and the November 2008 security agreement with Iraq, so that the provisions of the amnesty law can be applied to them. U.S.

forces held approximately 15,000 Iraqi detainees, as of January 2009, according to State and Department of Defense (DOD) officials. In addition, Iraq held provincial elections in 14 provinces on January 31, 2009.

	Laws drafted and reviewed	Draft referred to Council Representatives/Committee	First reading completed	Second reading completed	Third reading vote taken	Ratification completed; procedures	Law published in Gazette
De-Ba'athification	✓	✓	✓	✓	✓	✓	✓
Amnesty	✓	✓	✓	✓	✓	✓	✓
Provincial powers	✓	✓	✓	✓	✓	✓	✓
Elections							
Electoral commission	✓	✓	✓	✓	✓	✓	✓
Provincial election law	✓	✓	✓	✓	✓	✓	✓
Hydrocarbon laws							
Framework	✓	✓					
Revenue sharing	✓						
Ministry of Oil Restructuring	✓						
Iraq National Oil Company	—						
Disarmament and demobilization	—						

✓ Steps taken since February 2009.
— No legislation drafted

Source: GAO analysis of Department of State, Department of Defense, United Nations, and Iraqi government data.

Figure 1. Status of Enacting Iraqi Legislation.

The Iraqi government has not enacted laws to share oil revenues and disarm militias, and has not resolved issues in its constitutional review.

Some Legislation Has Yet to Be Enacted and Constitutional Issues Have Not Been Resolved

- Hydrocarbon legislation consists of four separate laws, but the key framework law is stalled, according to State. This law defines the control and management of Iraq's oil and gas sector. According to State, the delay illustrates struggles between the federal government and the Kurdistan Regional Government about how much control the Kurdistan Regional Government will have over its oil resources.
- As of February 2009, a law to disarm and demobilize militias had not passed. According to State, no legislation has been proposed, but militia activity, specifically from Jaysh al-Mahdi, has substantially declined. According to a December 2008 DOD report, some militias are considering reconciliation with the government.
- Iraq's Constitution was approved in a national referendum in October 2005, but this did not resolve several contentious issues, including the powers of the presidency

versus the prime minister, claims over disputed areas such as oil-rich Kirkuk, and the relative powers of the regions versus the federal government. Among these issues, a resolution on the status of Kirkuk remains a key issue for the Kurdistan Regonal Government and the United Nations ; Kurdistan Regional Government officials want resolved the issue of whether Kirkuk is to be part of Kurdistan. As of February 2009, the United Nations was working with a special committee to recommend mechanisms for sharing power in Kirkuk.

Oversight Questions

1. To what extent have new provincial elections helped stabilize Iraq and support national reconciliation?
2. What are the prospects of resolving the impasse on hydrocarbon legislation?
3. What challenges remain to implementing the laws that have already been passed?
4. What actions should the United States take to encourage the Iraqi government to pass the remaining legislation intended to promote national reconciliation?

Point of Contact

Joseph A. Christoff, 202-512-8979, christoffj@gao.gov

Enclosure XII:

Assisting Iraq's Refugees

Background

The United Nations (UN) reports that about 4.8 million Iraqis have been displaced from their homes, with about 2 million fleeing to neighboring countries. According to the UN High Commissioner for Refugees (UNHCR), Iraqi refugees pose an unprecedented burden on the economies and social infrastructures of the countries hosting them.

Issue

Despite security improvements, UNHCR has reported that conditions are not yet suitable for the safe return of Iraqi refugees, and most refugees that do return are settling in areas controlled by their particular sect. According to the Department of State (State), the United States has recognized the need to take the lead in mitigating the effects of this humanitarian crisis. As the administration further defines its plan for Iraq, it will need to consider how best to support the Iraqi government and the international community in addressing the needs of Iraqis displaced within Iraq, as well as those who have fled to neighboring countries.

Key Findings

The lack of reliable needs estimates impedes U.S. and international efforts to assist Iraqi refugees in Jordan and Syria. Official Jordanian and Syrian government estimates on the number of Iraqi refugees in each country may be overstated, with each country estimating up to 500,000 and 1,500,000 Iraqi refugees, respectively, in their countries. This is in contrast to the approximately 54,000 and 220,000 Iraqis that UNHCR had officially registered in Jordan and Syria, respectively, as of September 2008. Neither country has enabled an independent and comprehensive survey of refugees to be undertaken, asserting that assistance should not be targeted toward Iraqi refugees while they have populations that need help. Both countries have based requests for refugee assistance primarily on their countries' health and education needs rather than on the numbers of displaced Iraqis in their countries, and the U.S. government and UN have included Iraqi refugees and host country populations in their assistance programs. Donor country representatives further noted that the lack of objective and complete information on the numbers and needs of refugees has made it difficult to garner support for these efforts.

Lack of Reliable Needs Assessments Impedes Assistance

The U.S. government and UNHCR face challenges offering lasting solutions for Iraqi refugees. According to UNHCR, voluntary repatriation is the preferred solution, but conditions in Iraq are not yet suitable for Iraqis to return. The Iraqi government has cited improvements in security and offered financial incentives to returning families, but there is no clear trend on the number of Iraqis returning to or leaving Iraq. Difficulties renewing visas, lack of funds, and limited access to employment and public services affect Iraqis' decisions to stay in or return to Iraq. Another solution is resettlement in the host countries, though Jordan and Syria consider Iraqi refugees "guests" who should return to Iraq once the security situation improves. Resettlement to a third country is another option, according to State. The U.S. government has made progress resettling Iraqis under its U.S. Refugee Admissions Program. In 2007, the United States admitted 1,608 Iraqi refugees but did not achieve State's expectation of admitting 2,000 to 3,000 refugees; however, the U.S. government surpassed its fiscal year 2008 goal of 12,000 with the admission of 13,823 Iraqi refugees. According to UNHCR, as of September 30, 2008, other countries resettled 5,852 Iraqi refugees in calendar years 2007 through 2008.

U.S. Government Resettles Iraqis, but Lasting Solutions Remain a Challenge

A related issue for Congress to consider is the plight of Palestinian Iraqis who have been living, mostly under very harsh conditions, in three refugee camps in Syria and Iraq for about 3 years. As of December 31, 2008, about 2,540 refugees remained in these camps. About 446 camp refugees were resettled in 2007 and 2008, mostly in Chile and Europe. According to UNHCR, during the fall of 2008, Australia, Canada, the United States, and several European countries expressed interest in resettling these refugees.

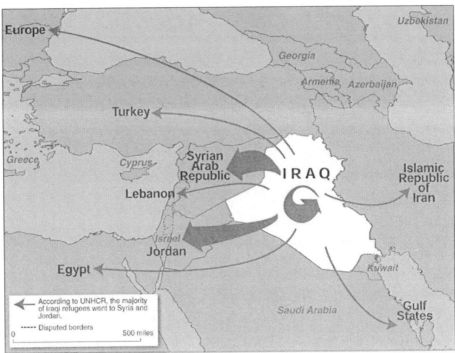

Sources: GAO based on maps from the United Nations High Commissioner for Refugees; Map Resources (map).

Figure 1. Neighboring Countries Hosting Iraqi Refugees.

GAO subsequently will issue a more detailed report on U.S. and international efforts to assist Iraqi refugees, including some of the key challenges faced in planning and delivering this assistance, such as determining the amount of funding provided for Iraqi refugee programs by the United States, Iraq, and UN agencies. GAO plans to issue a second report in 2009 that will discuss the challenges in assisting internally displaced persons within Iraq.

Oversight Questions

1. To what extent is the U.S. government helping Iraq address the needs of displaced Iraqis, bilaterally and in coordination with UN assistance efforts?
2. As U.S. military forces in Iraq draw down, how will the U.S. government aid Iraq in ensuring the security of internally displaced and returning Iraqis and support their access to housing and essential services?
3. How is the U.S. government working with the international community to improve conditions for Palestinian Iraqis in refugee camps and facilitate their eventual resettlement?

Point of Contact

Joseph A. Christoff, 202-512-8979, christoffj@gao.gov

APPENDIX I: OBJECTIVES, SCOPE, AND METHODOLOGY

The issues discussed in the 12 enclosures are based on completed and ongoing GAO work on Iraq security and reconstruction issues. They incorporate information from agency documents and interviews with U.S. officials in Iraq and Washington, D.C., including the Departments of Defense (DOD), Energy (Energy), State (State), and the Treasury (Treasury); the U.S. Agency for International Development (USAID); the Army Corps of Engineers; the Multinational Force in Iraq (MNF-I); and the Defense Intelligence Agency (DIA).

We conducted this performance audit in accordance with generally accepted government auditing standards. Those standards require that we plan and perform the audit to obtain sufficient, appropriate evidence to provide a reasonable basis for our findings and conclusions based on our audit objectives. We believe that the evidence obtained provides a reasonable basis for our findings and conclusions based on our audit objectives.

Enclosure I: Determining What Conditions Need to Be Met to Undertake a Responsible Drawdown of U.S. Forces

To discuss the change in approach that the U.S.-Iraq security agreement represents from prior strategies, we relied on previous GAO reporting and reviewed the security agreement and Strategic Framework Agreement that the U.S. and Iraqi governments signed in November 2008. We interviewed DOD and State officials to clarify the language and application of the agreements.

To present the levels of violence, we used MNF-I data on enemy-initiated attacks against the coalition and its Iraqi partners obtained from DIA. We determined the data were sufficiently reliable for establishing general trends in the number of enemy-initiated attacks in Iraq. To determine the reliability of the data, we reviewed MNF-I's attacks reporting guidance, compared the unclassified data to classified sources, and discussed how the data are collected, analyzed, and reported with DIA officials.

To report on the growth of Iraqi security forces, we relied upon DOD updates to weekly State reports. We used DOD's number of trained and equipped personnel for January 2007 data to represent the number of the Iraqi security forces. DOD changed its reporting metrics in November 2007 from "trained and equipped" forces to "authorized," "assigned," and "trained" forces. GAO determined that "assigned" data, based on payroll data, are the closest figures to the number of Iraqi security forces and are sufficiently reliable and similar to establish a general trend of growth in those forces under the previous metric. "Assigned" numbers show the same trend as other measures of Iraqi security forces growth—"trained" and "authorized" forces. However, as we have noted in previous reports, GAO recognizes limitations to these reported data. To display the change in Iraqi capabilities, we relied on unclassified DOD reporting of Iraqi Army units' "Operational Readiness Assessments." We have reviewed the Operational Readiness Assessments and, to the extent possible, corroborated the trends with classified data.

We based our discussion of administration plans for a responsible drawdown on public statements.

Enclosure II: Implementing Key Operational Requirements of the U.S.- Iraq Security Agreement

To discuss the implementation of the security agreement, we reviewed the text of agreement and the strategic framework agreement that the U.S. and Iraqi governments signed in November 2008, Coalition Provisional Authority Order 17, and the United Nations (UN) Security Council resolutions authorizing the U.S. presence in Iraq. We also interviewed State and DOD officials to clarify our understanding of the specific language and application of the agreements. We used our prior reports as background information for this enclosure.

Enclosure III: Managing the Redeployment U.S. Forces and Equipment from Iraq

To assess DOD's ability to manage the redeployment of U.S. troops from Iraq, we reviewed relevant documents, including command briefings and in-progress reviews, orders, joint and Army doctrine, relevant sections of the U.S. Code, and staff analyses that we obtained from several DOD organizations including U.S. Central Command, MNF-I, and U.S. Army Central. We also interviewed officials who were directly involved in the logistical planning efforts to determine the status and scope of these efforts. We traveled to Kuwait in May 2008 and met with DOD officials from a variety of organizations to discuss planning efforts. We also visited locations at which various aspects of the redeployment and removal process are performed and spoke with local commanders and on-site supervisors about their experiences and challenges.

Enclosure IV: Managing and Overseeing U.S. Government Contractors in Iraq during a Drawdown

To assess DOD's capacity to manage and oversee contractor performance, we relied extensively on our prior reports. In preparing these reports, we reviewed applicable DOD policies and guidance; interviewed DOD and contractor personnel in the United States, Iraq, and other locations; and reviewed contract-related information. We also reviewed the security agreement to identify provisions applicable to DOD's use of U.S. contractors in Iraq. We obtained updated information from DOD on the number of contractor personnel working under DOD contracts of as October 2008. Our prior work concluded that complete and reliable data on contractor personnel data were not available, but we presented the reported data along with their limitations as they established a minimum number of contractor personnel and provided insight into the extent to which agencies had information on the number of contractor personnel. Given the limitations we previously found, the data presented should not be used to reach conclusions about the total number of contractor personnel in Iraq.

Enclosure V: Determining the Department of Defense's Future Costs for Iraq

To discuss the costs associated with Operation Iraqi Freedom, we relied extensively on our prior reports related to reporting of overall Global War on Terrorism (GWOT) costs, estimating of GWOT funding needs, spending associated with the reset of equipment, and the redeployment of U.S. forces from Iraq, among others. Our prior work has found the data in DOD's reported obligations for GWOT to be of questionable reliability. Consequently, we are unable to ensure that DOD's reported obligations are complete, reliable, and accurate, and therefore any reported obligations contained in this enclosure should be considered approximations.

Enclosure VI: Transitioning from a Predominantly Military to a Civilian Presence in Iraq

To present the number of U.S. military personnel in Iraq, we relied on personnel data provided by DOD Joint Staff. We determined the data were sufficiently reliable for our purposes by comparing unclassified U.S. troop numbers to classified sources and discussing how the data are collected and reported with DOD officials. To determine the organization, missions, and tasks of U.S. military forces in Iraq, we reviewed documents from DOD, MNF-I, and MNF-I subordinate commands.

Enclosure VII: Rightsizing the U.S. Civilian Presence in Iraq

To develop the elements of the rightsizing framework, we analyzed previous reports on overseas staffing issues, including those of the Overseas Presence Advisory Panel (OPAP).[12] We interviewed officials from the Office of Management and Budget to discuss rightsizing initiatives in relation to the *President's Management Agenda*.[13] We discussed embassy staffing with rightsizing experts, including the Chairman of OPAP and former Undersecretaries of State for Management. We also interviewed officials from the State, DOD, Treasury, and the Departments of Commerce, Justice, and Agriculture, among others. To further develop and test the framework, we conducted a case study at the U.S. embassy in Paris (see our July 2002 report[14] for more details about this case study).

In the enclosure, we describe how elements of the rightsizing framework could be applied to the U.S. Embassy in Baghdad. We obtained agency documents and interviewed officials from State's Office of Rightsizing, the Bureau of Near Eastern Affairs, and the Bureau of Diplomatic Security regarding rightsizing challenges at Embassy Baghdad. We obtained data on the staffing levels at Embassy Baghdad from State's Bureau of Near Eastern Affairs, as its data were the most comprehensive. To assess the reliability of these data, we talked with agency officials about data limitations. We determined the data were sufficiently reliable to demonstrate that Embassy Baghdad is one of the largest U.S. embassies worldwide with an estimated 1,300 total authorized positions.

Enclosure VIII: Considering the Level of Engagement of the International Community

To present the number of non-U.S. troops participating in the coalition, we analyzed data from State and DOD from December 2003 to December 2008. The departments did not have information on coalition troops in Iraq from March to November 2003. We determined that the data were sufficiently reliable for estimating the number of troops contributed by other countries.

To discuss the international community's financial contributions to Iraq's reconstruction, we updated information previously reported by reviewing State documentation and consulting with State and UN officials.

To report on Iraq's foreign debt, we examined documents from the International Monetary Fund (IMF), the Paris Club of international creditors, and relevant U.S. agencies and international organizations. To determine the amount of outstanding debt in 2004 (prior to debt restructuring) and 2006, we used official IMF estimates of Iraq's external debt. Since the IMF estimates for 2006 included debt restructuring by non-Paris Club official creditors that had not been completed, we used the IMF estimate from 2004 for these countries. We worked with Treasury officials to update this information.

Enclosure IX: Building Iraq's Capacity to Assume a Greater Cost Share of Its Security, Reconstruction, and Economic Needs

To identify Iraq's estimated revenues and expenditures from 2005 through 2008, and Iraq's financial deposits and budget surpluses through 2008, we relied on the data sources and methodology outlined in our August 2008 report.[15] To update 2008 revenues, we used actual crude oil export revenues data through December 2008 as reported by the Central Bank of Iraq and provided by Treasury and a December 2008 update of the IMF's forecast of net revenues from oil-related public enterprises and taxes and other revenues. To update total expenditures for 2008, we reviewed Iraqi Ministry of Finance monthly budget and expenditure data through December 2008, which were provided by Treasury.

Enclosure X: Building Iraq's Capacity to Improve Critical Service Sectors

To assess Iraq's capacity to provide essential services, we relied extensively on our prior reports and updated the information as necessary. To do so, we interviewed officials and reviewed documents from the U.S. Embassy in Baghdad, DOD, and the UN. We have determined that the data were sufficiently reliable for identifying production goals and whether actual production is meeting these goals. We updated the data on U.S. and Iraqi spending for the oil, electricity, and water sector that we used in our August 2008 report. Our data on U.S. spending includes appropriations for the Iraq Reconstruction and Relief Fund, Iraq Security Forces fund, Economic Support Fund, Commander's Emergency Response Program, Iraq Freedom Fund, Democracy Fund, other agency program funds used for Iraq activities, and operating expenses from the Coalition Provisional Authority.

Enclosure XI: Enacting Iraqi Legislation to Promote National Reconciliation

To determine progress made on actions related to Iraq's constitutional review and enacting and implementing key legislation, we used prior GAO reporting and updated information where appropriate. In updating the information, we reviewed reports and documentation and spoke with officials from the UN, the U.S. Institute for Peace, nongovernmental organizations, USAID, DOD, and State. We reviewed draft laws and enacted legislation, as well as analyses of the laws.

Enclosure XII: Assisting Iraq's Refugees

To identify key challenges to providing humanitarian assistance and offering solutions to Iraqi refugees, we reviewed and analyzed reports and data from the U.S. government, the United Nations High Commissioner for Refugees (UNHCR), the International Organization for Migration (IOM), other UN agencies, foreign governments, nongovernmental organizations (NGOs), and research institutes. During our fieldwork in Washington, D.C., we met with officials from State and the Department of Homeland Security regarding refugee assistance, refugee admissions, special immigrant visa programs, and the challenges they have encountered. We also met with research institutions and NGOs and held discussion groups with NGOs conducting work in Jordan, Syria, and Iraq to discuss strategic planning and program implementation challenges. Through our fieldwork in Geneva, Switzerland; Rome, Italy; Amman, Jordan; and Damascus, Syria, we met with officials from the U.S., Jordanian, Syrian, and Iraqi governments; UNHCR and other UN umbrella agencies, including the World Food Program and IOM; international and local NGOs; and research institutions. Also, with the help of UNHCR, we held discussion groups with Iraqi refugees in Jordan and Syria to discuss their situations, needs, assistance received, and challenges encountered. We toured and observed assistance projects and activities in resettlement processing centers. We analyzed U.S. funding, refugee admissions, and visa data, and found the data to be sufficiently reliable for the purposes of this report.

APPENDIX II: LEVELS OF VIOLENCE AND U.S. FORCE LEVELS IN IRAQ

This appendix provides information on (1) the levels of violence in Iraq, as measured through trends in enemy-initiated attacks from May 2003 through January 2009 and (2) the number of U.S. troops deployed to Iraq from January 2006 through January 2009 and projected troop levels through October 2010.

Levels of Violence

As shown in figure 1, security conditions in Iraq deteriorated following the February 2006 bombing of the Golden Mosque in Samarra, but then improved following the surge of U.S. forces in Iraq during 2007. Specifically, the average daily number of enemy-initiated attacks has declined from about 180 in June 2007 to about 25 in October 2008 and has remained about the same through January 2009. This change accounts for a decrease of about 85 percent over a period of a year and a half— primarily due to decreases in violence in Baghdad and Anbar provinces. From 2003 through 2007, enemy-initiated attacks had increased around major political and religious events, such as Iraqi elections and Ramadan. In 2007 and 2008, attacks did not significantly increase during Ramadan. According to early reporting from the Multinational Force-Iraq (MNF-I), the provincial elections in January 2009 were not associated with significant increases in violence.

The enemy-initiated attacks counted in the Defense Intelligence Agency's (DIA) reporting include car, suicide, and other bombs; ambushes; murders, executions, and assassinations; sniper fire; indirect fire (mortars or rockets); direct fire (small arms or rocket-propelled grenades); surface-to-air fire (such as man-portable air defense systems, or MANPADS); and other attacks on civilians. They do not include violent incidents that coalition or Iraqi security forces initiated, such as cordon and searches, raids, arrests, and caches cleared.

According to DIA, the incidents captured in military reporting do not account for all violence throughout Iraq. For example, they may underreport incidents of Shi'a militias fighting each other and attacks against Iraqi security forces in southern Iraq and other areas with few or no coalition forces. DIA officials stated, however, that they represent a reliable and consistent source of information that can be used to identify trends in enemy activity and the overall security situation.

Reports from the Departments of Defense (DOD) and State, as well as the United Nations, have attributed the reduction in violence since June 2007 to three key factors. First, the U.S. surge of troops allowed a change of tactics and contributed to improvements in the security environment (see the following section). Second, according to DOD and MNF-I reports, the establishment of local nongovernmental security forces that oppose al Qaeda in Iraq has helped decrease the levels of violence in parts of Iraq, most notably in Anbar province. Third, the cease-fire declared in August 2007 by Moqtada al Sadr, the leader of the Mahdi Army, an extremist Shi'a militia, contributed significantly to the decline in violence in the second half of 2007, according to DOD and UN reports.

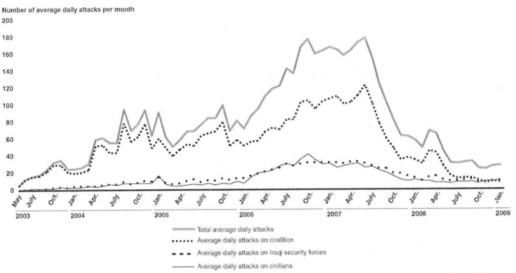

Source: GAO analysis of Defense Intelligence Agency-reported Multinational Force-Iraq data, January 2009.

Figure 1. Average Daily Enemy Initiated Attacks, May 2003 through December 2008

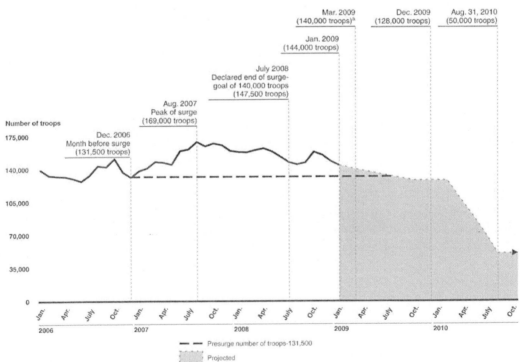

Sources: DOD, Joint Staff, and State Department data, and Presidential speech Feb. 27, 2009.

Note: Projections of troop drawdowns between March 2009 and October 2009 and between March 2010 and August 31, 2010 reflect an average rate of troop reductions over that period.

[a] DOD has not yet provided the final, unclassified number of U.S. troops in Iraq for February and March 2009. The March 2009 number is based on a projection provided by DOD officials.

Figure 2. U.S. Troops in Iraq, January 2006 through October 2010.

U.S. Force Levels in Iraq

In January 2007, the prior administration called for an increase of over 20,000 U.S. combat and other forces, including an additional five brigades, to help Iraqis clear and secure neighborhoods and protect the local population. Figure 2 shows the increase of U.S. forces in Iraq from about 131,500 in December 2006 to about 169,000 in August 2007, an overall increase of about 37,500 troops—almost 30 percent above the December 2006 force level.

In September 2007, President Bush announced that the United States would draw down the surge forces by July 2008—the end of *The New Way Forward* strategy—resulting in a decline in U.S. brigade combat teams from 20 to 15 and a projected force level of about 140,000 U.S. troops. By December 2008, another brigade combat team was removed from Iraq, bringing the total number of brigade combat teams in Iraq to 14, as of March 2009. The number of U.S. troops in Iraq has remained above projected levels for the end of the surge, and as of January 2009, there were about 144,000 U.S. troops in Iraq.

In February 2009, the President announced a significant drawdown of U.S. forces by August 31, 2010. According to DOD and MNF-I officials, the United States plans to reduce the number of combat troops from about 140,000 projected in March 2009 to about 128,000 by September 2009. This troop drawdown would represent 2 combat brigades and their support units, reducing the number of U.S. brigades from 14 to 12. Based on conditions in Iraq, the MNF-I Commanding General may recommend further reductions prior to Iraq's national election scheduled for December 2009. A few months after the election, the United States plans to further reduce U.S. forces to at most 50,000 troops by August 31, 2010. According to DOD officials, the remaining force will consist of 6 brigades and additional support units.

APPENDIX III: COMMENTS FROM THE DEPARTMENT OF THE TREASURY

Note: GAO's comment supplementing those in the report text appears at the end of this appendix.

See comment 1.

DEPARTMENT OF THE TREASURY
WASHINGTON

ASSISTANT SECRETARY

March 13, 2009

Mr. Joseph A. Christoff
Director, International Affairs and Trade
Government Accountability Office

Dear Mr. Christoff,

Thank you for the opportunity to review and comment on the March 2009 draft of the GAO's report, *Iraq – Key Issues for Congressional Oversight*. We welcome the GAO's close attention to the way forward in Iraq, and particularly the fiscal issues that impact Iraq's reconstruction, economic stability, and self-reliance. Treasury continues to be closely engaged with the Iraqi Ministry of Finance, other ministries, and the provincial governments on improving Iraq's fiscal processes to help ensure that Iraq's resources are being spent efficiently and responsibly for the betterment of the Iraqi people.

Despite lower oil prices and a changing fiscal environment, Iraq is still able to shoulder the burden of its own development, reconstruction, and security programs in 2009. The report correctly states that although Iraq's end-2008 cumulative surplus fell well short of the GAO's earlier projection of $67-79 billion, Iraq's $45 billion in cumulative budget surpluses will sufficiently cover the budgeted 2009 budget deficit of about $16 billion. However, if oil prices remain at current levels, Iraq will likely have difficulty financing large fiscal deficits in 2010 and 2011, which could impact spending on security and reconstruction. Therefore, in addition to improving budget execution, Iraq will need to better prioritize spending to help maintain fiscal sustainability in the medium term.

Iraq's expenditures have increased significantly in 2008

The report is correct to point out that Iraq's inability to fully execute its budgets hampers the government's efforts to further reconstruction and economic growth. But the report should draw attention to the significant improvements Iraq has recently made in budget execution. In 2008, Iraq made the following improvements in budget execution, particularly in spending its investment budget.

- Iraq spent $50 billion in 2008, compared to just $27 billion in 2007 (an 86% increase). While public sector wage increases contributed to the higher spending, spending on goods and services and investment projects also increased substantially. In Iraqi dinar terms, government spending increased by 77%, taking into account the 5% appreciation of the Iraqi dinar in 2008.

- Iraq's investment spending was almost $9 billion in 2008, which is 150% greater than 2007 investment spending. Including commitments, total investment spending in 2008 likely approached $12 billion (compared to roughly $6 billion in 2007).

- Iraq approved one-third of the investment budget in the August 2008 supplemental. Fully executing the original budget plus the supplemental by the end of the year would be very ambitious by any standard.

Integrated strategy to help improve Iraq's budget execution

Nonetheless, Iraq has further work to do to improve its ability to spend its own resources promptly and effectively. This issue remains a key priority for Treasury. We appreciate the report's highlighting of Treasury's work with the Embassy to deliver coordinated technical assistance to help improve Iraqi budget execution. The U.S. Government created the Public Financial Management Action Group (PFMAG) to better integrate the many U.S. civilian and military parties active in budget execution assistance. The group is dedicated to achieving four goals that are critical to facilitating Iraq's reconstruction:

- Partnering with the Iraqis to mobilize Iraq's substantial financial resources;
- Supporting budget formulation and execution through a broad-based engagement with ministries, provincial governments, and other spending units;
- Facilitating the development of a coherent budgetary framework in Iraq, incorporating municipal, provincial, and ministerial spending; and
- Integrating coalition public financial technical assistance into a coherent capacity-building effort across all levels of the Iraqi Government.

Treasury's technical advisors are a critical piece of the PFMAG, as they work with Iraqi officials at the ministries, at the Council of Representatives, and in the provinces to help achieve these stated goals. Treasury's cadre of technical advisors will continue to support the Iraqis in 2009 as the Iraqis further develop their budget formulation, execution, and monitoring processes. However, Treasury agrees with the GAO's assertion that agencies may need to reassess staffing levels if they are required to pay ICASS costs related to security and other expenses.

Andy Baukol
Acting Assistant Secretary for International Affairs
U.S. Department of the Treasury

The following is GAO's comment to the Department of the Treasury's letter dated March 13, 2009.

GAO Comment

1. GAO's estimate of Iraq's cumulative surplus differs from the Department of the Treasury's estimate because we use different sources to determine a small a portion of Iraq's 2008 government revenues—specifically, non-oil export related revenues. GAO and Treasury both use data from the Central Bank of Iraq concerning revenue generated from exports of crude oil, which represents about 90 percent of the government's revenue. However, GAO uses the International Monetary Fund's estimate of Iraq's government revenue that is derived from all other sources, such as oil-related public enterprises and taxes. In contrast, Treasury is utilizing information gathered by the U.S. Embassy in Baghdad. GAO asked Treasury officials for documentation validating their estimate, but they could not do so in time for this report's publication. GAO will work with Treasury to validate the Ministry of Finance's data for subsequent work in this area.

End Notes

[1] This figure includes appropriations for domestic and overseas military operations in support of the Global War on Terrorism, such as Operation Noble Eagle, Operation Enduring Freedom, and Operation Iraqi Freedom, as well as stabilization and reconstruction appropriations for Iraq and Afghanistan. See GAO, *Global War on Terrorism: Reported Obligations for the Department of Defense*, GAO-09-233R (Washington, D.C.: Dec. 15, 2008).

[2] Of this $49 billion, about $22 billion was provided to DOD for improving Iraqi security forces and is included in the $808 billion provided primarily in support of the Global War on Terrorism.

[3] GAO, *Securing, Stabilizing, and Rebuilding Iraq: Progress Report: Some Gains Made, Updated Strategy Needed*, GAO-08-837 (Washington, D.C.: June 23, 2008).

[4] GAO, *Stabilizing Iraq: DOD Should Identify and Prioritize the Conditions Necessary for the Continued Drawdown of U.S. Forces in Iraq*, GAO-08-700C (Washington, D.C.: June 23, 2008). In December 2008, DOD declassified the recommendations GAO made in this report. The body of the report remains classified.

[5] Activities at the strategic level include establishing national and multinational military objectives, as well as defining limits and assessing risks for the use of military and other instruments of national power. In contrast, activities at the operational level establish objectives that link tactics on the ground to high-level strategic objectives.

[6] *Agreement Between the United States of America and the Republic of Iraq on the Withdrawal of United States Forces from Iraq and the Organization of Their Activities during Their Temporary Presence in Iraq*, November 17, 2008, that took effect January 1, 2009. DOD also refers to the security agreement as a status of forces agreement (SOFA).

[7] The agreement also defines Iraqi jurisdiction over U.S. forces, DOD civilian employees, and U.S. forces' contractors in Iraq.

[8] Subsequently, four countries joined the coalition.

[9] The Paris Club is a group of 19 creditor nations and includes the United States.

[10] Under UN Security Council Resolution 1483, 5 percent of Iraq's annual oil export revenue is earmarked to finance payment of these reparations.

[11] The central government ministries include the ministries of oil, water, electricity, public works, health, housing and construction, defense, and interior. These figures therefore exclude the Kurdistan Regional Government and provincial governments.

[12] Former Secretary of State Madeline Albright established OPAP following the 1998 embassy bombings in Africa to consider the organization of U.S. embassies and consulates. Department of State, *America's Overseas Presence in the 21st Century, The Report of the Overseas Presence Advisory Panel* (Washington, D.C.: November 1999).

[13] Office of Management and Budget, *The President's Management Agenda, Fiscal Year 2002* (Washington, D.C.: August 2001).

[14] GAO, *Overseas Presence: Framework for Assessing Embassy Staff Levels Can Support Rightsizing Initiatives*, GAO-02-780 (Washington, D.C.: July 26, 2002).

[15] GAO, *Stabilizing and Rebuilding Iraq: Iraqi Revenues, Expenditures, and Surplus*, GAO-08-1031 (Washington, D.C.: Aug. 5, 2008).

Chapter 3

MEASURING STABILITY AND SECURITY IN IRAQ

Department of Defense Supplemental Appropriations

EXECUTIVE SUMMARY

This report to Congress, Measuring Stability and Security in Iraq, is submitted pursuant to Section 9204 of the Supplemental Appropriations Act for 2008, Public Law 110-252.[1] This report is also submitted pursuant to Section 1508(c) of the Department of Defense Authorization Act for 2009, Public Law 110-417. The report includes specific performance indicators and measures of progress toward political, economic, and security stability in Iraq, as directed by legislation. This is the fifteenth report in this series of quarterly reports. The most recent report was submitted in January 2009. The report complements other reports and information about Iraq provided to Congress and is not intended as a single source of all information about the combined efforts or the future strategy of the United States, its Coalition partners, or Iraq.

The United States seeks an Iraq that is sovereign, stable, and self-reliant; an Iraqi Government that is just, representative, and accountable; neither a safe haven for, nor sponsor of, terrorism; integrated into the global economy; and a long-term partner contributing to regional peace and security. The United States is pursuing this goal along political, security, economic, diplomatic, and rule of law lines of operation. This report indicates progress along these lines from December 2008 through February 2009 and highlights the challenges in achieving both Coalition and Iraqi objectives.[2]

With the entry into force and implementation of the Strategic Framework Agreement (SFA) and Security Agreement (SA), this reporting period witnessed a historic transition in the nature of the relationship between the United States and Iraq. A comprehensive agreement, the SFA begins to normalize U.S.-Iraq relations through economic, diplomatic, cultural, and security ties, and it will serve as a foundation for a longterm bilateral relationship based on common goals and interests. The SA governs U.S. forces' presence in Iraq, provides Iraqi authority for combat operations and detention activities, and provided the time frame for withdrawal from Iraq. The successful transfer of security authority from Coalition forces to the Government of Iraq (GoI), conducted on January 1, 2009, marked an important milestone in the development of this relationship. There have been no major issues to date in the coordination of detention operations. Multi-National Forces-Iraq (MNF-I) continues to release security detainees captured prior to December 31, 2008, in a safe and orderly manner in consultation with the GoI.

On February 27, 2009, the President of the United States announced a plan to commence a phased drawdown of U.S. combat brigades from Iraq by August 31, 2010. By this time, U.S. forces will have completed the transition from combat and counterinsurgency activities to a more limited mission set that focuses on training and assisting the Iraqi Security Forces (ISF), providing force protection for U.S. military and civilian personnel and facilities, conducting targeted counter-terrorism operations, and supporting civilian agencies and international organizations in their capacity-building efforts. Further drawdowns will occur in accordance with the U.S.-Iraq SA. The pace of the drawdown takes into consideration Iraq's improved, yet fragile, security gains and provides U.S. commanders sufficient flexibility to assist the Iraqis with emerging challenges. As combat brigades are responsibly redeployed, the United States will also continue to pursue other aspects of its strategy, including sustained diplomacy with a more peaceful and prosperous Iraq.

Iraq continues to make progress, as Iraqis increasingly choose the political process over violence. On January 31, 2009, the people of Iraq demonstrated their confidence in both the political process and the improved security environment through active participation in provincial elections. Although the first provincial elections in 2005 marked an important step in Iraq's transition to democracy and representative governance, this year's provincial elections were the first to draw broad-based participation by all religious and ethnic groups. The Independent High Electoral Commission (IHEC), with significant support from the United Nations Assistance Mission for Iraq (UNAMI), organized, conducted, and monitored the process. The elections were deemed credible and legitimate by international monitors and observers, taking place with minimal violence or complaints of voter fraud or intimidation. The process of forming governing provincial coalitions is underway.

Despite these positive developments, national reconciliation and accommodation continue to be hindered by the pursuit of ethno-sectarian agendas and disagreements over the distribution of power and resources at all levels. This is underscored by significant distrust between partisan national leaders. Arab-Kurd tensions continue to grow, surrounding the debate over the centralization versus decentralization of power, the resolution of disputed internal boundaries, property rights and restitution, the status of the Kurdistan Regional Government's (KRG) Peshmerga, the status of Kirkuk, and the resolution of hydrocarbon policy. Tensions between the Iraqi Army (IA) and the Peshmerga in and around disputed territories continue to be a flashpoint for potential violence. In addition, longstanding Sunni-Shi'a discord remains, with some Sunnis suspicious of the extent of the Shi'a political parties' ties to Iran and doubtful of the GoI's long-term commitment to the Sons of Iraq (SoI) transition program and the implementation of the Amnesty and Accountability and Justice Laws. Intrasectarian political tensions also continue, as evidenced by the defection of some members of Tawafuq to other same-sect parties competing for voter support during the provincial elections. Furthermore, there is growing opposition between those favoring a strong central government versus a highly decentralized government. The GoI will also have to address the issue of resettling refugees and internally displaced persons. These issues will require Iraq's political blocs to overcome their fears and build coalitions that reach across ethnic lines to compromise on sensitive political issues. Additional efforts toward dispute resolution will be required for the development of a secure and stable Iraq.

The overall security situation continues to slowly improve, with security incidents remaining at the same low levels as experienced in early 2004. In much of the country, a sense of normalcy is returning to everyday life, and citizens are increasingly focused on economic issues and the delivery of essential services. With more Iraqis now describing their neighborhoods as calm, the environment is slowly growing more conducive to economic and infrastructure development. Numerous factors have contributed to improved security, including effective Coalition and Iraqi counter-terror operations, increasing capabilities of the ISF, and the rejection of violence and extremism by the Iraqi people. Insurgent- initiated attacks have decreased from an average of 22 per day during the previous reporting period to 12 per day during this reporting period, but insurgents still have the capacity to conduct high-profile attacks. Although these security achievements are increasingly positive, they remain fragile in some places, most notably in Ninewa and Diyala Provinces, as well as in some parts of Baghdad.

Several threat groups remain dangerous and require continued focus to prevent their resurgence. The long-term threat remains Iranian-sponsored Shi'a militant groups, Asa'ib Al-Haq (AAH), Ketaib Hezbollah (KH), and unaligned Shi'a extremists, including the newly-formed Promised Day Brigade. In addition, violent Sunni insurgent groups and Al Qaeda in Iraq (AQI) are still a major security concern.

Iran continues to pose a significant challenge to Iraq's long-term stability and political independence. Despite repeated promises to the contrary, Iran attempted to derail the negotiation of a security agreement between the United States and the GoI, but ultimately achieved little success in affecting the SFA or the SA. Iran continues to host, train, fund, arm, and guide militant groups that seek to bleed the U.S. in Iraq, and Tehran remains opposed to a long-term partnership between the GoI and the United States. Tehran's overarching policy goal for Iraq is to prevent the emergence of a threat to Iran from Iraqi territory, either from the GoI or the United States. Iran seeks a Shi'a-led government in which Tehran's Shi'a allies—such as the Islamic Supreme Council in Iraq (ISCI) and the Da'wa party—hold the majority of political, economic, and security power. Tehran would prefer the GoI remain stable but relatively weak, providing Iran with opportunities to exert political and economic influence in Iraq and preventing the emergence of a regional competitor. Tehran remains determined to build influence in Iraq as part of a strategy to attain a preeminent role in the region, but Iraqi nationalism may act as a check on Iran's ambitions.

Despite these challenges, Iraqi forces continue to steadily improve their ability to provide basic security to the Iraqi people and, with Coalition support, extend security toward Iraq's borders. During this reporting period, the number of ISF battalions capable of taking the lead in counterinsurgency (COIN) operations has increased, and ISF leadership has improved its ability to command and control multiple brigade-sized elements from both the Iraqi Army and the National Police. With decreased Coalition support, Iraqi forces are beginning to take the lead in eliminating terrorist safe havens and reducing the flow of foreign fighters into Iraq. Tactical successes in ongoing joint Coalition and ISF operations against AAH, KH, Special Groups (SG), and AQI in Baghdad, Basrah, Diyala, Maysan, and Ninewa Provinces have demonstrated ISF's slow, but steady, improvement in their capability to combat extremists. A good demonstration of this continued progress was the planning and execution of a well-crafted security plan in support of the provincial elections held in late January 2009 with limited Coalition assistance. The ISF continues to gain the trust, confidence, and support of the Iraqi populace.

While making significant gains, the ISF continue to rely on the Coalition for logistics, fire support, close air support, communications, planning assistance, and intelligence, surveillance, and reconnaissance capabilities, particularly in northern Iraq. The leadership of the Ministries of Defense (MoD) and Interior (MoI) are making improvements in these areas and have prioritized efforts to expand infrastructure and improve budget execution. However, the global economic downturn and steep drop in oil prices could curtail the rate at which Iraqi forces can become fully modernized, self sufficient, and COIN capable, particularly in the near term. Finally, the Coalition remains a moderating force in the sometimes tense areas near disputed internal boundaries.

In addition to the SFA and SA, the GoI has negotiated Memoranda of Understanding with the United Kingdom, Australia, and Romania for military forces from those countries to continue supporting operations in Iraq through July 31, 2009. The size of the U.S. and Coalition footprint in Iraq continues to be steadily reduced and reshaped. Since January 1, 2009, five U.S. military units have redeployed from Iraq without replacement to include military police, engineers, logistics, and explosive ordnance disposal units, varying in size from detachment to battalion headquarters. Similarly, Coalition forces from Albania, Armenia, Azerbaijan, Bosnia, Bulgaria, Czech Republic, Denmark, El Salvador, Estonia, Georgia, Japan, Kazakhstan, Korea, Latvia, Lithuania, Macedonia, Moldova, Mongolia, Poland, Tonga, and Ukraine successfully completed their missions and departed Iraq since the last report. The GoI and NATO have negotiated an arrangement to enable the NATO Training Mission – Iraq (NTM-I) to continue specified missions until July 2009; follow-on negotiations to extend this training program beyond July 2009 are ongoing.

Turnover of the SoI program to the GoI has proceeded smoothly thus far. On October 1, 2008, the GoI assumed responsibility for nearly 51,000 SoI in the Baghdad area. Since then, the GoI has taken control of SoI programs in Diyala, Babil, Wasit, Qadisiyah, and Anbar Provinces, marking an important step toward national reconciliation. As of January 31, 2009, 77% of Iraq's SoI members have been transferred to GoI responsibility, and by April 1, 2009, SoI from Ninewa, Salah ad Din, and Tamim Provinces are scheduled to be transferred. Of the 94,000 SoI members remaining as of October 1, 2008, the GoI has pledged that 20% will be transitioned to the ISF, with the rest to be vetted for other civil servant positions or provided training or other support for transitioning into private-sector employment. Since October 2008, more than 5,000 of these have transitioned to the ISF, other ministries, or other non-security education, training, and support jobs programs. Long-term plans include increased education, training, and private sector employment opportunities. Although these steps have been encouraging, successfully transitioning SoI to permanent employment remains a long-term challenge for the GoI, particularly in light of recent budget concerns.

The decline in world oil prices has presented a number of challenges forcing the GoI to adopt a more conservative fiscal approach and seek additional efficiencies. Revenue from oil production comprises over 90% of the GoI's revenues, making the economy highly vulnerable to changes in the market price of oil. This situation has alerted Iraqi leaders of the need to heavily invest in oil infrastructure capacity to ensure stable production levels in the short term and to increase non-oil sector growth in the long term. The GoI currently faces a budget deficit of $20 billion in 2009 based on a price of $50 per barrel and an export rate of 2.0 million barrels per day. Current oil prices and export levels fall short of these estimates and will increase the budget deficit if the price of oil remains at its current levels. These shortfalls forced several revisions of the 2009 Iraqi Budget, passed by the Council of Representatives (CoR) on March 5, 2009. Core inflation remains persistent, although the Central Bank of Iraq continues to appreciate its exchange rate gradually to quell inflationary pressures and stimulate employment.

The GoI continues to show improvement in managing and executing its operations budget and capital projects, though significant challenges remain. From January through the end of November 2008, the GoI had spent a total of $41.2 billion, significantly more the $23 billion spent over the same period in 2007. The Ministry of Finance's (MoF) special report on capital funds indicates that through the end of September 2008, a total of $7.6 billion had been spent or committed. GoI ministries and provinces spent or committed $1.5 billion in September 2008 alone, a 20% share of the 2008 total. Additionally, Iraq continues to reduce its external debt burden. Following three years of satisfactory performance under International Monetary Fund Stand-By Arrangements, the GoI received its final tranche of Paris Club debt relief.

Improvement continues, albeit slowly, in the provision of essential services. Recent electricity production has reached record highs, and although the overall average generation for 2008 was 14% higher than 2007, demand for electricity continues to increase and exceed supply. Similarly, many Iraqis continue to have limited access to clean water, and challenges continue with respect to sewage services and water treatment plant operations, maintenance, and sustainment. Also, the Ministry of Health (MoH) continues to face a severe shortage of healthcare professionals, though the much improved security environment and concerted efforts by the MoH have resulted in more than 1,000 Iraqi physicians being repatriated and returned to serve in Iraq during 2008.

The GoI continues to strengthen its bilateral diplomatic relationships with regional partners and the international community. Iraqi Ambassadors have been dispatched to Syria, Lebanon, Turkey, and Qatar; and in recent months, the Arab League, Bahrain, Jordan, Kuwait, Syria, and the United Arab Emirates appointed ambassadors to Iraq. Also, Egypt has pledged to re-establish its diplomatic mission. In addition, trilateral talks with Turkey and the United States are encouraging and are a positive step toward improving security conditions in northern Iraq. UNAMI and NTM-I are engaged in a broad range of ongoing efforts and are committing their support for Iraq. Iraq's diplomatic relations with its regional neighbors will become increasingly important for security and stability as the GoI and the United States transition to a long-term strategic relationship.

Establishing a foundation for the rule of law in Iraq continues to face a number of challenges, and helping the GoI to bolster programs for judicial security has become one of the highest priorities. To counter intimidation of judicial officials, the Higher Judicial Council currently provides transportation for judges who try cases away from their home districts as a temporary measure. Until the GoI can provide adequate security to allow the full-time posting of judges within all judicial districts, the exercise of a fair criminal justice system in Iraq remains at risk. Additionally, the court system faces severe capacity challenges, leaving courts that handle the most serious violent crimes overwhelmed. Despite these challenges, Iraq's judicial security and rule of law capacity continues to mature with the assistance of the U.S. Embassy and Provincial Reconstruction Teams throughout Iraq.

In summary, the political, security, economic, diplomatic, and rule of law trends in Iraq remain generally positive, though key challenges remain. With the conclusion and the implementation of the SFA and SA, this reporting period witnessed significant steps toward the development of a U.S.-Iraq strategic relationship, setting the stage for long-term cooperative efforts as Iraq continues to develop as a stable partner in the region. At the same time, continued reductions in violence have afforded Iraqis an environment in which political and economic development can occur, and the peaceful conduct of provincial elections in January 2009 was an indicator of progress. In accordance with the SA, the ISF have assumed primary security responsibility for Iraq and continue to improve their operational and tactical capabilities, although still relying on U.S. combat support enablers.

Despite the continued progress, these gains remain fragile and uneven throughout the country, and their durability has not been seriously tested. Iraq remains fragile, primarily because the underlying sources of instability have yet to be resolved—the nation's major power brokers do not share a unified national vision, they disagree on the nature of the state, and they are reluctant to share power and resources. As security has improved, underlying political disputes have risen to the forefront, and political tension remains a problem. The world witnessed issue-based provincial elections in Iraq in January 2009, signaling the emergence of unresolved problems, such as delivery of essential services and infrastructure improvement, as important to the Iraqi people. To institutionalize and sustain its sovereignty and stability, the GoI must build its legitimacy through the provision of basic services and improved security for the Iraqi people, as well as the continued resolution of political, ethnic, and sectarian divisions.

SECTION 1. STABILITY AND SECURITY

1.1. Political Stability

Iraq continued to make political and legislative progress, including through the intensive activity culminating in the approval of the Strategic Framework Agreement (SFA) and the Security Agreement (SA), and despite the resignation of the Speaker of the Council of Representatives (CoR), Mahmud al-Mashhadani, in December 2008. The most significant accomplishments this reporting period were the Government of Iraq's (GoI) ratification of the SFA and a SA with the United States on December 4, 2008, the successful transfer of security authority from Coalition forces to the GoI on January 1, 2009, as the Chapter VII mandate for the Multi-National Forces-Iraq (MNF-I), contained in UN Security Council Resolution (UNSCR) 1790, expired, the successful conduct of provincial elections in 14 of Iraq's 18 provinces on January 31, 2009, and the passage of the 2009 Iraqi Budget on March 5, 2009. Ongoing operations by Iraqi Security Forces (ISF) against Jaysh al-Mahdi (JAM), Special Groups (SG) and other Shi'a militant splinter groups, and Al Qaeda in Iraq (AQI) in Baghdad, Basrah, Diyala, and Ninewa Provinces have demonstrated the GoI's commitment to combating extremists, as well as its ability to plan and lead security operations. However, there still remains significant tension within the CoR and between the CoR and the Prime Minister.

National Reconciliation

National reconciliation efforts continue positive development with a decline in violence and increased participation in the political process by all political actors. The transfer of the Sons of Iraq (SoI) program from Coalition to GoI control has proceeded smoothly, despite initial misgivings by the Sunni community. The GoI's goal is the transition of 20% of the SoI into the ISF and the reintegration of the remaining 80% into public or private employment. The GoI and Coalition are jointly implementing a number of employment and training programs to support this goal.

Within Iraq, political and sectarian tensions are increasingly being resolved within the democratic political framework instead of through violence. Although Kurd-Arab tensions over the status of Kirkuk and disputed internal boundary regions remain high, these are being discussed between Kurdish leaders and Prime Minister Maliki with U.S. mediation. Intra-Shi'a tensions rose leading up to provincial elections; however, parties pledged to accept the outcome of the democratic vote. Similarly, Sunni-Shi'a tensions over the integration of the SoI program continue, as do Sunni concerns over the extent of Shi'a political parties' ties to Iran, but these issues remain as discussions within the political arena. These tensions have been further exacerbated through corruption and sectarian behavior, and Kurds, Shi'a, and Sunnis have all accused Prime Minister Maliki of over-centralizing power under his authority and, in some cases, using extra-legal entities to bypass legal or constitutional processes. Nonetheless, there has not been a regression into the ethnic violence seen in past years, and parties remain willing to work within the political and legal systems.

Political Commitments

The dispute over the Provincial Elections Law (PEL), the debates on the SFA and the SA, and the Article 140 debate dominated the legislative agenda through the end of 2008. Additionally, the resignation of Speaker Mashhadani in December 2008 and the lack of a replacement speaker affected the CoR's ability to pass outstanding legislation from the 2008 legislative calendar, specifically the 2009 Iraqi Budget, which was passed on March 5, 2009. Legislative priorities this period include setting a date for the district and sub-district elections and concluding the report on provincial elections in Kirkuk based on recommendations from a CoR-appointed commission (Article 23 Committee). Additionally, Article 140 of the Iraqi Constitution regarding internally disputed boundaries, along with the Hydrocarbon Laws and a Census Law, remain under discussion. The passage of a Census Law and conduct of an actual census could have profound implications on the division of power and resources within Iraq. During 2009, the CoR will need to pass a National Election Law to establish the rules for CoR elections in late 2009 or early 2010. These legislative priorities highlight the progress of the political system as Iraqis continue to resolve core contentious issues through the legislative process.

Strategic framework agreement and security agreement

A significant achievement during this reporting period was the ratification of the U.S.-Iraq SFA and SA. The SFA formalizes the U.S.-Iraqi relationship with strong economic, diplomatic, cultural, and security ties and serves as the foundation for a long-term cooperative relationship based on mutual goals. The SA governs U.S. forces' presence in Iraq, provides Iraqi authority for combat operations and detention activities, and provides the time frame for withdrawal from Iraq. It ensures vital protections for U.S. forces and provides operational authorities for U.S. forces to sustain the positive security trends in Iraq as they transition to a supporting role—SA implementation arrangements between the United States and Iraq are ongoing. The SA may be submitted for a nationwide referendum no later than July 2009. The President's 19-month drawdown plan for U.S. combat brigades is compatible with the SA, which requires U.S. combat forces to withdraw from Iraqi cities and localities by June 2009 and for a complete withdrawal of all U.S. forces by December 31, 2011. The initial transitional force to be put in place by August 31, 2010 to execute a more limited mission set (training and assisting the ISF, providing force protection for U.S. military and civilian personnel and facilities, conducting targeted counter-terrorism operations, and supporting civilian agencies and international organizations in their capacity-building efforts) is a step further in the process of the U.S. drawdown out of Iraq in accordance with the terms of the SA. In addition to the SFA and SA reached with the United States, the GoI has negotiated Memoranda of Understanding with the United Kingdom, Australia, and Romania for military forces from those countries to continue supporting Iraqi security efforts through July 31, 2009. The GoI and NATO have negotiated an agreement to enable the NATO Training Mission – Iraq (NTM-I) to continue specified training missions until July 2009; follow-on negotiations to extend this training package beyond July 2009 are ongoing.

Accountability and justice law (DeBa 'athification reform law)

Despite the January 2008 passage of the Accountability and Justice Law, the GoI has not begun implementation. The Council of Ministers (CoM) has yet to nominate the individuals to head the new De-Ba'athification Commission, leaving the original Coalition Provisional Authority-appointed commission in place, but with no authority. Even with universal agreement that the law needs to be amended, neither the CoM nor the CoR has made any effort to introduce the necessary legislation. Without this legislative attention, some Sunni groups have accused the Shi'adominated government of appointing former Ba'athists who are deemed politically reliable, while denying positions to those who are eligible but not politically acceptable.

Provincial powers law

The Provincial Powers Law (PPL), approved by the CoR in February 2008, will take effect with the seating of new provincial councils in March, following the January 31, 2009 provincial elections. Implementation of the PPL will transfer additional authority from the central government to the provincial councils. Provincial councils will be granted specific powers over the approval of provincial budgets, the nomination and dismissal of senior provincial officials, authority over non-federal security forces, and a formal means to remove corrupt officials. Additionally, the PPL grants local and sub-district councils oversight of administration, budget, and other issues within their jurisdiction. However, the PPL mandates the creation of a Higher Board for the Provinces to coordinate administration across Iraqi provinces. The board will be chaired by the Prime Minister and includes the provincial governors and heads of the provincial councils. The critical tests of the federal governance model in Iraq will be the relationships between the provinces and the central government, as seen with the implementation of the PPL.

Provincial elections

Provincial elections were held on January 31, 2009, in 14 out of Iraq's 18 provinces. Approximately 51% of registered voters voted. The elections were deemed legitimate and credible by local and international observers and UN monitors. The relative order and calm under which the Iraqi-planned and managed elections took place demonstrated the improved competence of the GoI and ISF, who took the lead in establishing a secure environment for credible and legitimate provincial elections.

Preliminary reporting suggests that large, well-organized and well-funded incumbent parties and secular parties performed strongly. Mixed ethno-sectarian provinces experienced the highest registered voter turnout (Ninewa, Salah ad Din, and Diyala Provinces), while Anbar and Baghdad Provinces experienced the lowest registered voter turnout. Although the leading vote-getters in some provinces won strong pluralities, no party won the majority of votes in any province. As a result, most of the 14 provinces where elections were held will face a period of complex coalition-building before they can form governments. Long-term challenges include a smooth handover of authority to the new provincial councils and lack of governing experience of victorious candidates.

Constitutional review

Constitutional reform is the responsibility of the 29-member Constitutional Review Committee (CRC). The original deadline for the completion of the CRC's work was March 2007, but it did not issue its final report until August 2008. The CRC's final report left all of the major constitutional issues, including revenue distribution, federalism, and the status of Kirkuk, entirely unresolved.

Disputed Internal Boundaries (Article 140)

There has been little progress on implementation of Article 140 of the Iraqi Constitution. Most stakeholders objected to UNAMI's first set of recommendations, released in June 2008. The second set of recommendations on the remaining disputed areas in northern Iraq, including recommendations for the status of oil-rich and highly-contested Kirkuk, is expected to be released in mid-April 2009.

Amnesty law

As of January 2009, the amnesty review committees have considered over 152,000 amnesty petitions and have granted amnesty for more than 121,000 of them (80%). However, the large number of petitions granted is misleading because it reflects the number of petitions granted amnesty rather than the number of individuals requesting amnesty (in many cases, individuals filed multiple petitions). A large number of Iraqis who were granted amnesty were on bail, parole, or facing warrants. The total number of Iraqis granted amnesty reached 23,500; approximately 6,300 of these have been released from detention.

A package of hydrocarbon laws

Negotiations between the GoI and the Kurdistan Regional Government (KRG) continue in an attempt to resolve the deadlock over the hydrocarbon legislation package. Although negotiations on this package, introduced to the CoR in 2007, continue to be stalled, Iraqi politicians are working on this issue through alternate dialogue mechanisms. It is unlikely negotiations will result in a legislative breakthrough before the end of the winter legislative term, as fundamental differences remain over federal and regional authorities in contracting and management of the oil and gas sector. In the absence of unified hydrocarbons legislation, both the KRG and the GoI have pursued development contracts with international oil companies, although the GoI has stated that contracts signed by the KRG are not valid.

Government reform

Ministerial capacity development

The GoI continues to develop its capacity to govern at the national, provincial, and local levels. The U.S. Embassy supports Iraqi ministerial development through technical assistance to 12 ministries and several Executive Offices with senior advisors and attachés. The U.S. Agency for International Development (USAID) assists with public administration and management capacity building, as well as governance support at the national, municipal, and provincial levels through the *Tatweer* program, the Community Action Program, and the Local Governance Program, respectively.

To support legislative capacity building, the Embassy's Constitutional and Legislative Affairs (CLA) office has received permission from the CoR to work directly with members of parliament and their staffs and committees. CLA provides training to the CoR on drafting legislation, improving legislative procedures, and executing legislative oversight of the GoI's executive branch. Beginning in fiscal year (FY) 2009, USAID launched a $24 million program to support capacity building of priority CoR functions, including budgetary review, executive oversight, and internal management systems. The highlight of the program will be a parliamentary center to provide research and technical assistance support to CoR members and committees.

Provincial reconstruction teams

The Provincial Reconstruction Team (PRT) program is a key element in an integrated approach to developing an Iraq that is sovereign, stable, and self-reliant with a government that is just, representative, and accountable and that provides neither support nor safe-haven to terrorists. PRTs improve governance at the provincial level by mentoring, advising, and providing training for the legislative branch of the provinces (provincial councils) and executive branch officials (governors, deputy governors, etc.), as well as Directors General (DG) from the central ministries. The past year has seen an increased focus on provincial and local capacity-building efforts, with particular attention to budget execution and project implementation and facilitating the transition of reconstruction funding from the U.S. Government to the GoI. Other PRT contributions include helping improve the understanding and mastery of democratic processes and promoting investment and business opportunities, micro- financing, and agricultural development.

There are currently 12 U.S.-led PRTs, two Coalition-led PRTs, and four provincial support teams. Additionally, there are 10 embedded PRTs (ePRT), which work alongside brigade combat teams and focus on local capacity building as part of Counterinsurgency (COIN) operations. PRTs have also been enhanced, in some instances, with the addition of UN staff members that provide governance support to provincial governments, particularly in relation to elections.

Rule of law and criminal justice development

Iraq's criminal justice system continues to face serious challenges. Judicial intimidation significantly hinders administration of the criminal justice system and has impeded rule of law in Iraq. Judicial intimidation has led to an overwhelming backlog of pre-trial cases—three years in some districts—and unfair criminal justice procedures in many parts of Iraq. To reduce judicial intimidation and accelerate case reviews, the Higher Judicial Council (HJC) has hired additional guards to increase protection for individual judges. Additionally, with Coalition assistance, the Ministry of Interior (MoI) and HJC have negotiated a comprehensive plan for establishing the Judicial Protection Unit within the MoI's Directorate of Dignitary Protection. The plan will be presented to the Minister of Interior for his approval and implementation. In the meantime, representatives from the U.S. Departments of Justice (DoJ) and Treasury are assisting in creating a draft budget to be presented to the Minister of Finance.

Representatives from Multi-National Security Transition Command – Iraq (MNSTC-I) and DoJ are also developing a curriculum to train the judicial protection officers. The Coalition has established a Community of Interest working group to address the issue of judicial assassinations. This resource allows for the sharing of information regarding possible targets among the judiciary. Additionally, the U.S. Marshal Service continues to provide judges and their security details with handguns and assist them in obtaining MoI weapons cards.

In addition to protection officers, the Coalition assists with securing courthouses and protecting judges and their families by locating judges in secure complexes throughout Iraq. Judges living in the first Rule of Law Complex (ROLC) in Rusafa are enthusiastic about this arrangement, and Chief Justice Medhat supports the ROLC program. Another initiative intended to overcome judicial intimidation is the Traveling Judge Program. Chief Justice Medhat continues to support travel for judges from Baghdad to local areas with significant case backlog. Recently, the Coalition assisted in transporting judges to Diyala to reduce the case load and relieve severe overcrowding at the 5th Iraqi Army Division pre-trial detention facility. The Coalition will continue to provide such assistance when requested by the HJC.

Courts hearing the most serious insurgent crimes continue to be overwhelmed, particularly in Baghdad. Approximately 9,000 pre-trial detainees in Baghdad detention facilities are awaiting trial. The courts' ability to process cases in a fair and timely manner is hampered by the sheer number of criminal cases, the lack of timely and complete investigations, insufficient detainee files, poor court administration, and judicial intimidation. However, the Central Criminal Court of Iraq (CCCI) offices located at Karkh and Rusafa are beginning to show improvement in case processing time.

MNF-I's Task Force 134 and the U.S. Embassy's justice attachés work closely with the judiciary and the GoI to improve the quality of the Iraqi juvenile justice system and the treatment of convicted women in Ministry of Justice (MoJ) prisons. Recent progress includes expanded vocational programs at juvenile detention facilities, access to defense services, and expedited review of languishing cases. Although the quality of Iraqi post-trial detention facilities and detainee treatment varies, nearly all still require improvements. Many MoJ facilities, particularly post-trial facilities, are overcrowded and understaffed. The GoI reopened the Abu Ghraib detention facility—renamed Baghdad Central Prison—in January 2009, providing much needed holding capacity. Five new USG-funded prisons are scheduled to open over the next six months, increasing prison capacity by more than 6,500 beds, bringing the total capacity to 43,119 beds by April 2009. Further, the GoI is in the preliminary stages of planning four new prisons for an additional 12,500 beds. These new prisons should help alleviate post-trial overcrowding by the summer of 2009, accommodate additional convicted detainee growth, and facilitate the closure of the GoI's most neglected facilities.

Anti-Corruption Efforts

Corruption in Iraq continues to be a significant problem. From January 4-8, 2009, the UN Development Program held its first workshop in Amman as part of its 2008-2010 Anti-Corruption Program for Iraq. The workshop included instruction on how to conduct self-assessments of Iraq's compliance with the UN Convention Against Corruption. The MoI's Major Crimes Task Force (MCTF) seeks to build capacity in investigating complex, high-profile crimes such as public corruption, assassinations, and attacks upon government officials. The GoI has assigned 12 experienced Iraqi investigators drawn from MoI's Internal Affairs, the Inspector General's Office, and the National Information and Investigations Agency. The GoI is also working to establish an MCTF-dedicated tactical team to support the work of the task force. U.S. federal agents serve as mentors, trainers, and advisors. The GoI is taking an increasingly active role in the MCTF, committing high-quality personnel and financial resources to create a sustainable, capacity-building training program.

International Issues

Arab Neighbors and Diplomatic Engagements

Iraq continues to develop and strengthen ties with other countries in the region. Arab countries with a diplomatic presence in Iraq now include Egypt, Bahrain, Jordan, Kuwait, Lebanon, Syria, Tunisia, the United Arab Emirates (UAE), and Yemen. Saudi Arabia, Qatar, and Oman have also indicated a willingness to reopen embassies in Baghdad when they assess the security situation has sufficiently improved.

The GoI has taken steps to match the efforts of its neighbors to strengthen diplomatic relations. On September 28, 2008, the GoI announced that it had named ambassadors to Syria, Saudi Arabia, Qatar, Bahrain, Lebanon, and Turkey. Although Iraq has previously posted ambassadors in Bahrain, Lebanon, and Turkey, the naming of ambassadors to Saudi Arabia, Qatar, and Syria represents an additional strengthening of ties. The new ambassador to Syria arrived in Damascus on January 29, 2009. Although the naming of these ambassadors is an important step forward for Iraq, a number of key Iraqi ambassadorships remain vacant and subject to internal GoI disagreement, including those for Egypt, the UAE, and Kuwait.

International Compact with Iraq

The International Compact with Iraq (ICI) remains the framework for coordinating international donor support for Iraq's development and reform process. Since the launching of the ICI, Iraq has made progress in reducing and rescheduling debts from the Saddam era. As reflected in the October 23, 2008 ICI progress report, Iraq continues to strengthen its economy through internal reforms and increased regional and international economic ties and assistance. Recently, the ICI Secretariat moved to the Prime Minister's office, and an annual ICI meeting is tentatively scheduled for midsummer 2009 in Baghdad. Additionally, increased international attention, as evidenced by visits from trade missions and foreign investors, demonstrates promise for future integration within the global economy.

Iranian Influence

Since 2003, Tehran has invested to gain and sustain political and economic influence in Iraq. Iran's close ties with Iraq's Shi'a parties have helped facilitate this effort. The strength of ties between Tehran and pro-Iranian elements has also enabled Iran to survive strained relationships with Iraqi officials caused by Iran's sponsorship of militia groups targeting Iraqi and Coalition forces. Iranian officials have therefore made tactical adjustments to their Iraq strategy, following complaints by Iraqi officials of Iranian interference. Although continuing to support JAM leader Muqtada al-Sadr's religious studies in Qom, Tehran has selectively reduced the number of militants it supports. However, Tehran has also simultaneously improved the training and weapon systems received by the proxy militants. These groups are now returning to Iraq and remain a potential threat to Iraqis, the Coalition, and others. Some of these groups may also be involved in criminal activity.

Tehran sought to perpetuate its influence over Iraq by identifying and supporting pro-Iranian individuals and parties in their bid to win elections. Tehran has attempted to pressure government officials privately, through media campaigns and through largesse, to adopt pro-Iranian positions on such matters as the U.S.- Iraq SA, provincial elections, and the disposition of the Mujahidin-e Khalq (MeK). The large number of visits exchanged by Iraqi and Iranian officials testifies to the degree of Iranian influence in Iraq, but also highlights Iraq's efforts to channel this influence into mutually beneficial cultural and economic ties. A recent example of this cooperation is the award by the GoI of a billion dollar plus contract to an Iranian firm to perform major reconstruction in Basrah, as well as the repair of ancient Persian historical sites in the South.

Syrian Influence

In September 2008, Syria appointed its first ambassador to Iraq in nearly three decades; the new Iraqi ambassador arrived in Damascus on January 29, 2009. Syria likely hopes these steps toward better diplomatic relations will help promote Syrian economic interests in Iraq, especially expanding energy cooperation, trade, and investment. The Syrians recently voiced their willingness to cooperate with Iraq on the rehabilitation of the Iraq-Syria oil pipeline to Baniyas, an effort that would improve the economic situation of both countries and provide another outlet for Iraqi oil.

The Government of Syria must do more to address border security and its alliance with Iran. Syria's continued tolerance of AQI facilitation activity obstructs further progress on joint economic or political fronts with Iraq. Although Syria has detained AQI facilitators and operatives for domestic security reasons, Syria remains the primary gateway for Iraq-bound foreign fighters. In a recent visit to Syria by Iraq's Vice President Hashimi, the GoI insisted upon more meaningful security cooperation prior to enhancing economic relations between the two governments.

Furthermore, both governments desire to facilitate the return of nearly 1.5 million Iraqi refugees in Syria who are straining Syria's weak economy. The GoI provides transportation assistance on a case-by-case basis for Iraqis interested in returning. In November 2008, the Iraqi Embassy in Damascus announced that it would offer money and flights to Iraqi refugees willing to return. The vast majority of refugees, however, are not currently returning to Iraq due to housing, employment, or security concerns. In the meantime, the social and economic burdens of refugees impede improvements in diplomatic, security, and economic relations between the two countries.

Tensions on the Border with Turkey

Cooperation among the GoI, the KRG, and Turkey to combat the Kongra Gel (KGK) improved during this reporting period. In November 2008, the Governments of Turkey, the United States, and Iraq initiated regular trilateral meetings to exchange intelligence and to coordinate security measures to combat the KGK. KRG officials participated in these discussions as integral members of the GoI delegation and have also made efforts within the KRG to erode support for the KGK. In addition to the trilateral dialogue, the GoI has increased its diplomatic and economic contacts with the Government of Turkey to bolster bilateral ties beyond border security. Iraqi Foreign Minister Zebari traveled to Ankara on January 23, 2009, to discuss recently-concluded trade and economic agreements. Turkish President Gul intends to visit Iraq in the near term, and both governments plan to convene a Turkish-Iraqi Ministers Council Meeting in the spring of 2009.

Internally Displaced Persons and Refugees

The steady return of internally displaced persons (IDP) continued through the end of 2008. The office of the UN High Commissioner for Refugees (UNHCR) estimated that 208,000 Iraqis returned in 2008: 185,000 IDPs and 23,000 refugees. The return of IDPs and refugees is a critical step toward reversing the loss of human capital and re-establishing Iraq's intellectual class.

Despite these returns, a significant number of Iraqis remain internally displaced. The International Organization for Migration (IOM) estimates that there are more than 1.6 million post-February 2006 IDPs and more than 1.2 million pre-February 2006 IDPs. Increases in IDP returns coincide with improved security and GoI-led property restitution initiatives, specifically the implementation of the Prime Minister's Order 101 and Decree 262. Order 101 directs the eviction of squatters from private residences and the establishment of two Returns Assistance Centers in Baghdad. These centers assist returnees to register and to resolve property issues they may encounter upon returning. Decree 262 authorizes a onetime grant to returnees and a six-month rental subsidy for squatters secondarily displaced by returning homeowners in Baghdad. However, returnees have reported little success accessing these benefits.

United Nations Assistance Mission – Iraq

The United States and the UN extended their standing support agreement for Iraq in January 2009. The agreement stipulates that the United States will continue to facilitate United Nations Assistance Mission for Iraq (UNAMI) operations with security and logistical support at the request of the GoI until December 31, 2011. UNAMI advised the IHEC and Iraqi political leaders in preparations for the January 2009 provincial elections that were deemed credible and legitimate. The UN continues to state its commitment to expanding its presence and activities outside Baghdad and is looking at enhancing staffing in Basrah and several other Iraqi cities.

Conclusion

During this reporting period, Iraq has made significant progress in the political and diplomatic arenas, the most significant being successful provincial elections, conclusion of the SFA and SA, increased assertion of its coequal authority by the CoR, and the bilateral agreements with the non-U.S. Coalition partners and NTM-I. On the political front, the various political blocs in the CoR continue negotiations to find a suitable replacement for Speaker Mashhadani. Provincial elections occurred successfully on January 31, 2009, in 14 of Iraq's 18 provinces. On the diplomatic front, Iraq's engagements with neighbors and the international community continue to strengthen through increased debt relief, greater economic support, and mutual cooperation. More nations have established a diplomatic presence in Baghdad.

However, numerous challenges remain. Despite efforts to increase coordination between the GoI and KRG, political tensions remain elevated, and key legislation, such as the Hydrocarbon Law, remains stalled. Intrasectarian tension is also on the rise in some areas following elections, as former allies, competing with each other for votes during the provincial elections, now reveal sectarian or divisive agendas. Iraqi political leaders must continue to manage lingering sectarianism, work to improve nascent institutions, engage with neighbors (some of whom are not yet fully committed to the GoI's success), and stay committed to resolving the complex task of constructing a democratic state.

1.2. Economic Activity

Iraq's near-term economic development depends largely on its success in managing the oil and gas sector. Although the rapid rise in oil prices and projected revenues led to the expansive 2008 supplemental budget, the collapse of oil prices in the last quarter of 2008 has caused an equally rapid GoI shift to a more conservative posture. Falling oil prices undermine the International Monetary Fund's (IMF) projected 9.8% GDP growth in 2008 and have created a serious fiscal crisis for Iraqi leaders. Positive real growth in 2009 remains possible, as the effects of substantial increases in government spending stimulate the economy.

The collapse in oil prices prompted several revisions to the recently-passed 2009 Iraqi Budget. Volatile oil prices have refocused the attention of Iraqi leaders on oil infrastructure, although the results of major improvements will not be felt for several years. The GoI continues to seek reductions in spending that can still generate positive economic growth and diversify Iraq's economy beyond oil revenues.

The GoI has improved national and provincial budget execution and the distribution of essential services, although spending on capital projects continues to fall short of needed investment. Investments in electrical generation have led to a stable national grid, improved reliability, and recent all-time highs in generation. Although private generation has helped to fill the supply-demand gap, providing up to 30% of Baghdad's supply, insufficient electricity from the national grid remains a source of dissatisfaction.

Iraq's non-oil commercial sector has expanded, with the IMF projecting 5% growth over 2008. Iraq's Central Organization for Statistics and Information Technology (COSIT) reports a significant fall in underemployment over 2008, despite a slight increase in unemployment, with significant improvement in the private sector. Agriculture, Iraq's second most important resource and about 10% of Iraqi GDP, is likely to show growth as Iraq recovers from the 2008 drought. Even with economic progress, Iraq's banking system continues to be a source of weakness. The USG continues to engage on banking sector reform issues along with the World Bank. Rafidain and Rasheed, the two large state-owned banks, are in the process of implementing a large restructuring program.

Budget Execution

The GoI has improved budget execution across the ministries and provinces, although improved spending of capital funds is still needed. In 2008, Iraq averaged $3.7 billion in monthly expenditures, compared to $2.2 billion in 2007. Although most improvement has come from increased operational spending, particularly higher wages, execution of capital investment funds has also increased significantly over 2007 spending. The unexpected collapse in oil revenue required several revisions to the 2009 Iraqi Budget, which the CoR passed on March 5, 2009.

Although spending units in Iraq show improvement in managing and executing capital projects, they continue to face difficulties with conducting feasibility studies, negotiating contracts that follow Iraqi laws, and ensuring that letters of credit match approved contracts. Moreover, the one-year budgeting process makes it difficult for spending units to plan and execute multi-year capital projects.

The Public Financial Management Action Group (PFMAG) is expanding technical assistance to ministries and provinces and provides training to Iraqi officials and members of the CoR's Finance Committee to improve Iraqi budget execution and comprehension of budget processes and reforms. Embassy Baghdad created the PFMAG in June 2008 to better coordinate civilian and military assistance on budget execution. Other initiatives, including USAID's Iraq Financial Management Information System and the Governorates Accounting and Project Tracking Information System, will provide an improvement from the manual systems currently in use.

2008 Budget Execution

The 2008 GoI baseline budget is $49.9 billion, an $8.8 billion (2 1%) increase over the 2007 budget of $41.1 billion. This includes $3.3 billion for provincial capital budgets and $9 billion for security budgets ($3.9 billion for MoI and $5.1 billion for MoD).

Through the end of November 2008, the GoI spent a total of $41.2 billion (83% of the base budget), significantly more than the $23 billion spent through November 2007 (56% of the budget). The Ministry of Finance's (MoF) special report on capital funds indicated that through the end of September 2008, a total of $7.6 billion (58% of the capital budget) had been spent or committed. GoI ministries and provinces spent or committed $1.5 billion in September 2008 alone, a 20% share of the 2008 total.

2008 Supplemental Budget

In August 2008, in response to the increase in projected revenue related to world oil prices, the GoI passed a $22.3 billion budget supplemental, adding $14.3 billion for operations and $8 billion for capital funds. Since mid-2008, however, the rapid decline of oil prices coupled with falling exports have returned actual revenues to near the original 2008 projections. Although the supplemental allowed for an increase in public sector salaries, most of this supplemental capital funding proved too large for ministries to execute, particularly given the late approval of the supplemental. Only two ministries, Education and Higher Education, have spent or committed portions of their 2008 supplemental budgets. To shore up the 2009 Iraqi Budget, the MoF has prohibited ministries from rolling over unspent funds.

2009 Budget

Falling oil prices prompted the GoI to lower the expenditures in the 2009 Iraqi Budget. After extended debate and another round of spending cuts, the CoR passed the 2009 Iraqi Budget on March 5, 2009. The budget, based on $42.5 billion in projected revenues, includes roughly $60 billion in expenditures. Although lower than initial drafts, the new budget continues the trend of an overall increase of approximately 19% in expenditures over the previous year. Approximately 17% of the 2009 Iraqi Budget is marked for the Ministries of Defense and Interior.

IMF Stand-by Arrangement and Debt Relief

In December 2008, the IMF completed a review of Iraq's economy under the current 15-month Stand-By Arrangement (SBA). The successful completion triggered the final 20% tranche of Paris Club debt relief, totaling nearly $42.3 billion (80% of total Paris Club debt). The GoI has expressed interest in discussing future engagement with the IMF beyond the end of the current SBA in March 2009.

Iraq has also continued to obtain debt relief outside of the Paris Club agreements. To date, Iraq has received roughly $11.8 billion in debt relief from non-Paris Club countries and $20.9 billion in commercial debt relief. Iraq's neighbors and China are its largest remaining creditors. The UAE committed to complete relief of nearly $7 billion with an agreement expected to be finalized in early 2009. Saudi Arabia has publically committed to debt relief comparable to Paris Club levels (80%), although owed interest remains a point of contention. The U.S. Treasury estimates that Iraq's remaining bilateral debt outstanding (including that owed to the Paris Club) is between $48.9 billion and $76.9 billion. Iraq is studying options to deal with claims of bilateral creditors that do not sign debt relief agreements by the end of 2009.

Indicators of Economic Activity

IMF projections made before the fall in oil prices estimate real GDP growth as high as 9.8% over 2008, including a 5% expansion in the non-oil economy. Although benefitting from improved security, Iraq's private sector remains highly dependent on government outlays. Corruption remains a constraint to reconstruction and economic development.

Inflation

In December 2008, year-on-year core inflation fell to 11.8%, slightly below the 2007 average of 12% and significantly lower than the inflation rate of 26% in 2006.[3] Core inflation was trending up slightly at the beginning of the 2008, but has leveled off and is beginning to trend downward. Stabilization of inflation is attributable to improved security conditions, steady appreciation of the dinar, and global inflation trends. From November 2006 through December 2008, the dinar appreciated against the U.S. dollar by more than 24%. Lower inflation rates and an appreciating dinar improved Iraqi purchasing power for basic needs and provided a more stable environment in which the private sector could grow.

Unemployment

GoI data released in December 2008 revealed strong gains in employment. COSIT reports that underemployment (less than 35 hours of work per week) fell to 29.4% (from 37.8% in 2007), while unemployment increased slightly to 18.3% (from 17.6% in 2007). Most notably, the data revealed that over a third of the full- time work force was employed in the private sector, an increase from only 24% in 2007. Based on population demographics, Iraq's labor pool is growing at a rate of more than 200,000 people per year. The resultant growth in jobs has roughly kept pace with the expanding labor pool. Additionally, Iraqis continue to be challenged by underemployment, as many are overqualified for the positions they hold or can only find part time employment. Unemployment may be exacerbated by the return of displaced persons to Iraq as security conditions improve, as well as by the release of detainees who will seek to re-enter the work force. Continued economic progress is vital, as the employed populace greatly adds to Iraq's economic stability and simultaneously decreases the ranks of disenfranchised citizens potentially willing to embrace violence.

Business Development

The National Investment Commission and the Provincial Investment Commission programs, established to develop the investment capabilities of national and provincial governments, are operational and promoting foreign investment in Iraq. The "Southern Opportunity" Basrah Investment Commission business seminar in Istanbul and the Dialogue on Business and Investment Conference (DBIC) in Baghdad reflect the Iraqi pursuit to improve the investment dialogue internationally and promote private investment and economic development. The DBIC led to another surge of international investment, with 13 new investment licenses signed after the conference. The Provincial Investment Commissions of Baghdad, Najaf, Karbala, Muthanna, Diwaniyah, Babil, and Dhi Qar have each contributed to the overall $2.4 billion private-sector development progress that started in 2008 and, to date, has resulted in a total of 39 investment licenses signed.

In November 2008, the Ministry of State for Tourism and Antiquities hosted World Tourism Week. This event opened with a ceremony and tours in Baghdad and continued with visits to tourist sites in Babylon, Karbala, and Najaf. Of the 200 participants, more than 100 of them were international tourism investors and professionals. This event was significant because it was planned, coordinated, and executed by the Minister's staff and showed the level of international interest in the Iraqi tourism industry. To date, there have been 13 investment licenses signed for a total of $497 million in the Iraqi tourism and hospitality industries, accounting for 20% of foreign direct investment tracked by the National Investment Commission.

The Joint Contracting Command-Iraq/Afghanistan (JCC-I/A) continues to assist Iraq's transition to a free market economy through the Iraqi First Program. Beginning in 2006, the Iraqi First Program has executed over 35,000 contract actions, totaling $6.6 billion, with host nation vendors. With over 8,000 Iraqi vendors registered and vetted by the Iraqi Central Contract Registry, the program supports Iraq's ongoing economic expansion, entrepreneurship, and business development.

The Department of Defense Task Force to Improve Business and Stability Operations (TFBSO) aids in the revitalization of Iraq's economy and in creating jobs. This organization includes business leaders, engineers, subject-matter experts, and accountants working alongside Iraqi business and engineering professionals nationwide. Through its established effective working relationships with the GoI, the TFBSO continues to develop business and economic opportunities in Iraq. In the last year, the TFBSO has helped 66 state-owned factories either restart or increase production, and an additional 30 factory revitalization projects are currently being executed, focusing on the recently-secured areas of Basrah, Kirkuk, and Mosul.

In recent months, TFBSO has facilitated the completion of seven joint ventures between state-owned factories and multinational private investment consortiums. Two more large joint ventures are ongoing, and the TFBSO anticipates completion of these undertakings in the next few months. These completed contracts represent $910 million in private investment that helped jumpstart idled factories in Iraq. Also, the TFBSO was instrumental in bringing together international investors and GoI participants, which resulted in the license award by the GoI to build a five-star luxury 300-room hotel in Baghdad's **International Zone (IZ)**. Groundbreaking took place in August 2008, and construction is now underway. The hotel will be managed by a luxury hotel chain from the UAE. This privately-financed hotel, 750-person conference center, and seven-restaurant complex will serve as a world-class meeting place for business leaders, government officials, and tourists.

Banking Sector

The Iraqi banking sector consists of 40 banks with over 700 branches. According to the Central Bank of Iraq, there are seven state- owned banks and 33 privately-owned banks conducting business in Iraq. Of the 33 privately-owned banks, six are considered foreign-owned (having more than 50% foreign ownership). The Banking Law of 2004 limited the number of foreign-owned banks to six until December 31, 2008. Currently, the two largest state-owned banks, Rafidain and Rasheed, are undergoing a comprehensive restructuring with World Bank and Treasury guidance. The effort consists of two focus areas—a financial restructuring of the two banks and a complete operational restructuring.

While state-owned banks continue with restructuring efforts, privately-owned banks have established a retail payments consortium with support from the TFBSO, which will allow for domestic and international use of debit cards and credit cards through ATMs and points-of-sale terminals. Almost 200 private bank branches have been automated and linked to international financial systems. State-owned banks are issuing, and have already begun paying, pensions through new biometric smart cards that will permit automatic deposits into individual accounts on the cards, ATM uses, and points-of-sale capabilities. Also driving the conversion to electronic banking is the JCC-I/A requirement to pay Iraqi contractors using electronic funds transfer in accounts they establish in Iraqi banks.

Oil Industry

Iraq's oil industry has shown continued progress in increasing the internal production of refined products, repairing critical infrastructure, and, stimulated by the fall in oil prices, investigating ways to increase crude oil production. Despite higher crude oil production and exports in 2008, technical issues relating to wellhead equipment, field infrastructure, and field management— complicated by poor maintenance—will likely cause reductions in production throughout 2009.

Overall, crude oil production peaked at 2.54 million barrels per day (mbpd) in July 2008 and leveled off at approximately 2.36 mbpd in the later months of the year. Iraq earned an estimated $41 billion from crude oil exports in 2007, an increase of about $10 billion over 2006. Oil revenues increased significantly to an estimated $61.6 billion in 2008, primarily because of high world oil prices in the first half of the year.

Security improvements have contributed to maintaining production, exports, and increased domestic distribution. Although there have been several minor pipeline interdictions over the last six months, none have impacted the production, export, or refining of crude oil. On the Bayji-to-Baghdad pipeline corridor, two repair teams of Iraqi technicians have conducted more than 2,100 repairs since May 2008, and in December 2008, decommissioned the 16-inch natural gas line, which has provided fuel to power plants in North Baghdad since May 2008. An Oil Pipeline Company (OPC) repair team is currently repairing the 16- inch refined product line from Bayji to the Hammam Al Aleel depot near Mosul, and another team has begun repairs on the 12-inch Naft Khana crude line. These repairs will increase the supply of crude to the Doura Refinery in Baghdad and greatly increase the Ministry of Oil's (MoO) ability to distribute fuel to the largest city in the North. The Pipeline Exclusion Zone (PEZ) projects are on track but incomplete due to MoD and MoI disagreements over contracts for guard towers along the PEZs. The Bayji-to-Baghdad PEZ program, currently 95% complete, remains on track. The USG-funded construction on the Doura-to-Hillah PEZ is 99% complete. However, both PEZs currently have less than 25% of the towers and barracks built.

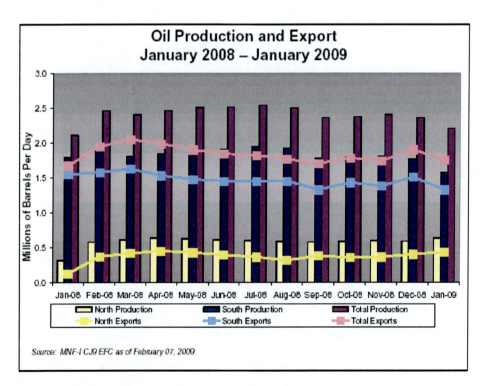

Despite improvements, much of Iraq's crude oil infrastructure remains outdated, poorly maintained, and under-resourced. The MoO is initiating a series of project proposals that aim to modernize and expand production, specifically in the refining sector. The CoM has approved renewal of a previously-signed $3 billion technical service contract with the China National Petroleum Corporation to jointly develop the Ahdab Oil Field in Wasit. In September 2008, the GoI signed a Heads of Agreement with Shell to implement a 25-year project to capture flared gas and provide it both domestically and for export. Moreover, the GoI has also launched two rounds of bidding on contracts to develop major oil fields; the second round was announced on December 31, 2008. Bids from international companies are due in mid-2009, after which the MoO will review and select. Given the length of the contract process, it is unlikely that there will be any significant foreign involvement in Iraqi oil infrastructure before mid 2010.

After long delays, Iraq has taken initial steps to bolster its southern oil export infrastructure. The Southern Export Redundancy Project will provide redundancy and expansion of the Basrah and Khor Al-Amaya Oil Terminals, rehabilitate undersea pipelines, and eventually increase export capacity from 1.6 mbpd to 4.5 mbpd. The front-end engineering design contract was signed on December 21, 2008, and surveys of geotechnical conditions and unexploded ordnance in the northern Gulf will began in mid-February 2009.

Agriculture

Iraq's **agricultural** industry, which accounts for 10% of the GDP and 25% of employment, is now rebounding in areas where security has improved, and access to working irrigation systems has counteracted the effects of the 2008 drought. Although agricultural output has increased, domestic food production remains below potential due to restrictive government policies, outdated technology, unstable electric power, and a breakdown of the long-standing irrigation water-management system. Traditional GoI farmer support programs will likely be limited in 2009 due to budget shortfalls. Still, Iraqi farmers have made gains in production, particularly those with access to private financing. In January 2009, for example, 87% of Iraqis have reported that they have enough to eat at least some of the time.[4]

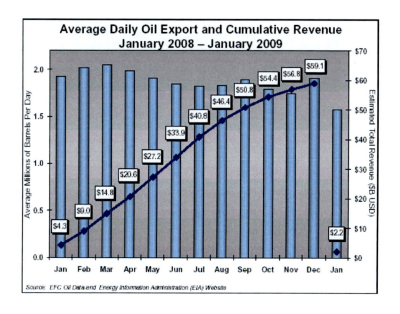

U.S. Government efforts have focused on building sustainable Iraqi agriculture through training, locally-owned farmer credit programs, and agriculture educational capabilities. The U.S. Department of Agriculture (USDA) is creating partnerships with universities and coordinating farmer association education with local PRTs. *Inma*, a $92.9 million USAID project launched in 2007, focuses on developing agribusiness and agricultural markets.[5] Now in its third year, this program has demonstrated the capability to rapidly grow the agriculture industry as security improves and electricity and water become more readily available. Since the beginning of the program, approximately 3,700 new agribusiness jobs have been created. In the Abu Ghraib area, *Inma* facilitated a 300% increase in vegetable yields by introducing improved seeds. Additionally, the TFBSO's agricultural initiative has partnered U.S. Land Grant University professors with Iraqi farmers. More than 30 faculty and staff are working on farms surrounding Baghdad and in western and northern Iraq. This relationship enables Iraqi farmers to increase production levels and teaches them new farming techniques.

Essential Services

The GoI has made mixed gains in delivering essential services, such as electricity, water, and healthcare, although progress varies by locale. Demand for electricity still outstrips supply; however, GoI investments in electrical generation have led to a stable national grid, improved reliability, and recent all-time highs in generation. Although many Iraqis still report limited access to potable water, 35 major new water supply and treatment plants are under construction. Improvements have been made to Iraq's telecommunications infrastructure, and initial steps are being taken to restore and expand the country's limited transportation infrastructure. The provision of essential services remains a key component of national reconciliation and a significant factor in building popular support for the GoI.

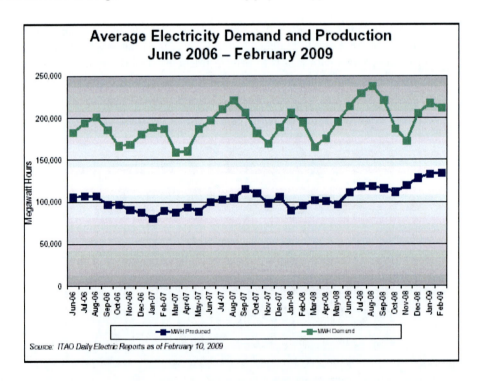

Electricity

The Iraqi Government continues to manage the electricity sector with increased effectiveness, as evidenced by the absence of blackouts in the national grid since May 2008. With the completion of hardening projects at key transmission towers, there have been no interdictions over the last six months. All transmission tower protection projects have either been completed or deemed infeasible and subsequently canceled. Progress continues on important transmission lines that will improve distribution and increase imports.

Despite gradual and steady increases in electricity generation, years of neglect and lack of maintenance continue to hamper electricity generation and distribution in Iraq. An average of 100 megawatts (MW) per day in capacity is lost due to the lack of fuel and the need for improvements in transmission. Only 43% of Iraqis feel they have been able to get the electricity they need at least some of the time, twelve percentage points less than the previous ten-month average.[6] Only 18% of Iraqis are somewhat or very satisfied by the amount of electricity they receive, down from 34% who felt satisfied in November 2007.[7]

Earlier investment by the GoI, the KRG, and the United States has added new generation to the grid. Average generation in 2008 was 14% higher than in 2007. Despite a 6% increase in average demand since 2007, improvements in the electrical sector led to a 17% increase in the average percentage of demand being met nationwide and increased the average national hours of power (HoP) a day from 12 HoP to 14 HoP, but this still translates into only a few hours of electricity per day for the average domestic consumer. A 41% increase in average gas turbine generation since 2007 (460 MW) more than offset the loss in hydroelectric power (250 MW) due to the 2008 drought.

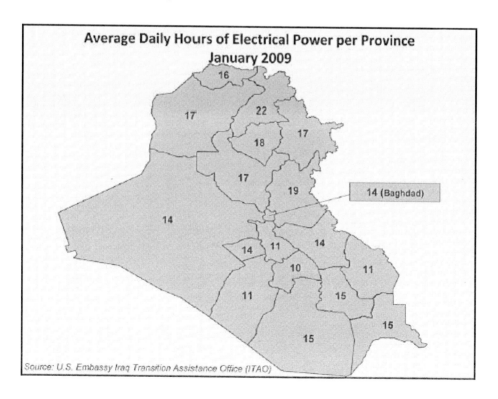

Iraq is taking long-term steps to close the electricity supply-demand gap, recently signing contracts for new gas turbine generation totalling more than 10,000 MW. The first set of units, from General Electric (GE), is expected to begin shipping in mid-2009. Although the purchase of these generators is a major step toward meeting the supply goal, the Ministry of Electricity (MoE) has yet to contract for the purchase of the balance of plant equipment or for the design and construction of the facilities. It is not known whether the budget will be able to support this volume of construction. Moreover, the full potential of these units depends on the availability of fuel, as well as proper operations and maintenance. Assuming all of this occurs, new generation should be online between 2012 and 2016. The MoE previously contracted Parsons Brinkerhoff to provide operations and maintenance services support, as well as training at several gas turbine plants. The six- month contract is expected to be renewed in the next few months. The MoE is also negotiating with GE and Siemens to provide maintenance and parts support for their respective units currently installed in power plants.

Water and Sewer

Poor water treatment plant operations, maintenance, and sustainment continue to stymie efforts to provide potable water to the Iraqi population. Poorly maintained water distribution systems are susceptible to contamination, increasing the potential for disease. Nearly 67% of Iraqis report being able to get safe, clean drinking water at least some of the time, down four percentage points from November 2007.[8] Although the majority of Iraqis can get safe drinking water, only 32% are satisfied with the availability of drinking water, a two-point reduction from November 2007.[9] Only 46% of Iraqis state that they have a working sewage disposal system at least some of the time, down two percentage points from November 2007.[10] The percentage of Iraqis satisfied with sewage disposal services is 26%, a one-point increase from November 2007.[11]

Several important projects enhancing water and sewer capability are underway. The Sadr R3 Water Treatment Plant has been operating at full capacity since mid-September 2008, and the Baghdad Water Authority has been operating the plant since the end of January 2009. In Najaf, the Mishkab Water Supply project, being executed under a $23 million grant to the Ministry of Municipalities and Public Works, is 45% complete and is due to be operational in 2009.

Healthcare

The Ministry of Health (MoH) faces serious human resource challenges across the spectrum of healthcare professionals and ancillary staff. With Iraq's improved security environment, the MoH has worked diligently to encourage the return of expatriate physicians; the Minister estimates that more than 1,000 physicians returned to Iraq in 2008. To increase skills, the MoH has sent 75 Iraqi medical specialists and subspecialists to various U.S. hospitals and clinics for month-long clinical rotations. Jointly, the MNF-I surgeon and the MoH are finalizing plans to rotate Iraqi healthcare providers through Coalition force hospitals and clinics throughout Iraq. The U.S. Army Corps of Engineers has transitioned 133 new Public Health Clinics to the MoH, although full potential remains limited by poor staffing and the lack of adequate essential services (i.e., electricity, water, and sewage) in some provinces.

Health awareness initiatives and responses to disease outbreaks have been very effective this year, reducing cholera cases by 80%, from 4,700 cases in 2007 to 925 cases in 2008. The MoH is also increasingly able to identify, diagnose, and treat diseases independently. Despite this initial progress, national polling indicates that only 26% of Iraqis are either somewhat or very satisfied with health services, 11 percentage points lower than in November 2007.[12]

Transportation

All airspace in Iraq at 24,000 feet and above was returned to Iraqi control on January 1, 2009. To facilitate a smooth transition, Iraq has asked the United States to assist with providing air traffic control services until it is fully capable of controlling all of its airspace. Planning and training for the next section of airspace that will be transferred to Iraqi control has already begun. Operations will continue to be assisted by the U.S. Air Force and U.S. contract controllers until there are enough qualified Iraqi controllers to assume responsibility.

Rehabilitation and expansion of Iraqi railroad track and station infrastructure continues. In addition, efforts to develop a state-of-the-art train control system for the railroad are nearing completion. This system will provide a positive means of communication with trains as they operate throughout the country. This technology is capable of preventing train-to-train collisions, over-speed derailments, and casualties to railroad workers when operating within the limits of their authority and will greatly add to the level of safety along the rail network.

Revitalizing the Port of Umm Qasr has continued with the support of MNF-I and Embassy Baghdad's Office of the Transportation Attaché (OTA). The GoI is employing port tender agreements to develop modern container-port facilities in Umm Qasr's South Port. The OTA is completing the last phase of the U.S.-funded repair of two container cranes in South Port to provide a major increase in capacity. The OTA and MNF-I, in conjunction with the U.S. Coast Guard, are also supporting offers by the GoI to achieve compliance for the Port of Umm Qasr with the International Ship and Port Facility Security Code of the International Maritime Organization.

Conclusion

It is expected that 2009 will be a pivotal year for economic development. The GoI will be challenged to create conditions for increased private-sector growth and job creation, while balancing the demands of capital investment, social spending, and security programs, amid shrinking oil revenue projections. Iraq's **ability to develop its oil** sector and reduce its vulnerability to oil-price changes simultaneously will be a critical test. Opportunities for foreign investment should increase, as security continues to improve. Iraq must take steps to develop a banking sector and a modern legal/regulatory framework to take advantage of new opportunities for investment and growth. In spite of falling revenue and increasing payroll costs, Iraq will need to continue its investment program to develop all sectors of its economy.

1.3. Security Environment

The security environment in Iraq continues to improve, as violence has dropped dramatically in the last two years, and normal life continues to return to the country. Many residents now express greater hope for the future and are demanding a better standard of living. The elections were an indicator of ISF progress since 2005, when Coalition forces played the primary role securing elections. However, for the January 31, 2009 provincial elections, the ISF were in the lead, with Coalition support, deploying outside polling centers in 14 of 18 provinces to ensure a safe and secure electoral process for Iraqi citizens. While progress has been significant, much work remains to be done.

The year 2009 will be a year of enormous opportunity for Iraq, and the GoI must capitalize on recent security gains and work to foster cooperation between political factions, resolve long-standing disputes, and improve the standard of living for its citizens. The events of 2009, which may culminate in national elections, are critical in consolidating the fragile security gains of the past two years and building the foundation for sustainable stability in Iraq.

Overall Assessment of the Security Environment

The insurgency in Iraq continues to decline but remains dangerous. Of primary concern are various Shi'a militia groups, including Asa'ib Al-Haq (AAH) and Ketaib Hezbollah (KH), Sunni resistance groups, and AQI. Coalition and ISF operations continue to impede AQI's and other insurgents' and militants' freedom of movement and re-supply capabilities. Security gains in Baghdad are allowing residents to enjoy an improved sense of personal freedom. Cafés remain open after dark and families now frequent public parks, in marked contrast to 2006 and 2007. ISF are taking the lead in operations in northern Iraq, and U.S. forces now carry out fewer missions in the lead, and instead, assist the ISF in supporting roles.

Security operations in Basrah, Baghdad, Ninewa, Maysan, and Diyala have produced encouraging results that further degraded the capabilities of AQI and reduced the activities of militias. Iraqi and Coalition forces have significantly extended control in more areas of Iraq, and ongoing operations have severely degraded AQI activities, finances, and supply networks, leading to the capture of several high-value individuals. Although Iraq has achieved progress, AQI retains limited capability to conduct high-profile attacks targeting civilians and ISF, mostly in the North.

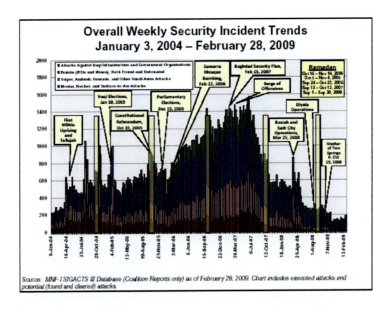

Sons of Iraq

The SoI have helped reduce overall levels of violence across Iraq since the Awakening Movement began in Anbar Province in September 2006. On September 8, 2008, Prime Minister Maliki signed an order that detailed the GoI plan to transition approximately 94,000 SoI from Coalition administration to GoI control. The Iraqi Army and Police will integrate 20% of SoI members, and the remainder will transition into non-security employment in ministries, municipalities, public works, or other employment. The transfer of SoI members to GoI control is complete in Multi-National Division-Baghdad, Multi-National Division-Center, and Multi- National Force-West areas. As of January 31, 2009, 77% of SoI members have been transferred to GoI responsibility, and by April 1, 2009, the remaining SoI from Ninewa, Salah ad Din, and Tamim Provinces will be transferred.

The SoI transition is complicated by many members' lack of skills and education, making it difficult for the GoI to integrate them into non-security positions or security positions that require literacy. To help mitigate this problem, the Coalition has invested $134 million into job programs such as vocational training centers, Civil Service Corps (CSC), and Civil Service departments that provide vocational training and apprenticeships for more than 9,000 SoI. Progress is being made with the CSC apprenticeship program, and the Coalition is actively working to ensure that SoI members learn valuable trade skills that will help them enter the job market. Other SoI continue to be wary of the transition process, as they are fearful the GoI will not adhere to its promises of integration. The Coalition is assisting to mitigate these fears by encouraging the GoI to carry out its commitments, and by facilitating face-to-face meetings with local SoI, and tribal leaders.

A majority of the SoI desire a long-term means to protect and provide for their families, underscoring the importance of the GoI ensuring all of the SoI are properly transitioned into longterm employment. However, this effort will require long-term emphasis and may be further complicated by recent budget concerns. Proper management of SoI groups to ensure their successful reintegration is critical for long-term stability in Iraq.

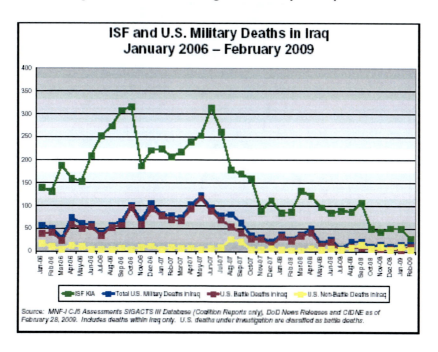

Daughters of Iraq

To mitigate an increasing trend of female suicide bombers in Iraq in 2008, MNF-I and community leaders began calling for women to join the Daughters of Iraq (DoI), a female counterpart to the SoI community policing program largely credited with reducing violence in Iraq. Although the DoI remain a small minority, their non-standard role in Iraqi society has attracted much attention. The GoI faces increased demand for female security personnel because of the large increase in female suicide bombings—41 women have carried out suicide attacks since this time last year, primarily in Diyala, Baghdad, and Anbar, compared to eight in 2007. The DoI program is specifically designed to fill the security gap that currently allows women to avoid scrutiny at checkpoints. To date, more than 600 women have joined the DoI, partnering with the SoI, to provide an added security capability in Anbar, Diyala, and some areas of Salah ad Din. Since November 2008, there has been a decrease in female suicide attacks. Also, the DoI played a prominent role in the provincial elections, searching large numbers of female voters as they went to the polls. On October 1, 2008, 345 Baghdad DoI transferred from Coalition control to the Baghdad Operations Command, where they continue to perform their important security work.

Attack Trends and Violence

Attacks have decreased dramatically from an average of 29 per day in September 2008 to 13.75 per day in February 2009, a 52% reduction. Civilian deaths across Iraq have also declined slightly to an average of 20 per week during this reporting period, but even a small surge in high-profile attacks could cause a spike in civilian deaths and potentially destabilize the environment. During this reporting period, there were 35% fewer civilian deaths than during the last reporting period, and Iraq's reported murder rates have dropped below levels that existed before the start of Operation Iraqi Freedom. Although periodic high-profile attacks continued throughout the reporting period, these attacks have not rekindled a cycle of ethno-sectarian violence.

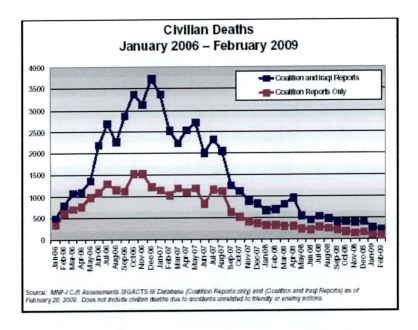

Since the last reporting period, the average number of attacks executed daily has decreased or remained relatively constant in all provinces. Of the 18 total provinces, Baghdad, Diyala, Ninewa, and Salah ad Din contain approximately half of Iraq's population and previously accounted for 78% of all attacks. Daily average attacks in Baghdad Province decreased 37%. The daily average attacks in the northern province s—Ninewa, Diyala, Tamim, and Salah ad Din—decreased 50%, largely due to ISF-led operations.

High-Profile Attacks

During this reporting period, the number of monthly high-profile attacks (HPA), including HPAs found and cleared, decreased 29% nationwide from the previous reporting period. The current level is lower than at any time since the spring of 2004; however, AQI retains the intent and capability to carry out spectacular attacks. During this reporting period, **49% of all casualties were from HPAs. AQI's use of person**-borne IED (PBIED) and female suicide bombers remains a key tactic, especially as population security measures and local opposition to AQI in some provinces make effective targeting using suicide vehicle- borne IED (SVBIED) more difficult. PBIEDs continue to be a deadly weapon in the insurgent arsenal and are most commonly associated with AQI, although they are not limited to that group.

Explosively-Formed Penetrator

With the exception of a slight increase in January 2009, explosively-formed penetrator (EFP) incidents have decreased over the past few months to the lowest rate since early 2006. With so many key extremist militant leaders detained, exiled, killed, or reverted to hiding, multiple intelligence reports indicate the remaining lower-level fighters are struggling to obtain and place EFPs to execute attacks. Increased border and clearing operations in south and central Iraq have also combined to disrupt the movement and storage of EFP components **to Shi'a militants. Over the past four months,** intelligence reports suggest arms and component facilitators are experiencing increasing difficulties in transiting the borders and accessing caches. However, those individuals and munitions that do make it into Iraq from Iran frequently have more sophisticated weapons and better training.

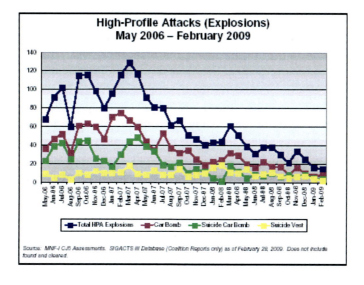

Insurgent and Militant Groups

Shi'a Militias

Ongoing ISF operations targeting AAH, KH, and Shi'a splinter extremist groups have impeded their operations, despite the return to Iraq of some of leaders in the fall of 2008. One of Muqtada al-Sadr's primary concerns has been ensuring his control over the Sadrist movement. In his November 14, 2008 statement, Sadr called for members of AAH to return to the Sadrist movement and implied that AAH was abandoning its resistance to the Coalition. Sadr's statement was intended to draw members of AAH back into his movement and undermine AAH as an independent entity. Sadr is continuing to assert his personal control over the direction of the Sadrist movement by attempting to call on AAH members to join his new armed wing, the Promised Day Brigade (PDB), which would continue to violently resist the Coalition. Progress on forming the PDB has been slow; however, the group has conducted some intermittent attacks. Sadrist movements, AAH, and KH continue to experience internal problems, including personal rivalries, disagreements over plans and policy, confusion over orders and operations, and an absence of leadership in Iraq to respond to increased ISF and Coalition operations. Despite these internal problems, Sadr will maintain a focus on the establishment and expansion of *al Mumahiddun*—Sadr's attempt to transform JAM into a social and cultural movement—and PDB as his top priority.

Sunni Insurgents

Sunni insurgent organizations draw much of their motivation for attacks from a few key factors. The largest motivators for Sunni-derived violence in Iraq are economic concerns and the lack of assistance from the GoI for the Sunni community. Due to high unemployment and underemployment rates and an overall suffering economy, many of the low-level Sunni insurgents choose to join or support local insurgent groups in order to earn an income. Regardless of ideologies and overarching objectives, inter-group cooperation at lower levels to achieve mutual goals is common. Frustration over the poor economic situation is directed at the current government and the Coalition for causing these problems. In a society that holds honor and pride in high regard, unemployed Sunni are disenfranchised and have few options to provide for their family. It is these individuals who make up the core fighting ranks of the Sunni insurgency. In addition to money, a small number of hard-line Sunni insurgents continue to draw motivation from a desire to return to power in Iraq. These individuals will continue to destabilize Iraq with the intent of discrediting the GoI. Secular motivated violence, a driver of instability in Iraq, lingers and is often dependent on local motivations. Personal grudges, ethnically charged incidents, or neighborhood pressure from other sects continue to spur violence. Secular attacks are often youthful reactions to events in their neighborhoods or cities. Religion and nationalism also play a part for a small number of Sunnis who conduct attacks either to expel the "occupiers," remove perceived Iranian influences, or highlight instances where *Sharia* Law may have been violated. There is also an unknown level of Sunni violence that is attributed to common criminal activities. These acts of violence often have no specific motivation other than greed, interpersonal relationships, and general discontent with the current situation.

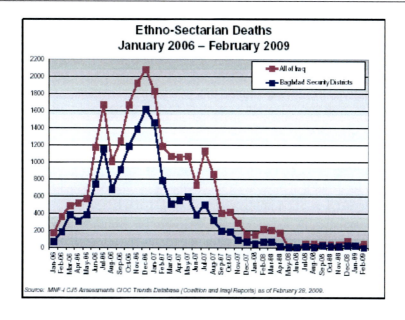

Al Qaeda in Iraq

Combined security efforts of Coalition forces and ISF, with SoI assistance, have significantly degraded AQI and reduced its ability to operate in population centers. Significant leadership losses, lack of public support, and the difficult operating environment have forced AQI from most population centers and limited its freedom of movement. However, AQI retains limited capability to conduct HPAs designed to demonstrate its viability and diminish GoI security advances. Subsequently, AQI has demonstrated its use of female suicide bombers to thwart improved security measures and conduct high-casualty producing attacks, especially against civilians. Further, AQI is targeting ISF to create an environment of instability and increase its freedom of movement.

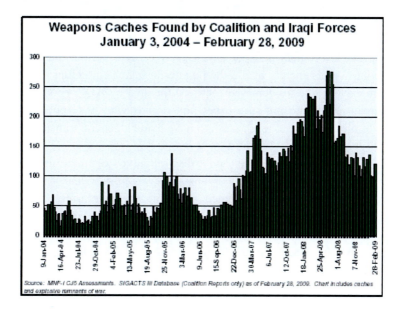

Although northern Iraq remains AQI's main area of activity, ongoing security operations in and around Mosul continue to pressure the group. These operations have also impeded AQI's ability to receive external support, and the influx of foreign fighters into Iraq continues to decline. Concurrently, further reducing exposure for the group, AQI's production of official media, primarily distributed through jihadist websites, has reduced dramatically.

Security Assessments by Region

Assessment of the Security Environment—Baghdad

It is currently assessed that most violent activity within the Baghdad Security Districts is conducted by either AQI or Shi'a militia elements. AAH and KH, among other insurgent and militant groups, continue to maintain cells in Baghdad but have had a difficult time conducting operations. The difficult operating environment has caused many operatives to stay in Iran or discontinue activities in Baghdad. However, neither of these groups has given up on Baghdad, and both continue attempts to reestablish networks despite recent arrests. These and other insurgent and militant groups continue low-level operations, and caches continue to be discovered. Overall, attacks by AAH and KH in Baghdad occur intermittently and mostly target Coalition forces. AAH and KH maintain the capacity for uncoordinated small scale insurgent and terrorist operations in Baghdad. AQI also maintains cells in and around Baghdad with the intent to re-ignite sectarian violence and undermine the GoI. Baghdad remains AQI's strategic center of gravity, although its ability to operate there has been significantly constrained by GoI security initiatives. Although AQI's presence continues to decline inside the capital, the group seeks to re-establish itself in the surrounding areas and maintains the ability and desire to carry out HPAs designed to cause high levels of casualties through the use of PBIEDs and SVBIEDs. Sunni resistance activity in Baghdad has steadily declined since early 2008, with more activity in the greater Baghdad area than in Baghdad proper.

Assessment of the Security Environment – Western Iraq

Since the previous report, attacks in Anbar Province decreased from an average of 1.5 incidents per day to fewer than one per day. Over the same period, the number of HPAs decreased to about two per month, as did the number of attacks targeting ISF within the city of Fallujah. This may be due to increased focus on the area by AQI or renewed attempts by remaining Sunni insurgents to pressure tribes and groups who have politically reconciled. Many elements of the Sunni insurgency seem to have made a general transition into either the political realm or the SoI, or have ceased attacks on the ISF.

Coalition, Iraqi Army, Iraqi Police, and tribal initiatives continue to make significant progress in the western region of Iraq against the capabilities and operations of AQI. Significant discoveries of caches, combined with key member arrests, have resulted in difficulties for AQI to carry out large-scale operations, as well as regain a foothold in the area. AQI in the West continues infrequent attacks in an effort to discredit ISF and the political process. AQI's attacks in the region focus on destabilizing security gains to intimidate and influence the local populace.

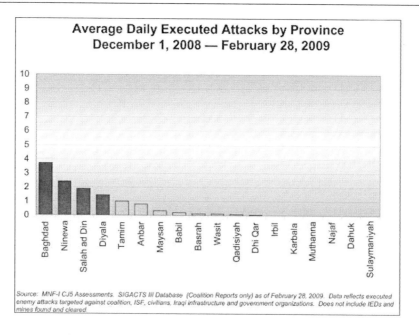

Assessment of the Security Environment – Northern Iraq/Central Iraq

Although trending down in the last few months, violence in northern and central Iraq remains an issue, particularly in Ninewa, where AQI remains focused on retaining an urban foothold and is actively targeting the ISF, local government leaders, and Coalition forces. Consistent with past tactics, techniques, and procedures, AQI continues to employ VBIEDs and suicide attacks to degrade security gains and improve its freedom of movement.

Despite continued activities, AQI has been heavily targeted by the GoI and the Coalition and continues to lose operational capability. AQI members occasionally cooperate with Sunni insurgent groups to maximize resources. The extent of the cooperation is mostly local, as Sunni insurgents make alliances with AQI and other groups often without input from strategic leadership. Both Sunni insurgents and AQI continue their campaign of intimidation of ISF, local government leadership, and local nationals throughout the region. All Sunni armed groups have propaganda campaigns designed to give the impression of strength to their members and future recruits.

Kurdish pressure on the GoI to implement Article 140 of the Iraqi Constitution continues to drive tensions between Kurds and Sunni Arabs in north and central Iraq, as well as bring about tensions with minorities, including Turkomen, Christians, and Yezidis. AQI and Sunni insurgent groups seek to exploit this tension and look for opportunities to increase ethno-sectarian violence. The presence of Kurdish Peshmerga and Kurd-dominated IA units beyond the KRG boundaries exacerbates tensions and fuels the belief that the GoI and the Coalition are allowing the Kurds to act unchecked.

With GoI assumption of responsibility for security across the country under the SA, ISF have moved to bases in areas from which they were long absent. These include areas adjacent to the KRG, such as northern Diyala, northern Tamim, and eastern Ninewa Provinces. This has created tensions between the newly-arrived ISF brigades and Peshmerga forces that have been providing security since 2003. Coalition forces present in the disputed areas continues to play a key moderating role between Peshmerga and GoI forces.

Attack levels in Ninewa have trended downward in the last few months, which are a good indicator that AQI is suffering losses in a key historical stronghold. As AQI has experienced a loss in operational capacity, Sunni insurgents throughout north and central Iraq have been less active due to Sunni involvement in provincial elections and positive effects from local SoI programs, although the group will likely continue to stage periodic HPAs, particularly against GoI targets.

Assessment of the Security Environment – Eastern Iraq (Diyala)

GoI-led operations from July 2008 through the end of 2008 forced AQI into the sparsely populated areas within the Hamrin Mountains, where AQI still maintains freedom of movement. AQI continues to exploit the province's diverse ethno-sectarian tensions, uneducated populace, and rural areas.

As it has throughout Iraq, Sadr's cease-fire is a contributing factor to the decrease in violence in the province, allowing ISF and Coalition forces to focus on targeting AQI, the Islamic State of Iraq (ISI), Sunni rejectionists, and other predominantly Sunni criminal elements. Although the ISF continues to make progress toward the GoI objective of improving security in the province by eliminating insurgent support and setting the conditions for economic recovery and the return of displaced citizens, the perception of disproportionate targeting of Sunnis has strained sectarian relations.

Despite the intention to remove extremists and militants and facilitate the return of displaced persons, GoI-led operations from late July through October 2008 strained the sectarian tension between Sunni and Shi'a and ethnic tension between Arabs and Kurds. Sunni leaders in Diyala perceived operations as an attempt to stunt their political development before provincial elections. Despite this perception, Sunnis, in general, remain engaged with the GoI and appear to have claimed a representative voice on several provincial councils following elections. Kurds reacted negatively to GoI operations into and north of the Hamrin Mountains, viewing this as a means for the GoI to exert Arab presence in one of the Article 140 disputed territories. The Kurds had maintained relative stability in Khanaqin district prior to GoI operations.

Assessment of the Security Environment – Southern Iraq

Although AAH and KH have experienced some difficulties in maintaining their networks and conducting operations in southern Iraq, Shi'a militant groups remain a primary threat to southern Iraq. Although members of both AAH and KH are able to return to Iraq from Iran, they face extremely difficult operating conditions. Reporting indicates that the population is supportive of the GoI's security initiatives and does not desire a return to the lawlessness and violence of the recent past. The ISF are in control over the vast majority of the Shi'a South, helping ensure violence maintains a downward trend. There is still low-level residual violence, and Shi'a militant groups are seeking to rebuild their damaged networks. Leading up to the provincial elections, tensions among competing parties increased and sporadic violence against rival political candidates occurred. These rivalries and the low-level violence will likely continue as the various Shi'a parties prepare for the SA referendum and national elections.

ISF assumed security responsibility for Basrah International Airport from UK forces on January 1, 2009. Following the transition of responsibility, commercial service at the airport, which is presently provided by Iraqi Airways, is expected to increase. Iraq's Ministry of Transportation intends to attract regional airlines and charter flights serving the pilgrim market.

Assessment of the Security Environment – Kurdistan Regional Government Area

The KRG remains the safest and most stable region of Iraq, although isolated acts of terrorism occasionally occur. The relatively homogenous Kurdish population and the presence of the Kurdish security forces mitigate the threat of AQI or other terrorist attacks in the North and reduce ethnic tensions that plague other cities in Iraq. Turkey and Iran continue to attack Kurdish terrorist groups along their borders with the KRG. These attacks have been conducted against sparsely populated areas in the mountains and have not led to significant numbers of refugees or collateral damage.

In disputed areas adjacent to the KRG in Ninewa, Diyala, and Tamim Provinces, tensions have increased between Kurdish Peshmerga and the ISF. These areas are ethnically mixed and resource-rich, and both the KRG and GoI assert security primacy but have not worked out a clear political arrangement. As U.S. forces depart and the profile of ISF units such as the 12th IA division rises, opportunities for miscalculation or provocation will be numerous. For now, it appears unlikely that the IA or Peshmerga will intentionally instigate a military confrontation, preferring to see whether negotiations and elections can manage results acceptable to both. However, continued Coalition involvement is critical to help manage the delicate situation.

Public Perceptions of Security

Iraqis generally believe the security situation is better locally than nationally. Research conducted in January 2009 reveals that 77% of Iraqis described the security situation in their neighborhoods as calm, a 15-percentage-point increase from November 2007.[13] When asked the same question about their province and Iraq as a whole, 57% said the situation was calm in their province, and 29% of Iraqis said the situation was calm nationwide.[14] There has been a five-percentage-point increase in the perception of security at the national level during the same period.

The majority of Iraqis (90%) feels that the security situation has remained constant or improved in their neighborhood over the last six months.[15] This is an eight-percentage-point increase when compared to November 2007. When asked about the security situation in the country as a whole, 85% felt it had either stayed the same or gotten better.[16] This is an increase of three percentage points since November 2007. January 2009 nationwide research indicates that 41% of Iraqis feel safe traveling outside of their neighborhoods.[17] This is a five-percentage-point decrease compared to November 2007.

When asked about their perceptions of the Iraqi Security Forces, 71% of Iraqis said they feel secure when they see the IA in their neighborhoods, and 62% said they feel secure when they see Iraqi Police (IP) in their neighborhoods.[18] This is a 21-percentage-point increase in trust in the IA, and a ten-percentage-point increase in trust of the IP since November 2007. Nationwide perceptions of the IA and the IP are nine percentage points apart from each other.

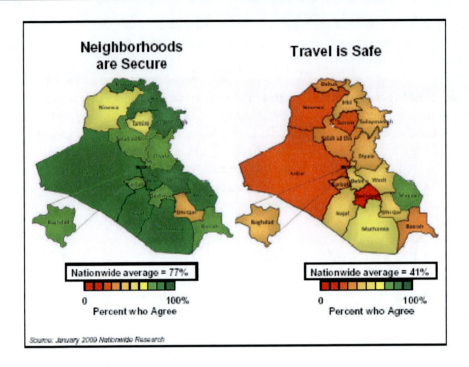

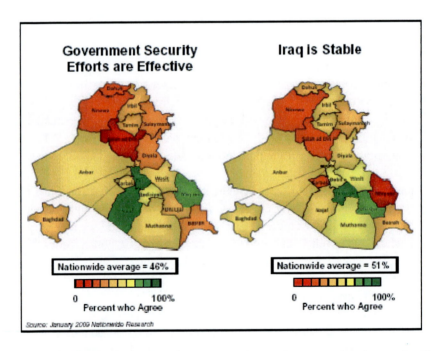

When asked in January 2009 if they believed the GoI was effective or ineffective at maintaining security, 46% of Iraqis said the GoI was effective; this represents a seven-percentage-point increase from the November 2007 data.[19] When asked to rate the level of peace and stability of the country, 51% of Iraqis said Iraq was stable, a 24-percentagepoint increase since November 2007.[20] Nationwide research in January 2009 also indicates that 72% of Iraqis believe that the IA is winning the battle against terrorists and that 61% of Iraqis believe the IP is winning the battle against crime.[21] This is a 20-percentagepoint increase in perception for the IA and a 12-percentage-point increase in perception for the IP since November 2007.

When asked who they would go to first to report a serious crime, 39% of Iraqis said the IP, while 30% stated the IA.[22] When asked who was most responsible for providing security in their neighborhoods, Iraqis responded that the IA (3 8%) and the IP (3 8%) are most responsible for providing security in their neighborhoods.[23] Relatively few Iraqis said the SoI (6%), people from their tribe (7%), neighbors (3%), militias (1%), religious leaders (2%), or Multi-National Forces (2%) were most responsible for providing security.[24]

When asked in January 2009 if they had confidence in specific groups to protect them and their families from threats, Iraqis had the highest confidence in the IA (86%).[25] When asked about other groups, 82% of Iraqis had confidence in the IP, 70% had confidence in their provincial government, 64% had confidence in their local government, and 71% had confidence in the national government.[26] Confidence in the Multi-National Forces, armed groups, and militias was much lower at 26%, 11%, and 12%, respectively.[27] In a continuation of trends from November 2007, Iraqis place their highest trust and confidence in the IA, the IP, and the GoI to protect them and to provide security.

Conclusion

Security trends across Iraq continue to be positive. There has been steady growth in the capacity, capability, and professionalism of the ISF. They are in the lead in operations across Iraq but continue to rely on Coalition forces for support. Where the security situation permits, Coalition forces have moved out of cities in Anbar Province and most southern Iraqi cities, though they remain visibly present in much of the country, especially in the disputed areas of northern Iraq. Coalition training and advising of the ISF continues, with increased emphasis on the development of the Iraqi Police.

Security incidents and civilian deaths have continued to decline, and joint Coalition and ISF operations have made progress against insurgent groups. Numerous extremist organizations, however, retain the capability and intent to conduct attacks, foment sectarian violence, and undermine the legitimacy of the GoI. In addition, Arab-Kurd tensions, intra-sectarian competition, and a climate of political divisiveness have the potential to destabilize the security situation. Sustainment of security gains will require broad-based political reconciliation, a fair, open, and non-violent political process, and an improved sense of human security and quality of life for the Iraqi people.

1.4. Transferring Security Responsibility

As of December 31, 2008, 13 of Iraq's **18 provinces had successfully transitioned to** Provincial Iraqi Control (PIC). On January 1, 2009, the SA between the U.S. and Iraq went into effect, transferring security responsibility to the GoI, even though not all of the provinces had completed the PIC transition process. At the request of the GoI, however, a new Joint Sub-Committee for Provincial Security was formed under the auspices of the SA to assess conditions in the remaining five Iraqi provinces that did not transition to PIC before January 1, 2009. This sub-committee met for the first time in January 2009.

Contingency Operating Base Turnover Status

MNF-I has delivered a list of all facilities and areas to the GoI that are currently occupied by Coalition forces, and will deliver a second list no later than June 30, 2009, to identify those remaining MNF-I bases after U.S. combat forces are removed from cities, villages, and localities in accordance with the SA. MNF-I will continue to return and close bases as security improves throughout Iraq but will ensure that sufficient facilities are maintained to support ongoing COIN efforts to ensure security gains are maintained or improved. The methodology for these closures and returns is to seek partial base turnovers with the ISF to maintain the partnership between the Coalition and the ISF. When agreeable, MNF-I will maintain forces as tenants at these locations and will continue transitioning from partnering to enabling and advising. As of February 21, 2009, MNF-I had a total of 50 large bases, including Contingency Operation Bases (COB) and Contingency Operation Sites (CO S) and approximately 202 Contingency Operation Locations (COL) and 134 other training facilities and sites. Since July 2008, MNF-I has returned or closed 36 bases in the IZ and across Iraq and is scheduled to return or close 11 COSs, 49 COLs, and four facilities over the next six months. The remaining bases will be returned on a "conditions-based" basis until all bases are returned in accordance with the SA (no later than December 31, 2011).

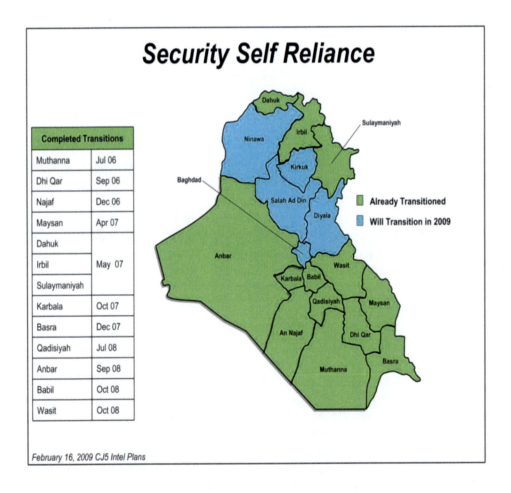

SECTION 2. IRAQI SECURITY FORCES TRAINING AND PERFORMANCE

Iraq's Security Forces (ISF) currently number approximately 615,000 forces in the Ministry of Interior (MoI), Ministry of Defense (MoD), and the Iraqi National Counter-Terrorism Force (INCTF).[28] The MoI desires growth to a total force of more than 400,000 personnel in the Iraqi Police Service (IPS), National Police (NP), and Directorate of Border Enforcement (DBE) by the summer of 2009 depending on additional resources provided by the GoI.[29] The MoI continues to make organizational and strength adjustments in its forces, as decreasing violence levels allow an increased focus on community policing, a growing recognition of the right of all Iraqi citizens to the impartial application of Iraqi law, and enforcement of Iraqi laws in concert with the judicial transition to evidentiary-based prosecution. Although there are delays in equipping and basing, the MoI's existing functional systems for procurement, budget, and real estate acquisition will, in time, meet force generation and organizational requirements throughout its forces, which include the NP, Station Police, Traffic Police, River Police, Border Police, Oil Police (OP), Facilities Protection Services (FPS), and other emergency response organizations. However, 2009 budget constraints will affect the ability of the MoI to fund any expansion of security force equipping and sustainment through 2009.

The MoD has approved a force structure for counterinsurgency (COIN) that includes 14 Army divisions (13 infantry and one mechanized) and support forces; a Navy of 2,700 personnel, including two marine battalions; and an Air Force of 6,000 personnel. Additionally, the INCTF, with projected end strength of 5,400, is contributing significantly to the COIN effort. Further modification in the military force structure appears likely, given the need to develop logistics units and enabling capabilities for tactical units, such as engineer, bomb disposal, medical evacuation, signal, and intelligence, surveillance, and reconnaissance (ISR) assets. Total ISF requirements are expected to grow as large as 646,000 by 2010, but challenges remain.[30] The MoI struggles with training throughput due to generally poor facilities and a lack of qualified instructors, while the MoD faces budget constraints. These factors will delay achieving the desired 2009 force levels required for the present planned structure.

The GoI continues to assume broader ownership for and increasing fiscal commitment to its security forces and to MoD and MoI programs. Budget execution, however, remains a significant concern. Although the MoI has demonstrated an improved ability to obligate its budget, the MoD struggles, particularly in the areas of support, sustainment, and infrastructure. Inter-ministerial budget coordination with the Ministry of Finance (MoF) is improving but remains problematic due to cumbersome procedures. In light of the decline in the market price of oil, MoD and MoI funding increases will be constrained by declining Iraqi revenues and large budgeted deficits. Further, the steady-state organizations for both the MoI and MoD beyond the year 2012 are facing significant funding challenges based on current budget projections that fluctuate with the price of oil.

Accelerating the growth of logistics-capable units and pursuing enabling capabilities remains a top priority, as does the effort to expand ministerial capacity within the MoD and MoI. Multi-National Security Transition Command – Iraq (MNSTC-I) advisory teams continue to work closely with both the MoD and MoI to improve the accuracy and frequency of their personnel reporting systems. The number of MoI personnel assigned continues to exceed personnel trained, as rapid hiring in 2007 and 2008 outstripped training center capacity and throughput. Also, as additional missions are transferred to the MoI (e.g., OP, Electricity Police, and FPS), personnel are transferred with limited training and inadequate equipment, creating a backlog of untrained and certified personnel. Ongoing efforts to expand MoI training throughput (e.g., training instructors, building infrastructure, etc.) will help remedy this training shortfall, while the focus on procurement, distribution, and sustainment will address equipping issues over time.

2.1. Assessed Capabilities of the Iraqi Forces

The Coalition's four areas of focus to develop the MoD, the MoI, and their forces remain unchanged: support force generation and force replenishment; improve the proficiency and professionalism of Iraqi forces; build specific logistic, sustainment, and training capacities; and develop ministerial and institutional capacity. The four near-term areas of emphasis through mid-2009 also remain unchanged: ensure Iraqi forces continue to improve in logistics, maintenance, and life support; ensure the size, capability, professionalism, and leadership of the ISF enable increasing assumption of additional security roles from Coalition forces; enhance the capabilities of Iraqi Special Operations Forces (ISOF) and Counter-Terrorism Forces (CTF); and ensure Iraqi Air Force (IqAF) and Navy (IqN) growth stay on-track.

Current ISF operations in Baghdad, Sadr City, Ninewa, Maysan, and Diyala continue to demonstrate the growth and the improving capabilities of the ISF. In particular, the ISF leadership has improved its command and control (C2) of multiple brigade-size elements from both the Iraqi Army (IA) and NP, while conducting simultaneous COIN operations throughout all regions of the country. IA brigade and division staffs continue to show steady improvement in planning and executing combined and joint operations, intelligence gathering, information operations, civil-military operations and limited post-conflict reconstruction operations. Operations Commands are more capable of planning and executing various types of combat operations, and they played a major role in the C2 of the security effort for the January 2009 provincial elections. Battalion- and company-level tactical COIN operation execution continues to improve. In New Baghdad, ISF units continue to plan and execute combined, targeted, cordon and knock operations, establish traffic control points, and conduct active patrolling and clearance operations. ISOF and Iraqi Special Weapons and Tactics (SWAT) units continue to conduct operations effectively to disrupt AQI and other foreign fighters. However, there remains a critical reliance on Coalition rotary wing assets and other enablers such as intelligence, close air support, and logistical sustainment during operations.

Ministerial Capacity

Both the MoI and MoD continue to show progress in developing ministerial capacity, albeit slowly and unevenly. To expand institutional capacity, Coalition mentorship and partnership will be necessary for sometime to overcome decades of isolation and stagnation in law enforcement and military education and training. A lack of capacity to train civilian management, a shortage of training staff, deterioration of some facilities, and an inability to fill many positions with trained personnel are challenges that continue to hinder the ministries. Currently, many of the Iraqi civilians working in positions inside the MoD and MoI are not yet fully trained and qualified for their positions. Although training on new processes and procedures with a focus on automation capability is being offered, many are reluctant to pursue technology-focused training.

The most significant difference between the MoD and the MoI budget execution success— and the reason the MoI is realizing greater progress—is that the MoI effectively delegates decision-making authority, including areas of budget execution, contracting, and hiring. In contrast, all management decisions within the MoD (e.g. approving all but very minor facility maintenance and all contracting requirements) must be approved by the Minister of Defense, and in some cases, by the Prime Minister. Until this process is replaced with delegated decision making, MoD's acquisition, force management, and logistics processes will continue to be hampered. Despite these challenges, both ministries achieved a near 100% budget execution for 2008. However, the increasing public friction between the Minister of Interior and the Prime Minister may produce unintended or unforeseen consequences in MoI functionality.

Operationally, both MoI and MoD forces are proving increasingly capable. In most areas, coordination between the two ministries and their subordinate organizations is improving with the implementation of operations centers in each of the provinces. These centers allow MoI and MoD forces to jointly coordinate operations and share information, which has resulted in the apprehension of suspects and the discovery and destruction of weapons caches, as well as successful security planning and mentoring for the provincial elections. ISF continue to actively cultivate community relationships and develop an environment of trust within their communities by performing humanitarian support and engaging in outreach and public information activities to solicit local help to combat insurgents. The ISF are gaining the acceptance of the Iraqi people by effectively demonstrating that their combined accomplishments against terrorist activities make Iraqi communities safer.

Iraqi Forces Proficiency

IA combat battalions continue to increase in both number and capability.[31] As of January 2009, there are 175 IA combat battalions conducting operations, with four newly-formed battalions (179 total). Five ISOF battalions are conducting operations, and five IA infrastructure battalions are conducting security support operations. The IqAF continues to expand its operational capability as the Iraqi Air Operations Center (IAOC) now provides scheduling, C2, and execution for over 350 operational and training sorties per week. The IqN continues to strengthen its ability to patrol Iraqi territorial waters and provide point defense for Iraq's two offshore oil platforms and security for the port and towns of Umm Qasr and Az Zubayr. The IqN will take responsibility of point defense for one of the two major oil platforms in the coming months. The IqN conducts an average of 42 independent patrols and 35 commercial ship boardings per week, and maintains an in-commission capability rate of 80% of the Iraqi fleet.

The NP continues to improve the effectiveness of its units. During this reporting period, 57 of 64 NP units were assessed and seven units were in force generation (these units will be assessed once they complete forming and are assigned areas of responsibility). Based on the improvement in capability and effectiveness of the NP, Coalition advisors have shifted their focus from battalion-level advising to brigade-level and above. The only exception to this approach is advisor assignments to the newly-formed NP battalions, as these battalions require more assistance to develop a capability for operations without Coalition support. Coalition advisors will continue to assess NP unit capabilities to distribute and realign teams more effectively to units requiring additional assistance. The Italian *Carabinieri* continue to train, advise, and assist with the professionalization of the NP, incrementally increasing NP training from 400 to 600, then to 900 police students every six weeks beginning in February 2009.

The long-term, nation-to-nation strategic relationship continues to mature with out-of-country training opportunities in the United States and many European-based NATO countries. The United States and NATO fund courses each year for security ministries to professionally develop their forces. Courses offered include: Basic Officer Leader Courses, Captain Career Courses, War Colleges, periodic security seminars at the National Defense University and the Marshall Center, General Officer Development Courses, and Civil Emergency Response Courses. The U.S. courses and many of the NATO courses require English language proficiency prior to enrollment, which has proven problematic. Consequently, MNSTC-I is working with the security ministries to establish a standard training framework and curriculum throughout Iraqi educational institutions to facilitate the development of a larger pool of English speaking professionals within the ISF.

ISF Intelligence Developments

The Coalition continues to support GoI development of the Iraqi Intelligence Community (IqIC), created to support senior policy makers and ISF operations. ISF intelligence organizations include the National Information and Investigation Agency (NIIA) in the MoI, the Directorate General for Intelligence and Security (DGIS), and the Joint Headquarters (JHQ) Directorate for Intelligence. They have shown substantial progress in conducting credible intelligence operations and improvements in providing legitimate, uncoerced physical evidence for the Iraqi judicial processes. However, at present, the Intelligence and Military Security School (IMSS), which provides training for ISF intelligence professionals and investigators, suffers from a lack of adequate cadre and sufficient curriculum to meet ISF intelligence specialization needs. The Coalition is working with ISF intelligence partners to address these and other specific shortfalls. Several significant challenges remain for the ISF intelligence organizations, including the absence of an Iraqi Intelligence Law that would delineate roles and responsibilities of organizations with clear legal mandates and C2 mechanisms, limited standardized security and clearance protocols to increase sharing of information among other IqIC members, and a need to standardize intelligence into common databases readily available to support operations.

Training Capacities

Operational since October 2007, the MoD's Ministerial Training and Development Center (MTDC) continues to provide valuable education and training to Iraqi security officials. Initially funded with Iraqi Security Forces Fund (ISFF) dollars, the MTDC has active ties with similar regional and international training and professionalism institutions. The MTDC offers courses in 11 different departments: Policy and Requirements, Intelligence and Security, Finance and Budgeting, Contracting, Inspector General and Human Rights,

General Counsel, English Language, Infrastructure, Information Technology, Personnel and Management, and Media and Communications. To date, the MTDC has conducted 130 classes, trained more than 2,500 GoI officials, developed 54 programs of instruction, and transitioned teaching responsibility for 20 courses to Iraqi instructors. The MTDC trains Iraqi Joint Forces (IJF) personnel, MoD civilians, and officials from the Ministries of Interior, Finance, and National Security, as well as the Counter-Terrorism Command and the Prime Minister's National Operations Center.

Logistics and sustainment capacities

Logistical and sustainment capability remains a major area of focus and is essential for enduring ISF self-sufficiency. ISF have become more competent and self-sufficient over time and have made appropriate organizational adjustments during more recent operations. Although this is an encouraging development at the tactical level, much effort must be directed to the sustainment and logistical support capability within the ISF at the operational and strategic levels. The MoD continues to develop a national supply and distribution network, with one Location Command in direct support of each IA division. The MoD will co-locate regional life-support assets at these sites to enhance warehousing and distribution capacity. Eight of these Location Commands are either complete or are being refurbished. The remaining five bases are under construction or pending contract and will be operational by mid-2009.

The MoI began fielding a NP Sustainment Brigade in October 2008 with the purchase of property and Coalition force-contracting for construction of facilities commencing in March 2009. The NP Sustainment Brigade will be a mobile organization providing support to the four NP divisions and separate brigades during operations. The NP will complete organic support units in each division during 2009.

The Taji National Depot Complex remains the centerpiece for national supply and maintenance services to the ISF. When complete, the complex will maintain line stock across all classes of supply for issue to the 13 Location Commands. Other organizations at the Taji Depot (e.g., engine and transmission repair workshops, repair parts warehouses, wheeled and tracked vehicle maintenance facilities, etc.) will begin operations as construction is completed, currently envisioned by the end of 2009. The theater-capable General Transportation Regiment (GTR) began performing transportation missions from its new base at the Taji National Supply Depot in December 2008. Accelerated fielding of the final Motor Transport Regiment (MTR) has significantly reduced Iraqi dependency on Coalition support to move supplies to Location Commands and training site warehouses.

Acquisition Capabilities

The MoI is increasing its equipment distribution, procurement capability, and service contracting. Additionally, it has executed significant purchases of materiel and services using the foreign military sales (FMS) process. A multimillion-dollar repair parts contract for commercial vehicles was established within the Baghdad Police College warehouse complex. This commercial spare parts contract will significantly affect parts distribution processes and ultimately improve vehicle readiness rates within the MoI.

MNSTC-I continues to use ISFF to supplement GoI logistics sustainment capacity development for the ISF. ISF funding of this critical area, which includes salaries, training, equipping, and sustainment of the ISF, continues to increase in parallel with the development of a detailed transition and sustainment plan. When complete, the plan will establish sustainment logistics and budgetary requirements that are necessary to ensure the long-term health of the ISF. It will also help guide the development of annual budgetary input for the recurring operations and maintenance (O&M) requirements of the force. As Coalition funding support to ISF O&M reduces to zero, Iraqi funds will be required to maintain the force. This process is deliberately advancing Iraq toward management and funding of its own forces.[32]

Foreign Military Sales

As of December 2008, the FMS program included 121 Iraqi-signed cases in execution valued at $5.8 billion since its inception in 2005. The latter part of 2008 saw a shift toward FMS as the GoI's preferred procurement strategy. An additional 80 FMS cases, valued at over $8 billion, were either offered or being developed in response to GoI Letters of Request. With assistance from the MNSTC-I Security Assistance Office (SAO), the GoI transferred just over $1 billion to its FMS account at the end of 2008 to pay for additional equipment and services.

Throughout 2008, many of the initiatives recommended by the FMS Task Force to improve the U.S. process and implementation became a solid foundation for FMS in Iraq. The biggest improvements included the arrival of experienced FMS, acquisition and security cooperation personnel to provide training on the FMS program and processes and to work as the primary interface between the Iraqis and their advisory and training teams and the U.S. Security Assistance and Acquisition Agencies. Additionally, the MNSTC-I SAO grew and improved its performance markedly. Consequently, FMS case processing timelines in the United States improved significantly.

Although room for improvement remains, FMS cargo delivery times have also been reduced. In-transit visibility and delivery dates still need to be improved; however, the U.S. Security Cooperation organizations worked hard during the last two months of 2008 to provide the SAO and the GoI an accurate picture of in-transit visibility of the equipment they purchased. Overall, the common operational picture has improved as a result of daily communications supported by weekly teleconferences, better coordination, and use of the Defense Transportation System.

Execution of FMS in Iraq continues to be hindered by several factors. These factors include the lack of ministerial capacity in all aspects of defining requirements generation and processing of FMS Letters of Offer and Acceptance, the lack of a budget planning and execution process that allocates funds for needed requirements (leading to insufficient funds for must-pay requirements), and unrealistic accounting expectations of total system ownership costs, including equipment purchase, training, sustainment, and operations costs. These areas are all being addressed through an increased focus on building ministerial capacity through MNSTC-I advisors and increased training from the SAO team.

Marking a new milestone in developing the ISF, in September 2008, the Minister of Defense signed the first force modernization cases for M1A1 Tanks, Armed Scout Helicopters, and C130-J Personnel and Cargo Aircraft, estimated to be valued at over $1.6 billion in equipment. Along with the F-16s, which are under review, these major end-item cases will provide the Iraqi military with increased mobility, airlift capability, and an enhanced COIN capability, enabling the development of a broader, full-spectrum national defense force. Additional cases in support of these three cases are valued at $1 billion in initial training, sustainment, and spare parts, and will need to be signed and funded in early

2009. The MoD Force Generation and Modernization plan for 2009 currently exceeds the projected spending authorizations for 2009, requiring the security ministries to either significantly reduce their vision to grow, develop, and equip their forces or to petition the GoI for an additional $8 to $10 billion to support desired growth.

2.2. Ministry of Interior

Ministerial Planning Capacity

The MoI's 2009 Strategic Plan represents a substantial improvement over past planning efforts, but it still does not link planning and goals to resource allocation and program management. To remedy this weakness, the MoI's 2010 Strategic Plan developmental team commenced planning in January 2009. The team's work is expected to be a major step forward in both planning and budgeting to better prepare the MoI for future success and autonomy, particularly as funding levels could become tight as the MoF handles other GoI budgetary constraints.

Budget Planning and Execution (Finance and Contracting)

The MoI received $3.9 billion for its 2008 budget, with approximately $3.1 billion (80%) allocated for salaries and $148.3 million (4%) allocated for capital expenditures. MoI budget execution struggles are due to a late budget allocation process (MoF released the budget to the MoI in late April 2008), slow design and contracting procedures, slow starts on construction projects, and a lack of progress on invoice and payment procedures at the provincial and national unit levels. Increased emphasis and active assistance from the Assistant Deputy Minister of Finance has resulted in improved timeliness of monthly financial reporting. According to MoF data, the MoI executed approximately 68% of its combined 2008 base and supplemental budget through November 2008, with increased wage payments approved in the supplemental budget, driving the MoI's higher expenditures.

The MoI continues to be burdened by antiquated Iraqi financial laws that make direct contracting procedures a time consuming process that simply cannot handle the amount of contracts required to obligate the funds for needed equipment and services. Also hampering execution was the late allocation of the 2008 budget supplemental and the refusal of the MoF to accept electronically-generated tracking and reporting data. One immediate success has been the end-of-year transfer of $674 million into the FMS account, with $271 million allocated for operational purchases and $403 million allocated for investments. This action will ensure these funds will continue to be available for MoI use in 2009.

Acquisition

The Ministry of Planning (MoP) continues to struggle with acquiring land deeds, which causes delays in project planning, design, and contracting phases prior to the start of construction. During this reporting period, the MoP reported initial expenditures on several construction programs, including a national headquarters for the Customs Police, land purchases for Karbala and Kirkuk police stations, construction of five police stations in Dhi Qar, multiple checkpoints in Maysan, Karbala, and Muthanna, and border forts for the Border Police.

Human Resources

As of January 2009, there are approximately 486,000 personnel assigned to MoI forces, of which approximately 382,000 personnel are IPS, NP, and Border and Port Forces. In September 2008, the MoI announced a future authorization of 476,562 personnel, including the IPS, NP, Border and Port Forces, FPS, and ministry staff. Consequently, the MoI has hired 16,231 personnel since September 2008. The hiring process continues to appear to follow fair vetting procedures and special care is taken to ensure comparable demographic representation in the MoI security forces.

Operations

Command Centers

The MoI's National Command Center (NCC) is improving coordination with other national-level command centers, other ministries, and Provincial Joint Coordination Centers (PJCC). A major renovation of the NCC, completed in November 2008, enhanced effectiveness through improved connectivity and coordination capabilities. The present C2 reporting system at the Director General of Police (DGoP)-level begins at the PJCC and flows through the NCC and on to the Prime Minister's National Operations Center (PMNOC). In addition, the reporting system facilitates information sharing with the MoD Joint Operations Center (JOC) and the Baghdad Operations Command.

MoI capacity to plan, coordinate, conduct, and sustain operations continues to improve, though planning efforts remain highly centralized and not thoroughly integrated with MoD plans. However, joint planning capabilities continue to improve between the MoD, MoI, and other GoI entities and will produce positive dividends in upcoming operations. A recent example of this improvement in planning capability was the successful coordination and movement of more than 31,000 Hajj pilgrims at the beginning of the reporting period. Additionally, the recent provincial election security operations were successfully coordinated and controlled through the Operation Centers network with no significant violence in any of the provinces.

Logistics

The MoI's National Vehicle Maintenance Plan is still under revision. The overall end state of this plan is to provide policy guidance and assistance in maintaining vehicle readiness to support police operations across Iraq. To that end, the MoI is executing a $48 million FMS case to create a computer-based supply-chain management system. The first step is the $160,000 FMS vehicle maintenance training case to provide maintenance training on non-tactical vehicles assigned to the MoI. As part of this FMS case, the MoI began delivery of spare parts to subordinate units in January 2009.

The NP Sustainment Brigade, scheduled to be operational by September 2009, will be capable of accomplishing a wide range of missions, including line-haul transportation, deployable maintenance, supply receipt, storage, and issue for NP divisions, combat health treatment, and mobile fuel storage and distribution. The brigade currently consists of a headquarters (HQ) and medical, transportation, maintenance, and logistics companies.

Training

As the MoI continues to make progress toward increasing training capacity to eliminate the backlog of *Shurta* (non-commissioned entry-level police men and women) requiring completion of Basic Recruit Training (BRT), the focus is moving more toward specialized training. The MoI Training Qualification Institute (TQI) has launched several initiatives to improve professionalization and quality of training, as well as address specific skill sets needed by its operational forces. Specifically, programs are being developed in English language training, criminal investigation techniques, ethics and human rights, forensics and crime scene management, community policing, police information and intelligence, and technology applications.

The MoI training base is currently capable of training more than 88,000 *Shurta* per year. In addition, 5,600 resident and 9,720 non-resident officers can be trained annually, with a total student capacity of nearly 25,000 students at any given time. In early 2009, resident capacity will increase to 8,900 as Phase II of the Baghdad Police College (BPC) expansion is completed on the main campus and branches are opened in Mosul and Basrah. In 2008, 3,430 officers and commissioners attended professional and leadership development courses at the BPC. TQI courses have graduated police in human rights instruction (955), instructor certification (385), basic criminal investigation (193), advanced criminal investigation (439), leadership development (1,389), and internal affairs (69). Since the previous report, the MoI has added additional training facilities, with 17 of 19 training facilities now under its full control. The jointly-funded MoI training-base expansion plan includes building 12 new training centers, as well as expanding six existing training centers. In the meantime, the Coalition and the MoI have collaborated to develop temporary training facility options to further reduce the training backlog.

The Iraqi BPC instructor cadre train all basic officer and commissioner tasks, provide a basic *Shurta* curriculum for all MoI forces, and continue to take on an increasing proportion of the specialized and advanced course loads. MNSTC-I advisors and International Police Advisors (IPA) continue to assist by providing advice, overwatch, and quality control assistance in each of these courses. Coalition advisors assist the MoI TQI in a continuous review of BRT and officer curricula to ensure the course standards are consistent with internationally acceptable practices and that courses meet the dynamic needs of the field.

Ongoing professionalization of the basic police forces is crucial to develop and maintain a credible police force. Coalition IPAs work closely with Iraqi curriculum development committees chaired by members of the BPC faculty. A training program curriculum for basic officer leadership is complete, with a successful pilot class in December 2008 and full program fielding currently underway. In addition, a mid-level officer leadership course and commissioner basic and advanced leadership courses are under development, with fielding anticipated in April 2009. The MoI is also pursuing partnerships with established international police academies for the development of an executive leadership course in 2009. Furthermore, the BPC has established working partnerships with the MoI's Directorate of Human Resources to develop options for embedding leader-training requirements in personnel management policies and recording completed training in personnel files.

The Ethics and Human Rights Center at the BPC already offers six different programs. All curricula integrate lessons on values-based policing, human rights, detainee operations, and principles of community policing. The newly-passed ISF Penal Code standard of conduct for police officers is integrated throughout MoI policing courses. In 2008, the Ethics Center trained 2,101 officers, commissioners, and *Shurta*. Curricula developed by the Human Rights Center are also used in ethics programs of instruction for all officer, commissioner, and *Shurta* basic accession courses. In 2009, TQI also has plans to expand the center to teach more police students. Recently, the Human Rights Center has begun exploring possible collaboration with the Ministry of Human Rights for a curriculum review and a guest lecture series.

The Minister of Interior is personally taking an active role in training; he directed that more training be focused on ethics and human rights, leadership, management, and administration, as well as core policing skills such as community policing and responsiveness to local citizen concerns. Training in the areas of investigative and forensic skills; intelligence data collection, analysis, and reporting; English language proficiency; and specific investigative training to counter corruption, organized crime, and drug trafficking is a priority. The MoI is actively developing a program designed to expand training and education opportunities abroad for IPS officers to expose them to best practices and techniques in other countries. This will supplement over 750 European-based training courses arranged by Coalition partners, the UK Department for International Development, and the European Union's integrated rule of law and police training mission to Iraq. An example program with select U.S. city police organizations is in development

Health Service Support

The Assistant Deputy Minister of Interior for Social Welfare and Health has the responsibility for providing healthcare to MoI employees, including the NP, IPS, and Border Police. Outpatient health services for MoI employees are provided by two MoI clinics and seven NP clinics in Baghdad and by the MoH in provincial areas. All inpatient care for the MoI is provided by the MoH. The fledgling MoI health system still requires concentrated Coalition support. One of the most challenging components to further expansion of military medical capabilities and infrastructure is a shortage of healthcare professionals. As of January 2009, the MoI has 6% of physicians authorized and is affected by the same national physician shortage as that experienced in the MoD.

Iraqi Police Services

The IPS mission to enforce the rule of law, safeguard the public, and provide local community security remains unchanged. IPS operational performance has improved with each operation, and the IPS is now becoming a professional force that can, with limited Coalition support, begin to operate and support the rule of law throughout Iraq in conjunction with the court system. The disparate elements that make up the IPS are starting to provide cross-department support to each other, further enhancing their ability to operate.

The IPS consists of all provincial police forces (station, patrol, traffic, and special units) assigned to the 18 Iraqi provinces. The Director General of Police (DGoP) for each province oversees operations and sustainment of more than 1,300 police stations across Iraq. The IPS directs policy and strategic planning and has technical control over the training, vetting, and hiring of *Shurta* and officers. Other significant departments and directorates within the IPS are the Criminal Evidence Directorate, SWAT/Emergency Response Unit, and the General Directorate of Crime Affairs.

The MoI's ability to address basic equipping shortfalls remains a concern. As of January 2009, one IP provincial headquarters and ten IP districts showed improvement in their readiness assessment over the last reporting period. The reason for the improvement is mere effective leadership, in addition to planning, training, and sustained police operations independent of Coalition support. Training challenges, with equipment shortfalls, while improving, also remain a concern. To address training challenges, the Minister of Interior held a training conference on November 29, 2008, resulting in the creation of a special training commission to determine the best way to utilize MoI human and material resources. The result of this commission was the MoI 2009 training plan, which addresses all untrained IP with improvements expected by December 2009.

National Police

Depending on funding, the NP will expand with the completion of the 3rd Division units in the northern region, and begin generation of the 4th Division HQs and subordinate units in the southern region. Additionally, the NP has assumed three new security force missions. The new special security unit missions are the Central Bank of ISF, Embassy Protection Force, and the Antiquities/Ruins Security Force. With the planned addition of these units, the 2009 authorization for the NP has increased to over 60,000 members. The NP had 43,000 personnel assigned as of January 2009 and will continue to recruit and train to meet the generation of the new 3rd and 4th Division units. Based on projected MoI budget shortfalls for 2009, the NP will likely struggle with hiring, training, and equipping the additional personnel required to reach the desired end strength of approximately 60,000.

The 3rd Division units will expand to provide a presence in Diyala, Mosul (to add to existing units in Salah ad Din), and Anbar. The 4th Division will generate units in Wasit, Maysan, and Dhi Qar in addition to the units already in Basrah. As part of the plan to regionalize the NP and provide direct support to Provincial Directors of Police (PDoP), it is projected that the NP will have a battalion or larger presence in nine of 15 provinces by the end of 2009. The NP continues to have success in recruiting across all of Iraq's ethnic and religious sects in each province, and the NP leadership is dedicated to a diverse ethnic force that represents the Iraqi population.

In Baghdad, the 1st and 2nd NP Divisions, as part of the Rusafa Area Command (RAC) and Karbala Area Command (KAC), continue to assume greater responsibilities as the Coalition withdraws to an overwatch status. In the KAC, in East and West Rashid, the 5th and 7th NP Brigades have assumed most of the security responsibility from the Coalition and are in the lead. Progress continues in the RAC, with the NP Brigades expected to assume full security responsibility from the Coalition by mid-year 2009.

Continued expansion of the NP into the provinces is supported by a three-year plan to base a brigade-sized NP force into each of the provinces, with a regionally based division HQ and division support battalions controlling these units and providing logistical support. The NP HQ is aggressively seeking available properties in the provinces to base these new units and has had initial success in acquiring properties. However, there remains much work to provide basing locations to all current and planned units. The continued support of the MoI is required to plan the equipping and infrastructure improvements required for the new units, as well as the ongoing need to replenish existing units' equipment and improve their basing locations.

Directorate of Border Enforcement and Ports of Entry Directorate

The DBE and Ports of Entry Directorate (PoED) continue in their respective responsibilities to protect Iraq's 3,650 kilometers of international borders and 28 air, land, and sea ports of entry to prevent smuggling, sabotage, and infiltration activities. These organizations continue to enforce compliance with international treaties and protocols, with respect to international agreements and boundaries. The PoED is responsible for administration and security of 13 land ports of entry throughout Iraq, as well as ports of entry in six international airports and four seaports. There are an additional five ports of entry in the Kurdish Region that are not recognized or managed by the GoI.

The DBE is divided into five regions, 13 brigades, and 52 battalions, as well as the Coastal Border Guard, which is assigned to Region 4 at Basrah. Seven of the DBE battalions are mobile commando battalions that perform operations based on the orders of the DBE Regional Commander. There is no current plan for additional force generation by the DBE, which is authorized 45,000 personnel with more than 40,000 currently assigned. More than 34,000 have completed BRT. The PoED is authorized 2,500 personnel and is fully staffed at this time. The DBE is a part of the MoI training commission that was recently appointed to seek Iraqi solutions to eliminate the backlog of personnel who had not received BRT by the end of 2009.

To overcome these challenges to progress, the MoI has instituted a training commission to address ineffectiveness issues based on training and leadership shortcomings. The Coalition has placed Logistical Training and Border Transition Teams in all regions to work on solutions to ISF logistical challenges. In addition to leadership and personnel issues, several Iraqi ministerial Directorates, including DBE and the PoED, continue to struggle with claims of corruption. With Coalition support, the GoI is combating this challenge through ongoing ethics training for PoED employees and has responded to corruption allegations with select re-assignments of personnel.

Oil Police

The OP is responsible for protecting all oil production infrastructure, including oil fields, pipelines, refineries, convoys, and retail stations. The OP mission requires forces to be located throughout Iraq along distribution lines in both remote and urban areas. Consequently, there is no standardized unit organization or coverage area. The OP operates 12 Battalions in three districts—south, central, and north. With additional funding, the MoI plans to form (funding permitting) an additional seven battalions over the next year and an additional 13 battalions by 2012 to provide nationwide infrastructure security coverage to this critical national resource. During this reporting period, the OP completed formation of two new battalions. Currently, select units of the IA guard designated areas of the oil production infrastructure, with the MoI scheduled to resume full responsibility for this mission in late 2010.

The OP lack the basic equipment required to perform its mission. The MoI and the OP are acquiring weapons and uniforms, as well as specialty equipment such as busses, fuel tankers, water tankers, road graders, and tow trucks. Much of the needed equipment was delivered in February 2009, on a cost share basis with the Coalition.

Approximately 78% of the existing force has achieved training certification through the three-week OP course. Discussions are underway to establish a surge training capability to ensure capacity keeps pace with growth projections. Additionally, there is a plan to begin training OP in the 240-hour IPS course to increase professionalism. OP leaders are actively involved in their organizations and are qualified for their positions with most officers trained in a police or military academy. The only significant shortfall in leadership is found in the junior officer and non-commissioned officer (NCO) ranks. This problem must be reviewed and a detailed plan developed in conjunction with the MoI.

Facilities Protection Services

The FPS is responsible for the protection of critical infrastructure throughout Iraq, including government buildings, mosques and religious sites, hospitals, schools and colleges, dams, highways, and bridges. Under CPA Order 27, FPS forces were decentralized within each ministry and province. If the FPS Reform Law is passed by the CoR, the GoI will consolidate all FPS within the MoI except those FPS forces currently detailed to the MoO and MoE, as well as the HJC. The law still lingers between the CoM and the CoR. The FPS Directorate is spread across three divisions providing oversight of 28 ministry facilities and various other facilities in 14 provinces.

The MoI FPS numbers just over 16,000 employees. Another 110,000 FPS employees work in other ministries and approximately 89,000 of these are expected to meet MoI hiring criteria and transfer to the MoI when consolidation occurs. During this quarter, the MoI FPS began signing contracts with the other ministries' FPS, which marks a significant step toward consolidation. The projected end strength of this force is expected to be around 108,000 when consolidation is complete in 2009.

The MoI's FPS is currently trained in the 240- hour IP course. The MoI has also provided training to other ministry FPS personnel in a three-week course, with 1,934 personnel and 83 instructors trained since the beginning of 2008. The FPS plans to continue training in the three- week FPS course once consolidation occurs. The FPS has traditionally been the unit with the lowest priority for equipment issue within the MoI and currently has less than 10% of its authorized equipment on hand.

2.3. Ministry of Defense

The MoD has approximately 203,000 personnel authorized and almost 221,000 assigned as of January 2009. As the ground force nears completion, lack of a sustainment funding plan and a cumbersome centralized decision-making process continue to inhibit MoD forces improvements. The Defense Minister still reviews almost all procurement and maintenance funding decisions and approves most equipment purchases.

From January through November 2008, the MoD executed approximately 97% of its $5.295 billion budget; the major challenge facing the MoD in 2009 is a limited "proposed" budget, currently projected to be below $5 billion. The projected 2009 MoD budget is barely sufficient to sustain the current ground force. Exacerbating these difficulties are expanding expenditures from growing employee lists, rising wages, the need to purchase logistics support and enabling unit equipment, and ballooning sustainment costs that squeeze capital growth programs beyond 2009. In short, the economic downturn and concurrent drop in oil prices will drastically curtail the rate at which the Iraqi military forces can achieve full COIN capabilities and begin to focus on modernization.

Ministry of Defense and Joint Headquarters

The JHQ is developing greater capability to provide operational-level advice to the MoD and is developing its capacity to plan and logistically resource operations. Despite the JHQ's progress, the Iraqi national security C2 architecture continues to be poorly defined and overly centralized, which inhibits planning, decision making, and the ability to execute coordinated operations at all levels. Coalition advisors continue to provide mentorship and partnership to the IJF, working closely with Iraqi staffs to increase their capacity to conduct rudimentary operational and strategic-level planning and execution.

Policy and Plans

The MoD General Directorate for Policy and Requirements has limited capability to generate relevant and applicable defense policies and plans. Although capability exists within some of these staffs to produce their respective policies and plans, there is no institutional process for feedback, approval, and implementation of such guiding documents. Senior Iraqi leadership has resisted publishing formal policy documents, which results in sluggish decision-making practices at all levels. The MoD leadership often disregards the requirements generated by its subordinate staffs and is resistant to tying capability requirements to national security documents.

Acquisition

The MoD's acquisition branches lack the capacity to routinely acquire the goods and services necessary to sustain and modernize the IJF. The MoD faces numerous challenges, including the lack of a multi-year acquisition strategy, weak requirements determination, late release of requirements funding, overly centralized decision making, inadequately trained and inexperienced staff, and insufficient use of technology to optimize processes. There exists limited ability to conduct simple contracts with a single vendor, with major overseas contracts and purchases personally negotiated by senior ministerial staff. Due to these limitations, the MoD continues to rely heavily on FMS to equip and sustain its forces. Several contracts for Organizational Clothing and Individual Equipment have been let internal to Iraq with state-sponsored companies. This was a Prime Minister-directed procurement initiative focused on strengthening Iraqi manufacturing capabilities while providing for the Iraqi Ground Forces.

To address these limitations, the Coalition is providing course instruction and on-the-job training to the MoD's acquisition staff in contracting, purchasing, and acquisition. Additionally, acquisition-trained subject-matter experts began deploying in December 2008 to support the Iraqi contracting branches.

Infrastructure

The MoD General Directorate of Infrastructure has limited ability to build new, or maintain current, infrastructure due to lack of experienced and qualified engineers, currently manned at 22% of authorization, and lack of authority to execute requirements. The Minister of Defense-mandated hiring freeze further compounds this situation. Obligation of funds to maintain infrastructure is problematic as well. In the latter part of 2008, the MoD received a supplemental to its infrastructure account, increasing the total budget authorization to $374 million; however, a total of only $31 million was actually obligated and executed.

Finance and Budget

Manual processes continue to dominate budgetary management in the absence of networked computer solutions. However, an automated stand-alone software package that will enhance the MoD Directorate General of Programs and Budget (P&B) capacity to execute its key financial management missions in support of the MoD and significantly reduce the need for external assistance is being considered. The principal weakness of the P&B Directorate remains a limited capacity to provide forecasts of ministerial budget execution. This branch is capable of iterative planning with the MoF to finalize and subsequently reconcile the MoD's annual budget, accurately track expenditures, and collate monthly reports to the MoF, while ensuring compliance with GoI accounting guidelines, policies, and regulations.

Personnel

The MoD General Directorate for Personnel continues progress toward implementing a computer-supported, comprehensive personnel management system. Lack of decentralized decision-making authority affects this and other initiatives, including hiring. Approximately 40% of civilian positions across the MoD remain unfilled. However, a positive trend is emerging whereby more civilian positions are being recognized and validated for fill. The areas needing skilled people are contracts, communications, infrastructure, and acquisition.

The Coalition has trained MoD staff to operate and maintain the Human Resources Information Management System (HRIMS), which began operating in December 2008. Continued testing, system validation, and expanded user training will occur over the next several months. HRIMS provides MoD the capability to pull personnel status reports, such as present for duty soldiers, number of soldiers trained, number of soldiers by Military Occupational Skill Qualification (MOSQ), and pay and other human lifecycle management reports. However, HRIMS will not be capable of full lifecycle management for approximately three years. Therefore, the MoD must use current paper-based systems until HRIMS matures sufficiently as a system of record to take over human resource lifecycle management. HRIMS will serve as the database for personnel identification and weapons accountability and interface with the network where biometric information is stored. The Minister of Defense recently committed nearly $5 million to pay all costs associated with the HRIMS fielding and operation.

The National Reconciliation Program, which allows qualified former soldiers the option to re-join the Iraqi forces, is not encumbered by the hiring freeze and is progressing. Once complete, the program should yield a moderate increase in the number of mid-grade officers and NCOs within the Iraqi Ground Forces Command (IGFC). The Prime Minister's initiative to form a National Reconciliation Committee (NRC) led to a process to reduce the backlog of 160,000 retirement applications from veterans of the previous regime. MNSTC-I continues work with the NRC to improve the retirement process, develop plans to revise and fill the modified table of organization and equipment (MTOE) with capable employees to work veteran programs, and establish automation processes to include ultimately utilizing HRIMS.

Inspector General

The MoD Inspector General's anti-corruption efforts still lack transparency and need to be professionalized. The MoD recently sought Coalition assistance in the development of initiatives to fight corruption and criminal influences within MoD. Chief among these initiatives is implementation of a department- wide ministerial Inspector General (IG) inspection plan. The JHQ IG, on the other hand, completed its ambitious inspection goals for 2008, conducting 110 unit readiness inspections, despite delayed hiring actions to achieve approved manning levels.

Human Rights

The MoD maintains about 30 small detention facilities but does not have the institutional mission, authority, or dedicated resources to adequately operate large or long-term detainee populations. Presently, about 96% of the approximately 2,195 pre-trial MoD-held detainees are in its eight largest facilities, and they are typically over-capacity. Detainee living conditions suffer accordingly. However, a vigorous bilateral inspection program, including joint Coalition-GoI key leader engagements and the re-establishment of the MoD Detainee Operations Committee, have led to increasing visibility of challenges and consensus building for improvement of detainee conditions. A notable success is the recent increase to 90% of MoD facilities now permitting family visitation. Although the MoD has begun to implement some improvements in its detainee operations, enduring, wide-scale progress depends on a MoD and MoJ cross-ministry solution.

Military Justice

Military justice continues to improve with operational courts hearing cases in Baghdad, Basrah, Mosul, Najaf, and Ramadi. In December 2008, the number of cases tried increased to more than three times the number tried in any previous month as the courts worked to clear a backlog of intentional absence cases. The increased number of cases continued through February 2009. In January 2009, the Minister of Defense authorized an additional military court in Baghdad to supplement the existing court in the al Karkh district. In February 2009, the Peshmerga and MoD successfully concluded negotiations and selected judges for the military court in Irbil. The Minister of Defense is taking measures to make the Irbil and Diyala courts operational by spring 2009 and has appointed a Chief Judge, who will be responsible for establishing the nascent Joint Military Court with judges appointed from all ministries. This court should begin hearing cases within the next several months. The Military Court of Cassation in Baghdad continues as the functioning appellate court

Operations

JHQ is slowly improving operational C2 capabilities; however, the Iraqi Forces JOC remains heavily reliant on Coalition sources for both friendly and insurgent unit disposition, situational awareness, and general intelligence gathering. Coalition forces are working to enhance training and advisory support of Iraqi organic capabilities in the JOC. Staff planning is improved but underutilized outside of the JHQ. MoD planning is hampered by a lack of delegation through the JHQ chain of command to appropriate directorates, and when accomplished, is ad hoc and based on personal and ethnic affiliation. Although some progress is being made, logistics, sustainment of ISF personnel, equipment distribution, infrastructure maintenance, and force generation continue to pose obstacles to long-term operational capability as more Iraqi forces operate without support from Coalition forces.

The Minister of Defense has recently directed that the IA assume sole responsibility for humanitarian demining operations within Iraq. This undertaking will severely degrade the IA's ability to conduct route clearance and counter the improvised explosive devise (IED) threat that is still prevalent in Iraq. To be successful, the MoD will have to enlist the help of the UN, as well as non-governmental organizations that are subject-matter experts in demining operations.

Logistics

Coalition and Iraqi forces have created a strategic logistics task force under the direction of a MNSTC-I senior logistician to hasten the implementation and integration of a comprehensive strategy. Critical components of this strategy include a strategic logistics doctrine supported by a requirements-based acquisition strategy, capable procurement specialists, and logistics managers. Without these elements, the MoD will not be able to sustain or modernize the IJF. The IJF is now able to sustain itself with refined petroleum products used to fuel its ground combat vehicles, support vehicles, and generators. This capacity is a key to successful transition to full self-sufficiency

Construction has begun on a facility for the Combined Logistics Operation Center, providing a structure to facilitate tracking, coordination, and reporting of IJF logistics operations, and will include a materiel management control element. Essential equipment for 13 field workshops ($90 million) and 13 Locations Commands ($134 million) procured by the Coalition recently began arriving and will continue through November 2009. The incremental delivery will prevent these units from reaching full strength for at least nine months. To improve repair parts flow and stimulate overall maintenance operations, repair parts packages were distributed to assist in establishing stock objectives and replenishment procedures. The difficulty in maintaining IA vehicles is exacerbated by the large variety of vehicle manufacturers and types. An effort is underway to alleviate this problem by identifying suitable vehicle types to retain and develop spare parts stock levels to aid their sustainment.

A collaborative effort between Coalition partners and the Iraqi Deputy Chief of Staff (DCoS) for Logistics' to re-establish Iraqi logistics doctrine using a systematic approach, established fundamental principles of logistics concepts, organization, methods, and procedures is continuing. The Coalition finalized a review of previous Iraqi Logistics doctrine and manuals and is working with the Iraqis to develop an updated architecture of logistics doctrine. Procedures are being validated through training exercises prior to approval and distribution. The DCoS-Logistics is now addressing doctrine and systems development at the strategic level. The combined Iraqi Logistics Development Committee of Coalition and Iraqi logistics leaders is continuing to recommend procedures and policies to reestablish doctrinal solutions that will address current gaps in the Iraqi Logistics Concept.

The Logistics Military Advisor Team and Logistics Training Advisor Team programs are successful, and their efforts are improving the logistical readiness posture of the MoD units with whom they partner. This process has identified that the key inhibitors to Iraqi logistical self-reliance reside at the Ministerial or JHQ level, not the tactical level. Iraqi logisticians are generally capable operators. Unfortunately, current Iraqi acquisition and distribution policies and procedures continue to prevent effective stock replenishment, subsequent maintenance, and repair operations. The DG Acquisition-Sustainment, DG Infrastructure, and DCoS-Logistics all lack contracting and purchasing expertise and authority necessary to replenish stocks, repair equipment, or renovate infrastructure facilities. These authorities reside solely at the MoD level.

Training

The JHQ implemented a training assessment program and is generating a new Training Assessment Manual that will codify the inspection and assessment procedures; thus, laying the groundwork for future analysis and improvement.

Doctrine

The JHQ developed a documented and functioning doctrine process, a key factor in standardizing and institutionalizing practices across the IJF. Under DCoS Training M7, the doctrine section is tasked with coordinating the development, approval, printing, and distribution of doctrine and technical manuals for the IJF. Once a month, DCoS-Training chairs the Doctrine Review Committee that approves doctrine for the Chief of Staff's signature. JHQ continues to work on improving these processes, and the advisory team is assisting the JHQ in conducting gap analysis and prioritizing future doctrine development.

Surgeon General

The Directorate of Military Medical Services is led by the Joint Forces Surgeon General who has the responsibility of providing Health Service Support to the IA, IqN, and IqAF. The single most challenging component to further expansion of military medical capabilities and infrastructure is a shortage of health professionals. As of January 2009, the Surgeon General Organization has 20% of physicians authorized and is affected by the same national physician shortage that plagues the MoI. The MoD is awaiting legislative relief via the Iraqi Law of Military Service and Retirement, which should be signed in early 2009. This proposed Iraqi law will grant authority to the MoD for providing salary, rank, and educational incentives to attract and retain physicians to military service.

In January 2009, MNSTC-I awarded a $3 million final-phase contract in support of the highly-effective MoD Prosthetics and Rehabilitation Clinic. MNSTC-I assisted with the construction and move to a new clinic, which was paid for with GoI funds using the FMS process. Using the new support contract in this final phase of a two-year effort, MNSTC-I will continue to develop and mentor 11 designated Iraqi nationals in prosthetics, increasing autonomy of physical therapists and technicians for this important service to the ISF.

In January 2009, the MoD opened the first Iraqi Military Hospital in Muthanna. This 50-bed facility adds key capability that will allow reduction of Iraqi inpatient population in Coalition medical facilities. The Coalition is working with the GoI to improve Iraqi medical evacuation capability to allow maximal use of this facility.

Iraqi Army

Organization

The IA currently has 13 infantry divisions and one mechanized division organized under the IGFC. Ground forces include 201 fully generated and trained IA battalions and 55 IA brigades with a force generation focus on enabler units to complete the divisional force structure. Of the 201 battalions, 179 comprise the IGFC combatant battalions. The other 25 battalions make up the Iraqi Infrastructure Battalion (5), the Presidential Brigade (5), the Baghdad Brigade (1), and the Independent Security Force battalions (13). Of the 55 brigades, 53 comprise the IGFC combatant brigades. The remaining two belong to the Presidential Brigade and Baghdad Brigade, respectively.

Budgetary constraints will present a major hurdle to the IA's ability to recruit new members and to add new units. As of January 2009, 175 IA combat battalions are conducting operations, with four newly-formed battalions (179 total), an increase from 165 in the last report. The hiring freeze based on budget challenges will impact the manning of enabler units.

Despite the current hiring freeze, the IA was able to generate three battalions, two brigade headquarters, one brigade headquarters service company, and one MTR with soldiers who were already in the training pipeline. As the hiring freeze continues, however, force generation of key enablers essential for completing the COIN force will be adversely affected, particularly mortars, light artillery, signal, engineer, ISR units, field service regiments, as well as the remaining MTRs. To develop the IA's capabilities and capacity to engage in force management and acquisition activities, the Coalition is partnering with the IA leadership and the Minister of Defense to establish a joint M1A1 Program Manager Office, which will provide life-cycle management, new-equipment training, and follow-on training for the 140 M1A1 tanks recently purchased through FMS. It will also ensure the integration of the M1A1s into the Iraqi maintenance system.

Training

In October 2008, the IA suspended Basic Combat Training (BCT) after it surpassed its mandated manpower authorization. Approximately 73,000 Iraqi soldiers completed BCT in 2008. To maintain and improve institutional training capacity, MNSTC-I has shifted its focus to professionalizing the force. This effort emphasizes enhancing special skills, enabler units, unit-level, and recurring training to develop depth and improve the quality of individual soldier skills. The on-going Warfighter Exercise (WFX) training program is indicative of continued improvement in training capacity and capability at the Divisional, Regional, and Combat Training Centers. Since the program began in June 2008, four battalions have completed this training.[33] These exercises are now scheduled and conducted by the IA with the Coalition prepared to support, as necessary. The MOSQ courses for maintenance, transportation, signal, supply, administration, weapons armorer, military police, and medical personnel are other examples of continued progress. More than 14,400 soldiers have completed training in one of these eight different courses. The requirement for specialty MOSQ training will increase significantly in 2009 as the focus continues to shift toward generating enabler units and skill sets. The Iraqi Army Service and Support Institute (IASSI) continues to provide advanced education and technical training in multiple support disciplines and supply, maintenance and repair specialties. More than 7,200 soldiers graduated from IASSI courses in 2008. In a separate effort, the IA conducted three cycles of Transition and Reintegration (TNR) training with vetted former Iraqi militia. These 1,659 officers and 1,705 NCOs graduated from TNR training in December 2008, adding 16% to officer and 4% to NCO current strengths.

Materiel

The IA self sustainment capability continues to improve through multiple programs. The single channel ground and airborne radio systems (SINCGARS) and Harris radio fielding provide the IA with a secure tactical communication and an increased C2 capability. Although combat units were initially the priority for distribution, service and service support units are now receiving these assets. The IA is now responsible for continued fielding of M16s and M4s and uses the Weapons Training Wing at each of the Regional Training Centers for this purpose. More than 50,000 of these weapons have been issued through December 2008. Currently on hold, the M16A4 and M4 fielding will resume in April 2009. The IA is also preparing to assume the training portion of the fielding and training program. Weapons accountability is maintained through frequent inventories and multiple checks of proper identification, including biometric data.

During the last quarter, the IA Deputy DCoS-Logistics emphasized information sharing and synchronization among the DCoS, the Commanding General of each Location Command, and the Chief of Supply Depot Management. This coordination effort significantly improved distribution management and asset visibility of ISFF and FMS procured materiel and equipment. This effort directly contributed to more efficient equipping of IA units and increased IA combat capability.

Finally, the IA fielded a key strategic enabler unit, the GTR, which is designed to transport equipment and supplies throughout the theater. The GTR is increasingly assuming responsibility from the Coalition and recently added a standard shuttle mission between locations where second- and third-level support is provided.

Leadership and Education

The IA continues to develop a NCO Education System (NCOES) that emphasizes small unit leadership. To date, nearly 14,000 NCOs have graduated from NCOES courses. The IA approved its NCOES Campaign Plan in October 2008 after a 12-month planning effort and began implementation on January 1, 2009. The new NCOES is controlled by the DCoS - Training Directorate, which standardizes all IA NCOES education in Iraq. The system is based on the recently developed Iraqi leadership doctrine and is intended to link promotions to graduation from IA NCO-producing schools. A planning team of combat-proven IA officers and NCOs developed and refined NCOES courses for corporals, squad leaders, and platoon sergeants. The goal is to increase professionalism of the NCO Corps by improving leadership, training, and combat skills.

The Basic Combat Training Campaign Plan generated a review of the basic combat training modules and improvement in the quality of graduating soldiers. It identified the requirement to develop Drill Instructors and a Basic Combat Instructors Course to improve course instruction quality. The Basic Combat Instructors Course, designed to reinforce skills required to instruct basic combat trainees through the use of practical exercises is under development.

In November 2008, the NATO Training Mission-Iraq (NTM-I) conducted the initial three-week course for Iraqi Senior NCOs. This course served as a "proof of principle" for future courses and lessons learned will lay the foundation for future senior NCO courses. The Iraqi Center for Military Values, Principles, and Leadership Development (CMVPLD) continues to provide the capability to professionalize the IA, offering instruction in five areas, including Professional Military Values, Leadership, the Profession of Arms, Law of Armed Conflict/Human Rights, and the Role of the Military in a Democracy. Ethics training is now included in basic combat and leader training programs, during unit set fielding and as part of WFX exercises. The center has generated more than 400 new instructors at Regional Training Centers and the four Iraqi Military Academies. An additional 82 Joint Staff College students were also trained in 2008. In 2009, CMVPLD plans to deliver ethics training at the division level, as well as conduct training assessment visits to the Regional Training Centers (RTC) and the Divisions.

Personnel

As of November 2008, the IA is currently manned to 57% of its authorized officers, 45% of its authorized NCOs, with 148% of total authorizations. IA personnel statistics reflect an average of 62% present for duty at any given time. The current attrition rate of assigned personnel is 1.7% per month. The average leave rate is currently 23% of assigned personnel, well within the policy limit of 25%. The absent-without-leave rate is less than 1% of the assigned strength per month. The most critical personnel issues continue to be the need for a documented manpower management strategy, improved procedures for paying soldiers, accurate accountability procedures, and the need to transparently promote individuals based on merit. The 2008 BCT graduation total of just over 70,000 was well below the original goal of 114,600 established at a time of accelerated growth. Nevertheless, adequate recruits were on hand to meet 2008 force generation requirements, which were adjusted due to budgetary factors.

Facilities

Currently, nine of 10 planned Divisional Training Centers (DTC) and Regional Training Centers (RTC) are complete. Each of these centers includes a range complex, combat assault course, live fire shoot house, and outdoor classrooms. They support both BCT and WFX exercises for the IA. Billeting continues to be limited, however, which restricts usage of the centers. The current combined capacity is limited to 14,600 students. Facilities planned in 2009 include dedicated after-action review and medical training classrooms, as well as weapons cleaning stations.

The construction of 13 Location Commands, one for each IA division, continues. These commands consist of warehousing, 3rd line maintenance, fuel storage, billeting, and life-support facilities. In 2009, the MoD is also planning to build 14 life-support base sustainment warehouses to provide food storage capacity. Location Commands are targeted for completion in the spring of 2010, once Coalition funding is approved.

Despite significant improvements, several shortfalls remain in IA infrastructure. The most significant shortfall is the availability of electricity. Only one base is connected to the national power grid, and all rely on generator-produced power, which is inconsistent at best and costly. Moreover, few bases have centralized power and sewage treatment plants. Although generators are used to offset this problem, connecting the remaining bases to the power grid will greatly reduce the cost of fuel and maintenance for the generators.

Iraqi Air Force

The challenge for the IqAF will be to expand current capabilities and build the foundation of a credible and enduring IqAF for the future. Currently, the IqAF has minimal capability across the spectrum of capabilities, but progress is being made in ISR, airlift (fixed/rotary wing), and developing its Airmen, with a focus on the COIN fight. These areas should achieve foundational capability by December 2010. Ground attack, airspace control, and C2 lag behind, with these foundational capabilities expected by December 2012. Despite its rapid growth in the past year, the IqAF lags behind all major Middle Eastern air forces, and achieving a credible and enduring IqAF will require continued Coalition support.

Doctrine

The IqAF has taken important steps to develop its doctrine. Iraqi and Coalition partners have begun codifying their ISR lessons learned in tasking, collecting, processing, exploiting, and disseminating information. In kinetic operations, the IqAF is preparing for operations of its first precision air-to-ground attack aircraft by establishing preliminary rules of engagement. Coalition airpower planners are actively contributing to the development of rules of engagement.

Organization

Over the past 12 months, the IqAF aircraft sortie rate has increased significantly, and its proficiency in scheduling and conducting flight operations continues to improve. Today, the IAOC provides C2 of over 350 sorties per week, spanning training, ISR, and airlift missions.

Training

Training remains a top priority within the IqAF as it strives to reach 6,000 personnel accessed and trained by 2010. Today, the IqAF has 100 officer and enlisted specialties spread across ten functional areas and anticipates adding approximately 15 more over the next 12 months. Over the past quarter, IqAF officer initial-entry and enlisted technical training has advanced. Enlisted Basic Technical Training (BTT) courses in communications, flight medicine, fire fighting, aircraft maintenance, aircraft structures, aerospace ground equipment, aircraft weapons, aircrew gunners, and professional military education were successfully accomplished, many for the first time. Several BTT syllabi currently in development will expand training in operations, maintenance, supply, and infrastructure support personnel.

In addition, the IqAF commissioned 165 officers after successfully completing Basic Military Training (BMT) and the Air Force Officer Course at the Iraq Military Academy at Rustamiyah (IMAR). An additional 107 IqAF cadets are forecast to graduate from IMAR by the end of 2009. To satisfy the demand for more officers, the IqAF has increased its officer class size to 250 personnel.

The Flying Training Wing at Kirkuk Air Base expanded to reach an annual basic flight training capacity of 128 students with 65 currently enrolled. During the first quarter of 2009, the IqAF graduated nine pilots, the largest pilot class to date. Also, four instructor pilots successfully completed basic flight instructor training. Despite rapid growth of its flight training capacity, the IqAF aircrew manning will continue to lag behind requirements as IqAF inventory of aircraft grows. This aircrew shortage will only be met by further expansion of domestic flight training resources and use of appropriate foreign training opportunities.

English Language Training (ELT) continues to be a top training priority for IqAF leaders. ELT currently focuses on aircrew, aircraft maintenance, air traffic control, and communications personnel. Although the Coalition continues to provide the vast majority of ELT instruction, efforts are underway to generate an Iraqi ELT program with an annual ELT training capacity of nearly 800 students.

Materiel

The IqAF added 36 aircraft in 2008 to reach a total of 89 assigned aircraft. [34] Plans call for adding another 34 aircraft in 2009. The IqAF's inexperience in acquisition continues to make procurement a challenge. This is complicated by a process that requires the Defense Minister to make most acquisition decisions. The IqAF has shown a nascent capability in requirements generation, FMS case development, and source selection, but significant staff development is still necessary. Work continues in building robust institutional processes for the GoI to obtain the aircraft, materiel, and support necessary to build and sustain its force. The IqAF will achieve an initial precision air-to-ground attack capability, forecast for early 2009, with the delivery of 20 Hellfire air-toground missiles for use with the AC-208 Combat Caravan. On December 9, 2008, Congress was notified that Iraq may purchase 26 additional Armed Scout Helicopters, 36 AT- 6C Texan light-attack aircraft, and 20 T-6A Texan II training aircraft through the FMS process.

Personnel

The IqAF continues to slowly increase its personnel but has still filled only 57% of its authorized military and civilian strength. Those numbers must grow significantly in the future to match anticipated growth in aircraft numbers. Such growth is slowed by the time required to recruit, access, and train airmen on complex aircraft and ground support systems.

Of particular concern is a severe shortage of mid-career officers. More than 50% of pilots and 35% of ground officers will reach retirement age before 2020, and the few remaining mid-career pilots lack flying experience. These numbers point to a shortage of senior IqAF leaders in ten years. This could be partly mitigated by the review and accession of some of the more than 2,400 former Iraqi military members currently being evaluated for either return to active duty or retirement. Finally, the IqAF must identify mid-career officers with potential to serve in the highest ranks and guide them through rigorous professional military development.

Facilities

On-going projects at Taji, Kirkuk, and New alMuthana Air Base will increase training capacity and adequately support the requisite growth in IqAF personnel through the spring of 2010. Over the next four years, the IqAF plans to expand to 11 main operating bases. Coalition turnover of key infrastructure, including aircraft parking ramps, hangars and dormitories is critical to growth, but the IqAF has limited capability to conduct infrastructure maintenance. Coalition advisors are helping the IqAF fill this capability gap by creating training programs for engineers.

Iraqi Navy

Organization

The IqN headquarters is co-located in the Baghdad MoD buildings, from where it sets maritime policy and provides strategic guidance for the Navy. To counter 2009 budgetary constraints, the staff developed a phased approach to deliver capabilities within the projected fiscal limits. Subject to budgetary approval, this strategy would see a contract for Patrol Boats and Offshore Support Vessels that will result in a phased delivery from 2011 through the beginning of 2013. The headquarters focus in 2009 is to improve its staff capability to support the new fleet and prepare the institutional IqN for future growth.

Training

The 80 Coalition trainers, led by a British Royal Navy Captain, continue to provide training for the IqN. The arrival of 16 eight-meter DEFENDER fast boats, 24 eight-meter boarding craft, and ten eight-meter rigid hull inflatable boats will complete replacement of the IqN's old small boat fleet. Once training is complete, these craft will give Iraq an enhanced boarding capability in the North Arabian Gulf and allow the IqN to conduct increased patrols of Iraq's inland seas. The Iraqi crew of the first 55-meter Patrol Ship is in Italy, preparing to sail the 5,500-mile passage back to Iraq in June 2009.

Officers training in the UK are meeting with mixed success. The younger, junior officers have tended to do well because the courses assumed a lower basis of fundamental seamanship knowledge. The more senior officers, on the other hand, fell short of the required standards, as the courses assumed a level of capability beyond their expertise and competence. This training experience reinforced the requirement for continued IqN training and underscored the need to significantly improve IqN standards. Budget constraints will limit the 2009 UK class to eight officers.

Progress has been made in growing and professionalizing the Iraqi Marines this quarter. The force gained 250 basic training graduates. In addition, the training of the Oil Platform Defense and Vessel Board Seize and Search Marine Platoons is almost complete. Five platoons of the Second Battalion have completed an enhanced "Warfighter" enhanced training program at the Shaibah DTC. The training focus for the remainder of 2009 will be on the Versatile Marine Training Program.

The Basrah Maritime Academy is now under MoD control and negotiations have begun between the MoD and MoI to rebuild the faculty and curriculum. The IqN aspires to rebuild this facility, regain International Maritime Organization accreditation, and resume its position as the single academy in Iraq to train all maritime related personnel (ports, merchant marine, coastguard, and police). This will re-establish the New Entry Training institution for the IqN and ensure the long-term well being of the service. The Coalition team, led by a UK officer, is developing a plan to assist in the reconstruction and rehabilitation of both the faculty and curriculum.

Material

Delivery of 44 small craft this quarter provided a much needed boost to IqN morale but will strain both the training and logistics sustainment capabilities. The arrival of the first two Patrol ships from Italy towards the end of 2009 will see the first real capability increase for the IqN. Without significant improvement in the HQ command and staff capacity, the IqN will find it increasingly difficult to support its growing fleet. The medium-term solution is to obtain a contract logistics and engineering support arrangement to assist Iraqi engineers while they build their capability.

Personnel

The IqN has approximately 2,000 personnel out of an authorized 3,596, with an additional 500 marine recruits due by April 2009. In the spring of 2009, 275 naval recruits will start basic training at Umm Qasr. An additional 250 naval recruits will then follow them in the fall. This will bring the IqN total to 2,900 personnel by the end of 2010, which is consistent with plans to achieve the objective of 6,500 personnel by 2015.

Facilities

The final design for the new pier and seawall is complete and construction on track to conclude in September 2009. Resolution of legal difficulties tied to repairing an existing pier and building a repair workshop and ship-lift facility will allow renovations to be complete by July 2009. Iraqi funding was secured for additional barracks, dining facilities, training aids, and simulators. Coalition assistance, in partnership with the Iraqi MoD, will deliver warehouse facilities, a command headquarters, and an ammunition storage magazine. By the end of 2009, the IqN should have sufficient infrastructure and training facilities to support and train crews with its new fleet of vessels.

2.4. Iraqi National Counter-Terrorism Force

The Iraqi National Counter-Terrorism Force (INCTF) is headed by the ministerial-level Counter-Terrorism Bureau (CTB) and includes the Counter-Terrorism Command (CTC) and the ISOF Brigade. Under Prime Minister Directive 61, signed in April 2007, the INCTF is independent of both the MoD and MoI. A bill still awaits CoR approval to establish the CTB as a separate ministry, formalizing a ministerial-level position for the CTB Director.

Organization

The CTB continues to improve coordination with the MoD and MoI on strategic-level planning, targeting, and intelligence fusion. The proposed CTB law was approved by the CoM in July 2008 and submitted to the CoR. However, in September 2008, the proposal was returned to the CoM to incorporate rule of law provisions, among them that the CTB Director be appointed a special rank with "minister-like powers." There has been resistance in the CoR and from the MoD in granting ministerial-level status to the CTB, and the bill is still pending. Beginning in 2008, the CTB was granted semiautonomous budget authority, and it submitted a 2009 budget for $580 million to the MoF. The MoF has since informed the CTB that because of the effect of falling oil prices on the national budget, it was likely the non-payroll budget for INCTF would be the same as in 2008, $167 million.

Besides its payroll, INCTF continues to rely on MoD support for finance, logistics, medical, aviation, and engineer support and training. In December 2007, the CTB and MoD concluded a MOA by which the IqAF provides air support for ISOF operations. The MOA is in effect until the CTB law is passed but does require MoD and CTB to revisit the MOA each year to discuss possible updates or changes. The MoD's IqAF provides Mi-17 helicopter and Cessna KingAir ISR support for ISOF training and operations. In October 2008, air elements were incorporated for the first time in initial ISOF training, and in November 2008, the first of two ISOF personnel completed the Iraqi Forward Air Control training.

The CTC is the operational headquarters for combating terrorism in Iraq. CTC exercises C2 of ISOF units that execute combat operations. The ISOF Brigade conducts tactical operations in conjunction with U.S. advisors. The brigade is composed of nine battalions: the 1st Battalion (Bn) (Commando); 2nd Bn, which is designated the Iraqi Counter-Terrorism Force (ICTF); 3rd Bn (Support); 4th Bn (RECCE); and 5th Bn, which conducts the Iraqi Special Warfare Center and School (ISWCS). In 2008, the ISOF Brigade underwent expansion to include four 440-man regional commando battalions: the 6th (Basrah), 7th (Mosul), 8th (Diyala) and 9th (Al Asad). The 6th and 7th Bns achieved full operational capability (FOC) in mid-2008. The 8th Bn is to achieve FOC in March 2009 and the 9th Bn in December 2009. The four regional battalions will be housed on regional commando bases, each of which will also incorporate a regional counter-terrorism center (RCC), a regional reconnaissance team, and a garrison support unit (GSU). These RCCs will have intelligence fusion cells that will be linked to the CTC, but as yet, they have not been integrated into the MoD and MoI intelligence networks. A separate RCC is also planned for Baghdad. The Coalition has provided secure communications and information networks for use throughout INCTF. The Coalition also has Military Training Teams at all three echelons that have 24-hour contact with their Iraqi counterparts.

Both the CTC and the ISOF Brigade have IG staff sections. The CTC IG has conducted inspections of more than 95% of INCTF's units, including the RCCs and the detention facility where ISOF transient detainees are held. The IG conducts staff assistance visits and formal inspections, as well as monitoring for human rights violations and internal affairs issues.

Training

The ISWCS conducts three rotational courses to meet force generation requirements. The first is the three-week Selection Course; the attrition rate for candidates in this rigorous screening course is greater than 40%. Of those who graduate, the top 10% are sent to the eight- week Operators Training Course, and from there they are assigned to the 2nd Bn (ICTF). The next 20% are earmarked for the six-week Commando Course. The remainder is assigned to the Support Battalion and the GSU. Most recruits for the Selection Course are nominated by Shi'a, Sunni, and Kurdish tribal leaders from among candidates who have no prior military experience.

The ISOF brigade currently has 824 soldiers who passed the Selection Course in May 2008 but cannot be added to the official rolls due to the hiring freeze. These personnel would be sufficient to bring all units to full operational capability by July 2009 and complete force generation. However, the ISWCS has encountered persistent difficulties obtaining support from the MoD for ammunition, equipment, and pay for the trainees, causing courses to be postponed. Failure to resolve the funding issue for the 824 Selection graduates is already having a significant impact on INCTF's sustainment capability. INCTF advisors have made this a priority in the months ahead.

Materiel

In 2008, the ISOF Brigade, including the ISWCS, relied on the MoD for ammunition and vehicle and weapons spare parts. As of mid-January 2009, the ISOF Brigade had 1,443 vehicles, including 306 High Mobility Multipurpose Wheeled Vehicles (HMMWV), delivered to its units. An additional 249 HMMWVs are expected by August 2009 under the Cascade Program, by which U.S. vehicles are shipped home, refurbished and up-armored, and shipped back for delivery to the Iraqis. The ISOF Brigade has received 95% of all ISF funded materiel in eight of its nine battalions.

Leadership and Education

In September 2008, INCTF submitted to the MoD a list of college-educated candidates for admission to the four regional military academies to help alleviate a critical officer shortage in the ISOF brigade; the MoD approved seven names. At the direction of the Prime Minister, ten graduates from each of the four military academies (Rustamiyiah, Zahko, Nasiriyah, and Qualachulon) and the staff college at Rustamiyiah were to be assigned to INCTF. However, the MoD assigned only 21 military academy graduates to INCTF and only three staff college graduates. INCTF is participating in an International Military Education and Training program for officer development where areas of focus are NCO and MOS training. Currently, NCO training within the ISOF Brigade is accomplished by on-the-job training at the unit level. In addition, in December 2008, NTM-I approved including CTB for its out-of-country training.

Personnel

INCTF is a non-sectarian force, as reflected in its leadership, its personnel, and the methodologies with which it conducts operations. INCTF personnel generally reflect the Shi'a, Sunni, Kurdish, and other minorities' breakdown in the general populace, according to recent statistics. INCTF's non-sectarian approach is also seen in the internal vetting of personnel in key positions. As of September 2008, CTB and CTC were well ahead of any other ISF organizations with respect to the number of personnel voluntarily screened by U.S. counterintelligence assets. This screening consisted of both interviews and polygraphs to verify background investigations.

The INCTF's manning increased 30% over the last year—CTB is currently manned at 40%, CTC at 48%, and the ISOF Brigade at 67%, as of February 2009. Overall, INCTF is manned at 61%, and all battalions are expected to be steady-state by December 2009. Currently, officer manning is at 34% and NCO strength is at 44%. Unit strengths remain low due to a decision in May 2008 to double authorized strength, and it will take several years to achieve the increased manning levels because of the timelines associated with the specialized training requirements for these personnel. INCTF advisors monitor personnel accountability, promotions, and personnel policies of ISOF. This is a command priority that continues to be emphasized at all senior leader engagements. At steady state, the INCTF will consist of more than 8,500 operators, staff, and support personnel.

Facilities

The CTB is housed in two compounds in the IZ. The ISOF Brigade is housed in a base near Baghdad International Airport that includes offices and billeting for the 1st, 2nd, 3rd, 4th, and 5th Battalions and the GSU. Construction was completed in October 2008 for 12 barracks, a company headquarters, and a maintenance bay. The INCTF expansion plan includes establishing four regional commando bases (RCB) located at Al Asad, Basrah, Diyala, and Mosul to provide force projection throughout Iraq. Each RCB template contains a commando battalion with a platoon-sized reconnaissance unit and a company-sized GSU. The RCB at Al Asad was completed on December 20, 2008, and is one of the premier facilities of its kind in Iraq. The RCBs in Diyala and Basrah are both scheduled for completion in December 2009.

ANNEX A

List of Acronyms and Abbreviations

AAH	Asa'ib Al-Haq
AQI	Al Qaeda in Iraq
BCT	Basic Combat Training
BMT	Basic Military Training
Bn	Battalion
BPC	Baghdad Police College
BRT	Basic Recruit Training
BTT	Basic Technical Training
C2	Command and Control
CBI	Central Bank of Iraq
CCCI	Central Criminal Court of Iraq
CMVPLD	Center for Military Values, Principles, and Leadership Development
COB	Contingency Operating Base
COIN	Counterinsurgency
COL	Contingency Operating Location
CoM	Council of Ministers
CoR	Council of Representatives
COS	Contingency Operating Site
COSIT	Central Organization for Statistics and Information Technology
CRC	Constitutional Review Committee
CSC	Civil Service Corp
CTB	Counter-Terrorism Bureau
CTC	Counter-Terrorism Command
CTF	Counter-Terrorism Force
DBE	Directorate of Border Enforcement
DBIC	Dialogue on Business and Investment Conference
DCOS	Deputy Chief of Staff
DG	Directors General
DGIS	Directorate General for Intelligence and Security
DGoP	Directorate General of Police
DoI	Daughters of Iraq
DoJ	Department of Justice
DTC	Division Training Center
EFP	Explosively-Formed Penetrator
ELT	English Language Training
ePRT	Embedded Provincial Reconstruction Team
ERU	Emergency Response Unit
FMS	Foreign Military Sales
FOC	Full Operational Capability
FPS	Facilities Protection Service
FY	Fiscal Year

GDP	Gross Domestic Product
GE	General Electric
GoI	Government of Iraq
GTR	General Transportation Regiment
GSU	Garrison Support Unit
HJC	Higher Judicial Council
HMMWV	High Mobility Multipurpose Wheeled Vehicle
HoP	Hours of Power
HPA	High-Profile Attack
HQ	Headquarters
HRIMS	Human Resource Information Management System
IA	Iraqi Army
IAOC	Iraqi Air Operations Center
IASSI	Iraqi Army Support and Service Institute
ICI	International Compact with Iraq
ICTF	Iraqi Counter-Terrorism Force
IDP	Internally Displaced Person
IED	Improvised Explosive Device
IG	Inspector General
IGFC	Iraqi Ground Forces Command
IHEC	Independent High Electrical Commission
IJF	Iraqi Joint Forces
IMAR	Iraqi Military Academy at Rustamiyah
IMF	International Monetary Fund
IMSS	Intelligence and Military Security School
INCTF	Iraqi National Counter-Terrorism Force
IOM	International Organization for Migration
IP	Iraqi Police
IPA	International Police Advisor
IPS	Iraqi Police Service
IqAF	Iraqi Air Force
IqIC	Iraqi Intelligence Community
IqN	Iraqi Navy
ISCI	Islamic Supreme Council of Iraq
ISF	Iraqi Security Forces
ISFF	Iraqi Security Forces Funds
ISI	Islamic State of Iraq
ISOF	Iraqi Special Operations Forces
ISR	Intelligence, Surveillance, and Reconnaissance
IZ	International Zone
JAM	Jaysh al-Mahdi
JCC-I/A	Joint Contracting Command – Iraq / Afghanistan
JHQ	Joint Headquarters
JOC	Joint Operations Center
KAC	Karbala Area Command
KGK	Kongra Gel

KH	Ketaib Hezbollah
KRG	Kurdistan Regional Government
mbpd	Million Barrels Per Day
MCTF	Major Crimes Task Force
MeK	Mujahedin-e Khalq
MNF-I	Multi-National Force-Iraq
MNSTC-I	Multi-National Security Transition Command-Iraq
MoD	Ministry of Defense MoE Ministry of Electricity
MoF	Ministry of Finance
MoH	Ministry of Health
MoI	Ministry of Interior
MoJ	Ministry of Justice
MoO	Ministry of Oil
MoP	Ministry of Planning
MOSQ	Military Occupational Skills Qualification
MTOE	Modified Table of Organization and Equipment
MTR	Motor Transport Regiment
MW	Megawatts
NCC	National Command Center
NCO	Non-Commissioned Officer
NCOES	Non-Commissioned Officer Education System
NIIA	National Information and Investigation Agency
NP	National Police
NRC	National Reconciliation Committee
NTM-I	NATO Training Mission-Iraq
O&M	Operations and Management
OP	Oil Police
OPC	Oil Pipeline Company
OTA	Office of the Transportation Attaché
P&B	Programs and Budget
PBIED	Person Borne Improvised Explosive Device
PDB	Promise Day Brigade
PDoP	Provincial Director of Police
PEL	Provincial Elections Law
PEZ	Pipeline Exclusion Zone
PFMAG	Public Finance Management Action Group
PIC	Provincial Iraqi Control
PJCC	Provincial Joint Coordination Center
PMNOC	Prime Minister's National Operations Center
PoE	Ports of Entry
PoED	PoE Directorate
PPL	Provincial Powers Law
PRT	Provincial Reconstruction Team
RAC	Rusafa Area Command
RCB	Regional Commando Bases
RCC	Regional Counter-Terrorism Centers

ROLC	Rule of Law Complex
RTC	Regional Training Center
SA	Security Agreement
SAO	Security Assistance Office
SBA	Stand-By Arrangement
SFA	Strategic Framework Agreement
SG	Special Groups
SINCGARS	Single Channel Ground and Airborne Radio Systems
SoI	Sons of Iraq
SVBIED	Suicide Vehicle-Borne Improvised Explosive Device
SWAT	Special Weapons and Tactics
TFBSO	Task Force to Improve Business and Stability Operations-Iraq
TNR	Transition and Reintegration
TQI	Training Qualification Institute
UAE	United Arab Emirates
UNAMI	United Nations Assistance Mission Iraq
UNHCR	United Nations High Commissioner for Refugees
UNSCR	UN Security Council Resolution
USAID	U.S. Agency for International Development
USDA	U.S. Department of Agriculture
USG	U.S. Government
WFX	Warfighter Exercise

End Notes

[1] This report was previously submitted pursuant to Section 9010 of the Department of Defense Appropriations Act 2007, Public Law 109-289, as amended.
[2] The data cutoff date for this report, unless otherwise stated, is February 28, 2009.
[3] Core inflation excludes fuel, electricity, transportation, and communications prices.
[4] Nationwide Survey, January 2009. For security reasons, to protect the integrity of the data and the anonymity of the individuals involved with the polling data and their association with the USG, the survey questions and supporting data can be found in the classified annex to this report. This note applies to footnotes 6 through 27.
[5] *Inma* translates as "growth" in Arabic.
[6] Nationwide Survey, January 2009.
[7] Nationwide Survey, January 2009.
[8] Nationwide Survey, January 2009.
[9] Nationwide Survey, January 2009.
[10] Nationwide Survey January 2009.
[11] Nationwide Survey, January 2009.
[12] Nationwide Survey, January 2009.
[13] Nationwide Survey, January 2009.
[14] Nationwide Survey, January 2009.
[15] Nationwide Survey, January 2009.
[16] Nationwide Survey, January 2009.
[17] Nationwide Survey, January 2009.
[18] Nationwide Survey, January 2009.
[19] Nationwide Survey, January 2009.
[20] Nationwide Survey, January 2009.
[21] Nationwide Survey, January 2009.
[22] Nationwide Survey, January 2009.
[23] Nationwide Survey, January 2009.

[24] Nationwide Survey, January 2009.
[25] Nationwide Survey, January 2009.
[26] Nationwide Survey, January 2009.
[27] Nationwide Survey, January 2009.
[28] DoD previously reported on the number of Iraqi Security Forces personnel authorized and assigned by the Ministries of Defense and Interior and trained with the assistance of Coalition forces. With the expiration of the mandate of UNSCR 1790, the data is now included in the classified annex because specific military personnel strength for a sovereign nation is considered sensitive.
[29] MoI employees not included in Iraqi Security Force numbers: Civil Defense forces, Facility Protection Service forces, Oil Police, and headquarters and administrative personnel—a total of approximately 112,000 other MoI employees.
[30] Four separate studies informed these Iraqi force end strength estimates. The first was the May 2007 MNSTC-I In-stride Assessment of growth required in 2008 to protect the population, overmatch the insurgent and terrorist threat, provide the depth necessary to deploy forces across the country, and implement an annual retraining and reconstitution program. The second was Iraqi Military Service plans focused on the 2010-2015 period, and MoI Plan that addressed near-term police force growth. The third was a Multi-National Corps – Iraq assessment of the Iraqi Army's required enduring posture by 2010. The fourth was a MNSTC-I directed, MNF-I sponsored Iraqi force analysis conducted by the Center for Army Analysis. The primary objective of this assessment was to determine if the projected, near-term (2010) Iraqi forces were capable of overmatching the anticipated threat. The assessment concluded that the ISF was incapable of overmatching the threat and recommended additional force structure growth and development of specific capabilities.
[31] DoD previously reported on readiness posture of Iraqi Security Forces with accompanying charts. With the expiration of the mandate of UNSCR 1790, the data is now included in the classified annex because military operational readiness for a sovereign nation is considered sensitive.
[32] This paragraph is pursuant to Section 1508(c) of the Department of Defense Authorization Act for 2009, Public Law 110- 417.
[33] The War Fighter Exercise (WFX) program rotates battalions through four-week long collective training cycles focused on platoon and company level skills, staff leader training, and battalion collective training.
[34] The current IqAF fleet consists of 36 fixed-wing aircraft and 53 rotary-wing aircraft (17 Mi-1 7, 16 UH-1, 10 Bell Jet Ranger, 10 OH-58C, 3 C-130E, 6 King Air 350 ISR/LTA, 10 C-172 Cessna, 5 TC-208 Caravan, 4 ISR Caravans and 8 CH- 2000.)

In: Iraq: Forward, Backward or Nowhere?
Editor: Frederick M. Golenberg

ISBN: 978-1-60741-018-8
© 2010 Nova Science Publishers, Inc.

Chapter 4

OPERATION IRAQI FREEDOM: STRATEGIES, APPROACHES, RESULTS AND ISSUES FOR CONGRESS

Catherine Dale

SUMMARY

Operation Iraqi Freedom (OIF), the U.S.-led coalition military operation in Iraq, was launched on March 20, 2003, with the immediate stated goal of removing Saddam Hussein's regime and destroying its ability to use weapons of mass destruction or to make them available to terrorists. Over time, the focus of OIF shifted from regime removal to the more open-ended mission of helping the Government of Iraq (GoI) improve security, establish a system of governance, and foster economic development.

In 2009, the war in Iraq appears to be winding down, as security gains made since the height of the insurgency in 2006 and 2007 continue to be sustained, and as Iraqis increasingly seek management of their own affairs. A new U.S.-Iraqi security agreement that went into effect on January 1, 2009, which confirmed the Iraqis' responsibility for their own security, introduced a new era in OIF and in US-Iraqi bilateral relations. Secretary of Defense Robert Gates called the agreement a "watershed, a firm indication that American military involvement in Iraq is winding down." U.S. military commanders on the ground have indicated that in most parts of Iraq, the focus of U.S. military efforts has shifted from counterinsurgency (COIN) to stability operations, including advising the Iraqi Security Forces (ISF), and supporting security, economic, and governance capacity-building. On February 27, 2009, at Camp Lejeune in North Carolina, President Obama delivered a speech addressing "how the war in Iraq will end," in which he announced the drawdown of U.S. combat forces by August 2010 and the transition of the rest of the military mission to training and advising Iraq security forces, conducting counter-terrorism operations, and providing force protection for U.S. personnel.

The United States begins this transition from a position of significant commitment – including some 140,000 U.S. troops deployed in Iraq, in addition to civilian experts and U.S. contractors, who provide substantial support to their Iraqi counterparts in the fields of security, governance, and development. Senior U.S. officials, including outgoing U.S. Ambassador to Iraq Ryan Crocker, and Secretary Gates, have suggested that lasting change in Iraq will require substantially more time, and that while the U.S. military presence will diminish, U.S. engagement with Iraq is likely to continue. The Government of Iraq (GoI), for its part, still faces challenges at the operational level, in countering the lingering strands of the insurgency; and at the strategic level, in achieving a single, shared vision of the Iraqi state, and in improving its capacity to provide good governance, ensure security, and foster economic development for the Iraqi people.

Key policy issues the Obama Administration may choose to address, with oversight from the 111th Congress, include identifying how U.S. national interests and strategic objectives, in Iraq and the region, should guide further U.S. engagement; monitoring and evaluating the impact of the changes in the U.S. presence and role in Iraq; and laying the groundwork for a future, more traditional bilateral relationship.

This report is intended to provide background and analysis of current developments and options, and will be updated as events warrant.

OVERVIEW

In 2009, the war in Iraq appears to be winding down, as security gains made since the height of the insurgency in 2006 and 2007 continue to be sustained, and as Iraqis increasingly seek management of their own affairs. A new U.S.-Iraqi Security Agreement that went into effect on January 1, which confirmed the Iraqis' responsibility for their own security, introduced a new era in Operation Iraqi Freedom (OIF)—the US-led coalition military operation in Iraq—and in US-Iraqi bilateral relations. Secretary of Defense Robert Gates called the Agreement a "watershed, a firm indication that American military involvement in Iraq is winding down."[1] U.S. military commanders on the ground have indicated that in most parts of Iraq, the focus of U.S. military efforts has shifted from counterinsurgency (COIN) to stability operations, including advising the Iraqi Security Forces (ISF), and supporting security, economic, and governance capacity-building. On February 27, 2009, at Camp Lejeune in North Carolina, President Obama delivered a speech addressing "how the war in Iraq will end," in which he announced the drawdown of U.S. combat forces by August 2010 and the transition of the rest of the military mission to training and advising Iraq security forces, conducting counter-terrorism, and providing force protection for U.S. personnel.[2]

The United States begins this transition from a position of significant commitment – including some 140,000 U.S. troops deployed in Iraq as of March 2009, in addition to civilian experts and U.S. contractors, who provide substantial support to their Iraqi counterparts in the fields of security, governance, and development. Senior U.S. officials, including outgoing U.S. Ambassador to Iraq Ryan Crocker, and Secretary Gates, have suggested that lasting change in Iraq will require substantially more time, and that while the U.S. military presence will diminish, U.S. engagement with Iraq is likely to continue.[3] The Government of Iraq (GoI), for its part, still faces challenges at the operational level, in countering the lingering threads of the insurgency; and at the strategic level, in achieving a single, shared vision of the Iraqi state, and in improving its capacity to provide good governance, ensure security, and foster economic development for the Iraqi people.

Key policy issues the Obama Administration may choose to address, with oversight from the 111th Congress, include identifying which U.S. national interests and strategic objectives, in Iraq and the region, should guide further U.S. engagement; monitoring and evaluating the impact of the changes in the U.S. presence and role in Iraq; and laying the groundwork for a future, more traditional bilateral relationship.

BACKGROUND

OIF was launched on March 20, 2003. The immediate goal, as stated by the George W. Bush Administration, was to remove Saddam Hussein's regime, including destroying its ability to use weapons of mass destruction or to make them available to terrorists. The broad, longer-term objective included helping Iraqis build "a new Iraq that is prosperous and free."[4] In October 2002, Congress had authorized the President to use force against Iraq, to "defend the national security of the United States against the continuing threat posed by Iraq," and to "enforce all relevant United Nations Security Council resolutions regarding Iraq."[5]

After the initial combat operations, the focus of OIF shifted from regime removal to the more open-ended mission of helping an emerging new Iraqi leadership improve security, establish a system of governance, and foster economic development. Over time, challenges to the emerging Iraqi leadership from homegrown insurgents and some foreign fighters mounted. Sectarian violence grew, catalyzed by the February 2006 bombing of the Golden Mosque in Samarra.

In January 2007, in an attempt to reverse the escalation of violence, President Bush announced a new strategic approach, the "New Way Forward," including a "surge" of additional U.S. forces, together with additional civilian experts. The troop surge included five Army brigade combat teams (BCTs), a Marine Expeditionary Unit (MEU), and two Marine battalions. More importantly, most observers agree, Ambassador Crocker and the Commanding General of Multi- National Force-Iraq (MNF-I), General David Petraeus, institutionalized counterinsurgency approaches across the force and the U.S. effort as a whole. Those approaches emphasized population security, empowering the Iraqi Security Forces (ISF) through close partnership, and building GoI capacity to govern and foster economic development in order to capitalize on security gains.

Over the course of the surge, observers generally agreed, security conditions on the ground improved markedly. In August 2008, GEN Petraeus agreed that there had been "significant progress" but argued that it was "still not self-sustaining." "We're not celebrating," he commented, and there are "no victory dances in the end zone."[6]

Practitioners and observers have identified a number of factors that may have contributed to the security improvements, including the additional surge forces; new and institutionalized counterinsurgency approaches concerning population security and reconciliation; the application of highend technological capabilities by Special Operations Forces (SOF) and closer integration between SOF and conventional forces; the accumulated experience of U.S. leaders at all levels after multiple tours in Iraq; the growing numbers and capabilities of the Iraqi Security Forces; the ground-up rejection of violence and support for the coalition by many Sunni Arabs; and the ceasefire declared by Shiite cleric Moqtada al-Sadr and the abandonment of violence by many of his followers.

While conventional, force-on-force wars tend to end with the unequivocal defeat of one party, the parameters for "mission success" in counter-insurgency efforts like OIF tend to be less definitive and more subject to qualitative interpretation. OIF appears poised to end with policy decisions by the U.S. and/or Iraqi governments, rather than with a decisive military victory on the battlefield.

Revised U.S.-Iraqi Strategic Partnership

On November 17, 2008, U.S. and Iraqi officials signed two key new agreements, designed to define the terms of their future partnership at the strategic and operational levels. On November 27, the Iraqi parliament voted its support for the two agreements, and on December 4, the Iraqi Presidency Council approved them.[7]

Strategic Framework Agreement and Security Agreement

The first document was the broad Strategic Framework Agreement, designed to provide a basis for future cooperation in multiple fields including diplomacy, culture, economics and energy, health and the environment, information technology, and law enforcement. This Agreement was based broadly on a declaration of principles, signed by President Bush and Iraqi Prime Minister Nouri al-Maliki, on November 27, 2007.[8]

The second document, the Security Agreement, was similar to a status of forces agreement (SOFA). It was the product of a contentious negotiations process that began in spring 2008. It elaborated the terms of the bilateral security partnership at the operational level, and provided the legal basis for the U.S. troop presence in Iraq. When approving the two agreements, the Iraqi parliament made the Security Agreement subject to a popular referendum, scheduled to be held by July 2009. The Agreement went into effect on January 1, 2009, at the expiration of the United Nations mandate that had provided the legal basis for the presence of the multi-national force in Iraq.[9]

Security Agreement Provisions

The Security Agreement underscored both Iraqi sovereignty and the "temporary" nature of the U.S. military presence, and it imposed a number of constraints on the presence and operations of U.S. forces. It provided for the withdrawal of all U.S. combat forces from Iraqi cities and towns by June 30, 2009, and for the withdrawal of all U.S. forces from Iraq by December 31, 2011.[10] This language was a stricter version of earlier drafts that reportedly had provided for time "horizons" or target dates.

The Security Agreement stipulated that the United States shall not use Iraqi land, sea or air as a "launching or transit point for attacks against other countries."[11] The Strategic Framework Agreement, which echoed this language, also provided that the United States shall not seek a "permanent military presence" in Iraq. The negotiations process reportedly considered various formulations regarding external threats to Iraq's sovereignty. The agreed language, in the Security Agreement, required bilateral consultations in case of such a threat, but made no other actions compulsory.[12]

The Security Agreement required that U.S. forces coordinate all military operations with Iraqi authorities.[13] It tightly constrained the role of U.S. forces in detaining Iraqis and mandated the transfer of current detainees to Iraqi custody.[14] It also granted Iraq some legal jurisdiction over U.S. servicemembers and defense civilians – specifically, in cases of "grave, premeditated felonies" committed off base and "outside duty status."[15] As senior officials on the ground have underscored, the Security Agreement acknowledged that many of its provisions would require further interpretation. To that end, it established a committee structure to provide implementation guidance.[16]

Drawdown and Transition

On February 27, 2009, at the Marine Corps Base Camp Lejeune, President Obama announced "a new strategy to end the war in Iraq through a transition to full Iraqi responsibility."[17] The setting for the speech quietly echoed its theme of transition. U.S. Marines entered Iraq at the start of OIF and helped lead both major combat and counterinsurgency (COIN) efforts. Recently, senior Marine Corps officials have argued that significantly increasing the Marine deployment to Afghanistan will require drawing down in Iraq—"during calendar year 2010."[18]

The President's policy calls for the withdrawal of all U.S. combat forces by August 31, 2010. That decision marked the culmination of a comprehensive strategic review of Iraq war efforts that President Obama ordered on his first full day in office. Military commanders were reportedly asked to review alternative 16-month, 19-month, and 23-month timeline options for the withdrawal of U.S. combat forces. The announced withdrawal timeline will mark 18 months from the time of the announcement, and approximately 19 months from the Inauguration— slightly longer than the 16-month timeline suggested by then-Senator Obama during the presidential campaign.

According to the new policy, after August 2010, the U.S. forces' focus in Iraq will shift to a three-pronged mission: training, equipping, and advising the Iraqi security forces (ISF); conducting targeted counter-terrorism operations; and providing force protection for both civilian and military personnel. That so-called "transitional force" will initially included between 35,000 and 50,000 troops. All remaining U.S. forces are expected to be withdrawn by the end of 2011, in accordance with the U.S.-Iraqi Security Agreement.

At the time of the announcement, there were approximately 140,000 U.S. troops deployed in Iraq, including 14 Brigade Combat Teams (BCTs) or equivalents, as well as a significantly larger number of support forces.[19] On March 8, 2009, Administration officials announced that 12,000 U.S. troops would redeploy from Iraq without replacement by September 2009.[20] Administration officials have suggested that between 10 and 12 BCTs would remain on the ground at the time of Iraq's national elections tentatively planned for the end of 2009.

The key components of the "transitional force" are expected to be "Advise and Assist Brigades" (AABs).[21] Some officials have suggested an initial target figure of six AABs but have noted that the number could be adjusted. Officials have explained that each AAB will be built on the chassis, or foundation, of a BCT, and it will be augmented with capabilities required for the stability operations-focused mission in Iraq, including training and advisory capabilities and significant enablers. Each unit is expected to prepare and train as an organic whole before deploying. AABs are expected to work closely with U.S. civilian counterparts, including Provincial Reconstruction Teams (PRTs); those relationships, including co-location and the degree and kind of support provided to civilian efforts, is likely to vary geographically across Iraq.

The troop withdrawal policy does not imply that no further deployments of U.S. military units to Iraq will take place. Some U.S. units schedule to redeploy from Iraq in the near term will be replaced by fresh U.S. units. In addition, some units may end up serving shorter tours in Iraq than the now-standard 12 months of "boots on the ground."

The drawdown and transition plans are expected to include a consolidation of three key military headquarters in Iraq: Multi-National Force-Iraq (MNF-I), the overall strategic-level command currently led by General Raymond Odierno; Multi-National Corps-Iraq (MNC-I), the operationallevel command led since April 4, 2009, by Lieutenant General Charles Jacoby and Ft. Lewis-Washington-based I Corps; and Multi-National Security Transition-Command-Iraq (MNSTC-I), led by Lieutenant General Frank Helmick. Some officials have suggested that the headquarters consolidation is likely to take place after the Iraqi national elections, but well before the August 2010 transition. The new entity is expected to be significantly smaller in terms of personnel. The consolidation would reflect not only an elimination of redundancy, but also, as one official described it, discretely "choosing not to do some things."[22]

The Obama Administration's drawdown and transition policy was widely considered to reflect a compromise between two broad schools of thought—advocates, respectively, of a relatively gradual or a relatively accelerated drawdown. Many observers have suggested that the policy splits the difference by maintaining a relatively robust force on the ground through the political hurdles of 2009, which preparing to draw U.S. forces down relatively rapidly in 2010.

One school of thought, which included many military commanders, supported a relatively longer timetable.[23] Secretary of Defense Robert Gates acknowledged, "I think that, if the commanders had complete say in this matter, that they would have preferred that the combat mission not end until the end of 2010."[24] One key concern was reportedly a desire to retain a robust force through the Iraqi political hurdles of 2009 to ensure their success and their ability to serve as catalysts of further stabilization. In December 2008, U.S. military commanders reportedly had recommended beginning the drawdown slowly, by withdrawing two BCTs over the first six months of 2009.[25] Before the President's policy announcement, GEN Odierno, MNF-I Commanding General, stated, "I believe that if we can get through the next year peacefully, with incidents about what they are today or better, I think we're getting close to enduring stability, which enables us to really reduce."[26]

Proponents of a gradual approach also argued that it is important to take every remaining opportunity to train, advise, and mentor the Iraqi security forces (ISF). MNSTC-I Commanding General LTG Helmick commented in February 2009 that the ISF still had "a long way to go." He argued that if they continue to focus on logistics—their "Achilles heel"—and there are no major surprises from the enemy, then the ISF could have "a sustained ground capability to fight the insurgency" by the end of 2011.[27]

Some military commanders were also reportedly concerned that any significant drawdown would be complicated and would require substantial time and attention from U.S.

military leadership on the ground. They urged delaying the bulk of the drawdown until 2010, to allow MNF-I to focus primarily on its substantive mission in 2009.

The other broad school of thought urged the adoption of a relatively accelerated timeline. Some advocates of an accelerated timeline sought simply to end the U.S. military commitment in Iraq as soon as reasonably possible. Other proponents of this school argued that the U.S. troop presence in Iraq—and the antipathy that might be generated among the Iraqi population by the presence of a de facto occupier—could be hindering further progress. Announced troop withdrawal plans, it was argued, could spur progress by encouraging Iraqi leaders to accelerate their own efforts to assume more responsibility and make progress toward reconciliation, and by urging international partners to increase their constructive involvement.[28] They stressed that it would be particularly helpful to reduce the visible presence of U.S. combat forces before the rest of the political "hurdles" Iraq faces in 2009, to reduce the risk that the U.S. presence might become the target of politically-motivated rhetoric and opposition.[29]

Some accelerated timeline advocates underscored the strain that simultaneous war efforts in Iraq and Afghanistan have placed on U.S. military forces—a strain likely to grow as the United States increases troop deployments to Afghanistan in 2009.[30] The high demand for forces for the ongoing U.S. troop commitments in Iraq and Afghanistan has meant, for many servicemembers, repeated deployments, extended deployments, and/or short "dwell times" at home between tours. Military Departments, responsible in accordance with Title 10, U.S. Code, for "organizing, manning, training and equipping" the force, and some key observers, have expressed concerns about the stress these demands have placed, and may continue to place, on the force.[31] Over time, DOD has introduced a series of policies designed to manage that stress—for example, limiting active duty Army deployments to 12 months for those deploying after August 1, 2008.

Some observers from each school of thought have expressed concerns about the Obama Administration policy. At the time of the policy announcement, some Democratic Party leaders in Congress, including Senate Majority Leader Harry Reid and House Speaker Nancy Pelosi, questioned the need for a residual force as large as 50,000 troops.[32] Some gradualists, in turn, urged the Administration to remain flexible about the timeline in execution, cautioning that "it cannot be carried out rigidly" and urging a readiness to "slow the pace next year if necessary."[33]

Current Strategic and Operational Dynamics

The Obama Administration announced its Iraq transition policy, and the U.S.-Iraqi Security Agreement came into force, against a backdrop of ongoing strategic-level challenges to the Government of Iraq, and multiple operational-level transitions in the counter-insurgency effort.

Current Strategic Dynamics: Tests and "Spoilers"

Most observers agree that the GoI faces several major tests in 2009. These began with the provincial elections held in most parts of the country on January 31, 2009, and are also scheduled to include district-level elections in June; a national referendum on the security agreement in July; and national-level elections at the end of the year. These events carry some risk of unrest, but, many observers contend, should these hurdles be cleared safely and successfully, they might serve to further catalyze the consolidation of the Iraqi state.

In addition, the GoI still faces several persistent strategic challenges – potential "spoilers" – that could disrupt not only security conditions on the ground but also progress toward a unified and stable Iraq.

One major challenge, increasingly prominent in 2009, is a portfolio of tensions and competing claims in "the north," particularly between Iraqi Kurds and Arabs. The set of related issues includes resolving the political status of the multi-ethnic and oil-rich city of Kirkuk, together with other "disputed territories" along the Green Line that divides the Kurdistan Regional Government (KRG) from the rest of Iraq.[34] The problems are complicated by the forced resettlement policies of Saddam's regime, which moved Kurds out of their homes and resettled Arabs in those areas; and by Kurdish efforts in the post-Saddam era to reclaim those areas. Further, the KRG and GoI continue to dispute the proper dispensation of oil revenues generated by the areas rich oil reserves. While Kirkuk city itself has been relatively calm, coalition and Iraqi officials in Kirkuk have noted with concern that outside players with strong vested interests, including ethnically based Iraqi political parties, and Turkey-based supporters of Iraqi Turkmen, sometimes use inflammatory language to stir up tensions in the city.[35] Elsewhere, violence has flared—in 2008, Iraqi security forces skirmished with KRG *peshmerga* forces in the restive town of Khanaquin, in Diyala province, on the GoI side of the Green Line.[36] The year 2009 is likely to prove pivotal in this ongoing set of debates. UNAMI is expected to present a comprehensive set of recommendations for resolving tensions in the north, as a basis for discussion. Provincial elections, held elsewhere on January 31, 2009, remain to be scheduled for At Ta'amin province, which includes Kirkuk.

A second major challenge concerns how effectively Sunni Arabs, are incorporated socially, economically, and politically into the Iraqi polity. Sunni Arabs, who are concentrated in western and central Iraq, were a disproportionately privileged minority under Saddam's rule but lost much of that status after regime change. The provincial elections held on January 31, 2009, marked a positive step, by increasing Sunni Arab political representation at the provincial level. A particular concern is the ongoing integration of members of the Sons of Iraq (SoI) "community watch" program. A majority of the SoIs were Sunni Arabs— including some former insurgents— and key Shiite officials in the GoI were long wary of the SoI program. On October 1, 2008, the GoI began assuming responsibility for the SoIs, including paying their salaries, and this transition was expected to be completed by April 2009.

The integration of former SoIs into the Iraqi security forces and civilian jobs has proceeded very slowly, and participants have reported serious delays in the payment of salaries. Some practitioners and observers have expressed concerns about the possible security repercussions if the GoI were to shut down the program, cease paying salaries, or fail to secure alternative employment for the SoIs.[37] More seriously still, SoIs have reported a "campaign of arrests" against their members by Iraqi Security Forces (ISF), in Baghdad and Diyala provinces. In late March 2009, the detention of a key SoI leader in Baghdad by the ISF led to localized armed clashes, the detention of scores of SoIs, and the GoI decision to disband that SoI group.[38]

A third major challenge is the potential for violence in "the south," home to a long-standing and growing competition for power and resources between well-established Shiite political factions backed by militias that have sometimes used violence, and also to tribal Shi'a who may be beginning to find a public voice. Against that volatile backdrop in southern Iraq, both U.S. and Iraqi officials remain concerned about Iranian interventions—economic, social, and sometimes "military" in the form of the provision of lethal aid and sponsorship of proxies including Asa'ib al-Haq and Ketaib Hezbollah.[39] Tensions in the south have the potential to be exacerbated by elections, and also by potential drives to form multi-provincial "regions" that would enjoy special access to authorities and resources.

Current Operational Dynamics: Transitions

By the start of 2009, several major but uneven transitions were underway at the operational level in Iraq. First, the substantial security improvements achieved over the course of the "surge" had further deepened, with some fluctuations during combat operations in 2008 in specific parts of Iraq, and some remaining insurgent activity, particularly in north central Iraq.[40] In March 2009, the outgoing Commanding General of MNC-I, LTG Austin, characterized the overall situation this way: "We are close to sustainable security but we're not there yet."[41] Concerning the restive north, LTG Austin commented that the problems in Iraq's third-largest city Mosul, in Ninewah province, could still "put us off track and cause violence to really reignite in a greater way."[42] East-central Diyala province, along the Iranian border, with its volatile mix of Kurds, and both Shi'a and Sunni Arabs, also remained a potential flashpoint. Second, accordingly, the focus of U.S. military operations shifted toward stability operations in the south and west, with greater remaining emphasis on COIN in north-central Iraq.

Third, the operational capabilities of the Iraqi Security Forces (ISF) continued to grow, reflected in—and catalyzed by—ISF operational experiences in 2008 in Basra, Sadr City, Amarah, Mosul, and Diyala. According to U.S. commanders, the March 2008 ISF operations in Basra, targeting Shiite militias, were poorly planned and required a strong rescue effort by coalition forces. The August 2008 operations in Diyala, targeting affiliates of Al Qaeda in Iraq (AQI), were planned by the Iraqis in advance but still required coalition forces to provide enablers and to help hold areas once they were cleared.[43]

A fourth transition was a growth in 2008 in formal Government of Iraq (GoI) security responsibility, antedating the Security Agreement, as additional provinces transitioned to "provincial Iraqi control" (PIC). In practice, PIC arrangements varied from province to province but as a rule gave the GoI lead security responsibility—and practice exercising that responsibility—and mandated increased coordination of coalition operations and activities with the GoI.[44] Fifth, as the ISF's basic capabilities improved, the coalition's approaches to training and partnering with the ISF evolved substantially though unevenly across Iraq. In terms of substance, many embedded "transition teams" shifted their training focus away from basic "move, shoot, and communicate" skills, toward more advanced skills including staff functions and the use of enablers. In terms of organization, the use of various forms of unit-to-unit partnering, which allows advising by example as well as by instruction, and complements the work of transition teams, grew substantially.

Sixth, by early 2009, MNF-I was a far less "multi-national" force than in the past. By the end of 2008, most remaining coalition partner countries had brought their deployments in Iraq to a close. Major redeployments in late 2008 included the 2,000-strong Georgian contingent;

the Poles, who had led Multi-National Division-Center South; and the South Koreans, who had led Multi- National Division-Northeast. Faced with the expiration of the UN mandate authorizing the multinational force in Iraq, several coalition partners—the United Kingdom, Australia, and Romania— each signed a Memorandum of Understanding with the GoI, providing a new legal basis for the presence of their troops, but each of their mandates is set to expire on July 31, 2009. Seventh, the geographical focus of U.S. forces in Iraq shifted somewhat from north to south, as U.S. forces assumed some battlespaces in the south previously held by coalition partner forces.[45] On March 31, 2009, the Multi-National Division-Center absorbed UK-led Multi-National Division- Southeast, to form the new Multi-National Division-South, under U.S. command, with responsibility for nine provinces.[46]

Eighth and finally, as civilian-led Provincial Reconstruction Teams (PRTs) grew, they increasingly took the lead in some efforts formerly spearheaded by the U.S. military. In some cases, including Najaf and Karbala provinces, PRTs operated without a significant nearby U.S. forces presence. Nevertheless, the military's extensive presence on the ground at district and local levels, compared with the limited number of U.S. civilian experts, meant that in practice, the military continued to play a strong "supporting" role in helping Iraqis develop civil capacity.

Diminishing U.S. Leverage

Meanwhile, U.S. practitioners in Iraq, both civilian and military, have suggested that the appetite of GoI officials to be mentored, advised, or guided by U.S. officials—and thus the leverage that the U.S. government is able to exercise – is diminishing. In 2008, as Iraqi civilian and military capacity and capabilities grew, and as Iraqi confidence in those capabilities increased, GoI officials demonstrated growing assertiveness and less inclination to consult with U.S. officials before taking action.[47] That approach was manifested, for example, in the decision by Prime Minister Nouri al Maliki to launch military operations in Basra in March 2008, and the GoI's unilateral decision to assume full responsibility for Sons of Iraq in fall 2008. Most practitioners and observers expect that U.S. leverage is likely to diminish further in 2009, under the new sovereignty regime and as the U.S. presence decreases.

Future Strategic Considerations

President Obama's drawdown and transition policy charts a new strategic course but also raises several questions about the future U.S.-Iraqi relationship. At the same time, OIF experiences as a whole raise additional strategic questions about U.S. Government preparations to undertake future complex contingencies.

Clarifying and Updating U.S. Interests and Strategic Objectives

Announcing the drawdown and transition policy, President Obama stated that the goal is "an Iraq that is sovereign, stable and self-reliant." To that end, the President added, the United States would:

- Work to promote an Iraqi government that is just, representative, and accountable, and that provides neither support nor safe haven to terrorists;
- Help Iraq build new ties of trade and commerce with the world; and
- Forge a partnership with the people and government of Iraq that contributes to the peace and security of the region."[48]

Under that broad rubric, as the U.S. role in Iraq transitions, it might be useful to confirm key U.S. national interests regarding Iraq, and the crucial strategic objectives that, at a minimum, it is important for the United States to achieve to support those interests. Such broad objectives might address the following elements:

- U.S. interests in Iraq's domestic political arrangements. Some might argue that a democratic or broadly representative and inclusive Iraqi polity is essential as a key to Iraq's stability, while others might argue that the nature of Iraq's domestic political arrangements is much less important than simply a unified and stable Iraq.
- U.S. interests in Iraq's role in the fight against global terrorist networks. Some might argue that the most important goal is simply ensuring that Iraq does not serve as a safe haven for terrorists. Others might stress the importance of active intelligence-sharing by Iraq with the United States. Still others might argue that it is in U.S. interests that Iraq couple the counter-terrorism skills it is currently developing as part of its domestic counter-insurgency effort, with expeditionary capabilities, so that it could participate in future regional counter-terrorist activities.
- U.S. interests in the regional balance of power. Some might argue that Iraq's strength, relative to that of its neighbors, is important. Others might simply stress the importance of an absence of conflict—that is, as a long-stated U.S. goal puts it, an "Iraq at peace with its neighbors."

Furthermore, it may prove judicious to update the formulation of U.S. strategic objectives as the U.S. mission and presence in Iraq change and results of those changes are assessed. In his policy announcement, President Obama stressed that the situation in Iraq remains dynamic and challenging: "But let there be no doubt – Iraq is not yet secure, and there will be difficult days ahead. Violence will continue to be a part of life in Iraq."[49]

Applying Strategic Leverage

As the Iraqi appetite for accepting guidance and advice from international partners continues to wane, U.S. policy makers may wish to reassess how the U.S. government might most effectively apply political, economic, and security "levers" to help shape Iraq's transformation into a stable and prosperous state. One challenge is an apparent mismatch in Iraq between those who are most susceptible to leverage and those making key decisions. Iraqi warfighting commanders, as a rule, recognize the extent to which they rely on U.S. military enablers, and remain eager for a continuation of U.S. support. At the same time, Iraqi political leaders—those who make the decisions—tend toward overconfidence in the capabilities of Iraqi security forces, and a less urgent sense of the need for close mil-to-mil partnership with the United States.

Shaping a Long-Term U.S. Relationship with Iraq

Another strategic consideration concerns the kind of long-term partnership the United States wants to have with Iraq, including the traditional panoply of diplomatic and economic as well as security ties, and the kind of U.S. presence in Iraq that would be required to support such a relationship. On January 27, 2009, Secretary Gates told the Senate and House Armed Services Committees that "...we should still expect to be involved in Iraq on some level for many years to come."[50] One particular challenge for both states may prove to be the cultural or psychological adjustment from an essentially paternalistic relationship to a partnership on equal footing.

In the security field, decisions about the shape of that future partnership could suggest different possible forms for a future U.S. presence. In theory, one option would be establishing permanent U.S. military bases in Iraq, to support broader U.S. policy in the region, possibly on the model of those in Japan, South Korea, Germany, and Italy. Kurdish leaders have reportedly long proposed a permanent U.S. military presence in northern Iraq. However, the "permanent basing" option does not appear to enjoy support from the Obama Administration, Members of Congress, or from the Government of Iraq as a whole. A presence of U.S. forces beyond December 2011 would require revisiting and amending the U.S.-Iraqi Security Agreement.

Another option would be a particularly robust U.S. Office of Security Cooperation (OSC), responsible for some combination of training, advising, and mentoring Iraqi security forces, and helping build the capacity of Iraqi security ministries. Following the usual pattern, the OSC would be responsible to both the U.S. Ambassador to Iraq and to the Commanding General of U.S. Central Command. One possible model might be the U.S. Military Training Mission to Saudi Arabia, which operates on the basis of a bilateral Memorandum of Understanding with the Government of the Kingdom of Saudi Arabia and serves to train, advise, and assist the Saudi Arabian Armed Forces.

Defining U.S. Policy toward Iranian Intervention in Iraq

According to U.S. and Iraqi officials, Iraq, particularly in the south, continues to face a potential threat from Shi'a Iraqi proxy groups trained by Iran's Quds forces, and other forms of lethal aid from Iran.[51] In March 2009, U.S. forces reportedly shot down an Iranian unmanned aerial vehicle over Iraqi territory, in eastern Diyala province.[52] Meanwhile, Multi-National Corps-Iraq (MNC-I) is in the process of shifting its focus somewhat from north to south in Iraq, including relocating a Division headquarters to Basra and increasing the U.S. troop presence in southern Iraq as coalition partner troops withdraw or draw down. According to U.S. military commanders on the ground, the growing U.S. footprint in southern Iraq is not likely to be lost on Iran.[53] Any such Iranian concerns might be exacerbated by the growing U.S. forces presence across Iran's eastern border, in Afghanistan.

It is not clear to what extent U.S. "Iran policy" factors in current and potential Iranian activities in southern Iraq. In the context of growing potential for low-level U.S. military confrontations— "shadow-boxing"—with Iranian proxies in southern Iraq, as the U.S. force presence in that area grows, it may be important to consider scenarios in which tactical-level developments might escalate into strategic-level concerns.

Assessing the Implications of OIF Lessons for the Future of the Force

How Military Departments fulfill their Title 10 responsibilities to organize, man, train, and equip the force – how they make decisions about endstrength and capabilities required—may depend in part on lessons drawn from OIF, and on how applicable those lessons are deemed to be to potential future engagements. For example, lessons might be drawn from OIF concerning how to most effectively train foreign security forces and to prepare U.S. forces for that mission; how increasing the intelligence assets available to commanders on the ground affects their ability to identify and pursue targets; how "dwell time" policies for the Active and Reserve Components can best be implemented; and what closer operational integration between Special Operations Forces and conventional forces might suggest about the most effective division of labor between them.

President Obama's drawdown and transition policy for Iraq has pressed the Army, in particular, to address the question of how and whether to institutionalize key capabilities developed, often through trial and error, for use during OIF. The policy calls for the deployment to Iraq, by mid- 2010, of Advise and Assist Brigades (AABs). According to DOD officials, AABs are to be built on the chassis of existing BCTs and augmented as necessary with capabilities appropriate for the new stability operations mission in Iraq.

The near-term requirement to prepare and deploy such units does not resolve a more fundamental question – how permanent should AABs be? In theory, for potential future contingencies, the Army could simply plan to use and adapt its standard force structure to meet new requirements as they arise, or it could dedicate resources to establish a standing capacity of some kind.

Secretary of Defense Robert Gates has underscored that "…building the security capacity of other nations through training and equipping programs has emerged as a core and enduring military requirement,"[54] suggesting the need to institutionalize such capabilities. Dr. John Nagl has proposed one possible institutional solution – creating a permanent, standing Advisory Corps of 20,000 combat advisors, which would be organized, equipped, educated and trained to develop host nation security forces.[55]

Meanwhile, some officials suggest that Army leaders remain reluctant to make permanent changes to the Army's force structure, not least because such changes could mean assuming increased risk in more traditional areas of warfighting. The Army has advocated, as a substitute for "AAB," the term Brigade Enabled for Stability Operations (BESO).[56] In March 2009, the Army announced that new BESOs would deploy from Fort Bliss, TX, to Iraq and Afghanistan later in the year. BESOs, Army officials stressed, would not depart radically from the familiar BCT construct—they would "remain full-spectrum capable," and would be "…a matter of augmentation … slight modifications to gain skill sets."[57]

For the Department of Defense as a whole, in turn, OIF experiences may be used to help frame future discussions about the Department's force planning construct—a shorthand description of the major contingencies the Department must be prepared to execute simultaneously—which is used to shape the total force. Drawing conclusions, however, is not simple. Analytical challenges include deciding what kind of contingency OIF represents, how likely it is to be representative of future contingencies, and which chronological "slice" of OIF requirements (given the great variation in troop commitment and equipment over time) to use to represent the effort. Recent DOD guidance documents—including DOD Directive 3000.07 "Irregular Warfare IW" issued on December 1, 2008, which stated that "it is DoD policy to recognize that IW is as strategically important as traditional warfare"; the 2008

National Defense Strategy; and the 2009 *Quadrennial Roles and Missions Review Report*—all suggested a relatively strong future DOD emphasis on capabilities required for complex contingencies like Iraq and Afghanistan.[58]

Applying OIF Lessons to Interagency Coordination

A further strategic consideration concerns how lessons are drawn from OIF regarding U.S. government coordination in complex contingencies, including decision-making, planning and execution.[59] Just as the executive branch's responsibilities in this area are divided among different agencies, congressional oversight responsibilities are divided among different committees of jurisdiction, such that achieving full integration can be a challenge for both branches of government.

One set of questions prompted by OIF experiences concerns the decision-making process about whether to go to war and if so, how to do so. Key issues include the rigor of the interagency debates, the effectiveness of the provision of "best military advice" to key decision-makers, and the thoroughness of congressional oversight in general.[60]

Another set of questions raised by OIF concerns balancing roles, responsibilities, resources, and authorities among U.S. government agencies to support implementation of activities required in complex contingencies—such as security forces training, local governance work, and economic reconstruction.[61] In security forces training, OIF experiences included several different patterns for the distribution of responsibilities between the Departments of Defense and State. In OIF, governance and economic reconstruction work, in turn, have been carried out by Provincial Reconstruction Teams (PRTs), by civilian U.S. government agencies operating separately from PRTs, and by military units—not always in close conjunction with one another.[62] Based in part on OIF experiences, many observers have concluded that the capacity of U.S. Government civilian agencies, including deployable capabilities, should be enhanced; and that the modalities for coordinating and integrating civilian and military efforts in the field should be improved.

Future Operational Considerations

The President's drawdown and transition announcement left open a number of operational issues that U.S. practitioners, policy makers, and Members of Congress may wish to consider.

How Much Help Is Enough?

The Obama Administration transition policy generally calls for a diminishing U.S. government role in Iraq, but senior U.S. civilian and military officials on the ground are likely to continue to face myriad small choices about exactly how much support to provide, in various circumstances, to their host nation partners.

During the formal occupation of Iraq, from 2003 to 2004, the coalition was responsible for all facets of Iraqi public life. In the early post-occupation days, the coalition's general approach was to do everything possible to get Iraqi institutions up and running, limited primarily by resources and personnel available to implement the efforts. As Iraqi capacity grew, the role of Iraqi civilian and military officials and institutions shifted, to various degrees, from sharing responsibilities to leading, with some support or back-up from the coalition.

By 2008, U.S. civilian and military officials in Iraq were seriously discussing a fundamental question: how much U.S. help is enough? The debates addressed both the U.S. military's relationship with the Iraqi Security Forces, and U.S. government civilian expert assistance provided through Provincial Reconstruction Teams and at the national level.

A number of U.S. officials, both civilian and military, argued that, in the words of one military commander, "it's time to take the training wheels off," that it is okay to "let the Iraqis fail." Taking a step back, they argued, is not only a key to reducing the U.S. commitment over time—it may also be the best way to reduce the risk of Iraqi dependence on U.S. help, and to encourage Iraqis to assume more responsibility and to learn to solve problems themselves. One former brigade commander in Iraq, from this school of thought, argued, "It's time to let go," and added the observation: "The coalition has a very difficult time having the restraint and discipline to refrain from intervening."[63]

Some officials countered that, given the shrinking U.S. presence as U.S. forces draw down, and the diminishing Iraqi appetite to be advised and mentored, it is important to facilitate the growth of Iraqi capacity as much as possible while the window of opportunity is still open.[64]

Further Troop Drawdowns

President Obama's drawdown and transition policy prescribes the withdrawal of all U.S. combat troops from Iraq by the end of August 2010, and the U.S.-Iraqi Security Agreement mandates that all U.S. forces withdraw from Iraq by the end of 2011. Further, in March 2009, the Obama Administration announced plans to withdraw a total of 12,000 U.S. troops from Iraq by September 2009.

Within those parameters, remaining key remaining decisions include:

- When, before the end of August 2010, to transition the U.S. force presence in each geographic area of Iraq from combat troops to Advise and Assist Brigades (AABs).
- How large of a residual transition force, between roughly 35,000 and 50,000 troops, to leave in Iraq after August 31, 2010.
- How quickly to draw down the residual force between August 2010 and the end of 2011.
- Whether the basic parameters of the Obama policy timeline, including the August 2010, could be adjusted, should changing circumstances on the ground appear to make that advisable.

Future of the Iraqi Security Forces Training Mission

Supporting the development of the Iraqi Security Forces (ISF) is a critical focus of U.S. military operations in Iraq. Counterinsurgency (COIN) theory emphasizes the importance of conducting operations "by, with and through" host nation forces; and helping to build such forces when their capacity or capabilities are not adequate. From the outset, the organization and focus of the coalition's efforts to train, equip, and mentor the ISF varied across the battlespace of Iraq, depending on the conditions on the ground, the level of development of the locally based ISF, and the availability of coalition forces for training missions. A key operational consideration, looking ahead, is how to accomplish the ISF training mission as U.S. forces draw down and AABs are established.

Transition Teams

The "standard" approach to training the ISF has been the use of embedded "transition teams" that typically live and work with a host nation unit. One key point of variation over time has been the size of these teams. Transition teams working with the Iraqi Army, for example, typically included between 11 and 15 members, depending on the size of the Iraqi unit they embedded with. In practice, however, the numbers have varied—for example, in western Anbar province, Multi-National Force-West (MNF-W), led by U.S. Marines, consistently used larger teams, with between 30 and 40 members.[65] One key development over time, in the view of U.S. commanders on the ground and many experts, has been an overall improvement in the quality and effectiveness of the transition teams—in part a reflection of standardization and improvements in the training "pipelines" used by the Military Departments to produce the trainers.[66]

In 2008, as the basic operational capabilities of the ISF grew, the use of embedded transition teams shifted toward higher-level ISF headquarters, including brigades and divisions. The substantive efforts of the teams also shifted, from basic skills like patrolling to leadership and enablers. For example, teams working with the Iraqi Army increased their focus on staff functions and logistics, and teams working with the Iraqi Police increased the emphasis on specialized skills like forensics. In effect, transition teams work themselves out of a job, as their host nation partner unit improves.

The U.S. military may not, in every case, have the full spectrum of skills required to staff all types of embedded teams. While logistics experts in the U.S. military are well-placed to share that expertise with Iraqi Army counterparts, U.S. Military Police (MPs) generally do not have the requisite specialized policing skills and have thus relied on collaboration with civilian International Police Advisors, who have been in short supply.

Unit Partnering

In addition to transition teams, coalition forces throughout Iraq have made substantial use of various forms of "unit partnering," in which coalition maneuver units work side-by-side with Iraqi units of equal or larger size. Commanders on the ground have stressed the value of unit partnership, as a complement to the use of embedded teams, as an effective way to "show" rather than just "tell" ISF unit leaders how they might most effectively organize their headquarters, lead their troops, and manage staff functions.[67] Unit partnership has not been envisaged as a permanent arrangement – any individual unit partnership has been designed to be temporary, a catalyst to the development of that Iraqi unit.

As conditions permitted, commanders extended unit partnering beyond the Iraqi Army to Ministry of the Interior (MoI) forces, including the Iraqi Police and the Department of Border Enforcement. That outreach to the MoI was initially more common in Multi-National Division- Center, south of Baghdad, and in Multi-National Force-West in Anbar, than in Multi-National Division-North, which was still actively engaged in combat operations, together with ISF counterparts, in Diyala and Ninewah provinces, in late 2008.

Capacity-Building

Coalition forces have also provided substantial support to the "capacity-building" of the key security institutions of the Government of Iraq—the Ministry of Defense, the Ministry of the Interior, and the Counter-Terrorism Bureau. This support, led by the Multi-National Security Transition Command-Iraq (MNSTC-I), part of MNF-I, has included mentoring Iraqi senior leaders in leadership and management skills, as well as providing technical assistance to ministry personnel.

Coalition officials have stressed the growing importance of maximizing such capacity-building efforts while Iraqis are still receptive to receiving such training. With appropriate leadership skills, they argued, Iraqi senior leaders in the security sector could make substantially greater and more effective contributions to the development of the ISF, gradually reducing the need for U.S. advice and support. Coalition commanders have also underscored the importance of utilizing the right U.S. and coalition personnel for the mission, including senior "mentors" with enough leadership experience and stature to carry weight with their Iraqi counterparts.[68]

ISF Training and Advising Under Transition

The Obama transition policy for Iraq underscores the importance of the ISF training and advisory effort, naming it one of the three missions of the U.S. transition force from August 2010 forward. The increasingly smaller U.S. military footprint and the reduction in senior U.S. military leadership in Iraq could complicate that mission somewhat.

One issue may be the ability of the U.S. AABs, spaced thinly across Iraq, to continue to provide ISF counterparts with key enablers, such as logistics; Intelligence, Surveillance and Reconnaissance (ISR); and the ability to call in close air support (CAS). On the other hand, over time, ISF units are expected to rely increasingly on their own capabilities for such support.

A related issue may be the ability of AABs to continue the practice of providing mentorship through close relationships with equivalent Iraqi units. For example, under MNC-I, Multi-National Divisions (MND) were often able to provide a BCT to partner full-time with an Iraqi Army (IA) Division based in the same province; and MND Commanding Generals themselves developed close relationships with their IA counterparts. One option, under the AAB footprint, might be a transition from a relationship of "partnership" to one of "liaison" with less senior U.S. officers.

Future of the U.S. Forces Footprint

The U.S.-Iraqi security agreement requires that all U.S. combat forces withdraw from Iraqi "cities, villages, and localities" no later than the time when the ISF assume security responsibility in the relevant province, and in any case no later than June 30, 2009. By early 2009, many U.S. forces had already pulled out of major urban areas, consolidating at large Forward Operating Bases (FOBs) and handing over to the ISF the responsibility to provide continual presence.[69] The Obama drawdown and transition policy, including the planned withdrawal without replacement of 12,000 U.S. troops by September 2009, might serve to accelerate this shift.

This dynamic marks a sharp departure from a basic premise of COIN in Iraq. Top U.S. commanders in Iraq long argued that "living where we work" is what made the counterinsurgency effort a success. This phrase refers to establishing a security presence in cities and towns, including small command outposts of U.S. forces, and Joint Security Stations that include both U.S. and various Iraqi forces. That presence, commanders have noted, allowed ongoing collaboration between U.S. and Iraqi forces, making those partnerships more effective, and it facilitated frequent interaction with the local population, building trust and confidence. In 2008, before the terms of the U.S.-Iraqi Security Agreement were finalized, U.S. commanders generally favored "thinning" the ranks in cities and towns over time – that is, using a progressively lighter but still dispersed U.S. footprint, as the ISF gradually assumed responsibility for providing the "presence" in each area.

Looking ahead, one option is that some U.S. forces might retain a light, distributed presence in some urban areas, after the June 2009 deadline, in advisory capacities to the ISF. In December 2008, Commanding General of Multi-National Force-Iraq (MNF-I), General Raymond Odierno, noted that some U.S. forces were likely to remain inside cities and towns after June 2009, in order to continue to train and mentor Iraqi security forces.[70] In March 2009, Deputy Commanding General of Multi-National Division-Baghdad, Brigadier General Fred Rudesheim, noted that somewhere under 10% of U.S. troops based in Baghdad, for example training teams that work with the Iraqi Army and National Police, might remain in the city past June 30, 2009.[71] At the end of March 2009, MNC-I Commanding General LTG Austin noted that based on joint assessments, Iraqi officials were likely to request for a continuation of some U.S. force presence in Mosul and Diyala, beyond the deadline.[72]

Coordination on Operations under the Security Agreement

The U.S.-Iraqi Security Agreement required the coordination of all U.S. military operations— including ground operations, air operations, and detainee operations—with Iraqi authorities. The Agreement required the establishment of a committee structure to elaborate more detailed implementing instructions; by February 2009, such a structure of committees and subcommittees, including Iraqi and U.S. civilian and military participation, was in place and functioning.[73]

In a December 2008 letter to the force, regarding the new Agreement, GEN Odierno noted that the new environment would "require a subtle shift in how we plan, coordinate, and execute missions throughout Iraq," and that new rules of engagement would be issued.[74] In early 2009, MNF-I officials noted that the Security Agreement was the fundamental theme of current U.S. efforts in Iraq.[75] The premise for future U.S. operations, according to MNC-I, is to "figure out how to get it done through Iraqis."[76] A key issue is the further impact that the Security Agreement will have on U.S. operations.

In practice, according to commanders on the ground, before the Security Agreement went into effect, the vast majority of U.S. operations were already closely coordinated with the GoI. Further, most of those operations were already "combined" with Iraqi forces. These transitions had been facilitated by the Provincial Iraqi Control (PIC) process, in which, by decision of the GoI in consultation with MNF-I, lead security responsibility for a given province was transferred to Iraqi control, based on assessments of security conditions and local ISF capabilities. Before the Security Agreement went into effect, 13 of 18 provinces had transitioned to PIC, and PIC arrangements generally required that U.S. operations be coordinated with the GoI. Another common practice, before the Security Agreement, was that the GoI granted approval in advance for U.S. forces to carry out certain categories of activities, or to take action against certain targets. The use of warrant-based arrests—now required—was already frequently practiced in 2008.

As of early 2009, U.S. commanders on the ground, particularly those in PIC provinces, have reported a smooth transition to operations under the Security Agreement. One U.S. BCT commander, based in Qadisiyah province where the 8th Iraqi Army Division is headquartered, stated: "We do all of our operations ... by, with and through the Iraqi security forces. They're all joint. Anybody that we detain, we detain with a warrant."[77]

Concerning the use of Iraqi air space, the Security Agreement stated: "Surveillance and control over Iraqi airspace shall transfer to Iraqi authority immediately upon entry into force of this Agreement". It added a caveat: "Iraq may request from the United States forces temporary support for the Iraqi authorities in the mission of surveillance and control of Iraqi air space."[78] The caveat is important because the capabilities of the Iraqi Air Force are still in the very early stages of development and training. In addition, that training has focused, first of all, on skills relevant to the ongoing counter-insurgency (COIN) fight, such as moving troops and supplies, and providing some ISR. U.S. officials have noted that Iraqi officials and commanders on the ground remain aware that they still lack key COIN capabilities such as sufficient ISR and CAS; that they acknowledge that they do not yet have the ability to defend Iraqi airspace; and that they remain eager for the support of U.S. air assets. In late 2008, U.S. officials expressed some confidence that it would be possible to reach agreements on shared use of air space.[79]

The Security Agreement did not address a parallel concern related to operational coordination: Iraqi coordination with U.S. forces concerning ISF operations. U.S. commanders on the ground report that it is increasingly common for ISF commanders to inform U.S. forces only after they have carried out local operations; some commanders add that these are positive developments in terms of growing ISF capabilities and initiative.[80] At the same time, it could be helpful for U.S. forces to know in advance about significant ISF operations, for two reasons: first, the ISF might call on U.S. forces suddenly, during such operations, to provide key enablers; second, such operations could have an impact on U.S. force protection.

Article 22 of the Security Agreement described provisions for detainee operations. One set of provisions placed tight constraints on the circumstances under which U.S. forces may take Iraqis into physical custody.[81] Another set of provisions, of even more concern to U.S. commanders on the ground, specified how the cases of those detainees held by coalition forces would be further adjudicated. The Security Agreement mandated that U.S. forces provide information about all detainees held, and stated that Iraqi authorities would "issue arrest warrants for persons who are wanted by them." The agreement required U.S. forces to turn over custody of all "wanted" detainees, and then to release all remaining detainees "in a safe and orderly manner."[82]

In anticipation of a more stringent new detention regime, throughout 2008, MNF-I carried out a detainee release program, releasing detainees to their homes and communities whenever possible. As of late November 2008, U.S. forces held approximately 15,800 detainees in theater internment facilities, after releasing more than 17,500 during 2008.[83]

Some U.S. military commanders expressed concerns about the remaining "legacy" population. In many cases, for the detainees it held, the coalition lacked releasable evidence with legal sufficiency in Iraqi courts. Scrupulous collection of evidence—such as photographs, diagrams, eye-witness accounts—common in civilian law enforcement, was not always an integral part of coalition combat operations in Iraq. Such legacy detainees could pose real security threats to the Iraqi population, or to the coalition, commanders warned. Some coalition officials and outside observers also expressed concerns that the GoI adjudication of legacy detainee cases, whether or not legally sufficient evidence exists, might evince a sectarian bias—in particular, a tendency to treat Shiite Arabs more leniently than Sunni Arabs.[84]

In January 2009, Iraqi and U.S. officials reached an agreement that the U.S. military would transfer 1,500 detainees per month to Iraqi authorities. At the first such transfer, Iraqi officials had warrants for 42 of the 1,500; they chose to keep about 70 others for further investigation; and they planned to release the remaining persons to their home communities at a rate of about 50 per day.[85]

Some detainees have expressed fears that they may face harm if they return to their home communities, as part of the new release process; in those cases, the GoI reportedly agreed to help them resettle elsewhere.[86] In March 2009, it was reported that six recently released detainees were abducted and killed by local police officers, in an apparent act of retaliation.[87] Some local Iraqi officials, in turn, have expressed concerns that some released detainees may return to violence—for example, the deputy police chief in Fallujah, Anbar province, commented, "Of course they represent a threat."[88]

Civil-Military Roles and Responsibilities

Over the course of Operation Iraqi Freedom, the balance of U.S. civilian and military roles and responsibilities has evolved to include a larger civilian footprint and a stronger civilian role, and integration between U.S. civilian and military efforts has increased over time. Looking ahead, as U.S. forces draw down, a key operational issue is the most effective future balance and pattern of U.S. civilian and military efforts in Iraq.

As a rule, the military has played the preponderant role in OIF, including in non-traditional fields such as governance and reconstruction. As of 2008, the U.S. military remained the *de facto* default option in many cases, though military officers were usually the first to note that they lacked the requisite expertise.[89] One key role of the U.S. military in Iraq throughout has been supporting civilian-led efforts to provide Iraqis with governance mentorship, and in particular, to build linkages among the national, regional, and local levels. As MNC-I officials noted, "Our job at Corps is to establish the connective tissue between the center and the provinces."[90] As a rule, while PRTs focused on governance at the provincial level, military units, with far more boots on the ground, worked on a daily basis to foster governance at the district and local levels, and to help link those levels to higher levels of Iraqi government.[91] Through early 2009, the U.S. military continued to provide some support for small-scale reconstruction initiatives, though unevenly across Iraq. Some commanders continued to facilitate the reopening of small businesses—and to use the number of reopened businesses as a metric of economic progress— while others decided to "give back," that is, "not spend," their Commanders Emergency Response Program (CERP) funds, in order to encourage Iraqis to budget and spend their own money.[92]

As security conditions on the ground in Iraq improved, civilian and military officials all pointed to increased opportunities for civilian assistance initiatives, particularly capacity-building at all levels. As one U.S. commander argued, "Embassy people should be out more every day now, like we are."[93] Some provincial Iraqi officials, for their part, appear eager to welcome additional U.S. civilian expertise.[94]

In theory, one option, as U.S. troops draw down, would be to increase the U.S. civilian effort in Iraq in terms of personnel and resources, taking advantage of the improved security climate to boost support for Iraqi civilian capacity-building at the national, provincial, and local levels. In 2008, some key steps were taken to amplify U.S. government civilian assistance efforts at the provincial level, including authorization to add 66 civilian subject matter experts, in technical fields including agriculture and business development, to work with the PRTs.[95] However, officials at U.S. Embassy Baghdad and at the Department of State noted that it was likely that peak PRT staffing levels in Iraq had already been reached. In 2008, the Embassy—in response to direction from Congress—began working on "PRT strategic drawdown" plans.[96]

The Obama Administration's drawdown and transition policy calls for consolidating PRT personnel at fewer locations, and for closely integrating the work of the PRTs and the AABs. In testimony before the House Armed Services Committee in January 2009, describing future plans, Secretary Gates noted: "The plans that General Odierno has developed in conjunction with Ambassador Crocker foresee that as we consolidate our forces, we would also consolidate our PRTs ... so that the two would be stationed together and our forces would be in a position to continue to protect the civilian element."[97] Some officials have suggested that those civil-military relationships might vary geographically, including closer integration—including co-location or even full integration into a single staff structure—where security conditions remain unsettled, and looser partnerships in relatively permissive areas.

Good test cases are already available, in Najaf and Karbala provinces, for the ability of PRTs to function without a substantial co-located U.S. forces presence. In May 2008, the personnel of the PRTs for Najaf and Karbala provinces, who had been operating from a remote base in Hillah, in Babil province, relocated to their respective areas of operation. Najaf and Karbala were both PIC provinces at that time, with limited U.S. military presence. In Najaf, for example, in late 2008, the PRT, including a diverse team of civilian experts and a small U.S. military team that provided them with movement, was based at a small Forward Operating Base (FOB), together with a U.S. Army transition team that worked with the local Iraqi Army battalion and a small U.S. military "mayor's cell" that managed the installation.[98] A team of private security contractors from Triple Canopy provided static security. In early 2009, U.S. officials in both Baghdad and Washington also pointed to Najaf as a possible model for the future.[99]

Role of Contractors

Over the course of OIF, the role of contractors supporting the operation has varied in both scope and scale. According to DOD, as of the first quarter of 2009, DOD had a total of 148,050 contractors in Iraq, including 39,262 U.S. citizens; 70,875 third-country nationals; and 37,913 host country nationals.[100] A key operational issue looking ahead is the likely role of contractors supporting U.S. operations in Iraq as U.S. forces draw down.

While some substantive requirements for contractor support may diminish, others could increase. For example, one of the three pillars of the mission of Advise and Assist Brigades, after August 2010, is to provide force protection to U.S. government civilians. As of early 2009, that function was performed, in many cases, by private security contractors. At the same time, requirements for some specialized contractor skills—for example, training and advisory support to the ISF – may increase as the U.S. force presence decreases.

Another factor shaping the role of contractors may be explicit U.S. policy decisions. On January 31, 2009, MNF-I Commanding General, GEN Odierno, issued a directive instructing subordinate commanders to begin reducing their reliance on international contractors, including both U.S. and "third-country national" contractors, by five percent per quarter. The Directive noted that commanders should seek to replace them, where possible, with Iraqi contractors, and added, "As we transition more responsibility and control to the government of Iraq, it's time to make this change."[101]

A third factor shaping the role of contractors may be decisions stemming from provisions in the U.S-Iraqi Security Agreement that mandate, "Iraq shall have the primary right to exercise jurisdiction over United States contractors and United States contractor employees."[102] In some instances, concerns about legal jurisdiction have reportedly prompted efforts by U.S. government agencies to transition key contractors to U.S. Government "term employee" status. For example, members of Human Terrain Teams—small teams of academic social scientists who support military units by engaging with the local population and "mapping" population characteristics and trends—were employed as contractors by BAE Systems. But in early 2009, reportedly in response to concerns about jurisdiction, the jobs were shifted to term appointments under the Department of the Army.[103]

Equipment

One of the key operational issues with great potential impact on costs is the future disposition of U.S. military equipment as U.S. forces draw down. Several factors, in combination, are likely to shape equipment disposition decisions:

- Costs: In some cases, it may be more expensive to ship an item home than to leave it behind and replace it.
- Support to the ISF: Some U.S. military equipment and supplies may be required by the ISF to further develop their force—or even urgently required by the ISF to help prosecute the current COIN fight.
- Support for the war in Afghanistan: Some equipment, no longer required in Iraq, may be needed by U.S. military forces in Afghanistan. For example, U.S. Army engineering assets, urgently needed in Afghanistan, may be sent directly from one theater to the other.
- Stockpiles for future contingencies: Some equipment—particularly heavy equipment—may remain stockpiled in the CENTCOM theater, to support possible future contingencies, pending approval by host nations.[104]
- Availability of Logistical Support: Redeploying equipment requires logistical support in the form of heavy equipment transports (HETs), whether military or commercial, to provide ground transportation; air assets; sea port capacity, including Kuwait and the Iraqi port of Um Qasr; as well as diplomatic permission from all other relevant host nations for basing, access, and/or overflight.

Options Available to Congress

A number of tools are available to Congress to help shape U.S. government policy toward Iraq, and the execution of that policy.[105] One tool is limiting or prohibiting funding for certain activities. For example, the *Duncan Hunter National Defense Authorization Act for Fiscal Year 2009* stated that no funding appropriated pursuant to authorizations in the Act could be used "to establish any military installation or base for the purpose of providing for the permanent stationing of United States Armed Forces in Iraq," or "to exercise United States control of the oil resources of Iraq."[106]

Congress may also make some funding contingent on achievement of certain milestones. For example, in the *Supplemental Appropriations Act, 2008* (P.L. 110-252), Congress required that funding under Chapter 4 of the Act, "Department of State and Foreign Operations," be made available for assistance to Iraq "only to the extent that the Government of Iraq matches such assistance on a dollar-for-dollar basis."[107]

More broadly, in the *U.S. Troop Readiness, Veterans' Care, Katrina Recovery, and Iraq Accountability Appropriations Act of 2007,* Congress established 18 benchmarks for the performance of the Government of Iraq, and provided that further U.S. strategy in Iraq would be conditioned on the Iraqi government's meeting those benchmarks.[108]

Another tool is holding oversight hearings, to ask Administration officials to account for the progress to date on policy implementation.

For example, on September 10, 2008, the House Armed Services Committee invited Secretary of Defense Robert Gates and Chairman of the Joint Chiefs of Staff Admiral Michael Mullen to testify at a hearing entitled "Security and Stability in Afghanistan and Iraq: Developments in U.S. Strategy and Operations and the Way Ahead." On September 23, 2008, the Senate Armed Services Committee held a hearing on the situation in Iraq and Afghanistan, with Secretary Gates and General James Cartwright, Vice Chairman of the Joint Chiefs of Staff.

Congress may also shape policy by establishing reporting requirements. For example, in the *Supplemental Appropriations Act, 2008* (P.L. 110-252), Congress required the Secretary of Defense to provide to Congress, every 90 days beginning not later than December 5, 2008, until the end of FY2009, a "comprehensive set of performance indicators and measures for progress toward military and political stability in Iraq." The *Act* lists detailed reporting requirements in two areas, stability and security in Iraq, and the training and performance of Iraqi security forces, and also required an assessment of "United States military requirements, including planned force rotations, through the end of calendar year 2009."[109]

Structure and Aim of the Report

This report is designed to support congressional consideration of future policy options for the war in Iraq by analyzing strategies pursued and outcomes achieved to date, by characterizing current dynamics on the ground in Iraq, and by identifying and analyzing key strategic and operational considerations going forward. The report will be updated as events warrant. Major topics addressed include the following:

- Analysis of future strategic and operational considerations.
- OIF war planning, including stated objectives, key debates in the major combat and post-major combat planning efforts, and the impact of apparent shortcomings in the planning efforts on post-war developments.
- Major combat operations, including both successes and challenges encountered.
- Post-major combat military activities—combat operations, Iraqi security forces training, and an array of "reconciliation," governance, and economic reconstruction efforts—including analysis of evolutions over time in strategy and approaches.
- Assessments of the results of strategy and operations to date.

DECISION TO GO TO WAR IN IRAQ

The Administration's decision to launch Operation Iraqi Freedom had antecedents stretching back to the 1991 Gulf War and its aftermath.

Antecedents in the 1990s

In the 1990's, the United States shared with other countries a concern with the Iraqi government's weapons of mass destruction (WMD) programs. Iraq had demonstrated a willingness to use WMD against its neighbors during the 1980-1988 Iran-Iraq war, and against its own citizens, as it did, for example, against Iraqi Kurds in Halabja in 1988. U.S. policy after the Gulf War supported the United Nations-led weapons inspection regime and the economic sanctions imposed to encourage Iraq's compliance with that regime. Before they were withdrawn in 1998, U.N. weapons inspectors located and destroyed sizable quantities of WMD in Iraq.

U.S. post-Gulf War policy also included containment initiatives—"no fly" zones—imposed by the United States together with the United Kingdom and, initially, France. The northern "no fly" zone, Operation Northern Watch was designed to protect the Iraqi Kurdish population in northern Iraq and international humanitarian relief efforts there. Operation Southern Watch was designed to protect the Shiite Arab population in southern Iraq.

These containment measures were periodically marked by Iraqi provocations, including troop build-ups and attempts to shoot down allied aircraft, and by allied responses including attacks on targets inside Iraq.[110] In December 1998, the United States and the United Kingdom launched Operation Desert Fox, whose stated purpose was to degrade Iraq's ability to manufacture or use WMD.

Also during the late 1990s, a policy climate more conducive to aggressive action against the Iraqi regime began to take shape in Washington, D.C., as some policy experts began to advocate actively fostering Iraqi resistance, in order to encourage regime change.[111] In 1998, Congress passed the Iraq Liberation Act, authorizing support to Iraqi opposition organizations.[112] Some supporters of this policy approach gained greater access, and in some cases office, under the Bush Administration after the 2000 presidential elections.

Bush Administration Strategy and Role of the United Nations

For many U.S. policy makers, the September 11, 2001, attacks catalyzed or heightened general concerns that WMD might fall into the hands of terrorists. Reflecting those concerns, the first National Security Strategy issued by the Bush Administration, in September 2002, highlighted the policy of preemptive, or anticipatory, action, to forestall hostile acts by adversaries, "even if uncertainty remains as to the time and place of the enemy's attack."[113]

Throughout 2002, the stated position of the Administration was to aggressively seek Iraqi compliance with U.N. Security Council Resolutions concerning the inspections regime, while holding out the possibility of U.N Chapter VII action if Iraq did not comply.[114] In September 2002, addressing the U.N. General Assembly, President Bush stated: "The Security Council Resolutions will be enforced ... or action will be unavoidable." On that occasion, President Bush also articulated a list of conditions that Iraq must meet if it wanted to avoid retaliatory action: give up or destroy all WMD and long-range missiles; end all support to terrorism; cease persecution of its civilian population; account for all missing Gulf War personnel and accept liability for losses; and end all illicit trade outside the oil-for-food program.[115]

On November 8, 2002, following intensive negotiations among its "Permanent 5" members,[116] the U.N. Security Council issued Resolution 1441. In it, the Council decided that Iraq remained in "material breach" of its obligations; that the Council would afford Iraq "a final opportunity to comply"; that failure to comply would "constitute a further material breach"; and that in that case, Iraq would "face serious consequences."[117]

This language, though strong by U.N. standards, was not considered by most observers to imply "automaticity"—that is, that Iraqi non-compliance would automatically trigger a U.N.-authorized response under Chapter VII.

While the Iraqi government eventually provided a large quantity of written materials, the Administration deemed Iraqi compliance to be insufficient. The Administration chose not to seek an additional U.N. Resolution explicitly authorizing military action under Chapter VII, reportedly due to concerns that some Permanent Members of the Council were prepared to veto it.

Ultimatum to Saddam Hussein

The Administration's intent to take military action against Iraq was formally made public on March 17, 2003, when President Bush issued an ultimatum to Saddam Hussein and his sons to leave Iraq within 48 hours. "Their refusal to do so," he said, would "result in military conflict."[118]

WAR PLANNING

As the Prussian military theorist Karl von Clausewitz wrote, war planning includes articulation of both intended goals and how they will be achieved.[119] In the case of Operation Iraqi Freedom, Administration goals included both short-term military objectives and longer-term strategic goals. To meet that intent, the Administration planned—though apparently in unequal measure—for both combat operations and the broader range of operations that would be required on "the day after" regime removal.

Strategic Objectives

The Administration's short-term goal for OIF was regime removal. As President Bush stated in his March 17, 2003, Address to the Nation, "It is too late for Saddam Hussein to remain in power." In that speech, he promised Iraqis, "We will tear down the apparatus of terror ... the tyrant will soon be gone."[120]

In his March 2003 speech, President Bush declared that in the longer term, the United States would help Iraqis build "a new Iraq that is prosperous and free." It would be an Iraq, as he described it, that would not be at war with its neighbors, and that would not abuse its own citizens.[121] Those were the basic "endstate" elements typically used by war planners. The U.S. Central Command (CENTCOM) OIF campaign plan, for example, described the strategic objective this way: "A stable Iraq, with its territorial integrity intact and a broad-based government that renounces WMD development and use and no longer supports terrorism or threatens its neighbors."[122]

Over time, the Administration's longer-term strategic objectives were fine-tuned. In the November 2005 *National Strategy for Victory in Iraq,* the Administration stated the long-term goal for Iraq this way: "Iraq is peaceful, united, stable, and secure, well-integrated into the international community, and a full partner in the global war on terrorism."[123]

In January 2007, at the time the "surge" was announced, the White House released an unclassified version of the results of its late 2006 internal review of Iraq policy. That document states: "Our strategic goal in Iraq remains the same: a unified, democratic, federal Iraq that can govern itself, defend itself, and sustain itself, and is an ally in the war on terror."[124]

In January 2009, in its regular quarterly update to the Congress, the Department of Defense (DOD) used almost the same language, with additional words to reflect the new security agreement: "The goal of the strategic partnership between the United States and Iraq remains a unified, democratic and federal Iraq that can govern, defend and sustain itself and is an ally in the war on terror."[125] In March 2009, in its first Iraq report issued under the Obama Administration, DOD stated: "The United States seeks an Iraq that is sovereign, stable, and self-reliant; an Iraqi Government that is just, representative, and accountable; neither a safe haven for, nor sponsor of, terrorism; integrated into the global economy; and a long-term partner contributing to regional peace and security."[126]

Military Objectives

To support the stated U.S. strategic objectives, CENTCOM, as it planned military operations in Iraq, defined the OIF military objectives this way: "destabilize, isolate, and overthrow the Iraqi regime and provide support to a new, broad-based government; destroy Iraqi WMD capability and infrastructure; protect allies and supporters from Iraqi threats and attacks; destroy terrorist networks in Iraq, gather intelligence on global terrorism, detain terrorists and war criminals, and free individuals unjustly detained under the Iraqi regime; and support international efforts to set conditions for long-term stability in Iraq and the region."[127]

Planning for Major Combat

From a military perspective, there are theoretically many different possible ways to remove a regime—using different capabilities, in different combinations, over different timelines. The 1991 Gulf War, for example, had highlighted the initial use of air power in targeting key regime infrastructure. The more recent war in Afghanistan had showcased a joint effort, as Special Operations Forces on the ground called in air strikes on key targets. Key debates in OIF major combat planning concerned the size of the force, the timelines for action, and the synchronization of ground and air power.

According to participants, throughout the planning process, Secretary of Defense Donald Rumsfeld played an active role, consistently urging the use of a streamlined force and a quick timeline.[128] Secretary Rumsfeld reportedly came into office with a vision of defense transformation, both operational and institutional.[129] A basic premise of that vision, captured in the 2002 *National Security Strategy*, was that "... the threats and enemies we must confront have changed, and so must our force."[130] In general, that meant transitioning from a military "structured to deter massive Cold War-era armies," to a leaner and more agile force. At issue in the OIF planning debates was not only how to fight the war in Iraq, but also—implicitly—how to organize, man, train and equip the force for the future.

For military planners, the guidance to use a streamlined force reflected a fundamental shift away from the Powell Doctrine, named after the former Chairman of the Joint Chiefs of Staff, which stressed that force, if used, should be overwhelming.[131]

The planning effort started early. Just before Thanksgiving, 2001, President Bush asked Secretary Rumsfeld to develop a plan for regime removal in Iraq, and Secretary Rumsfeld immediately gave that assignment to the commander of U.S. Central Command (CENTCOM), General Tommy Franks.[132]

The planning effort for combat operations was initially very "close hold," involving only a few key leaders and small groups of trusted planners at each level. As the effort progressed, the number of people involved grew, but key elements of the plans remained compartmentalized, such that few people had visibility on all elements of the plans.[133]

The starting point for the planning effort was the existing, "on the shelf" Iraq war plan, known as 1003-98, which had been developed and then refined during the 1990's. That plan called for a force of between 400,000 and 500,000 U.S. troops, including three Corps (or Corps equivalents), with a long timeline for the deployment and build-up of forces beforehand. When General Franks briefed Secretary Rumsfeld on these plans in late November 2001, Secretary Rumsfeld reportedly asked for a completely new version—with fewer troops and a faster deployment timeline.[134]

In early 2002, General Franks briefed Secretary Rumsfeld on the "Generated Start" plan. That plan called for very early infiltration by CIA teams, to build relationships and gain intelligence, and then the introduction of Special Operations Forces, particularly in northern Iraq and in Al Anbar province in the west. The main conventional forces effort would begin with nearsimultaneous air and ground attacks. The force would continue to grow up to about 275,000 troops.[135]

CENTCOM's air component—the Combined Force Air Component Command (CFACC)— reportedly urged modifying the plan to include a 10- to 14-day air campaign at the start, to target and hit Iraq's missile, radar, command and control, and other leadership sites, on the model of the Gulf War.[136] But the early introduction of ground forces—rather than an extended exclusively air campaign—was apparently intended to take Iraqi forces by surprise.[137]

Later in the spring of 2002, CENTCOM and subordinate planners developed an alternative plan called "Running Start," which addressed the possibility that the Iraqi regime might choose the war's start time through some provocation, such as the use of WMD. "Running start" called for a smaller overall force and a shorter timeline. It would still begin with infiltration by CIA teams, followed by the introduction of SOF. Air attacks would go first, and as ground forces flowed into theater, the ground attacks could begin any time after the first 25 days of air attacks. The ground war might begin with as few as 18,000 ground forces entering Iraq.[138]

In the summer of 2002, planners developed a so-called "hybrid" version of these two plans,[139] which echoed key elements of the "Running Start" plan—beginning with an air campaign, and launching the ground war while other ground forces still flowed into theater. Specifically, the plan called for: Presidential notification 5 days in advance; 11 days to flow forces; 16 days for the air campaign; the start of the ground campaign as ground forces continued to flow into theater; and a total campaign that would last up to 125 days. This plan, approved for action, continued to be known as the "5-11-16-125" plan even after the numbers of days had changed.[140]

By January 2003, at the CENTCOM Component Commanders Conference hosted by General Franks in Tampa, the plans had coalesced around a modified version of "Generated Start." They featured a very short initial air campaign, including bombs and missiles—a couple of days, rather than a couple of weeks. The ground campaign would begin with two three-star-led headquarters—U.S. Army V Corps, and the I Marine Expeditionary Force—and some of their forces crossing the line of departure from Kuwait into Iraq, while additional forces continued to flow into theater. Meanwhile, the 4th Infantry Division would open a northern front by entering Iraq from Turkey.

The number of forces that would start the ground campaign continued to be adjusted, generally downward, in succeeding days. On January 29, 2003, Army commanders learned that they would enter Iraq with just two Divisions—less than their plans to that point had reflected. At that time, V Corps and its subordinate commands were at a training site in Grafenwoehr, Germany, rehearsing the opening of the tactical-level ground campaign at an exercise called "Victory Scrimmage."

During that exercise, commanders and staff concluded that should they be required to "secure" cities in southern Iraq, they would have insufficient forces to do so.[141]

The V Corps Commander at the time, then-Lieutenant General William Scott Wallace, reflected after the end of major combat in Iraq: "I guess that as summer [arrived] I wasn't real comfortable with the troop levels."[142]

Post-War Planning

Most observers agree that the Administration's planning for "post-war" Iraq—for all the activities and resources that would be required on "the day after," to help bring about the strategic objective, a "free and prosperous Iraq"—was not nearly as thorough as the planning for combat operations.

For the U.S. military, the stakes of the post-war planning efforts were very high. In theory, civilian agencies would have the responsibility for using political, diplomatic, and economic tools to help achieve the desired political endstate for Iraq, while the Department of Defense and its military forces would play only a supporting role after the end of major combat operations. But by far the greatest number of coalition personnel on the ground in Iraq at the end of major combat would be U.S. military forces, and the U.S. military was very likely to become the default option for any unfilled roles and any unanticipated responsibilities.

A number of participants and observers have argued that the Administration should have sent a larger number of U.S. troops to Iraq, to provide security in the post-major combat period. Ambassador L. Paul Bremer, who served as the Administrator of the Coalition Provisional Authority (CPA) throughout the formal occupation of Iraq, leveled this criticism after departing Iraq. Asked what he would have changed about the occupation, he replied: "The single most important change—the one thing that would have improved the situation—would have been having more troops in Iraq at the beginning and throughout."[143]

A logical fallacy in the number-of-troops critique is that "How many troops do you need?" is not an especially meaningful question, unless what those troops will be expected to do is clarified. By many accounts, the OIF post-war planning process did not provide commanders, before the start of combat operations, with a clear picture of the extent of their assigned post-war responsibilities.[144]

Inter-Agency Post-War Planning

A primary focus of the interagency post-war-planning debates was who would be in charge in Iraq, on "the day after." For the military, decisions by the Administration about who would do what would help clarify the military's own roles and responsibilities. Before making such decisions—in particular, what responsibilities would be carried out by Iraqis—the Administration cultivated Iraqi contacts.

Based on months of negotiations, in conjunction with the government of the United Kingdom, the Administration helped sponsor a series of conferences of Iraqi oppositionists, including expatriates and some Iraqis—notably Iraqi Kurds—who could come and go from their homes. The events included a major conference in London in December 2002, and a follow-on event in Salahuddin, Iraq, in February 2003.[145] At these events, Iraqi oppositionists agreed on a political statement and self-nominated a "leadership council," bu the events did not directly produce U.S. policy decisions about post-war roles and responsibilities.[146]

During the same time frame, the Departments of State and Defense were locked in debate about post-war political plans for Iraq. The State Department supported a deliberate political process, including slowly building new political institutions, based on the rule of law, while, in the meantime, Iraqis would serve only in advisory capacities. Through the second half of 2002, the State Department's "Future of Iraq" project brought together Iraqi oppositionists and experts, in a series of working groups, to consider an array of potential post-war challenges. While a tacit goal of the project was to identify some Iraqis who might serve in future leadership positions, it was not designed to produce a slate of leaders-in-waiting.[147] The project was also not designed to produce formal plans. However, some of the ideas it generated did reportedly help operationallevel military planners refine their efforts, and the project might have had a greater impact had more of its output reached the planners.[148]

The Department of Defense (DOD)—more specifically and accurately the Office of the Secretary of Defense (OSD)—favored putting Iraqis in charge of Iraq, in some form, as soon as possible, based loosely on the model of Afghanistan. A "real" Iraqi leadership with real power, some officials believed, might find favor with the Iraqi people and with neighboring states, and might shorten the length of the U.S. commitment in Iraq.[149] As Secretary Rumsfeld reportedly told President Bush in August 2002, "We will want to get Iraqis in charge of Iraq as soon as possible."[150]

In the fall of 2002, no clear decision emerged about the role of Iraqis in immediate post-war Iraq. Discussions among senior leaders apparently focused on the concept of a U.S.-led "transitional civil administration" that would govern, or help govern, Iraq. However, no agreement was reached at that time about what authority such a body would have, what its responsibilities would be, how long it would last, or which Iraqis would be involved.[151]

In January 2003, Administration thinking coalesced around a broad post-war political process for Iraq, captured in what was universally known at the time as the "mega-brief." The approach favored the State Department's preference for a deliberate process that would give Iraqi post- Saddam political life a chance to develop organically, but it also acknowledged DOD's concern to provide a visible Iraqi leadership—though very weakly empowered—as soon as possible. The "mega-brief" process would include creating a senior-level Iraqi Consultative Council (ICC) to serve in an advisory capacity; dismissing top Iraqi leaders from the Saddam era but welcoming most lower-ranking officials to continue to serve; creating an Iraqi judicial council; holding a national census; conducting municipal elections; holding elections to a constitutional convention that would draft a constitution; carrying out a constitutional referendum; and then holding national elections. It was envisaged that the process would take years to complete.[152]

The "mega-brief" approach—which gained currency just as U.S. troops were conducting final rehearsals for the war—implied that many governance tasks would need to be performed by coalition (non-Iraqi) personnel, whether civilian or military, for some time to come.[153]

Military Post-War Planning

Military commanders and planners typically base operational plans on policy assumptions and clearly specify those assumptions at the beginning of any plans briefing. For OIF planners, the critical policy assumptions concerned who would have which post-war roles and responsibilities. OIF preparations reversed the usual sequence, in that military planning began long before the key policy debates, let alone policy conclusions.

During their planning process, military commanders apparently sought to elicit the policy guidance they needed by briefing their policy assumptions and hoping for a response.[154] In December 2001, in his first OIF brief to President Bush, General Franks included as one element of the mission: "establish a provisional Iraqi government," but this measure was neither confirmed nor rejected. General Franks wrote later that as he briefed this to the President, he had in mind the Bonn Conference for Afghanistan.[155] In August 2002, still without a policy decision about post-war responsibilities, CENTCOM included in its war plans briefing the assumption: "DoS [Department of State] will promote creation of a broad-based, credible provisional government prior to D-Day."[156]

Unable to determine what Iraqi civilian structure they would be asked to support, the military sought to elicit guidance about the coalition's own post-war architecture and responsibilities. According to General Franks, the CENTCOM war plans slides briefed to President Bush and the National Security Council on August 5, 2002, included the intentionally provocative phrase, "military administration," but no decision about post-war architecture was made at that time.[157]

Two months later, the OIF plans slides included, for the first time, a full wiring diagram of the coalition's post-war structure, describing post-war responsibilities in a "military administration." A "Joint Task Force" would be responsible for security, a civilian "High Commissioner" would be responsible for all other functions; and both would report to CENTCOM. This chart still failed to prompt a decision, although Office of the Secretary of Defense staff reportedly spent the ensuing weeks considering "High Commissioner" candidates, just in case.[158]

By late 2002, in the absence of detailed policy guidance, military commanders at several levels had launched "Phase IV" planning efforts, to identify and begin to prepare for potential post-war requirements. In January 2003, based on a recommendation that came out of the "Internal Look" exercise conducted in Kuwait in December 2002, Brigadier General Steve Hawkins was named to lead a new "Task Force IV." TFIV, an ad hoc organization, was tasked to conduct post-war planning, and to prepare to deploy to Baghdad as the nucleus of a post-war headquarters. TFIV was dispatched immediately to Kuwait, to work under the operational control of the Combined Forces Land Component Command (CFLCC)—the ground forces component of CENTCOM— and its commanding general, Lieutenant General David McKiernan.[159] TFIV thus provided skilled labor, but no connectivity to the still on-going Washington policy debates about the post-war division of responsibilities.

In March 2003, CFLCC launched a dedicated post-war planning effort of its own, led by Major General Albert Whitley (UK), who was part of the CFLCC leadership. His more comprehensive effort—known as Eclipse II—benefitted from close connectivity with its sister-effort, CFLCC's combat operations planning, but lacked direct access to the broader Washington policy debates.

In addition to lacking policy guidance about post-war roles and responsibilities, these operationallevel planning efforts lacked insight into key aspects of the current state of affairs in Iraq. For example, planning assumed that Iraqis, in particular law enforcement personnel, would be available and willing to resume some civic duties on the "day after." Also, plans did not recognize the deeply degraded status of Iraqi infrastructure, such as electricity grids.

Organizational Decisions

On January 20, 2003, by National Security Presidential Directive 24, the President created the Organization for Reconstruction and Humanitarian Assistance (ORHA), to serve first as the postwar planning office in the Pentagon, and then to deploy to Iraq. Throughout, ORHA would report to the Department of Defense. Retired Army Lieutenant General Jay Garner, who had led Operation Provide Comfort in northern Iraq after the Gulf War, was appointed to lead ORHA. He quickly brought on board a team of other retired Army general officers to serve in key leadership positions.[160]

ORHA held its founding conference on February 20 and 21, 2003, at the National Defense University. Participants included the fledgling ORHA staff, representatives of civilian agencies that would contribute to the effort, and representatives of the military commands—long since deployed to Kuwait—that would become ORHA's partners.

As briefed at NDU, ORHA would be responsible for three pillars of activity in post-war Iraq— Civil Affairs, Humanitarian Affairs, and Reconstruction—while the military would be responsible for security. Those ORHA efforts would commence in each area as soon as major combat operations ended. The most important constraint was time—the civilian agencies were not organized or resourced to be able to provide substantial resources or personnel by the start of major combat operations.

ORHA's command relationships with other Department of Defense bodies were initially a topic of dispute. During ORHA's "post-war planning office" days inside the Pentagon, General Garner reported directly to Secretary Rumsfeld. It was generally agreed that, once in the field, ORHA would fall under CENTCOM. CFLCC insisted that ORHA would also fall under CFLCC, but ORHA resisted that arrangement.[161]

Shortly after the founding conference at NDU, ORHA deployed to Kuwait with a skeleton staff and limited resources, and set up its headquarters at the Kuwait Hilton.

MAJOR COMBAT OPERATIONS

Major combat operations in Iraq, launched in March 2003, roughly followed the course that had been outlined at the CENTCOM Component Commanders Conference in January that year. The coalition force was both joint—with representatives from all the U.S. military services—and combined—with participants from coalition partner countries.[162]

Early Infiltration

As long planned, the effort had actually begun before the full-scale launch, with early infiltration into Iraq by the CIA, including the so-called Northern and Southern Iraq Liaison Elements (NILE and SILE), whose task was to gather intelligence, form relationships, and lay the groundwork for the early entry of Special Operations Forces (SOF).[163]

SOF, in turn, had also entered Iraq before the formal launch. Among other missions, SOF secured bases in Al Anbar province in western Iraq, secured suspected WMD sites, pursued some of the designated "high-value targets," and worked closely with Iraqi Kurdish forces in northern Iraq— the *pesh merga*—to attack a key stronghold of the designated Foreign Terrorist Organization, Ansar al-Islam.[164] Special operations forces in OIF, like the conventional forces, were both joint and combined—including contingents from the United Kingdom, Australia and Poland. Defense expert Andrew Krepinevich estimated that "nearly 10,000" SOF took part in OIF major combat.[165]

The Launch

The visible public launch of OIF took place on March 20, 2003, shortly after the expiration of President Bush's 48-hour ultimatum to Saddam Hussein and his sons (see above, "Ultimatum to Saddam Hussein").[166] After months of debate about the sequencing of the air and ground campaigns, the planned sequence shifted in two major ways at the last minute.

By early 2003, the plans called for beginning with a short air-only campaign, followed by the ground invasion. However, late-breaking evidence gave rise to stronger concerns that the Iraqi regime would deliberately destroy its southern oil wells, so the timing of the ground forces launch was moved up, ahead of the scheduled air campaign launch.

Then, even closer to launch time, the CIA obtained what seemed to be compelling information about Saddam Hussein's location—at Dora Farms near Baghdad. In the early hours of March 20, just as the ultimatum expired, a pair of F-117 fighters targeted the site. That attack narrowly followed a barrage of Tomahawk missiles, launched from ships at key leadership sites in Baghdad.

That night, coalition ground forces crossed the line of departure from the Kuwaiti desert into southern Iraq. The following day, March 21, 2003, brought the larger-scale "shock and awe" attacks on Iraqi command and control and other sites, from both Air Force and Navy assets. Early Iraqi responses included setting a few oil wells on fire, and firing a few poorly directed missiles into Kuwait, most of which were successfully intercepted by Patriot missiles.[167]

The Ground Campaign

The ground campaign was led by Army Lieutenant General David McKiernan, the Commanding General of the Combined Forces Land Component Command (CFLCC), the ground component of CENTCOM. The strategy was a quick, two-pronged push from Kuwait up through southern Iraq to Baghdad.

Under CFLCC, the ground "main effort" was led by U.S. Army V Corps, under Lieutenant General William Scott Wallace. V Corps was assigned the western route up to Baghdad, west of the Euphrates River.[168] Meanwhile, the 1st Marine Expeditionary Force (IMEF), led by Lieutenant General James Conway, was assigned the eastern route, closer to the border with Iran. From a tactical perspective, for both the Army and the Marines this was a very long projection of force— over 600 kilometers from Kuwait up to Baghdad, and more for those units that pushed further north to Tikrit or to Mosul. Those long distances reportedly strained capabilities including logistics and communications.

The Marines were assigned the eastern route up to Baghdad—with more urban areas than the Army's western route. The basic strategy still called for a quick drive to Baghdad. Just across the border into Iraq, IMEF took the far southern port city of Umm Qasr.

The UK First Armored Division, which fell under IMEF, was tasked to take Basra, Iraq's second largest city. The UK Division faced resistance from members of the paramilitary force Saddam Fedayeen and others still loyal to the Ba'ath Party. To limit casualties in the large urban area, rather than enter the city immediately in full force, the Division used a more methodical elimination of opponents, combined with outreach to the population to explain their intentions. IMEF supported the Division's use of a slow and deliberate tempo. After several weeks of gradual attrition, the Division pushed into Basra on April 6, 2003.

The main IMEF force encountered some resistance as they pushed north, in particular at the town of Nassiriyah, a geographical choke-point. At Nassiriyah, "there were a number of things that seemed to hit us all about the same time, that dented our momentum," LtGen Conway later noted. There, the Marines suffered casualties from a friendly fire incident with Apaches. As widely reported, the Army's 507th Maintenance Company lost its way in the area and stumbled into an ambush, in which some personnel were killed and others, including PFC Jessica Lynch, were taken hostage. The area was blanketed by fierce desert sandstorms. And the Saddam Fedayeen put up a determined resistance—"not a shock, but a surprise," as LtGen Conway later reflected. Evidence suggested that additional Iraqi fighters, inspired by the ambush carried out by the Fedayeen, came from Baghdad to Nassiriyah to join the fight.[169] After the defeating the resistance at Nassiriyah, the Marines pushed up to Baghdad along their eastern route.

In the west, the Army faced a longer distance but a less-populated terrain. V Corps began combat operations with two divisions under its command, the Third Infantry Division (3ID), under Major General Buford Blount, and the 101st Airborne Division (101st), under Major General David Petraeus.

The 3ID rapidly led the western charge to Baghdad, moving speedily through the south and reaching Saddam International Airport on April 4. The division launched its first "thunder run"— a fast, armored strike—into Baghdad on April 5, and the second on April 7. The purpose of the first, according to the Brigade Commander in charge, Colonel David Perkins, was "to create as much confusion as I can inside the city." The purpose of the second was "to make sure, in no uncertain terms, that people knew the city had fallen and we were in charge of it."[170]

The 101st followed the 3ID up the western route through southern Iraq, clearing resistance in southern cities and allowing the 3ID to move as quickly as possible. Soldiers from the 101st faced fighting in key urban areas—Hillah, Najaf, Karbala. Just after mid-April, the division arrived and set up its headquarters in Mosul, in northern Iraq.[171]

Like the Marines, the Army was somewhat surprised by the resistance they encountered from the Saddam Fedayeen. LTG Wallace apparently caused some consternation at higher headquarters levels with his candid remarks to the press in late March: "The enemy we're fighting is different from the one we'd war-gamed against." He explained, "The attacks we're seeing are bizarre—technical vehicles with .50 calibers and every kind of weapon charging tanks and Bradleys."[172] Coupled with major sand storms, these attacks posed challenges to the ground forces' long supply lines—"lines of communication"—running up from Kuwait over hundreds of miles through southern Iraq.[173]

In the north, on March 26, 2003, about 1,000 soldiers from the 173rd Airborne Brigade, part of the Army's Southern European Task Force based in Italy, parachuted into northern Iraq. They began their mission by securing an airfield so that cargo planes carrying tanks and Bradleys could land. Once on the ground, the 173rd, working closely with air and ground Special Operating Forces and with Kurdish *pesh merga* forces, expanded the northern front of OIF.

Initial coalition plans had called for the heavy 4th Infantry Division (4ID) to open the northern front by crossing into Iraq from Turkey. The intended primary mission was challenging Iraqi regular army forces based above Baghdad. A more subtle secondary mission was to place limits on possible Kurdish ambitions to control more territory in northern Iraq, thus providing some reassurance to the Government of Turkey and discouraging it from sending Turkish forces into Iraq to restrain the Kurds.

By early 2003, 4ID equipment was sitting on ships circling in the eastern Mediterranean Sea, waiting for an outcome of the ongoing negotiations with the Turkish government. But on March 1, 2003, the Turkish parliament rejected a proposal that would have allowed the 4ID to use Turkish territory.

Iraqi Contributions to Major Combat

Iraqi opposition fighters made a very limited contribution to coalition major combat efforts. Before the war, the Office of the Secretary of Defense had launched an ambitious program to recruit and train up to 3,000 Iraqi expats, to be known as the "Free Iraqi Forces." Training, by U.S. forces, took place in Taszar, Hungary. Ultimately, the number of recruits and graduates was much lower than originally projected. Most graduates did deploy to Iraq, where they served with U.S. forces primarily as interpreters or working with local communities on civil affairs projects.[174]

Meanwhile, in late March 2003, Iraqi expatriate oppositionist Ahmed Chalabi contacted U.S. officials with a request to send a group of his own fighters from northern to southern Iraq to join the fight. After some discussion, agreement was reached and a U.S. military flight was arranged. In early April, Chalabi and 600 fighters stepped off the plane at Tallil air base in southern Iraq. The forces were neither equipped nor well-organized. Accounts from many observers, in succeeding months, suggested that some members of the group engaged in lawless behavior.[175]

End of Major Combat

On April 9, 2003, the statue of Saddam Hussein in Firdos square in Baghdad was toppled. Two days after the second 3ID "thunder run," this event signaled for many observers, inside and outside Iraq, that the old Iraqi regime had ended.

Consistent with the war plans from "Generated Start" onward, U.S. forces continued to flow into Iraq. The 4th Infantry Division (4ID), diverted from its original northern front plans, had re-routed its troops and equipment to Kuwait. 4ID forces began entering Iraq on April 12, 2003. The 1st Armored Division (1AD) also began arriving in April 2003. According to the planning, the 1st Cavalry Division (1CD) was scheduled to be next in line. However, in April 2003, Secretary Rumsfeld, in coordination with General Franks, made the decision that 1CD was not needed in Iraq at that time—a decision that apparently caused consternation for some ground commanders.[176]

As soon as it became apparent that the old regime was no longer exercising control, widespread looting took place in Baghdad and elsewhere. Targets included government buildings, and the former houses of regime leaders, but also some private businesses and cultural institutions.Leaders of the Iraqi National Museum in Baghdad reported, for example, that "looters had taken or destroyed 170,000 items of antiquity dating back thousands of years."[177] Looters and vandals also targeted unguarded weapons stockpiles largely abandoned by former Iraqi security forces.[178] Some observers and coalition participants suggested that the coalition simply did not have enough troops to stop all the unlawful behavior.[179]

Meanwhile, U.S. senior leadership attention had turned to Iraq's political future. In April, the President's "Special Envoy for Free Iraqis," Ambassador Zalmay Khalilzad, chaired two "big tent" meetings of Iraqis. The first was held on April 15, 2003, at the ancient city of Ur, near Tallil air base, and the second was held on April 28, at the Baghdad Convention Center. Participants include expatriate opposition leaders and Iraqi Kurds, together with a number of in-country community leaders who had been identified by the CIA and other sources. The sessions focused on discussion of broad principles for Iraq's future, rather than specific decisions about Iraqi leadership roles.[180]

On May 1, 2003, President Bush, standing aboard the USS Abraham Lincoln, declared an end to major combat operations in Iraq. He stated, "In the battle of Iraq, the United States and our allies have prevailed."[181] At that point, the old Iraqi regime, though not completely dismantled, was no longer able to exercise control over Iraq's territory, resources, or population. Saddam Hussein was captured later, on December 13, 2003, by units of 4ID, outside his hometown Tikrit.

POST-MAJOR COMBAT: BASIS AND ORGANIZATION

This Report uses the term "post-major combat" to refer to the period from the President's announcement of the end of major combat, on May 1, 2003, to the present. This period has not been monolithic—it has included evolutions in national and military strategy, and in the specific "ways and means" used to pursue those strategies on the ground, as described below. From a political and legal perspective, the major marker after May 1, 2003, was the June 28, 2004, transition of executive authority from the occupying powers back to Iraqis. From a military perspective, the period after May 1, 2003, has included a continuation of combat operations as well as the introduction of many new missions.

Legal Basis for Coalition Presence

Formal Occupation

From the time of regime removal until June 28, 2004, the coalition was formally an occupying force. Shortly after the end of major combat, in May 2003, the United Nations Security Council recognized the United States and the United Kingdom as "occupying powers," together with all the "authorities, responsibilities, and obligations under international law" that this designation entails.[182] Somewhat belatedly, in October 2003, the United Nations authorized a "multi-national force under unified command to take all necessary measures to contribute to the maintenance of security and stability in Iraq."[183] That language referred to the coalition military command in Iraq at the time—the Combined Joint Task Force-7 ("CJTF-7").

Iraqi Request for a Multinational Force

As the deadline for the "transfer of sovereignty"—June 30, 2004—approached, U.S. and new interim Iraqi officials negotiated the terms for the presence and activities in Iraq, after that date, of the newly re-organized multi-national force, now called the Multi-National Force-Iraq ("MNFI").

Agreement was reached to reflect the terms of that presence in the unusual form of parallel letters, one from U.S. Secretary of State Colin Powell, and one from Iraqi Prime Minister Ayad Allawi, to the President of the UN Security Council. Those letters were appended to U.N. Security Council Resolution 1546, issued on June 8, 2004.[184]

That U.N. Resolution reaffirmed the authorization for the multi-national force and extended it to the post-occupation period—on the grounds that it was "at the request of the incoming Interim Government of Iraq."[185] It repeated the authorization language used in the October 2003 Resolution, with an important qualifier: the force was now authorized to "take all necessary measures to contribute to the maintenance of security and stability in Iraq *in accordance with* the letters annexed to this resolution."[186]

The U.S. letter spelled out the tasks the multi-national force would undertake, including combat operations, internment, securing of weapons, training and equipping Iraqi security forces, and participating in providing humanitarian assistance, civil affairs support, and relief and reconstruction assistance.

Some of the early U.S.-Iraqi discussions had considered the possibility that Iraqi forces might, in some cases, fall under the command of the multinational force.[187] However, the U.N. Resolution and the appended letters made clear that the command-and-control relationship between the Iraqi government and the multi-national force would be strictly one of coordination, not command. The Resolution called the relationship a "security partnership between the sovereign Government of Iraq and the multinational force."[188]

Both letters described coordination modalities to help ensure unity of effort. Both stated the intention to make use of "coordination bodies at the national, regional, and local levels," and noted that multi-national force and Iraqi officials would "keep each other informed of their activities."

Further parameters of the MNF-I presence in Iraq were spelled out in a revised version of Order 17 of the Coalition Provisional Authority, issued on June 27, 2004. The document addressed issues including legal immunities, communications, transportation, customs, entry and departure, for government civilians and contractors as well as military forces. Issued by the legal executive authority of Iraq at the time, the Order was to remain in force "for the duration of U.N. Resolution mandates including subsequent Resolutions, unless rescinded or amended by Iraqi legislation."[189]

Security Agreement

The final U.N. authorization, issued on December 18, 2007, extended through December 31, 2008. In requesting that authorization, in a letter appended to the UN Resolution, Iraqi Prime Minister Nuri al-Maliki made clear that it would be the final request by the Government of Iraq for an extension of the current mandate. The Iraqi Government, he wrote, "expects, in future, that the Security Council will be able to deal with the situation in Iraq without the need for action under Chapter VII of the Charter of the United Nations."[190] In November 2008, the U.S. and Iraqi governments concluded a new status of forces-like agreement – the "security agreement" – which took effect on January 1, 2009, and which defines the legal terms of the presence of U.S. military forces, and the civilians who support them, in Iraq.[191]

Coalition Command Relationships

Since the declared end of major combat operations, the formal relationships among U.S. military and civilian organizations operating in Iraq have shifted several times, in important ways.

The period of formal occupation was characterized by multiple, somewhat confusing relationships.[192] In late April 2003, LTG McKiernan, Commanding General of the Combined Forces Land Component Command (CFLCC), issued a proclamation stating: "The coalition alone retains absolute authority within Iraq."[193] CFLCC, the military face of the coalition in Iraq, maintained a small headquarters presence in Baghdad, at the Al Faw Palace at Camp Victory, while the majority of its staff remained in their pre-war location at Camp Doha, Kuwait.

The civilian face of the coalition in Iraq, in that time frame, was the Organization for Reconstruction and Humanitarian Assistance (ORHA), whose small staff had arrived in Baghdad in late April. The basic civil-military division of labor was clear—CFLCC was responsible for security, while ORHA focused on reconstruction and humanitarian issues. The command relationship between the two, debated before the war, was never clearly resolved during the very short duration of their partnership on the ground in Iraq.

In early May 2003, President Bush announced his intention to appoint a senior official to serve as Administrator of a new organization, the Coalition Provisional Authority, which would serve as the legal executive authority of Iraq—a much more authoritative mandate than ORHA had held. On May 9, 2003, Ambassador L. Paul "Jerry" Bremer arrived in Baghdad with a small retinue, to take up the assignment. By mandate, Ambassador Bremer reported through the Secretary of Defense to the President. Later, in fall 2003, the White House assumed the lead for coordinating efforts in Iraq, and Ambassador Bremer's direct contacts with the White House became even more frequent.

On June 15, 2003, the headquarters of U.S. Army V Corps, now led by Lieutenant General Ricardo Sanchez, assumed the coalition military leadership mantle from CFLCC— and the new body was named the CJTF-7.[194] CJTF-7 reported directly to CENTCOM, and through it to the Secretary of Defense. At the same time, CJTF-7 served in "direct support" to CPA.[195] In the view of many observers, that dual chain of command and accountability was not a recipe for success— particularly when the CENTCOM Commanding General and the CPA Administrator disagreed with each other. In May 2004, CJTF-7 separated into a higher, strategically focused headquarters, the Multi-National Force-Iraq (MNF-I), still led by LTG Sanchez, and a lower, operationally focused headquarters, the Multi-National Corps-Iraq (MNC-I). MNF-I retained CJTF-7's "direct support" relationship with CPA until the end of the formal occupation.

CJTF-7 itself was a combined force, including a UK Deputy Commanding General, and many key staff members, as well as contingents, from coalition partner countries. As a rule, those representatives maintained direct communication with their respective capitals. CPA, too, was "combined," including a senior UK official who shared the leadership role, though not executive signing authority, with Ambassador Bremer, and who maintained a regular and full channel of communication with the UK government in London.

On June 28, 2004, at the "transfer of sovereignty," the Coalition Provisional Authority ceased to exist. The new U.S. Embassy, led by Ambassador John Negroponte, inherited none of CPA's executive authority for Iraq—like other U.S. Embassies around the world, it simply represented U.S. interests in Iraq. The relationship between the Embassy and MNF-I—led by General George Casey beginning on July 1, 2004—was strictly one of coordination.

POST-MAJOR COMBAT: THE FORCE

The Multi-National Force-Iraq (MNF-I), like its predecessor CJTF-7, is a joint, combined force. It includes some Department of Defense civil servants, and it is supported by civilian contractors.

Structure and Footprint

The MNF-I headquarters, located in Baghdad, is the strategic-level headquarters, currently led, as of September 16, 2008, by U.S. Army General Raymond Odierno. The position of MNF-I Deputy Commanding General (DCG) has always been filled by a general officer from the United Kingdom—since March 2009, Lieutenant General Chris Brown has served simultaneously as MNF-I DCG and Senior British Military Representative to Iraq. The MNF-I staff is an ad hoc headquarters, including senior leaders and staff provided individually by the U.S. military services and by coalition partner countries.

The Multi-National Corps-Iraq (MNC-I), also located in Baghdad, is the operational-level headquarters, reporting to MNF-I.[196] Its role is synchronizing coalition forces actions throughout Iraq. MNC-I is built around a U.S. Army Corps. As of April 2009, the nucleus of MNC-I is I Corps, led by Army Lieutenant General Charles Jacoby, which replaced the XVIII Airborne Corps led by Lieutenant General Lloyd Austin. In each rotation, the Army Corps staff is augmented by additional U.S. and coalition partner senior leaders and staff.

The structure and staffing of both MNF-I and MNC-I have evolved significantly from the early days of OIF. When U.S. Army V Corps became the nucleus of CJTF-7, in June 2003, its pre-war planning and exercising, and its OIF wartime experience, had been focused on the tactical-level ground campaign. Its senior staff positions were filled by Colonels; those senior positions were only gradually filled by General Officers over the course of summer and fall 2003.

Under the command of MNC-I, Divisions or their equivalents are responsible for contiguous areas covering all of Iraq. The boundaries of the divisional areas of responsibility have shifted somewhat over time, to accommodate both shifting security requirements and major changes in deployments by coalition partner countries.

U.S. Forces in Iraq

The total number of U.S. forces in Iraq peaked early, during major combat operations, at about 250,000 troops. Since then, the number has varied greatly over time, in response to events on the ground, such as Iraqi elections, and to strategic-level decisions, such as the 2007 surge. The peak surge level of U.S. troops was about 168,000, in October 2007, up from a relative low of 135,000 troops in January 2007 just before surge forces began to arrive.

As of February 1, 2009, the total number of U.S. troops in Iraq was about 146,000.[197] The lower total, compared to October 2007, reflects the redeployment from Iraq without replacement of all five of the Army's "surge" brigades: the 2nd brigade combat team (BCT) of the 82nd Airborne Division; the 4th BCT of the 1st Infantry Division; the 3rd BCT of the 3rd Infantry Division; the 4th BCT of the 2nd Infantry Division; and the 2nd BCT of the 3rd Infantry Division.

In September 2008, President Bush had announced that an additional Army BCT would withdraw from Iraq, in early 2009, without replacement. In November 2008, DOD announced that that unit—the 2nd BCT of the 101st Airborne Division, based in western Baghdad—would redeploy about six weeks earlier than planned. Their departure left 14 U.S. BCTs or BCT-equivalents in Iraq, before President Obama's February 2009 announcement of his Iraq drawdown and transition policy.

Well before the surge, by many accounts, the demand for forces in Iraq had placed some stress on both the active and reserve components. The operational benefits of maintaining continuity, and keeping forces in place long enough to gain understanding and develop expertise, competed against institutional requirements to maintain the health of the force as a whole, including the ability to recruit and retain personnel.

An additional challenge was that pre-war assumptions only very incompletely predicted the scope and scale of post-war mission requirements, which meant in practice, especially early in OIF, that individuals and units deployed without certainty about the length of their tours. U.S. Army V Corps, for example, was not specifically given the mission, before the war, to serve as the postwar task force headquarters, let alone a timeline for that commitment. As the press widely reported after the end of major combat operations, some members of the 3rd Infantry Division (3ID), which had led the Army's charge to Baghdad, publicly stated their desire to redeploy as soon as possible. Major General Buford Blount, the 3ID Commanding General, commented: "You know, a lot of my forces have been over here since September, and fought a great fight and [are] doing great work here in the city. But if you ask the soldiers, they're ready to go home."[198]

Sometimes, changes in the security situation on the ground—rather than anticipated political events like Iraqi elections—have prompted decisions to extend deployments. The earliest and possibly most dramatic example took place in April 2004. The young Shiite cleric Muqtada al-Sadr and his militia, the *Jaish al-Mahdi* (Mahdi Army), staged uprisings in cities and towns throughout Shi'a-populated southern Iraq, just as the volatile, Sunni-populated city of Fallujah, in Al Anbar province, simmered in the wake of the gruesome murders of four Blackwater contractors. The 1st Armored Division (1AD), which had served in Baghdad for one year, and was already in the process of redeploying, was extended by 90 days—and then executed a remarkable series of complex and rapid troop deployments to embattled southern cities.

In early 2007, in an effort to provide greater predictability if not lighter burdens, the Department of Defense, under the leadership of Secretary of Defense Robert Gates, announced new rotation policy goals. Active units would deploy for not more than 15 months, and return to home station for not less than 12 months.[199] Reserve Component units would mobilize for a maximum of 12 months, including pre- and post-deployment responsibilities, rather than 12 months of "boots on the ground," with the goal of five years between deployments.[200]

In April 2008, partly in anticipation of some reduction of stress on the force from the redeployment of the surge brigades, President Bush announced that active component Army units deploying after August 1, 2008, would deploy for 12 months, rather than 15. The President also recommitted to "...ensur[ing] that our Army units will have at least a year at home for every year in the field."[201]

Coalition Partner Forces[202]

Since its inception, OIF has been a multinational effort, but the number, size, and nature of contributions by coalition partner countries has varied substantially over time.

Four countries provided boots on the ground for major combat—the United Kingdom, Australia, and Poland, in addition to the United States. Coalition forces contributions then reached their peak, in terms of the number of both countries and troops contributed, in the early post-major combat period. After that period, some countries withdrew their forces altogether. A number of other countries, as they reduced their contributions, withdrew the bulk of their contingents, but left a few personnel in Iraq to serve in headquarters staff positions.

Past decisions to draw down forces may have been shaped, in some cases, by a perception that the mission had been accomplished. However, far more frequently, decisions seem to have been informed by domestic political considerations, sometimes coupled with apparent pressure from extremists seeking to shape those decisions. Most notable was the Spanish troop withdrawal, catalyzed by the March 11, 2004, commuter train bombings in Madrid, which killed nearly 200 people. The attacks took place just days before scheduled Spanish parliamentary elections, in which the ruling party of Prime Minister Jose Maria Aznar Lopez, who had supported OIF, was voted out of office. The new Prime Minister, Jose Luis Rodriguez Zapatero, gave orders, within hours after being sworn into office, for Spanish troops to come home from Iraq.

In 2008, several major contributors redeployed or significantly drew down their forces. In June, Australia withdrew its battle group of combat forces, which had been based at Tallil Air Base in Nassiriyah province, in southern Iraq, but other Australian troops continued to serve in and around Iraq, including providing maritime surveillance, intelligence assistance, and logistics operations.[203] In August, Georgia withdrew its 2,000-strong contingent, which had been deployed in Wasit province along the border with Iran, after Russian troops invaded Georgia. In October, Poland withdrew its remaining contingent of about 900 soldiers from Qadisiyah province in southern Iraq, where Poland had led the Multi-National Division Center-South. And in December, the Republic of Korea concluded its deployment in northern Iraq, focused on reconstruction, as the nucleus of Multi-National Division-North East.

As of December 2008, the largest remaining non-U.S. coalition partner was the United Kingdom, which had approximately 4,100 troops on the ground and continued to lead Multi-National Division-Southeast, headquartered in Basra. That month, however, British defense officials indicated that the UK contingent would draw down to 400 by summer 2009.[204]

The expiration of the UN mandate as of December 31, 2008, forced all remaining coalition partners either to negotiate a bilateral status of forces agreement with the Government of Iraq, or to withdraw their forces. Most remaining partners chose to bring their deployments to a close. In December, the GoI signed agreements with the UK and Australian governments, authorizing their troops to remain in Iraq for the first six months of 2009.[205] In late January, the Governments of Iraq and Romania reached agreement on the continued deployment of approximately 350 Romanian troops.[206] Both Estonia and El Salvador reportedly sought to reach agreements with the GoI but ultimately decided to withdraw their contingents.[207]

In addition to MNF-I, foreign troops serve in two other organizations in Iraq. One of those is the NATO Training Mission-Iraq (NTM-I), which falls under the dual supervision of MNF-I and NATO. As of January 2009, 14 countries were contributing staff to NTM-I in theater, including: Bulgaria, Denmark, Estonia, Hungary, Italy, Lithuania, Netherlands, Poland, Romania, Slovenia, Turkey, Ukraine, the UK, and the United States.[208] NATO reached an agreement with the GoI to allow the continuation of specific NTM-I missions until July 2009. The other is the United Nations Assistance Mission for Iraq (UNAMI), to which New Zealand and Fiji contribute forces in Iraq to provide security.

POST-MAJOR COMBAT: SECURITY SITUATION

The security situation in Iraq is multi-faceted, geographically varied, and constantly evolving. In a society where the rule of law is not completely established, politics—the struggle for power, resources and influence—more readily and frequently takes the form of violence. Iraqi people are often faced with imperfect, pragmatic decisions about who is best suited to protect them and their interests. As a general trajectory, after a brief period of relative quiet in 2003 following major combat operations, forms of violent expression grew in variety, intensity, and frequency, hitting peaks in 2005 and 2006. By 2008, indicators of violence had tapered off to markedly lower levels. By the end of 2008, DOD assessed, "the strength of the insurgency continues to decline."[209]

Major Sources and Forms of Violence

Sunni Extremism
One major form of violence that has been practiced in post-Saddam Iraq is terrorism carried out by Sunni Arabs with stated Islamic extremist goals. Al Qaeda in Iraq (AQI) has been the most prominent named organization, but the threat may be better characterized as a loose network of affiliates, including both Iraqis and foreign fighters. Within the networks, assigned roles range from financiers, and planners of coordinated attacks, to unskilled labor recruited to emplace improvised explosive devices (IEDs). Their efforts to recruit primarily

young males have capitalized on Iraq's widespread under-employment, which can make the prospect of one-time payments appealing,[210] and general disaffection spurred by a perceived lack of opportunities in the new Iraq. The infrastructure used by AQI and its affiliates has included safe houses and lines of communication reaching, especially, through central and northern Iraq.[211]

The network has capitalized on Iraq's porous borders. In 2008, U.S. military commanders confirmed that the flow of foreign fighters continued, from Syria into Iraq.[212] In its March 2009 quarterly report to the Congress, the Department of Defense stated, "Syria remains the primary gateway for Iraq-bound foreign fighters."[213]

Over time, the AQI network demonstrated adaptability, quickly shifting its tactics and its footprint as circumstances change. Pushed out of urban areas, they typically sought refuge and an opportunity to re-group in deep rural settings. As surge operations pushed AQI and its affiliates out of Baghdad in late 2007, they sought new bases of operation to the east and to the north, in the Diyala River Valley in Diyala province, and in the northern Tigris River Valley in Ninewah province.[214] In early 2008, some AQI elements attempted to regroup in Mosul, but coalition and Iraqi operations pushed AQI elements out of the city and deeper into rural areas.[215]

As of August 2008, U.S. commanders in Iraq assessed that AQI was in disarray but still capable of conducting spectacular attacks. AQI was making increasing use of "surgical" attacks, such as sniper attacks, and using intimidation tactics, which may require fewer resources and less coordination that large-scale catastrophic attacks. In western Anbar province, where significant security progress was achieved earlier than in the north, commanders noted—borrowing from Mao—that there's "no longer a sea for the AQI fish to swim in;" that is, popular support for AQI had so sharply diminished that they were forced to operate clandestinely.[216]

As of the end of 2008, DOD assessed that AQI retained "limited freedom of movement in rural and some urban areas," and that it had both the intent and the ability to "carry out limited highprofile attacks within key urban center."[217] Their strongest base of operations remained Ninewah province, where DOD assessed the city of Mosul to be "a logistical, financial and operational hub for AQI."[218] In January 2009, the new Commanding General of Multi-National Division-North, Major General Robert Caslen, noted that there was still "a viable insurgency" in Mosul.[219] February 2009 witnessed a series of attacks on U.S. troops in that region by men wearing Iraqi police uniforms.[220] In March 2009, DOD assessed that AQI "retain[ed] the intent and capability to carry out spectacular attacks."[221]

Shi'a Extremism

Some Shi'a militias have been another major source of violence in post-Saddam Iraq. A central figure since the days of major combat operations has been the young Shi'a cleric Muqtada al-Sadr, the head of the Office of the Martyr Sadr political organization and its armed militia, the *Jaish al-Mahdi* ("JAM"). During the year of formal occupation, al-Sadr frequently delivered Friday sermons at mosques, using a hardline nationalist message to condemn the coalition and its Iraqi partners and to call for action against them. In April 2004, his followers staged coordinated, violent uprisings in cities throughout southern Iraq, which were put down by coalition forces.

While continuing to voice staunch opposition to the U.S. force presence in Iraq, in August 2007, al-Sadr declared a ceasefire to which most of JAM adhered, and he repeated the call in February 2008. By the summer of 2008, al-Sadr was making efforts to shift the focus of his base organization to social, cultural and political activities, including an umbrella movement called *al Mumahiddun*, designed to provide social services. At the end of July 2008, Sadr issued a statement pledging his support and that of his followers to the Government of Iraq, if the GoI would refrain from signing any security agreement with the United States. He also urged his followers to refrain from any actions that would harm Iraqi civilians, or disrupt the provision of government services.[222]

Meanwhile, rogue elements of JAM—known euphemistically as "special groups" or "special groups criminals," including *Asa'ib Ahl al-Haq* (AAH) – defied al-Sadr's August 2007 ceasefire call and continued to practice violence. The Office of the Martyr Sadr, insisting that JAM itself was an "army of believers," described such elements as criminal infiltrators who find it useful to have the cover of the JAM name.[223] In November 2008, however, Sadr called for members of the renegade AAH to return to the fold; and he created a new armed wing of his own movement, known as the Promised Day Brigade.

According to U.S. and Iraqi commanders on the ground, the series of Iraqi-led military operations in southern Iraq, which began in Basra in March 2008, had the effect of isolating some Shiite extremists and forcing others to flee across the border into Iran. The Iranian government has reportedly pledged to help stop the further flow of lethal aid into Iraq, but reports suggest there has been no marked diminution.[224] However, in official reports, the Department of Defense stated that as of March 2009, some Shiite extremist groups, including AAH and Ketaib Hezbollah (KH), continued to receive funding and support from Iran. DOD added that while Tehran has reduced the number of militants that it supports, it has "simultaneously improved the training and weapon systems received by the proxy militants."[225]

According to officials from the Multi-National Divisions that border Iran, the cross-border flow varies geographically over time, tending to seek the path of least resistance. The deployment of the Georgian full brigade to Wasit province, for example, made that province harder to traverse and pushed traffic north and south.[226] As of August 2008, a key locus of cross-border smuggling—not only of lethal aid but also of consumer goods—was the border along Maysan province, where Marsh Arabs historically have traded goods for centuries.[227]

U.S. and Iraqi commanders have noted that Quds forces continue to train some Iraqi Shiite extremists, including former special groups members. They added that some infiltrations continued, with the apparent goal of carrying out assassinations or planting improvised explosive devices. They suggested that special groups may attempt to reassert themselves in Iraq, with help from Iran. As one Iraqi commander noted, "Sadly, our neighbors are not friendly." Some U.S. and Iraqi commanders commented that a special groups re-emergence might take the form of a streamlined, well-trained terrorist network with a cellular structure, operating under cover, rather than a mass movement with popular support.[228] In March 2009, Iraqi Interior Minister Jawad al-Bolani noted that the ISF had evidence that Shiite militants were regrouping in Baghdad and some locations in southern Iraq.[229]

Meanwhile, the Iranian government apparently continues to seek influence among Iraqi Shi'a through the exercise of "soft power," for example by continuing to foster relationships with political leaders, by providing social services, and through investments including purchasing a power plant in the Shi'a-populated Sadr City section of Baghdad.[230]

Militant activities in southern Iraq and Baghdad have taken place against the backdrop of a deeply rooted intra-Shi'a struggle for power and resources. Some observers assess that, more than the Sunni-based insurgency or any other issue, the struggle for the Shi'a-populated south may shape Iraq's future.[231] Other main protagonists include Prime Minister Maliki's Da'wa party, and the Islamic Supreme Council in Iraq (ISCI, formerly known as the Supreme Council for the Islamic Revolution in Iraq), which is backed by its Badr militia and which, like JAM, provides people with goods and services in an effort to extend its influence. The power struggle also includes smaller Shi'a political parties backed by militias, such as *Fadila al-Islamiyah* (Islamic Virtue), which is active in the major southern city and province of Basra.

Relatively new to the power struggle are the ground-up voices of southern tribal leaders, most of whom stayed in Iraq through the Saddam period, unlike many Iraqi Shi'a political party leaders who spent years in Iran. Recognizing the largely untapped potential political power of southern tribal Shi'a, in 2008 Prime Minister Maliki sought to form consultative tribal *isnad* ("support")councils, first of all in Shi'a-populated areas including the southern provinces, which were supposed to articulate tribal needs to the provincial councils.[232] In at least one case, Babil province, the governor sought to form a competing provincial tribal council.[233] By late 2008, Maliki had expanded the effort to mixed-population provinces including Ninewah, Kirkuk, and Diyala, prompting protests from some senior officials.[234] A number of observers viewed the support councils as a blatant "get-out-the-vote" initiative.

Key political events have the potential to exacerbate the contest for political power and influence in the south. In April 2008, an 18-month moratorium expired on the implementation of a 2006 law on federalism, which included provisions for the creation of "regions" based on one or more provinces. "Regional" status could prove important because it affects the distribution of economic resources and political power. Major Shi'a groups in the south have called for various approaches to regionalization, based on their popular bases of support – for example, ISCI has advocated the creation of a nine-province in southern Iraq.[235] Iran, too, has reportedly expressed interest in how southern Iraq might be regionally grouped. In 2008, local political parties and organizations in Basra took the first steps to seek regionalization of Basra province, by organizing a petition drive, but the effort failed to secure the required 140,000 signatures.[236]

In late 2008, some Iraqi provincial political leaders and security forces commanders in southern Iraq suggested that the several rounds of elections scheduled to be held in 2009—provincial, district, and national—carried the potential for violence, in part because many incumbents recognized that they might not have enough popular support to be elected. Others have stressed the importance of those elections as a safety valve for popular opinion.[237] The results of the provincial elections held on January 31, 2009, reshuffled the balance of political power in southern provinces. Prime Minister Maliki's Da'wa party substantially increased its representation, earning pluralities in Baghdad and southern provinces, while ISCI lost significant ground, and some parties backed by al Sadr secured some support. Without clear majorities, governing will require coalition-building throughout the south.

Nature of Sectarian Violence

Less a source than a type of violence, Iraq has struggled for years with sectarian violence, particularly along the fault lines between populations predominantly of different sectarian groups. Those fault lines, some observers suggest, are where local populations are likely to feel most vulnerable, and might in some cases be most open to assurances of protection from one organized armed group or another.

Sectarian violence skyrocketed in February 2006, following the bombing of the Golden Mosque in Samarra, one of Shiite Islam's holiest shrines. That attack prompted Shi'a reprisals targeting Sunnis and Sunni mosques in a number of cities. AQI responded in some locations by staging a series of further attacks.[238]

The sectarian-based displacement of many Iraqis from their homes, and the resulting greater segregation in urban areas, reduced the number of fault lines somewhat.[239] Displacement and esettlement are dynamic issues—the United Nations High Commissioner for Refugees estimated hat as of late 2008, there were nearly 2.8 million IDPs in Iraq.[240] Some GoI resettlement and restitution initiatives have been launched, but DOD reports that as of March 2009, "returnees have reported little success accessing these benefits."[241] In many instances, the usual challenges of displacement are compounded by both sectarian and class-based differences, between those who have fled, and those who have moved into the "abandoned" homes.[242]

Criminality

Another major category of violence is opportunistic criminality, practiced with a view to sheer material gain rather than political or ideological goals. The inchoate status of Iraq's judicial system and law enforcement organizations has left room for opportunists to steal, loot, smuggle, kidnap and extort.

Other Security Challenges

In addition to the primary adversaries during major combat operations—the regime's forces and security structures—and the primary sources of violence in the period after major combat, coalition forces in Iraq have had to contend with the presence of two groups, designated by the Department of State as Foreign Terrorist Organizations, which are largely unrelated to the rest of the fight but of deep interest to some of Iraq's neighbors. Both cases have consumed substantial time and energy from MNF-I staff in Iraq as well as senior leaders in Washington, D.C., and both have had the potential to destabilize the broader security environment.

Kurdistan Workers Party (PKK)

The first group is the Kurdistan Workers Party—the PKK, also known over time as KADEK, Kongra-Gel, and the KCK. The PKK is based in southeastern Turkey, but maintains a presence in northern Iraq and reportedly uses that area to rest and re-group from its operations inside Turkey. The PKK's stated goal is the establishment of an independent Kurdish state, and it has practiced terror to that end, targeting Turkish security forces and civilian officials.

Since 2003, the Turkish government has pushed for action against PKK members in northern Iraq. The U.S. and Iraqi governments have both strongly supported the Turkish government's stand against terrorism and the PKK in principle. In the past, both the Iraqi government and MNF-I reportedly expressed concerns that military action against the PKK in Iraq could open a new northern front, taxing their already thinly stretched forces.[243]

In 2007, the Government of Turkey received a one-year Turkish parliamentary authorization to conduct cross-border actions against the PKK, and in October 2008 the Turkish parliament extended the authorization for another year.[244] In December 2007, the Turkish Air Force launched a series of air strikes, targeting presumed PKK positions in northern Iraq, followed in February 2008 by a week-long series of coordinated air and ground attacks.[245] Initially, Iraqi government officials objected, stressing the need to respect the sovereignty of its territory and air space. U.S. senior leaders, reportedly informed in advance of the February 2008 attacks about Turkish intentions, publicly called on the government of Turkey to keep the operation as short as possible.[246] In July 2008, the Turkish Air Force conducted another series of air strikes on presumed PKK positions in northern Iraq.[247] In October 2008, following a PKK attack that killed 17 Turkish soldiers, Turkish forces launched another series of air strikes into northern Iraq. In November 2008, the U.S., Iraqi and Turkish governments launched a trilateral forum to exchange information and coordinate activities regarding the PKK.[248]

In March 2009, Turkish President Abdullah Gul visited Baghdad, the first visit by a Turkish head of state in 30 years. During the visit, at a joint press conference, Iraqi President Jalal Talabani called on the PKK to lay down its arms or leave Iraq. In public statements, PKK representatives rejected that call.[249]

Mujahedin-e Khalq (MeK)

During the year of formal occupation, the leadership of CJTF-7 and CPA, and senior officials in Washington, D.C., spent considerable time focused on the disposition of the Mujahedin-e Khalq ("MeK"). Formed by students in Iran in the 1960's, in leftist opposition to the Shah and his regime, the MeK later stepped into opposition against what it calls the "mullah regime" that took power after the 1979 Iranian Revolution. Over time, the MeK has sought opportunistic alliances, including moving its operational headquarters to Iraq, and making common cause with the Iraqi government, during the Iran-Iraq war in the 1980s.

Although the MeK is a designated Foreign Terrorist Organization, some U.S. officials reportedly have considered the possibility of using the MeK as leverage against Tehran. Several times, some Members of Congress—reportedly some 200 in the year 2000—signed letters expressing their support for the cause advocated by the MeK.[250]

This awkward policy history was magnified by awkward events on the ground during OIF major combat operations, when, on April 15, 2003, members of the U.S. Special Operations Forces signed a ceasefire agreement with MeK leaders. Subsequently, Department of Defense issued guidance through CENTCOM to forces on the ground to effect a MeK surrender. Following a series of negotiations with MeK leaders, the several thousand MeK members were separated from their well-maintained heavy weapons and brought under coalition control at Camp Ashraf in Diyala province. The key operational concern, in the early stages, was that MeK non-compliance could generate large-scale operational requirements, effectively opening another front. Efforts have been underway since that time, in coordination with the Iraqi government and the many countries of citizenship of the MeK members, to determine appropriate further disposition. The efforts have faced obstacles, because some countries are reluctant to receive members of the MeK, while MeK members who are still citizens of Iran insist that they cannot return home for fear of persecution. The MeK's presence in Iraq is an irritant in Iraq's bilateral relationship with Iran.

As of fall 2008, the Government of Iraq had initiated steps to transition responsibility for control of the MeK camp from U.S. to Iraqi security forces.[251] In a public statement in September 2008, Minister of Defense Abdul Qadr noted that the sovereign government of Iraq should be responsible for any such group inside the country—"The Iraqi government is entitled to be the guard around the borders of the camp."[252] After the security agreement took effect on January 1, 2009, U.S. forces handed control over the outer perimeter around Camp Ashraf to the ISF. MeK members told the press that in March 2009, ISF blockaded Ashraf, preventing the delivery of supplies including food and water.[253]

At the political level, the GoI has underscored its intent to close the facility. In January 2009, during a visit to Tehran, National Security Advisor Dr. Mowaffaq al-Rubaie stated, "The only choices open to members of this group are to return to Iran or to choose another country," and he added, "…the camp will be part of history within two months." In March 2009, Iran's supreme religious leader Ayatollah Khamenei reportedly expressed some impatience, telling visiting Iraqi President Talabani, "We await the implementation of our agreement regarding the expulsion of the hypocrites."[254]

POST-MAJOR COMBAT: MILITARY STRATEGY AND OPERATIONS

Over time, U.S. military strategy for Iraq—and thus also operations on the ground—have been adapted to support evolving U.S. national strategy. In turn, national strategy has directly drawn some lessons from OIF operational experience. Given the scope and scale of the mission, and its lack of precise historical precedents, there has been ample need and opportunity for learning and adaptation.

The Administration's basic national strategic objectives have remained roughly consistent over time. So have the major categories of activities (or "lines of operation")—political, economic, essential services, diplomatic—used to help achieve the objectives. What have evolved greatly over time are the views of commanders in the field and decision-makers in Washington, D.C., about the best ways to achieve "security" and how that line of operation fits with the others.

This section highlights key episodes and turning-points in the theory and practice of OIF military operations, including early operations during formal occupation, "Fallujah II," COIN operations in Tal Afar, Operation Together Forward, the operations associated with the 2007 "New Way Forward," and surge follow-on operations in 2008. The review suggests that the application of counter-insurgency (COIN) theory and practice grew over time, but by no means steadily or consistently.

Nomenclature: Characterizing the Conflict

Prussian military theorist Karl von Clausewitz argued: "The first, the supreme, the most farreaching act of judgment that the statesman and commander have to make is to establish ... the kind of war on which they are embarking."[255] In theory, how the "kind of war" is identified helps shape the tools selected to prosecute it. In the case of OIF after major combat operations, it proved difficult for senior Bush Administration officials and military leaders to agree on what "kind of war" OIF was turning out to be.

On July 7, 2003, General John Abizaid, an Arabic speaker who had served during OIF major combat as the Deputy Commanding General of CENTCOM, replaced General Tommy Franks as CENTCOM Commander. At his first press conference in the new role, GEN Abizaid referred to the challenge in Iraq as a "classical guerrilla-type campaign." Slightly more carefully but leaving no room for doubt he added, "I think describing it as guerrilla tactics is a proper way to describe it in strictly military terms."[256]

The Pentagon pointedly did not adopt that terminology. Two weeks later, asked about his reluctance to use the phrase "guerrilla war," Secretary Rumsfeld noted: "I guess the reason I don't use the phrase 'guerrilla war' is because there isn't one, and it would be a misunderstanding and a miscommunication to you and to the people of the country and the world." Instead, he argued, in Iraq there were "five different things": "looters, criminals, remnants of the Ba'athist regime, foreign terrorists, and those influenced by Iran."[257]

In his account of that year, CJTF-7 Commanding General LTG Sanchez wrote that by July 2003, he and GEN Abizaid, his boss, had recognized that what they faced was an insurgency.[258] A UK officer serving as Special Assistant to LTG Sanchez drafted a paper outlining the concepts of insurgency and counter-insurgency and their possible application to Iraq. The paper's ideas, and its nomenclature, gained traction and helped inform the command's planning.[259]

However, for years afterward, the Pentagon also resisted the terminology of "insurgency." At a November 2005 press conference, Chairman of the Joint Chiefs of Staff General Peter Pace, speaking about the adversary in Iraq, said, "I have to use the word 'insurgent' because I can't think of a better word right now." Secretary Rumsfeld cut in— "enemies of the legitimate Iraqi government." He added, "That [using the word "insurgent"] gives them a greater legitimacy than they seem to merit."[260]

Military Strategy and Operations during Occupation

During the formal occupation of Iraq from 2003 to 2004, the military command in Iraq, CJTF-7, was responsible for "security," while the civilian leadership, the Coalition Provisional Authority (CPA), was responsible for all other governance functions.[261] In the views of the CJTF-7 leadership, establishing "security" required more than "killing people and breaking things"—it required simultaneous efforts to achieve popular "buy-in," for example by rebuilding local communities and engaging Iraqis in the process.[262]

Accordingly, CJTF-7 built its plans around four basic lines of operation, or categories of effort— political (governance), economic, essential services, and security—which differed only slightly from the categories in use in early 2008. Those lines of operation were echoed in the plans of CJTF-7's subordinate commands. CJTF-7 would lead the "security" line, and support CPA efforts in the other areas.

Beginning in 2003, CJTF-7's basic theory of the case was that the lines of operation, pursued simultaneously, would be mutually reinforcing. Major General Peter Chiarelli, who commanded the 1st Cavalry Division in Baghdad from 2004 to 2005, argued after his tour that it was not effective to try to achieve security first, and then turn to the other lines of operation. He wrote: "... if we concentrated solely on establishing a large security force and [conducting] targeted counterinsurgent combat operations—and only after that was accomplished, worked toward establishing a sustainable infrastructure supported by a strong government developing a freemarket system—we would have waited too long."[263]

In the "security" line of operation, military operations under CJTF-7 included combat operations focused on "killing or capturing" the adversary. Aggressive operations yielded large numbers of Iraqis detained by the coalition—the large numbers, and frequent difficulties determining whether and where individuals were being held, were an early and growing source of popular frustration. In April 2004, the unofficial release of graphic photos of apparent detainee abuse at Abu Ghraib generated shock and horror among people inside and outside Iraq. Some observers have suggested that these developments may have helped fuel the insurgency.[264]

CJTF-7 military operations also included early counter-insurgency (COIN) practices for population control. Those practices included creating "gated communities"—including Saddam's home town of al-Awja—by fencing off a town or area and strictly controlling access through the use of check-points and ID cards. To make military operations less antagonistic, when possible, to local residents, units substituted "cordon and knock" approaches for the standard "cordon and search."[265]

The security line of operation also included early partnerships with nascent Iraqi security forces, including mentoring as well as formal training. Where troop strength so permitted, for example in Baghdad and in Mosul, Army Military Police were assigned to local police stations as de facto advisors.[266] GEN Abizaid's theory was that the very presence of U.S. forces in Iraq was an "antibody" in Iraqi society.[267] Therefore, to remove the possibility that insurgents could leverage the presence of an occupation force to win popular support, a key goal was to move quickly to an "overwatch" posture. Doing so would require an accelerated stand-up of Iraqi security forces. That approach shared with later COIN approaches the premise that U.S. forces alone could not "win"—that success in the security sphere would require acting by, with and through Iraqis. It differed sharply from later COIN approaches, however, in terms of implications for the U.S. forces footprint, size of presence, and many activities.

While the military command did not have the lead role for the non-security lines of operation, it made contributions to those efforts. To address the most pressing "essential services" concerns, the military command created Task Force Restore Iraqi Electricity, and Task Force Restore Iraqi Oil, which were later consolidated into the Gulf Region Division, under the Army Corps of Engineers.

To help jumpstart local economies—and to provide Iraqis with some visible signs of post-war "progress"—the military command launched the Commanders Emergency Response Program (CERP). As initially crafted, CERP provided commanders with readily available discretionary funds to support small-scale projects, usually initiated at the request of local community leaders.

In the "governance" field, commanders needed Iraqi interlocutors to provide bridges into local communities, and advice concerning the most urgent reconstruction and humanitarian priorities. Since official Iraqi agencies were no longer intact, and since the CPA did not yet have a sufficient regional presence to help build local governments, commanders helped select provincial and local councils to serve in temporary advisory capacities.[268]

By most accounts, by the end of the year of formal occupation, in June 2004, the security situation had worsened—catalyzed in April by the simultaneous unrest in Fallujah and al-Sadr-led uprisings throughout the south. Many observers have suggested that none of the lines of operation—whether civilian-led or military-led—was fully implemented during the year of formal occupation, due to a lack of personnel and resources. In particular, GEN Abizaid's goal of diminishing the presence of U.S. "antibodies" in Iraq society was not realized, since highly inchoate Iraqi security forces training efforts, led by CPA, had not had time to yield results. The basic assumption of CJTF-7—that establishing security required simultaneous application of all the lines of operation—may never have been fully put to the test.

Operation Phantom Fury (Fallujah II)

One of the first very high-profile military operations after major combat was Operation Phantom Fury, designed to "take back" the restive city of Fallujah in the Al Anbar province. In November 2004, Phantom Fury—or "Fallujah II"—highlighted the intransigence of the emerging Sunni Arab insurgency, early coalition military efforts to counter it, and the complex intersection of political considerations and "best military advice" in operational decision-making.[269]

During major combat operations and the early part of the formal occupation, the military command practiced first an "economy of force" approach to Al Anbar province, and then a quick shuffling of responsible military units, which left little opportunity to establish local relationships or build expertise.[270] Building relationships with the population is critical in any counterinsurgency, and it may have been particularly important in Al Anbar, where social structure is based largely on complex and powerful tribal affiliations.

Coalition forces in Al Anbar during major combat were primarily limited to Special Operations Forces. After CJTF-7 was established, the first unit assigned responsibility for the large province was the 3rd Armored Cavalry Regiment—essentially a brigade-sized formation. In fall 2003, the much larger 82nd Airborne Division and subordinate units arrived in Iraq and were assigned to Al Anbar, but their tenure was brief—after six months they handed off responsibility to the 1st Marine Expeditionary Force (IMEF).[271]

The city of Fallujah, like the rest of Al Anbar, is populated largely by Sunni Arabs. Under the old Iraqi regime, Fallujah had enjoyed some special prerogatives and had produced a number of senior leaders in Iraq's various security forces. Many residents therefore had some reason to be concerned about their place in the post-Saddam Iraq.

On March 31, 2004, four American contractors working for Blackwater, who were driving through Fallujah, were ambushed and killed—and then their bodies were mutilated and hung from a bridge. Photos of that grisly aftermath were rapidly transmitted around the world— riveting the attention of leaders in Baghdad, Washington, and other coalition country capitals.

What followed, in April 2004, was a series of highest-level deliberations in Baghdad and Washington concerning the appropriate response. Some key participants in the debates initially favored immediate, overwhelming military action, but those views were quickly tempered by concerns about the reactions that massive military action—and casualties—

might produce. Several key Sunni Arab members of the Iraqi leadership body, the Iraqi Governing Council— threatened to resign in the event of an attack on Fallujah.[272] And some senior U.S. officials expressed concerns about the reactions of other governments in the region, and of Sunni Arabs elsewhere in Iraq.[273]

The Administration's guidance, after the initial debates, was to respect the concerns of Iraqi leaders and to avoid sending U.S. military forces into Fallujah. What followed, instead, was a series of "negotiations" by CPA and CJTF-7 leaders with separate sets of Fallujah community representatives, some of them brokered by Iraqi national-level political leaders. And what emerged was a "deal" initiated by IMEF with a local retired Iraqi Army General and a group of locally recruited fighters, who formed the "Fallujah Brigade" and pledged to restore and maintain order.[274]

When the Fallujah Brigade collapsed that summer, the city of Fallujah had not been "cleared" by either the Brigade or IMEF. Over the summer, insurgents reportedly strengthened their hold on the city.

Decisive military action—Operation Phantom Fury—was launched by IMEF in November 2004. Several factors may have shaped the timing of the Operation. By November, the new interim Iraqi government, led by Prime Minister Ayad Allawi, had had some time to establish its credibility— perhaps enough to help quell citizens' concerns in the event of large-scale military action. Key Iraqi elections were scheduled for January 2005, and eliminating a hotbed of insurgency beforehand might increase voter participation. And earlier in November, President Bush had been re-elected, which may have reassured some Iraqi leaders that if they agreed to the military operation, the U.S. government—and coalition forces—would be likely to continue to provide support to deal with any aftermath.

The Marines began the Fallujah operations by setting conditions—turning off electrical power, and urging the civilians of Fallujah to leave the city. The vast majority of residents did depart— leaving about 500 hardcore fighters, who employed asymmetrical tactics against a far larger, stronger force. That coalition force included one UK battalion, three Iraqi battalions, six U.S. Marine battalions and three U.S. Army battalions. The operation reportedly included 540 air strikes, 14,000 artillery and mortar shells fired, and 2,500 tank main gun rounds fired. Some 70 U.S. personnel were killed, and 609 wounded. In Fallujah, of the city's 39,000 buildings, 18,000 were damaged or destroyed.[275]

In the aftermath, coalition and Iraqi forces established a tight security cordon around the city, with a system of vehicle searches and security passes for residents, to control movement and access. Fingerprints and retinal scans were taken from male residents. Observers noted that by spring 2005, about half the original population, of 250,000, had returned home—many of them to find essential services disrupted and their property damaged.[276] The scale of destruction was criticized by some observers inside Iraq and in the Middle East region more broadly.

The effects of the comprehensive "clearing" were not lasting. Al Qaeda affiliates gradually returned and made Fallujah a strong-hold and base of operations.

Counter-Insurgency in Tal Afar

Military operations in the town of Tal Afar, in 2005, marked an early, multi-faceted, and successful application of counter-insurgency (COIN) approaches, and successful results, in OIF. In Washington, "Tal Afar" gave birth to a new Iraq policy lexicon, and in Iraq—though not immediately—to the expanded use of COIN practices.

Tal Afar is located in Ninewah province, along the route from the provincial capital of Mosul to Syria. Its mixed population of about 290,000 includes Sunni Arabs, Kurds, Turkmen and Yezidis. From April 2003 until early 2004, the 101st Airborne Division had responsibility for Ninewah and Iraq's three northern, largely Kurdish-populated provinces. Because the north was relatively quiet, due in part to the effectiveness of the Kurdish *pesh merga* forces, the 101st was able to concentrate primarily on Ninewah—a relatively high troops-to-population ratio. In early 2004, when the 101st redeployed, responsibility for the area passed to a much smaller Stryker brigade. That brigade, in turn, was periodically asked to provide forces for operations elsewhere in Iraq, so the coalition force footprint in Ninewah was substantially reduced. Tal Afar—with a convenient trade route location, and a mixed population "perfect" for fomenting sectarian strife—become a base of operations for former regime elements and Sunni extremists, including suicide bombers.

In May 2005, the 3rd Armored Cavalry Regiment (3ACR), now commanded by Colonel H.R. McMaster, arrived in Tal Afar. COL McMaster was familiar with OIF issues from his previous service as the Director of GEN Abizaid's Commander's Action Group at CENTCOM.[277] At CENTCOM, he had helped the command to think through the nature of the Iraqi insurgency, and to craft appropriate responses including targeted engagements with key leaders. As the author of a well-known account of Vietnam decision-making, COL McMaster could also readily draw key lessons from that earlier complex engagement.[278]

In early 2005, the 3ACR began their deployment preparations at home in Fort Carson, Colorado—studying COIN approaches, training and exercising those approaches, and learning conversational Arabic. Later, in Iraq, COL McMaster described the Regiment's mission in the classical COIN lexicon of "population security": "...the whole purpose of the operation is to secure the population so that we can lift the enemy's campaign of intimidation and coercion over the population and allow economic and political development to proceed here and to return to normal life."[279]

In practice, that meant taking "a very deliberate approach to the problem," beginning with months of preparatory moves. Those preparatory steps included beefing up security along the Syrian border to the west, and targeting and eliminating enemy safe havens out in the desert. They also included constructing a dirt berm ringing Tal Afar, and establishing check points to control movement in and out of the city.

Before the launch of full-scale operations in September 2005, the Regiment urged civilians to leave Tal Afar. Then 3ACR cleared the city deliberately—block by block. After the clearing operations, 3ACR had sufficient forces to hold the city, setting up 29 patrol bases around town, every few blocks.[280]

Basing coalition forces among the population was an unusual approach at the time. Though common in the early days of OIF, by 2005, most coalition forces in Iraq had been pulled back to relatively large Forward Operating Bases (FOBs), secure and separate from the local population.

That strategy was driven in part by the theory that the visible presence of coalition forces—and their weapons and their heavy vehicles—could antagonize local communities.[281]

3ACR's COIN approaches also included working closely with their Iraqi security forces counterparts—the 3rd Iraqi Army Division. COL McMaster credited that partnership as essential to the strategy: "What gives us the ability to ... clear and hold as a counterinsurgency strategy is the capability of Iraqi security forces."[282] The key to the success in Fallujah, he added—and the major difference from "Fallujah II"—was popular support: "we had the active cooperation of such a large percentage of the population."

COL McMaster's use of the phrase "clear and hold" was not accidental—it had been the name of the counter-insurgency approach introduced in Vietnam by General Creighton Abrams, following years of General William Westmoreland's "search and destroy" approach.[283]

"Clear, Hold, Build"

A short time later, the Administration adopted and expanded on the "clear, hold" lexicon to describe the overall strategy in Iraq.[284] In October 2005, in testimony about Iraq before the Senate Foreign Relations Committee, Secretary of State Condoleezza Rice began by stating: "Our political-military strategy has to be clear, hold, and build: to clear areas from insurgent control, to hold them securely, and to build durable, national Iraqi institutions."[285] About three weeks later, in a major Veterans Day speech, President Bush echoed Secretary Rice's "clear, hold, build" language almost verbatim.[286]

The following month, November 2005, the Administration issued a new *National Strategy for Victory in Iraq*. The Strategy argued—roughly consistent with the military's long-standing lines of operation—that success required three major tracks, security, political and economic. Consistent with the basic theory of the case since 2003, these tracks were to be pursued simultaneously, and would be "mutually reinforcing." As the *Strategy* states, "Progress in each of the political, security, and economic tracks reinforces progress in the other tracks."[287].

The new *Strategy* prominently adopted the "clear hold build" lexicon, with a twist. "Clear, hold, build" was now the prescribed set of approaches for the security track alone. The political and economic tracks were also each based on a trinitarian set of approaches. In the security track, "build" now referred specifically to the Iraqi security forces and local institutions. "Build" also appeared in the other two tracks—capturing the focus on national-level institutions from the earlier public statements by President Bush and Secretary Rice.[288]

By March 2006, a complete, official narrative had emerged, in which Tal Afar operations had tested and confirmed both the "clear, hold, build" strategy, and the interdependence of the three major tracks. As a White House Fact Sheet, titled "Clear, Hold, Build," stated, "Tal Afar shows how the three elements of the strategy for victory in Iraq—political, security, and economic— depend on and reinforce one another."[289]

Operation Together Forward

In June 2006, Iraqi and Coalition forces launched "Operation Together Forward," officially based on "clear, hold, build" and aimed at reducing violence and increasing security in Baghdad. Baghdad was chosen as the focus because it was "the center that everybody [was] fighting for— the insurgents, the death squads ... the government of Iraq."[290] The Operation was predicated on basic counter-insurgency principles—"to secure the citizens' lives here in Baghdad."[291]

Together Forward included some 48 battalions of Iraqi and coalition forces—about 51,000 troops altogether, including roughly 21,000 Iraqi police, 13,000 Iraqi National Police, 8,500 Iraqi Army, and 7,200 coalition forces.[292] Iraqi forces were in the lead, supported by the coalition. The effort included clearing operations, as well as a series of new security measures including extended curfews, tighter restrictions on carrying weapons, new tips hotlines, more checkpoints, and more police patrols.[293]

Together Forward theoretically included the other major tracks of the November 2005 *National Strategy*—political and economic efforts, as well as security, although the coalition's primary focus was security. As MNF-I spokesman Major General William Caldwell noted in July 2006, "It's obviously a multi-pronged approach ... but those [other tracks] are mostly the government of Iraq side of the house."[294]

MNF-I stated publicly from the start that Together Forward was expected to take months, not weeks. For several months after the operation was launched, the levels of violence in the capital rose. As MG Caldwell explained in October 2006, "the insurgent elements, the extremists, are in fact punching back hard." Once the Iraqi and coalition forces cleared an area, the insurgents tried to regain that territory, so the Iraqi and coalition forces were "constantly going back in and doing clearing operations again."[295]

Many observers attributed that circle of violence to a lack of sufficient forces—whether coalition or Iraqi—to "hold" an area once it was "cleared." The vast majority of participating forces were Iraqi, and at that juncture, some observers suggest, their capabilities were limited. MNF-ISpokesman MG Caldwell noted in July 2006: "We are by no means at the end state, at the place where the Iraqi security forces are able to assume complete control of this situation."[296]

By October 2006, MNF-I admitted that Together Forward had not achieved the expected results—it had "not met our overall expectations of sustaining a reduction in the levels of violence."[297] In the event, from the experiences of Tal Afar, Operation Together Forward had applied the principle of close collaboration with host-nation forces, but only the "clear" element of the "clear, hold, build" mandate.

New Way Forward

By late 2006, senior diplomats and commanders in Iraq had concluded that the approaches in use were not achieving the intended results—indeed, levels of violence were continuing to climb. Several strategic reviews were conducted in parallel, some input from key observers was solicited, options were considered, and a decision was made and announced by the Administration—to pursue a "New Way Forward" in Iraq.[298]

"New Way Forward" National Strategy: Theory of the Case

While the Administration's basic long-term objectives for Iraq did not change, the New Way Forward introduced a fundamentally new theory of the case. Until that time, Iraq strategy had assumed that the major tracks of effort—security, political, economic—were mutually reinforcing, and should therefore be implemented simultaneously.

The New Way Forward agreed that all of the tracks—plus a new "regional" track—were important, but argued that security was a prerequisite for progress in the other areas.[299] As a White House summary of the results of the strategy review stated, "While political progress, economic gains and security are all intertwined, political and economic progress are unlikely absent a basic level of security."[300] And as President Bush stated in his address to the nation on this topic, in January 2007, "The most urgent priority for success in Iraq is security."[301]

This thinking, though new as the premise for U.S. Iraq strategy, was not new to practitioners on the ground. As early as 2003, some U.S. practitioners in Iraq had suggested that substantial political and economic progress could not be expected, absent basic security conditions that allowed Iraqis to leave their homes, and civilian coalition personnel to engage with local communities.[302] The New Way Forward institutionalized that view.

The theory of the case was that security improvements would open up space and opportunities for the Iraqi government to make improvements in other areas. As General David Petraeus described it in March 2007, one month into his tour as the MNF-I Commander, if security improves, "commerce will return and local economies will grow." And at the same time, "the Iraqi government will have the chance it needs to resolve some of the difficult issues it faces."[303]

By early 2008, the basic premise had met with broad if not universal support among practitioners and observers. For example, in October 2007, Commandant of the Marine Corps General James Conway told a think-tank audience, "Certainly you have to have a level of security before you can have governance."[304] Retired Marine Corps General James Jones, who led a congressionally mandated review of Iraqi Security Forces in 2007, described it differently. He suggested that the relationship between two major components of politics and security—national reconciliation and sectarian violence—is more complex: "It's a little bit of a chicken-and-egg question.... The real overall conclusion is that the government of Iraq is the one that has to find a way to achieve political reconciliation, in order to enable a reduction in sectarian violence."[305]

Surge Forces

In his January 10, 2007, address to the nation, President Bush announced that to help implement the New Way Forward, the United States would deploy additional military units to Iraq, primarily to Baghdad. Their mission, a paraphrase of the "clear, hold, build" language, would be "to help Iraqis clear and secure neighborhoods, to help them protect the local population, and to help ensure that the Iraqi forces left behind are capable of providing the security that Baghdad needs."[306]

The surge forces would grow to include five Brigade Combat Teams (BCTs), an Army combat aviation brigade, a Marine Expeditionary Unit (MEU), two Marine infantry battalions, a Division headquarters, and other support troops. The number of U.S. forces in Iraq reached a peak of about 168,000 U.S. troops in October 2007.

The surge effort also included a civilian component—increasing the number of civilian-led Provincial Reconstruction Teams (PRTs) and the size of their staffs. A White House Fact Sheet stated, "PRTs are a key element of the President's 'New Way Forward' Strategy."[307]

Surge Military Strategy: Theory of the Case

The fundamental premise of the Iraqi and coalition surge operations was population security. This marked an important shift from previous years, when the top imperative was transitioning responsibility to Iraqis.[308] The two efforts were not considered mutually exclusive—during the surge, efforts would continue to train, mentor and equip Iraqi security forces to prepare for transitioning increasing responsibilities to them. But the relative priority of the "population security" and "transition" efforts was adjusted.

In early 2008, close to the height of the surge, some Division Commanders commented that their guidance from their higher headquarters—MNC-I—was to practice patience, not to be in too much of a hurry to move to an overwatch posture or to transition responsibility to Iraqi security forces.[309] The January 2008 mission statement of one division provides a good illustration of the new priorities—population security first, with a view to laying the groundwork for future transition. The division, "in participation with Iraqi security forces and the provincial government, secures the population, neutralizes insurgents and militia groups, and defeats terrorists and irreconcilable extremists, to establish sustainable security and set conditions for transition to tactical overwatch and Iraqi security self-reliance."[310]

The surge aimed to provide "population security" not merely with greater troop strength, but also by changing some of the approaches those troops used. One major emphasis was population control—including the extensive use of concrete barriers, checkpoints, curfews, and biometric technologies for identification including fingerprinting and retinal scans.

In April 2007, some key Baghdad neighborhoods were entirely sealed off using these approaches, prompting the use of the moniker "gated communities." In an Op-Ed piece, Multi-National Corps-Iraq Commander Lieutenant General Ray Odierno explained that the gated communities were "being put up to protect the Iraqi population by hindering the ability of terrorists to carry out the car bombings and suicide attacks."[311] As counter-insurgency expert Dave Kilcullen described it, "once an area is cleared and secured, with troops on the ground, controls make it hard to infiltrate or intimidate ... and thus [they] also protect the population."[312]

Some initial press coverage took note of some citizens' dismay at the tighter controls that gated communities brought.[313] By early 2008, coalition and Iraqi leaders reported anecdotally that Iraqi residents were pleased at the added protection the "gated community" measures provided them— by "keeping the bad guys out."[314]

Another key set of population security approaches involved troop presence—including not only increasing the number of troops but also changing their footprint. From late in the formal occupation through 2006—including Operation Together Forward—coalition forces in Iraq had been consolidated at relatively large Forward Operating Bases (FOBs). Surge strategy called for getting troops off of the FOBs and out into local communities, to live and work among the population.

As Major General James Simmons, III Corps and MNC-I Deputy Commanding General until February 2008, stated, "You have to get out and live with the people."[315] Multi-National Force-West leaders agreed that the key is "living with the population," because "it makes Iraqis see us as partners in the fighting and rebuilding."[316] As MNF-I Commanding General

David Petraeus commented in July 2008, explaining surge approaches: "The only way to secure a population is to live with it—you can't commute to this fight."[317]

Accordingly, coalition forces established scores of small combat outposts (COPs) and joint security stations (JSSs) in populated areas. A JSS includes co-located units from coalition forces, the Iraqi police, and the Iraqi Army. Each component continues to report to its own chain of command, but they share space—and information. A COP is coalition-only, usually manned by a "company-minus." As of January 2008, for example, Multi-National Division-Center had established 53 such bases in their restive area south of Baghdad.

Senior commanders at all levels have stressed the critical role JSSs and COPs played during the surge. General Petraeus noted in March 2007 that they allowed the development of relationships with local populations.[318] Multi-National Division-Baghdad leaders called the creation of these outposts the "biggest change over time" in coalition operations in Iraq.[319]

Surge strategy still called on Iraqi and coalition forces to "clear, hold, build." Administration and coalition leaders admitted that in the past—in Operation Together Forward in 2006—insufficient forces had been available to "hold" an area once it was cleared. The surge was designed to correct that.

As the President noted in his January 10, 2007, address to the nation, "In earlier operations, Iraqi and American forces cleared many neighborhoods of terrorists and insurgents, but when our forces moved on to other targets, the killers returned. This time," he added, "we'll have the force levels we need to hold the areas that have been cleared."[320] General Petraeus confirmed the approach, and the contrast with past operations, in March 2007: "Importantly, Iraqi and coalition forces will not just clear neighborhoods, they will also hold them to facilitate the build phase of the operation."[321] Key outside observers agreed. Retired General Jack Keane, a strong surge advocate, noted, "We're going to secure the population for the first time. What we've never been able to do in the past is have enough forces to stay in those neighborhoods and protect the people."[322]

President Bush announced one other major change which would make surge military operations different from those of the past—the lifting of political restrictions on operations, which had been imposed in the past by an Iraqi leadership concerned about its own fragility. In the past, President Bush noted, "political and sectarian interference prevented Iraqi and American forces from going into neighborhoods that are home to those fueling the sectarian violence." But this time, Iraqi leaders had signaled that Iraqi and coalition forces would have "a green light" to enter those neighborhoods.[323]

Surge Operations in 2007

Enabled by the greater availability of U.S. and Iraqi forces in 2007, U.S. military commanders launched a series of major "combined" operations with their Iraqi security forces counterparts.

Baghdad Security Plan

In February 2007, just as surge forces began to flow into Iraq, U.S. and Iraqi forces launched Operation *Fardh al-Qanoon*, often referred to as the Baghdad Security Plan. Its primary emphasis was population security, and the primary geographical focal point was Baghdad, broadly defined.[324] As then-MNC-I Commander LTG Odierno put it, "The population and the government are the center of gravity."[325]

The basic theory of the case was another paraphrase of "clear, hold, build." At the outset of operations, Major General Joseph Fil, Commander of 1st Cavalry Division and the Multi-National Division-Baghdad, described the plan as "clear, control, and retain." That meant, he explained, clearing out extremists, neighborhood by neighborhood; controlling those neighborhoods with a "full-time presence on the streets" by coalition and Iraqi forces; and retaining the neighborhoods with Iraqi security forces "fully responsible for the day-to-day security mission."[326]

The specific targets of the Operation included Al Qaeda in Iraq (AQI) and its affiliates, and rogue Shi'a militia elements including the *Jaish al-Mahdi* "special groups."

"Baghdad" was defined to include the surrounding areas, or "belts," which had been providing bases of operation and transit points, with access into the capital, for both Sunni and Shi'a extremists. LTG Odierno's guidance to his subordinate commanders was to stop the flow of "accelerants of the violence" through those areas into Baghdad.[327]

Operating in the "belts" required shifting the footprint of coalition forces to cover all the major supply lines leading into Baghdad. Coalition presence in many of the belt areas had previously been very light. During the spring of 2007, incoming surge brigades were deployed into Baghdad and its belts. April 1, 2007, a new division headquarters was added—the Multi-National Division- Center, initially led by 3rd Infantry Division—to cover parts of Baghdad province and other provinces just south of Baghdad.[328]

"Phoenix" Series of Corps-Level Operations

Beginning in June 2007, once all the coalition surge forces had arrived in Iraq, coalition forces, in coordination with Iraqi counterparts, launched a series of operations: Phantom Thunder, followed by Phantom Strike, and then Phantom Phoenix. As "Corps-level operations," these were sets of division- and brigade-level actions coordinated and integrated across Iraq by MNC-I. They included close coordination with U.S. Special Operations Forces as well as with Iraqi military and police forces.

The city of Baghdad was the most complex battle space in Iraq, due to the strong presence of both AQI and JAM special groups, the many potential fault lines among different neighborhoods, and a security "temperature" that can vary on a block-by-block basis. In the series of Corps-level operations, the Multi-National Division-Baghdad, led by the 4th Infantry Division since December 2007, focused first on clearing the city, and then on establishing a strong presence to hold each neighborhood.[329]

The area just south of Baghdad and along the Tigris River, with its mixed Shi'a/ Sunni population, had long provided safe havens and a gateway to Baghdad for AQI and its affiliates from Al Anbar and Iraq's western borders, and for Shi'a extremists coming from southern Iraq or from Iraq's border with Iran. As part of the Corps-level operations, Multi-National Division- Center, led by 3ID, focused on clearing these restive areas, narrowing down to more specific pockets of resistance, including Salman Pak and Arab Jabour, as progress is made.

To the north, Multi-National Division-North, led by 1st Armored Division, focused on clearing and then holding those areas where AQI affiliates sought refuge as they were pushed out of Baghdad.[330] Many AQI affiliates, pushed out of Baghdad by surge operations, initially relocated to Baquba, the capital city of Diyala province east of Baghdad. Reports suggested they had renamed it the new "capital of the Islamic State of Iraq."[331] As operations by MND-North and Iraqi security forces pushed AQI out of that city, some AQI moved east up the

Diyala River Valley, into the so-called "breadbasket" of Iraq near the city of Muqtadiyah—a focal point for the Division's operations in January 2008. Working in Diyala in partnership with the Iraqi 5th Army Division, the combined forces uncovered a number of major weapons caches, and had "some very tough fights."[332]

In Al Anbar province to the west, the Multi-National Force-West, led by II Marine Expeditionary Force (Forward), working closely with Iraqi counterparts, focused its operations on a pocket of AQI concentration around Lake Thar Thar, northwest of Baghdad. As AQI was pushed out of major population centers including Ramadi and Fallujah, they tended to attempt to regroup in the desert, so another major coalition and Iraqi focus in Al Anbar has been targeting the AQI remnants in rural areas.[333]

Military Operations in 2008

Coalition and Iraqi military operations in 2008 have been characterized by growing ISF capabilities, and growing assertiveness of the GoI in employing the ISF. Operations have been carried out against both Al Qaeda in Iraq affiliates in north-central Iraq, and against extremist Shi'a militia members in the south and Baghdad.

The Fight against Al Qaeda in Iraq (AQI) Elements in the North

By the beginning of 2008, Corps-level operations had pushed AQI out of Anbar and Baghdad to the east and north. Operations by Multi-National Division-North in January 2008, in Diyala province, pushed AQI out of Diyala's capital city Baquba and further up the Diyala River Valley. Some members of AQI sought to establish the northern city of Mosul as their last stronghold— their "center of gravity."[334]

In 2007, through the height of the surge, Ninewah province and its capital city Mosul had been an "economy of force" area for both U.S. and Iraqi forces, as additional forces were sent south to Baghdad and nearby areas.[335] Ninewah province offered AQI affiliates some geographic advantages, including land routes out to Iraq's porous western border. It also offered a volatile mixed population, including governing structures largely controlled by Kurds, a sizable Sunni Arab population that felt disenfranchised, and Christian, Yazidi, and other minority groups.

On January 25, 2008, Prime Minister Maliki announced that there would be a major new Iraqi and coalition offensive against AQI in Mosul and stated that it would be "decisive."[336] The Prime Minister established a new Ninewah Operations Command (NOC), designed to coordinate operations by all ISF. The NOC was scheduled to reach full operating capacity in May 2008, but as one senior U.S. commander noted, "they just weren't ready." Nevertheless, ISF did launch some clearing operations and took steps to secure Mosul including setting up check points and maintaining a presence at combat outposts.[337] MNC-I noted its intent, once progress in Diyala province allows, to go back and complete the effort in Mosul, to "get it set."

In October 2008, U.S. and Iraqi forces struck a major blow against AQI in Mosul by killing Abu Qaswarah, the senior AQI emir of northern Iraq. According to U.S. commanders on the ground, that successful operation was made possible by a series of actions and information-gathering by U.S. and Iraqi forces over preceding months, and his death was expected to disrupt the AQI network significantly.[338]

According to U.S. commanders, operations in Mosul in 2008 benefitted from an initiative by Multi-National Corp-Iraq (MNC-I) in the Jazeera desert, west of Mosul. MNC-I formed a task force around a military intelligence brigade headquarters, based it in the desert, and tasked it to coordinate intelligence fusion, drawing on sources from the U.S. Marines in the west, and U.S. and Iraqi SOF, in addition to its own assets. Commanders note that the approach has facilitated identifying and interdicting fighters coming across the desert toward Mosul.[339]

Meanwhile, in January 2008, operations in Diyala province, east of Baghdad, had driven AQI affiliates out of major population centers into rural areas. One U.S. military commander, emphasizing AQI's lack of cohesive structure, described them as "a bunch of gangs under the Al Qaeda rubric."[340]

In late July 2008, ISF, supported by coalition forces, launched operations against AQI in Diyala. Before the operations began, Prime Minister Maliki publicly stated the intention to launch operations, and as a result, according to U.S. commanders, many of the "bad guys" simply ran away.[341] In the view of one U.S. commander, that approach may have "pushed the problem down the road," but on the other hand, he added, it might allow time for ISF capabilities to develop further. U.S. support to the operations included conducting blocking operations, to try to catch AQI affiliates attempting to flee,[342] as well as providing air support, some logistics, and engineering support.[343]

According to U.S. commanders, the Diyala operations were the first to include rehearsals by the ISF and joint planning with Multi-National Corps-Iraq. Iraqi officials noted that the Diyala operations more than two Iraqi Army divisions, and more than one division from the Ministry of Interior.[344] U.S. commanders add that while the Iraqi Army demonstrated some proficiency in "clearing," it has been harder for the Iraqis to figure out how to "hold" cleared areas—Iraqi planning for the "hold" portion of the operations was insufficient and hampered by a lack of Iraqi police.[345]

The Fight against Shi'a Extremists in the South

On March 25, 2008, based on direction from Prime Minister Nouri al-Maliki, Iraqi security forces launched a major operation, *Sawlat al-Fursan* (Charge of the Knights) in Basra, with the stated aim of targeting criminals operating under religious or political cover.[346] Some Muqtada al-Sadr loyalists apparently viewed the matter differently, and accused the government of using its armed forces, many of which are strongly influenced by the Islamic Supreme Council in Iraq (ISCI), to attack a political rival. International Crisis Group expert Joost Hiltermann characterized the operations as "a fairly transparent partisan effort by the Supreme Council [ISCI] dressed in government uniforms to fight the Sadrists and Fadila."[347]

Prior to the operations, by many accounts, key militias in Basra controlled local councils and much of the flow of daily life on the streets of the city.[348] In 2007, the UK-led Multi-National Division-Southeast (MND-SE), responsible for Basra, had determined that "the UK presence in Basra was a catalyst for violence." In August of that year, UK forces consolidated at the airport, outside the city, and assumed an overwatch posture.[349] In an apparent attempt at reconciliation, the division reportedly made an accommodation with the *Jaish al-Mahdi* (JAM), agreeing to limit its own presence in the city.[350]

The launch of the "Charge" was, by many accounts, precipitate. In March 2008, Iraqi forces in Basra, assisted by UK advisors, had been preparing a staged plan to take back Basra, including setting conditions first, and then launching operations in June. According to Iraqi civilian and military officials in Basra, and U.S. and UK military officials, the Iraqi operation was not wellplanned. Some officials, who were directly involved, note that when the Prime Minister arrived in Basra in March, he had been prepared only for a "limited operation" and was surprised by the magnitude of the challenge.[351] Some observers suggest that Maliki was emboldened by progress against AQI in the north, and somewhat over-confident in the abilities of the ISF.

The ISF applied considerable forces to the effort, including 21 Iraqi Army battalions and 8 National Police battalions—reportedly some 30,000 Iraqi forces altogether, including special operations and conventional army forces, as well as police.[352] Extremists in Basra mounted fierce resistance—including simultaneous attacks on 25 Iraqi police stations by JAM-affiliated forces.[353] Iraqi Minister of Defense Abdel Qadr Jassim was quoted as saying, "We supposed that this operation would be a normal operation, but we were surprised by this resistance and have been obliged to change our plans and our tactics."[354]

U.S. military officials report that without substantial assistance from the coalition, the operation would have been in jeopardy. As one senior U.S. commander explained it, Prime Minister Maliki had staked his reputation on the operation—if the operation failed, the government might collapse, so, he added, "We made sure that it would be successful."[355] Coalition support included the advice and support of embedded transition teams, air strikes, and air lift.[356]

According to coalition officials, while many of the ISF performed competently, some—as widely reported—did not. One newly formed Iraq Army brigade, the 52nd, which had no combat experience, seemingly collapsed under the pressure. In April 2008, the GoI noted that more than 1,000 members of the ISF had laid down their weapons during the fight. Accordingly, some 500 Iraqi Army Soldiers, and 421 members of the Iraqi Police in Basra, were fired.[357]

In the aftermath of the Basra operations, coalition and Iraqi commanders reported that the security situation had improved markedly. Accordingly to MND-SE, the ISF regained freedom of movement throughout the city.[358] According to an Iraqi Army commander, security was much better, and the main challenge now was to act against criminals and outlaws.[359]

In March 2008, as operations in Basra commenced, some JAM elements stepped up attacks targeting coalition and Iraqi forces in Baghdad. The attacks included significant targeting of the International Zone, primarily from the direction of Sadr City, a stronghold of supporters of Moqtada al-Sadr and the Sadr family.

To quell the attacks, U.S. and Iraqi forces launched operations, first of all targeting the southern part of Sadr City where many rocket attacks were originating. According to a senior U.S. military official, the Iraqi security forces, perhaps focused on the ongoing Basra operations, were reluctant to engage—he added, "We had to drag them to the fight."[360] U.S. forces, while largely remaining outside Sadr City itself, brought to the fight air weapons teams and substantial layered ISR.[361]

After simmering for nearly two months, with continual pressure applied by coalition and Iraqi forces, the fight in Sadr City ended in May 2008 with a deal struck between Moqtada al-Sadr and the GoI. The arrangements reportedly allowed the ISF full access to the area. They called for an end to the launching of rockets and mortars from Sadr City, and for the removal of any explosives that had been laid down. They did not require the disbanding or disarming of JAM forces—and JAM affirmed that it did not possess any medium or heavy weapons.[362] In the aftermath of the fighting in Sadr City, U.S. officials confirmed that ISF freedom of movement had been restored, and local residents reportedly confirmed that the grip of control by Shi'a militias over the local economy and public services had relaxed.[363]

In June 2008, the ISF launched clearing operations in Amarah, capital city of Maysan province just north of Basra. While little resistance was encountered, ISF found a number of weapons caches, assisted by information from the local population. The ISF followed by providing humanitarian assistance in the form of hot meals, and coalition forces introduced a temporary employment program, hiring local residents to remove trash and debris from city streets. U.S. commanders noted that the Amarah operations may have been the first that the ISF carefully planned.[364]

Counter-IED Efforts

Improvised explosive devices (IEDs) are the enemy's "weapon of choice" in Iraq. Usually made with technologically simple, off-the-shelf materials, they generally do not require deep expertise to construct. As of early 2008, over 78% of those detained by coalition forces were interned based on suspicion of some IED-related activity.[365] IEDs are the leading cause of coalition casualties in Iraq—and over time, they have driven changes in coalition operations, including an increased reliance on air lift for transportation of personnel and cargo.

Recognizing the threat from these asymmetric weapons, both the Department of Defense and the military command on the ground in Iraq have made countering IEDs a top priority.[366] At DOD, the Joint IED Defeat Organization, based in the Office of the Secretary of Defense and led since December 2007 by Lieutenant General Tom Metz, is mandated to facilitate the rapid development, production and fielding of new technologies and approaches.

In the field, the premise of the counter-IED efforts has been to "attack the network." That involves not just capturing the IED emplacers, usually hired for a one-time payment, but also, in the words of one Division Commander, "influencing the decisions of those who place IEDs."[367] More broadly, it includes mapping the relationships among emplacers, financiers, and overall strategists, including the support they receive from outside Iraq.

To help execute those efforts, Multi-National Corps-Iraq and its subordinate multi-national divisions created dedicated counter-IED cells, reinforced by experts provided by JIEDDO. Their efforts include information-sharing about the latest enemy tactics, techniques and procedures, distributing and providing training for the latest counter-IED technology, training the force to recognize how the network operates, and integrating all available intelligence assets to better define—and target—the networks.[368] MNC-I also includes a task force of technical experts who collect and analyze all found IEDs.[369]

MNF-I and MNC-I officials point to a dramatic decrease in enemy IED use, from September 2007 to September 2008, from about 110 incidents per day to about 26 incidents per day. Most of those incidents involved relatively unsophisticated devices, with key exceptions. According to U.S. officials, enemy IED use seems to follow cycles of innovation.[370] In late 2007, a key IED concern was the explosively formed penetrator (EFP), able to target vehicles with a particularly powerful blast, but EFP trend lines diminished markedly after January 2008. In late 2007, another worrisome form of IED appeared, the improvised rocket-assisted mortar (IRAM)—a rocket with a propane tank and ball bearings. IRAMs take a long time to build, and they have indiscriminate and catastrophic effects. The first two IRAM incidents took place in November 2007, and a total of 13 incidents had taken place by August 2008. In mid-2008, the use of "building-borne IEDs"— houses wired to explode—became more common.[371]

Carrying out IED attack requires, to some extent, the ability to operate within a local population. U.S. commanders note that the most fundamental factor in explaining the successes to date in the counter-IED effort is that "the Iraqi population has turned against the IED effort."[372]

Special Operations Forces

U.S. Special Operations Forces (SOF) have played an integral role throughout Operation Iraqi Freedom, including targeting key enemy leaders. MNF-I leaders note that as of 2008, SOF and conventional forces work in a much more closely integrated way than they did earlier in OIF. SOF is particularly well-suited to infiltrate difficult areas to reach key individual targets. But according to MNF-I and MNC-I leaders, SOF often rely, for targeting information, on conventional units' detailed, daily familiarity with their battle space, based on their long-standing relationships with local Iraqi counterparts. Further, commanders stress, after a SOF action, it is the conventional forces—in partnership with Iraqi forces—that stay to "hold" the area.[373]

Air Power

Most press coverage of the counter-insurgency effort in Iraq has focused on the role of ground forces—the Army and the Marine Corps—including the number of troops on the ground, the approaches they have used, and the stress on those two Military Services.[374] Air power has also been an integral element of the OIF counter-insurgency (COIN) effort— providing critical Intelligence, Surveillance and Reconnaissance (ISR) capabilities, and facilitating mobility— particularly given the lack of mass transit of troops by ground.[375] Importantly from an analytical perspective, the role of air power in Iraq has evolved over time.

One major shift over the course of OIF has been in the kinetic use of air power. Defense expert Anthony Cordesman has pointed to its "steadily more important role over time."[376] In November 2007, Major General Dave Edgington, then the MNF-I Air Component Coordination Element (ACCE) Director, confirmed a sharp spike, once all the surge troops had arrived in Iraq, in the number of weapons dropped from fighters and bombers.[377]

Statistics released in January 2008 by the Combined Force Air Component Command (CFACC), the air component of CENTCOM, provided further detail about the upswing in the use of weapons. The yearly number of close air support (CAS) strikes, with munitions dropped, in OIF, rose from 86 in 2004, to 176 in 2005, to 1,770 in 2006, to 3,030 in 2007. During 2007, the monthly number of CAS strikes rose from 89 in January, then 36 in February, to 171 in June, 303 in July, and 166 in August, before dropping back to double-digits for the rest of the year.[378]

In January 2008, Maj. Gen. Edgington explained that close air support—or "on-call" support—is the type of kinetic air power that has been most in demand in Iraq. Coordinated air/ground operations during the first several months after the arrival of the full surge force produced the heaviest CAS requirements, but afterward the demand tapered off. The significantly higher demand for CAS, he noted, was less a reflection of a deliberate strategy to use more air power, than a natural result of a significantly larger number of U.S. troops, working significantly more closely with Iraqi counterparts and in local neighborhoods, and getting better information that made target identification much easier. As of January 2008, in a shift from mid-2007, the majority of weapons dropped were targeting deeply buried IEDs.[379]

Some counter-insurgency specialists have questioned the use of kinetic air power in counterinsurgency operations because it risks civilian casualties that could fuel the insurgency. For example, Kalev Sepp has written, "These killings drive family and community members into the insurgency and create lifelong antagonisms toward the United States."[380]

Commanders have stressed, in turn, that although there is always a chance of accidental civilian casualties, the likelihood has greatly diminished with the development of precision capabilities. Further, the decision cycle before a weapon is dropped includes a series of decision points that give commanders the opportunity to stop an action if new and better information becomes available about a civilian presence in the target area.[381] In his December 2007 assessment of the use of air power in Iraq and Afghanistan, Anthony Cordesman concludes that "considerable restraint was used in both wars."[382]

Another major shift in the use of air in OIF, according to U.S. commanders, has been the growing availability of greater air assets—for example, significantly more full-motion video assets.[383] In 2008, U.S. air assets—ISR, kinetic, and mobility—proved essential to the increasingly "combined" coalition and Iraqi operations on the ground. In the Basra operations in March 2008, U.S. transition teams embedded with Iraqi units relied on ISR and some kinetic air as key enablers, and the coalition also provided some essential airlift.

U.S. and Iraqi military operations in the Sadr City section of Baghdad, in spring 2008, presented some specific challenges—a geographic area largely denied to legitimate Iraqi security forces but densely populated by civilians, serving as a launching pad for frequent attacks on Iraqi and coalition targets, in the middle of the nation's capital. In the judgment of some U.S. commanders, what helped make the U.S.-Iraqi Sadr City operations a success was pushing the control of air assets to lower levels in the U.S. chain of command.[384] Commanders on the ground had access to layered inputs from manned and unmanned sensors, and multiple options—both ground- and airbased —for taking out targets, if the decision was to "kill" rather than "follow and exploit."

IRAQI SECURITY FORCES (ISF)

As of the beginning of 2009, the Iraqi Security Forces (ISF) consisted of three major groups: the Army, Navy and Air Force under the Ministry of Defense (MoD); the Iraqi Police Service, the National Police, and the Department of Border Enforcement under the Ministry of Interior (MoI), as well as the Facilities Protection Service that was still being consolidated under the MoI; and the Iraqi Special Operations Forces that report to the Counter-Terrorism Bureau, under the office of the Prime Minister.

Developing the ISF and the security Ministries that oversee them is a critical component of the role of U.S. and coalition forces in Iraq—a role that has evolved over time in response to events on the ground and changes in U.S. strategy.

Requirement for New Iraqi Security Forces

The scope of the challenge has been extensive, since none of Iraq's pre-war security forces or structures were left intact or available for duty after major combat operations.

U.S. pre-war planning had foreseen an immediate and practical need for law enforcement, and for security more broadly, after major combat—particularly since some challenges to law and order might reasonably be expected after the collapse of the old regime. Planning had also stressed the need for security providers to have an "Iraqi face," to calm and reassure the Iraqi people.

However, pre-war planning had erroneously assumed that Iraqi local police forces would be available, as needed, to help provide security for the Iraqi people. Instead, in the immediate aftermath of major combat, coalition forces found that civilian law enforcement bodies had effectively disappeared.

Meanwhile, military pre-war planning had also assumed that Iraqi military units would be available for recall and reassignment after the war, as needed. Military plans counted on the "capitulation" of Iraqi forces, and included options for using some of those forces to guard borders or perform other tasks.[385]

Instead, on May 23, 2003, the Coalition Provisional Authority (CPA) issued CPA Order Number 2, which dissolved all Iraqi military services including the Army. That decision foreclosed the option of unit recall to support security or reconstruction activities, or to serve as building blocks for a new, post-Saddam army.[386]

Post-war Iraq was not, however, a blank slate in terms of trained and organized fighters. The Kurds in northern Iraq had long maintained well-trained and well-equipped forces—the *pesh merga*—which had worked closely with coalition forces during major combat. Somewhat more equivocally, a major Shi'a Arab political party, the Supreme Council of the Islamic Revolution in Iraq (SCIRI, later ISCI), maintained its own militia, the Badr Corps,[387] which had been trained in Iran during the Iran-Iraq war. Like the *pesh merga*, Badr members were trained and equipped, but unlike them, they had no history of cooperation with coalition forces in Iraq. In the early days of the formal occupation, in various contexts, both militias offered their services to help provide security. The coalition—then the executive authority of Iraq—thus faced the additional challenge of whether and how to incorporate these militias into official Iraqi security structures.

ISF Training Efforts during the Formal Occupation

During the year of formal occupation, Iraqi security forces training was led and primarily executed by the Coalition Provisional Authority. Particularly in the earliest days, the efforts were characterized by limited long-term strategic planning, and by resources too limited for the scope and scale of the tasks.

Police training began as a function of the CPA "Ministry of the Interior" office, initially under the leadership of former New York Police Commissioner Bernard Kerik. He was supported by a skeleton staff in Baghdad, and by some resources from the State Department's Bureau of International Narcotics and Law Enforcement Affairs (INL). Based on priorities articulated by Washington, the team focused initially on the capital city, including rebuilding the Baghdad Police Academy. The office also launched a limited call-back and re-training effort for former Iraqi police officers, but the effort was constrained by limited resources and staff—including a very limited presence outside Baghdad.[388]

Meanwhile, military units throughout Iraq had recognized an immediate need for some Iraqi law enforcement presence on the ground in their areas of responsibility. To the frustration of some CPA officials,[389] military commanders launched police re-training initiatives in their areas, initially in the form of three-week courses, with the goal of quickly fielding at least temporary Iraqi security providers. Ambassador Bremer eventually instructed CJTF-7 to cease police recruiting.[390]

CPA also initially had responsibility for rebuilding Iraq's Army, under the supervision of Walt Slocombe, the CPA Senior Advisor for National Security, and a former Under Secretary of Defense for Policy. In an August 2003 Order, CPA directed the creation of the New Iraqi Army (NIA).[391] The training effort, led day-to-day by Major General Paul Eaton, focused on recruiting and training Iraqi soldiers, battalion-by-battalion. The plan was to create higher headquarters later on—and in particular, once an Iraqi civilian leadership was in place to provide civilian control of the military. The initial, ambitious goal was the creation of 27 battalions in two years, which was adjusted to the even more ambitious goal of 27 battalions in one year.[392]

In early September 2003, as a stop-gap measure, at the urging of CJTF-7 with backing from the Office of the Secretary of Defense, CPA announced the establishment of the Iraqi Civil Defense Corps (ICDC). The ICDC would be a trained, uniformed, armed "security and emergency service agency for Iraq."[393] In accordance with the Order he signed, establishing the ICDC, Ambassador Bremer delegated responsibility for its development to the senior military commander in Iraq—LTG Sanchez. Under CJTF-7's authority, Division Commanders launched ICDC recruiting and training programs, supporting the efforts in part with their own organic assets, and in part with CERP funding.

Unity of Effort: Creation of Multi-National Security Transition Command-Iraq

In 2003 and early 2004, the various ISF training efforts—for the police, the NIA and the ICDC—proceeded in parallel, led by separate entities within the coalition, with little opportunity for integrated strategic planning and resourcing.

The military command in Iraq had sought for some time to be assigned responsibility for the entire ISF training mission, based on the view that CPA did not have the capacity to accomplish all of it, or to coordinate its many elements in a single strategy. Ambassador Bremer resisted this design, based on the view that the military was not trained to train police forces.[394]

On May 11, 2004, President Bush issued National Security Presidential Directive (NSPD) 36, which assigned the mission of organizing, training and equipping all Iraqi security forces (ISF) to CENTCOM. This included both directing all U.S. efforts, and coordinating all supporting international efforts. It explicitly included Iraq's civilian police as well as its military forces.[395]

CENTCOM, in turn, created the Multi-National Security Transition Command-Iraq (MNSTC-I), a new three-star headquarters that would fall under the Multi-National Force-Iraq (MNF-I), to bring together all Iraqi security forces training under a single lead in Iraq.[396]

Since December 2004, in keeping with the original NSPD mandate concerning international contributions, the MNSTC-I Commanding General has been dual-hatted as the Commander of the NATO Training Mission-Iraq (NTM-I). NTM-I provides training, both inside and outside Iraq, to Iraqi security forces; assistance with equipping; and technical advice and assistance. As of August 2008, its permanent mission in Iraq included 133 personnel from 15 countries. Major initiatives have included helping the Iraqi Army build a Non-Commissioned Officer Corps; helping establish and structure Iraqi military educational institutions; and—with a strong contribution from Italy's Carabinieri—helping update the skills and training of Iraq's National Police.[397]

On October 1, 2005, MNSTC-I was given the additional responsibility of mentoring and helping build capacity in the Ministries of Defense and Interior.[398]

ISF Training: Theory of the Case

At the heart of the ISF training mission is the practice of embedding coalition forces and other advisors and experts—now called "transition teams"—with Iraqi military or civilian units, to train, mentor and advise them.

That practice, though it has grown over time, is not new. In early 2004, under CJTF-7, some Army units embedded teams with the newly generated New Iraqi Army battalions. Under Commanding General George Casey, MNF-I initiated a more aggressive embedding strategy, and the effort expanded still further in scope when GEN Petraeus assumed command of MNF-I in February 2007.[399]

One thing that has changed over time is the strategic intent of the training mission. As the word "transition" in MNSTC-I's name suggests, the initial stated goal of MNSTC-I and the ISF training effort in general was to transition security responsibility to Iraqis. The sooner the Iraqis were capable of providing security for themselves, the sooner U.S. and other coalition forces could go home.[400] Accordingly, embedded teams worked with their Iraqi counterparts with a view to the earliest possible independence of those Iraqi units.

In early 2007, in keeping with the Administration's New Way Forward strategy and the surge emphasis on "population security" as a prerequisite for complete transition, the emphasis of the training and embedding mission shifted. The ultimate goal was still to transition security responsibility to Iraqis, but the timeline was relaxed. The primary focus, in the near term, would be working with Iraqi units to help them better provide population security. Working closely with U.S. counterparts on real-world missions, Iraqi units would be practicing the skills they would need to operate independently.[401]

ISF Training: Organizational Structure and Responsibilities

Under MNF-I, several key subordinate bodies share responsibilities for training and advising Iraqi Security Forces and their respective headquarters institutions.

MNSTC-I's broad mandate is to generate and replenish the ISF, improve their quality, and support the institutional capacity development of the security ministries—the Ministry of Defense, the Ministry of the Interior, and the Counter-Terrorism Bureau. In practice, MNSTC-I shares some of these responsibilities with the Multi-National Corps-Iraq (MNC-I), the three-star operational command that also reports directly to MNF-I. In working with the ISF, MNC-I's focus is operational, managing transition teams that embed with the Iraqi Army, the Department of Border Enforcement and the National Police, while MNSTC-I's focus includes both operational and institutional issues.

Under MNC-I, the Iraq Assistance Group (IAG), a one-star command created in February 2005, is the "principal coordinating agency for the Iraqi Security Forces" within MNC-I. Originally, the IAG "owned" the transition teams that embed with Iraqi units, but a major change was made in mid-2007. At that time, transition teams, while still assigned to the IAG, were attached to the brigade combat teams, also under MNC-I, which were responsible, respectively, for the areas in which the teams were working. As previous IAG commander Brigadier General Dana Pittard explained, the change provided "unity of effort and unity of command in a brigade combat team's area of operations."[402]

The IAG continues to serve as the executive agent for transition teams throughout Iraq, ensuring they have the training and support they need. This includes synchronizing the curricula at the transition team training sites inside and outside Iraq, providing the teams with equipment and related training, and supporting the teams' Reception, Staging, Onward Movement, and Integration (RSOI) as they arrive in Iraq. The IAG also directly supports transition teams working with three Iraqi headquarters staffs: the Iraqi Ground Forces Command, the National Police headquarters, and the Department of Border Enforcement headquarters. And the IAG is helping spearhead the creation of an Iraqi Non-Commissioned Officer (NCO) Corps—including training Iraqi NCOs to run a new NCO training course.[403]

As a corollary to President Obama's troop drawdown and transition policy, the mission and structure of MNSTC-I are expected to transition into a large version of a typical Office of Security Cooperation, focused on mil-to-mil partnership activities, capacity-building in the security ministries, and foreign military sales. The Advise and Assist Brigades scheduled to compose the transitional force are likely to assume day-to-day responsibility for advising the Iraqi Army; MNSTC-I could retain responsibility for partnering with other ISF forces.[404]

ISF Training: Transition Teams

Transition teams have been called the "linchpin of the training and mentoring effort."[405] The teams vary in size, composition and focus, based on the needs of the Iraqi forces they partner with and the specific local circumstances, but the theory of the case is consistent: the teams simultaneously "advise, teach, and mentor," and "provide direct access to Coalition capabilities such as air support, artillery, medical evacuation and intelligence-gathering."[406] They also provide continual situational awareness to coalition forces about the status of the ISF.

Transition teams work with units in each of the Iraqi military and police services, with key operational headquarters, and with the security ministries. Due to resource constraints, coverage of Iraqi units by training teams has not been one-to-one.

In 2008, as ISF capabilities grew, several shifts were underway, if unevenly across Iraq, in the focus of the embedded transition teams: from basic skills to more sophisticated capabilities, from lower-level units to higher-level headquarters, and from training to advising.[407]

In general, the embedded advisory effort is highly dynamic—work with any Iraqi unit is expected to be temporary. According to U.S. military officials, as of fall 2008, the embedded training effort was far from completed—while many Iraqi units had already "graduated" from the need for embedded advisors, others Iraqi units had just entered that form of partnership, and other units were still being generated by the Government of Iraq.[408]

Interior Ministry Transition Teams

For Ministry of Interior forces, the Department of Defense reported that as of August 2008, there were 27 border transition teams (BTTs) working with about two-thirds of Department of Border Enforcement units at battalion-level or above; and 41 National Police Transition Teams (NPTTs) which were partnering with about 80% of National Police units at battalion-level or above. For the Iraqi Police, there were 223 of 266 required Police Transition Teams (PTTs) working with Iraqi police at local, district and provincial levels.[409]

The Police Training Team mission is supported by a U.S. Military Police brigade, complemented by civilian International Police Advisors (IPAs) who provide expertise in criminal investigation and police station management. The IPA contracts are funded by DOD and managed by the Department of State. As of August 2008, MNSTC-I noted that about 400 IPAs were deployed in Iraq, at academies and with some units. Some contemporary observers have suggested—echoing the CPA's Ambassador Bremer—that military forces, including MPs, are not optimally suited to train civilian law enforcement personnel, and have urged the expansion of the IPA program.[410] Some U.S. military officials, while strongly supporting the IPA program, caution that some IPAs have more relevant backgrounds than others—a police officer from a relatively quiet U.S. town with a 30-member police force may not have the background to train and mentor "big city cops" preparing for a counter-insurgency fight.[411]

Approaches to police training have varied over time, and by U.S. battle space in Iraq. In Anbar province, for example, Multi-National Force-West (MNF-W), led by the Marines, decided early in the effort to triple or quadruple the normal size of the embedded PTTs. As one commander noted, "You need to be able to leave Marines at the police station while others are out on patrol." But by mid-2008, based on analysis of 109 police stations, MNF-W concluded that around-the-clock PTT presence at the level of the local station was no longer necessary.[412]

In general, by mid-2008, the focus of the police training effort had shifted, in many locations, from basic policing to the professionalization of the force. As local police mastered basic skills such as carrying out patrols, PTTs increasingly emphasized higher-end skills, including police intelligence and forensics. To help with this new focus, for example, in summer 2008, MNF-W brought in experts from the Royal Irish Constabulary.[413]

Defense Ministry Transition Teams

For Ministry of Defense forces, the Iraqi Navy is supported by a Maritime Strategic Transition Team (MaSTT) advising the headquarters, and a Naval Transition Team (NaTT) embedded with sailors at the Umm Qasr Naval Base. The Coalition Air Force Transition

Team (CAFTT) provides advisory teams to the Iraqi Air Staff, Air Operations Center, and individual squadrons.

For the Iraqi Army, as of September 2008 there were 183 Military Transition Teams (MiTTs) working with Iraqi units from battalion to division level.[414] At the Iraqi division level, the standard pattern calls a 15-member team led by a Colonel (or equivalent); at the brigade level—a 10-member team led by a Lieutenant Colonel; and at the battalion level—an 11-member team led by a Major. The teams, though small, include a wide array of specializations—including intelligence, logistics, maneuver trainers, effects, communications, and medical expertise.[415]

The MiTTs—like the PTTs—have varied, over time and by battle space, in number and composition. MNF-W consistently chose to use larger MiTTs—with 30 to 40 people.[416] In some instances, U.S. Army MiTTs have also been augmented to form larger teams.

In 2008, one major transition in the Iraqi Army training effort was a shift of focus from basic skills to enablers. MNC-I Commanding General LTG Austin made ISF logistics a top priority. To that end, MNC-I created Logistics Transition Assistance Teams (LTATs), drawing on Corps assets, to help jumpstart the development of Iraqi Army logistics capabilities. In mid-2008, U.S. commanders also stressed the Iraqi Army's continuing need for combat enablers, such as ISR, and the ability to call forward and adjust fires.[417]

A second major transition was a shift of focus from lower-level to higher-level Iraqi headquarters. Both U.S. Army- and Marine-led multi-national divisions are shifting some of their advisory efforts to the Iraqi brigade and division level, focusing on leadership and staff organization.[418]

A third transition was the shift, in the rhetoric of U.S. commanders, from "training" to "advising." In practice, that can mean decreasing the rank of the members of the embedded U.S. teams, and assigning them "liaison" rather than structured training functions.[419]

The methodology for forming the MiTTs and preparing them for their assignments has evolved significantly over the short duration of the program. Initially, in the push to field trainers quickly, teams were pulled together from individual volunteers and trained at seven different locations in the United States, without specific standards.

Subsequently, the Army consolidated a training program for Army, Navy, and Air Force transition team members, under the auspices of the 1st Infantry Division at Ft. Riley, Kansas. The program included 72 days at Ft. Riley, including 12 days of inprocessing and 60 days of training, followed by a theater orientation at Camp Buehring, Kuwait, and then by further counter-insurgency training and hands-on equipment training at the Phoenix Academy at Camp Taji, Iraq. The program sent new team leaders out to the field for a brief visit, at the very beginning of their training at Ft. Riley, and it solicited "lessons learned" from Transition Team members both midtour and at the end of their tours in Iraq.

While the program of preparation improved markedly, the participants were still individual volunteers, who could come from any occupational specialty. As one program leader commented, the curriculum at Ft. Riley includes a measure of "move, shoot, and communicate" skills, as a refresher for all the "professors and protocol specialists" who volunteer.[420]

The Marine Corps created a separate program to prepare trainers—the Marine Corps Training and Advisory Group (MCTAG). Its mission is to "coordinate, form, train and equip Marine Corps advisor and training teams for current and projected operations."[421] According to a senior Marine commander in Iraq, the individuals selected for the program are the "first team," with recent experience in command or in combat jobs such as battalion operations officer.[422]

The majority of MiTTs in Iraq are "external" teams—that is, they come out of the Ft. Riley and MCTAG systems. However, to help meet demand, about 20% of the MiTTs are "taken out of hide," or "internal"—that is, their members are pulled from U.S. units already serving in Iraq.[423]

The experiences with providing large-scale training to indigenous security forces in Iraq and Afghanistan prompted debates within the Department of the Army and DOD more broadly about likely future requirements to provide such training in general, and, more specifically, the best ways to continue to source the Transition Team mission in Iraq.[424]

ISF Training: Unit Partnering

In 2008, in addition to the work of embedded transition teams, the practice of "unit partnering"— that is, a one-to-one matching between a U.S. unit and an ISF unit of similar larger size—grew substantially. Unit partnering is an opportunity for U.S. units to provide an example of how a headquarters functions, how decisions are made, and how efforts are coordinated. The "lessons" are provided by fellow combat units that, like their Iraqi partners, practice the "curriculum" daily. Many U.S. commanders in Iraq describe unit partnering as the opportunity to "show," not just "tell."[425] In August 2008, one commander observed that there was "greater energy from partnering, than from the transition teams."[426]

While unit partnering became much more widely institutionalized in 2008, the practice had been used by some U.S. units in the past. In 2007, for example, in the turbulent area of Mahmudiyah and Yusufiyah south of Baghdad, Colonel Mike Kershaw, Commander of the 2nd Brigade of 10th Mountain Division, tasked his entire field artillery battalion to embed with the 4th Brigade of the 6th Iraqi Army Division and its battalions. The de facto transition team—350 soldiers, staff, and all of their enablers—was far more robust than a MiTT, and had the added value of providing a visible example of how a U.S. battalion is organized and functions. The results in terms of Iraqi operational capabilities were apparently positive. Near the end of the brigade's tour, COL Kershaw reported, "We really conduct almost no operations where we do not have Iraqi forces either embedded with us, or where they are in the lead."[427]

Unit partnering is most common—and the closest "fit"—with the Iraqi Army. In mid-2008, for example, both Multi-National Division-Center and Multi-National Division-North assigned a brigade to partner with each Iraqi Army division in their respective battle spaces.[428] Some brigades, in turn, such as the 1st BCT of 10th Mountain Division in Kirkuk, assigned one battalion to partner with each Iraqi Army brigade.[429] A U.S. BCT commander in Diyala reported in January 2009 that he partners with every Iraqi brigade, battalion, squad and platoon in his area of responsibility. He stated, "We take our tactics, techniques, procedures and our skill sets, and we rub up against them extremely hard. And the end result is that we rub off on them."[430]

Across Iraq, some U.S. units have also partnered with units from other Iraqi security forces—a brigade in Baghdad, for example, described a growing partnership with the Iraqi police.[431] However, unit partnering is both time- and personnel-intensive, and in some cases operational requirements have not permitted U.S. forces to unit-partner with all of the ISF in their battle space.[432]

Like ISF training in general, unit partnering is a dynamic endeavor—it is designed to boost the capabilities of Iraqi units, and at some stage of improvement a unit's need for a close partnership diminishes. As of early 2009, ISF units had reached quite varied stages of development—many, in the views of U.S. commanders, were very proficient, while others had just been formed, and the Government of Iraq has stated the intention to form still others.

More so than the use of embedded teams, unit partnership requires a robust U.S. forces presence, and it may become more difficult to practice as U.S. forces in Iraq draw down. It seems that U.S. commanders, in more widely institutionalizing unit partnerships in 2008, decided to make maximum use of time and presence remaining in Iraq—whatever that might be. As one senior commander noted in August 2008, "If we partner with the Iraqis for the next six to nine months, then maybe they will be good enough."[433]

Iraqi Security Forces: The Numbers

The Department of Defense reported that as of March 2009, there were approximately 615,000 assigned members of the Iraqi Security Forces.[434] As of October 31, 2008, the following numbers of ISF, by category, had been "authorized" by the Government of Iraq, "assigned" based on payroll data, and "trained."[435]

Table 1. Iraqi Security Forces as of October 31, 2008

Component	Authorized	Assigned	Trained
Ministry of the Interior			
Police	334,739	300,156	209,100
National Police	46,580	41,044	52,513
Border Enforcement	45,550	40,328	36,673
Total MoI	426,869	381,528	298,286
Ministry of Defense			
Army	174,280	196,236	235,606
Training and Support Forces	15,583	23,452	22,930
Air Force	3,690	2,006	2,843
Navy	3,596	1,898	1,494
Total MoD	197,149	223,592	262,873
Counter-Terrorism Bureau			
Special Operations	4,733	4,160	4,564
Total ISF	628,751	609,280	565,723

Source: Department of State, "Iraq Weekly Status Report," December 3, 2008.

MNSTC-I and MNF-I estimate that the ISF numbers are likely to grow further in the future. According to MNSTC-I, the GoI's target size for the ISF is between 600,000 and 650,000, by the end of 2010.[436]

The three categories—authorized, assigned, and trained—are not a continuum. Some of those "trained" may not currently be "assigned"—on the payroll—for example due to casualties, or having left the service for other reasons. Further, in some cases the numbers "assigned" have outstripped the numbers "authorized." In some cases, this due to hirings at the provincial level not yet approved at the national level.

The overall numbers of Iraqi Security Forces (ISF) continue to grow, driven by revised estimates by the Government of Iraq of the forces required to provide security; by provincial-level requests for more police forces; and by the consolidation of forces from other ministries under the Defense and Interior Ministries.

Iraqi Security Forces: Evaluating the Results

The total numbers of ISF alone provide only a partial gauge of progress toward the broadly recognized ultimate goal of independent and self-sustaining Iraqi security forces. Recent qualitative assessments of capabilities and gaps, by current officials and outside experts, provide a more complete picture.

Iraqi Security Forces as a Whole
Both internal and external assessments of the ISF point to growing evidence of demonstrated operational capabilities, but raise some questions about some institutional capabilities, and thus about how close Iraqi forces and their oversight ministries are to completely independent and competent functioning.

One of the most comprehensive external assessments of the ISF was carried out in late 2007 by the congressionally mandated Commission on the Security Forces of Iraq, led by retired Marine Corps General James Jones (the "Jones Commission").[437] The commission benefitted from the participation of many senior leaders with years of experience in policing as well as military matters, and from spending considerable time in Iraq with the ISF. In its September 2007 *Report*, the commission concluded, somewhat pessimistically, that "... in the next 12 to 18 months, there will be continued improvement in their [ISF] readiness and capability, but not the ability to operate independently."[438]

Later that year, retired General Barry McCaffrey concluded that the picture had improved somewhat, and that the ISF were making operational contributions. He wrote after the trip that while the Iraqi police were "a mixed bag," and "much remains to be done" in the Iraqi Army, overall, the Iraqi Security Forces were "now beginning to take a major and independent successful role in the war."[439]

By early 2008, U.S. commanders on the ground in Iraq were describing an operationally increasingly competent Iraqi force. As one leader with multiple tours in Iraq noted, improved ISF capabilities were the single biggest difference between January 2008 and several years earlier.[440] Operationally, another leader observed, "the Iraqis are holding their ground, responsible for their own turf."[441] Regularly in 2008, at the daily MNC-I Battle Update Assessments, Division Commanders described to the MNC-I Commander operations carried out unilaterally, or with coalition tactical overwatch, by Iraqi forces.

By fall 2008, U.S. commanders on the ground in Iraq were consistently praising the tactical-level capabilities of their Iraqi counterparts.[442] The Department of Defense argued in

June 2008 that in operations in Basra, Mosul and Sadr City, the ISF "demonstrated their capability to conduct simultaneous extensive operations in three parts of the country."[443] One senior U.S. commander noted, "They can move themselves around the battlefield."[444] In March 2009, DOD confirmed the assessment of growing ISF operational capabilities, including their increasing use of after action reviews (AARs) but added: "The ISF continue to rely on the Coalition for logistics, fire support, close air support, communications, planning assistance, and intelligence surveillance and reconnaissance capabilities."[445] In February 2009, Lieutenant General Frank Helmick, MNSTC-I Commanding General, stated that the ISF "are getting better every day, and they have in large measure provided much of the security posture that we have in this country right now. So they are doing okay, but we have a long way to go."[446]

Among Iraqis themselves, there appeared to be a range of views concerning the readiness of the ISF to operate independently. According to MNC-I, Iraqi operational commanders stress that they still want a close partnership with U.S. forces.[447] In August 2008, one Iraqi Army division commander asserted that the United States should maintain combat forces in Iraq for another five years, to work with Iraqi counterparts.[448] In contrast, according to some U.S. officials, the perception of some senior Iraqi civilian officials is that the ISF are ready, or very nearly ready, to maintain security independently. At a press conference in September 2008, seemingly striking a middle path, Minister of Defense Abd al-Qadir noted that the Government of Iraq expects to have a security force completely able to provide security to the Iraqi people on its own, by 2011 or the beginning of 2012.[449]

In the views of many coalition advisors, the biggest long-term challenges faced by the Iraqi Security Forces as a whole may be institutional, rather than operational. These include improving ministerial capacity and effectiveness; clarifying chains of command; and crafting long-term, integrated force modernization plans for personnel and equipment.

In early fall 2008, MNF-I and MNSTC-I officials stressed the critical importance of civilian ministerial capacity. The practical challenges of growing and developing the Iraqi force are likely to continue for many years, they noted. But if the right, able civilian leadership is in place, they will be able to make needed decisions and solve problems as they arise.[450] In March 2009, DOD flatly assessed: "Many of the Iraqi civilians working in positions inside the MoD and MoI are not yet fully trained and qualified for their positions."[451]

Current *de facto* chains of command within and among the Iraqi Security Forces reflect the exigencies of the GoI's ongoing counter-insurgency (COIN) efforts. To help coordinate the efforts of the various ISF in given geographical areas, the GoI created provincially-based operations commands that report up directly to the office of the Prime Minister.[452] For some observers, the Prime Minister's direct access to the operations commands has raised concerns about potential misuse of the ISF for personal or even sectarian purposes.

In some cases, the operations command arrangements have created tensions with provincial-level officials, who would ordinarily exercise greater control over some provincial-level security forces.[453] The arrangements have also created some tensions with parent ministries in Baghdad— and in particular with the Interior Ministry, which apparently views the IA-led operations commands as "MoD-centric."[454] The commands also create some practical confusion, since units still rely on their parent organizations for supplies and logistical support. For example, as of August 2008, Baghdad was divided into two area commands: "Karkh" and "Rusafa." Under each were two Iraqi Army (IA) divisions and one

National Police (NP) division. Each division staff included representatives of the IA, NPs, and the Iraqi Police. Both IA and NP brigades fell under both IA and NP division headquarters. U.S. commanders working closely with these Iraqi units reported that this Iraqi experiment with jointness was working well at the tactical level, but became complicated when units turned to their respective ministries for support.[455]

Long-term force modernization planning and execution is another challenge for the ISF, in terms of both cost and strategic requirements. The current force continues to train and prepare for the ongoing counter-insurgency fight against Sunni and Shi'a extremists. Eventually, it is envisaged that the force will shift into a more typical division of labor—and train and equip themselves accordingly—in which MoD forces focus externally, and the Iraqi police, backed up by the National Police, provide domestic security.

For civilian and military leaders of the ISF, one major challenge is balancing near-term security challenges with long-term requirements. In August 2008, Iraqi ground commanders were all focused completely on the current fight, while senior civilian ministry officials were looking out toward the future division of labor.[456] At a press conference in September 2008, Minister of Defense Abd al-Qadir, speaking about the Iraqi police, stated that "it is their job to protect the citizen and our job to protect the frontier."[457]

By mid-2008, the Iraqi MoD had demonstrated keen interest in buying equipment for a future, outward-looking force—including tanks and fighter aircraft. DOD assessed in December 2008 that the "MoD has been overly focused on purchases for its steady-state force (2012 and beyond) rather than fundamental training, equipping, and sustaining shortfalls for its current force."[458] Senior U.S. advisors have expressed concerns about still-nascent Iraqi abilities to effectively identify, fund, and contract for future requirements. Some add that the approach of some Iraqi officials appears to be based on traditional "bazaar culture," in which the goal is getting the lowest price, with little consideration for long-term maintenance or interoperability.[459] In September 2008, the MoD signed the first letters of offer and acceptance (LOA) through the foreign military sales (FMS) program, for M1A1 tanks, armored reconnaissance helicopters, and C-130J transport aircraft.[460]

Some coalition advisors have noted that one of the greatest challenges for the ISF may be overcoming lingering sectarianism. The ISF as a whole is one of the most powerful national-level Iraqi institutions. A resurgence of sectarianism in the ranks could potentially turn key tools of the Iraqi government—the capabilities of its security forces—into potential threats to the unified whole state.[461]

Some Iraqi government officials, in turn, have expressed concerns about the size and scope of the ISF compared to other Iraqi government institutions. The more resources dedicated to the ISF, the more powerful the ISF will become, and the fewer resources that will be available for other government institutions. One provincial Governor added, "I fear the ISF. They are recruiting too many people. They are a big draw on the state budget and they have too much power."[462]

Iraqi Army

Both the size and the overall capabilities of the Iraqi Army (IA) continue to grow. MNC-I noted that as of December 20, 2009, the IA had 166 combat battalions (BN) conducting operations, of which 124 were in the lead for operations. A total of 208 combat BNs was planned. Altogether, at that date the IA had 213 BNs.[463] DOD reported that by January 2009, the IA had 175 combat BNs conducting operations.[464] DOD reported in March 2009 that that

IA had 13 infantry divisions and one mechanized division, and 55 brigades, and 201 fully generated and trained BNs, all reporting to the Iraqi Ground Forces Command.[465]

In December 2006, the Iraq Study Group provided a very cautious overall assessment of the Army's capabilities, noting: "The Iraqi Army is making fitful progress toward becoming a reliable and disciplined fighting force loyal to the national government."[466] Nine months later, in September 2007, the Jones Commission noted more positively that the Iraqi Army was increasingly effective at COIN, and increasingly reliable in general, but that progress among units was uneven.[467]

By the end of 2007, coalition commanders in Iraq pointed to further improvements Iraqi Army operational capabilities. In December 2007, Major General Joseph Fil, the out-going commander of Multi-National Division-Baghdad (MND-B), commented on the status of the Baghdad Operational Command, which has responsibility for Baghdad province and the two Iraqi Army divisions then under its command. MG Fil noted, "They are making good tactical decisions. They are planning true operations that involve multiple forces, combined operations that are frequently intelligence-driven."[468] In January 2008, the Commanding General of Multi-National Division- North (MND-N), noted that the four different Iraqi Army divisions he partnered with were "growing in size and capacity every day." He commented, "Where we can't be, they can be, and in many cases we're conducting operations with them."[469]

By early 2008, some IA units had also developed the ability to move themselves across Iraq. As part of Operation Phantom Phoenix, the 3rd Brigade of the 1st Iraqi Army Division deployed independently, with less than a week's notice, from Al Anbar province in the west to Diyala in the east to support combat operations in the Diyala River Valley.[470] According to MNF-I leaders, while not as attention-grabbing as combat operations, the move demonstrated a different but very important set of capabilities that Iraqi units will need to master, to operate independently in the future.[471]

In August 2008, U.S. commanders noted that most of the IA units that had participated in operations in Basra, Sadr City, Amarah, Diyala, and Mosul had performed very well at the tactical level.[472] The Commanding General of Multi-National Force-West (MNF-W), in Anbar province, using a phrase common among U.S. forces, stated that the IA was not just "Iraqi good enough"— it was "Iraqi very good."[473]

By early 2009, U.S. commanders were reporting further growth in IA capabilities and initiative. In March 2009, DOD reported that "IA brigade and division staffs continue to show steady improvement in planning and executing combined and joint operations, intelligence gathering, information operations, civil-military operations, and limited post-conflict reconstruction operations."[474] One BCT commander stated: "It is now routine for the Iraqi brigade commanders that I partner with to develop their own plans for operations, issue their orders to their battalions, and then expect and demand that those orders are carried out…Increasingly they do it independently, and they come to me on a much more reduced basis for specific help with certain enablers that they may not have yet."[475]

The list of the major developmental challenges faced by the Iraqi Army—building a strong leadership cadre, and developing key enablers such as logistics—has remained relatively consistent over time, although commanders and advisors on the ground point to specific incremental marks of progress in each area.[476]

Like all the other Iraqi security forces, the Iraqi Army has faced the challenge of quickly developing a capable leadership cadre. As many U.S. military commanders in Iraq point out, a basic problem is that leadership abilities depend in part on experience—their production cannot easily be "accelerated." The IA's leadership challenge may be more acute than that faced by the other security forces, since it is both large and, unlike the Iraqi Police, a nationally based service whose leaders must be able to command diverse mixes of soldiers in all regions of Iraq.

In December 2006, the Iraq Study Group pointed out simply that the Iraqi Security Forces lacked leadership.[477] In September 2007, the Jones Commission also noted that the Army was "short of seasoned leadership at all levels," and pointed in particular to "marginal leadership at senior military and civilian positions both in the Ministry of Defense and in the operational commands."[478] In congressional testimony in January 2008, Deputy Assistant Secretary of Defense Mark Kimmitt indicated that the most important gap was in mid-level leadership[479]— non-commissioned officers and field grade officers, who are required in far greater numbers than senior leaders. To help redress the situation, the Iraqi Army launched several initiatives, including accelerated officer commissioning for university graduates, waivers to time-in-grade or time-inservice promotion requirements, and recruitment of former Army officers and Non- Commissioned Officers (NCOs).[480] It is possible that it will prove easier to generate leaders "on paper," than to accelerate generation of leadership qualities.

In practice, the quality of IA leadership varies somewhat. MND-N noted in August 2008 that the Commanding Generals of the four IA divisions in their area of responsibility were "very good."[481] One of the more impressive IA leaders, according to U.S. officials, is Major General Oothman, the Commanding General of the 8th IA Division, headquartered in Diwaniyah, in Qadisiyah province. In August 2008, echoing U.S. military counter-insurgency thinking—and helping institutionalize it in the IA—MG Oothman stated, "Today's fight is a 360-degree battlefield," and explained that "once you clear an area, you have to put in Iraqi Police, the Iraqi Army and coalition forces to hold it."[482]

On the other hand, MND-B officials noted that leadership selection processes varied in quality. In August 2008, the newly selected commanding general of the newly formed 17th IA division was a well-regarded, competent brigade commander—a good choice. But in some other cases, MND-B officials noted, the choices have been "terrible"—reflections not of competence but of political connections that make the selected leaders "untouchable" by their military chains of command.[483]

Another major challenge to the continued progress of the Iraqi Army is developing key enablers, ranging from intelligence to logistics—which are absolutely essential to an Army's ability to operate independently.[484]

In December 2006, the Iraq Study Group pointed out that the Iraqi Army lacked logistics and support to sustain their own operations.[485] Later, in September 2007, the Jones Commission called logistics the Army's "Achilles' heel," and observed: "The lack of logistics experience and expertise within the Iraqi armed forces is substantial and hampers their readiness and capability."[486] The Commission further concluded that the Army would continue to rely on coalition forces for combat support and combat service support—though the Commission did not estimate for how long that reliance would continue.

Testifying before Congress in January 2008, then-MNSTC-I Commander LTG Dubik agreed that the Army "... cannot fix, supply, arm or fuel themselves completely enough at this point."[487] As of March 2008, the Army was able to feed itself—a key component of life support. As of June 2008, the Army's maintenance backlog continued, but the backlog had been "stabilized" and the IA had better visibility than previously on what needs to be repaired.[488] As of August 2008, the IA was continuing to develop a national-level maintenance and supply system, including the new National Depot at Taji, to serve as the "centerpiece" for national supply and maintenance services. The Depot is scheduled to be completed by the end of 2009—a target date that has slipped several times.[489] In February 2009, LTG Helmick echoed the words of the Jones Commission, noting: "The Achilles heel of the Iraqi military is logistics."[490]

In June 2008, MNC-I Commanding General Lieutenant General Austin confirmed that the IA still had substantial room for improvement:

> There are still some things that need to be done, and those things include developing combat enablers that will enable them to do things like call for and adjust fires and integrate those fires into their formation, support themselves logistically, use their own intelligence, surveillance and reconnaissance assets to create intelligence and then be able to use that intelligence to plan operations. So there's some work to be done yet.[491]

Iraqi counterparts agree with this assessment. In August 2008, MG Oothman stated flatly, "I see no progress in logistics." He explained that the Iraqi Army started building its forces by concentrating first on operations, not on logistics or other enablers, such as repairing HMMWVVs, or providing spare parts, or building military hospitals.[492] In February 2009, MNSTC-I Commanding General LTG Helmick assessed, "the Achilles heel of the Iraqi military is logistics."[493]

Iraqi Air Force

As of October 31, 2008, the Iraqi Air Force had 2,006 personnel on its payrolls, up from 1,300 in March 2008, out of 3,690 authorized personnel.[494] According to MNSTC-I, the plan is for the Air Force to grow to 6,000 personnel by December 2009.[495]

As of December 2008, the small Iraqi fleet included 77 aircraft, 31 fixed-wing and 46 rotarywing: 16 UH-1HP "Huey-II" helicopters and 17 Ukrainian Mi-17 helicopters for battlefield mobility; 3 C-130E "Hercules" aircraft; 6 King Air 350's for both ISR and as light transport aircraft; 8 CH-2000 aircraft; and 10 Cessna C-172's, 5 Cessna 208 "Caravans" plus 4 ISR Caravans, 10 Bell Jet Rangers and 10 OH-58A/C's for training. The Iraqi Air Force plans to have a fleet of 123 aircraft by December 2009.[496]

By any measure, the Iraqi Air Force is still a fledgling institution in the early stages of recruiting, training, and development. The effort to develop the Iraqi Air Force in earnest began at the start of 2007, and coalition advisors note that it takes three to five years to train pilots, air traffic controllers, and maintenance personnel—longer than it takes to train ground forces.

The initial—and exclusive—focus of Iraqi Air Force training was counter-insurgency, including first of all battlefield mobility. In September 2007, the Jones Commission assessed that the Air Force was "well designed as the air component to the existing counterinsurgency effort, but not for the future needs of a fully capable air force."[497] By August 2008, MNSTC-I noted that Air Force training had expanded to include "kinetic air to ground attack capability," and ISR capabilities.[498] In early 2009, DOD reported that the Iraqi Air Force had made initial progress in COIN capabilities including ISR and airlift; capabilities still "lagging" included ground attack, airspace control, and command and control.[499]

In August 2008, the Iraqi Air Force was flying about 230 sorties per week, up from about 150 sorties per week one year earlier. The number had fallen slightly from a peak of over 300 sorties per week, in April and May of 2008, due to a combination of weather, sustainment challenges, and the grounding of Cessna 172s used for training.[500] By March 2009, the number had climbed again to over 350 operational and training sorties per week, and the Iraq Air Operations Center was providing scheduling, and command and control, for those missions.[501]

In 2008, regular Air Force training was augmented by real-world experience supporting Iraqi Army operations. During the Basra operations in March 2008, the Iraqi Air Force flew 353 missions, transporting personnel and cargo, dropping leaflets providing information to the local population, and helping provide ISR.[502]

An open question for the future is what sort of air force—with what capabilities, personnel, and equipment—the Iraqi Ministry of Defense will determine it needs, to meet its full spectrum of security requirements. In February 2008, then-Commander of the Coalition Air Force Transition Team, Air Force Major General Robert Allardice, noted that like all of Iraq's MoD forces, the Iraqi Air Force is eventually expected to turn its attention to external threats. The final stage of development would include the use of jet aircraft to defend Iraq's air space. He estimated that Iraqis could have a self-sustaining Air Force with that capability "in about the 2011 or 2012 timeframe," depending on the investments they make.[503]

Other senior U.S. officials have raised questions about the capabilities that a future, externally focused Iraqi Air Force might really need. One official suggested that air defense capabilities may be more important than fighter aircraft. One challenge, he added, is that Iraqi Air Force senior leaders are former fighter pilots eager to have a fleet of fighter aircraft.[504]

A number of senior U.S. officials point out that most senior Ministry of Defense officials have an Army background—the Minister of Defense himself is a former tanker. That background, officials argue, together with the exigencies of the ongoing COIN fight, leaves them with relatively little time and attention for guiding the long-term development of their air and maritime services.[505]

Iraqi Navy

Like the Iraqi Air Force, the Iraqi Navy is still in the early stages of development. As of March 2009, the Iraqi Navy had approximately 2,000 assigned personnel out of 3,596 authorized, with 500 more Marine recruits due by April 2009.[506] That number included 499 former Iraqi Army soldiers, who joined the Iraqi Navy to form the 2nd Iraqi Navy Marine Battalion. The small Navy is based primarily in the southern port city of Umm Qasr, and includes an operational headquarters, one squadron afloat, one support squadron, and two battalions of Marines.[507]

The missions of the Iraqi Navy as a whole include protecting Iraq's coastline and offshore assets. One of the Marine battalions provides port security at Um Qasr and Az Zubayr. The other Marine battalion provides oil platform security and conducts vessel boarding and search and seizure. As of December 2008, the Iraqi Navy was conducting an average of 42 patrols, and 35 commercial ship boardings, per week.[508] As of August 2008, the fleet included 15 vessels—5 small, 24-meter patrol boats, and 10 seven-meter fast assault boats. The Iraqi Navy expects to acquire an additional 21 vessels in 2009-2010.[509]

In November 2008, the Iraqi Navy spearheaded an early mil-to-mil partnership with one of Iraq's neighbors—joint patrols with counterparts from Kuwait in the Khawr Abd Allah waterway.[510]

One challenge the Iraqi Navy faces, according to MNSTC-I officials, is conducting the preparations required to more than double its fleet—ensuring that the infrastructure is in place, and the proper training conducted.

A longer-term challenge for the Iraqi Navy, and the MoD, is crafting a realistic and appropriate "future force vision" for the Navy. U.S. advisors note that, like the Air Force, the Navy faces the challenge of working for a Ministry that does not see their Service as a high priority, and that may not be "sophisticated enough" to define requirements and build a Navy. Iraqi Navy officials hemselves are reportedly eager to continue working with coalition advisors, and do not want to uild a force that would be likely to lead them into conflict.[511]

Iraqi Special Operations Forces

Iraqi Special Operations Forces (ISOF) were an early priority for Iraqi and coalition forces leaders. As of December 31, 2008, ISOF included 4,160 assigned personnel, of 4,733 authorized.[512] As of March 2009, the single ISOF brigade included nine battalions – one counter- terrorism battalion, five commando battalions, and support units. Four of the commando battalions are regionally based – in Basra, Mosul, Diyala, and Al Asad.[513]

According to both U.S. commanders in Iraq and outside assessments, the ISOF are extremely competent.[514] Since ISOF's inception, the selection process has reportedly been very competitive, and training—conducted by U.S. SOF—highly demanding.[515] In September 2007, the Jones Commission reported, "The Special Operations brigade is highly capable and extremely effective."[516] In August 2008, a senior MNSTC-I official confirmed, "ISOF is very capable, and increasingly so."[517]

ISOF has its own chain of command, separate from the Ministry of Defense. It reports to the Counter-Terrorism Command (CTC), an operational-level command that reports, in turn, to the Counter-Terrorism Bureau (CTB), the ministerial-level body under the Prime Minister that sets policy. Although this is not an uncommon arrangement in the region, one possible issue for Iraqi leaders in the future will be ensuring adequate integration of the ISOF and Iraqi conventional forces. Other observers have expressed concern that the ISOF, despite its several layers of headquarters, might be used by the Prime Minister for personal or political ends.

Looking ahead, the next practical challenges for the ISOF include continuing to improve its capabilities. U.S. advisors note that the ISOF is eager to have access to the assets they have seen U.S. SOF counterparts employ, including specialized rotary air assets, ISR, and signals intelligence (SIGINT). One official noted in August 2008, "They're more conscious than others of how much they need US enablers."[518]

Iraqi Police Service

The Iraqi Police Service includes three categories—patrol police, station police, and traffic police. All are based on the principle of local recruitment and local service. The GoI's broad future vision is that the Iraqi Police (IPs) will eventually assume responsibility for providing internal security, backed up by the National Police, while the Iraqi Army turns its focus toward external security challenges.

As of October 31, 2008, 300,156 Iraqi Police (IPs) were assigned, of 334,739 authorized. Those IPs serve at approximately 1,300 police stations across Iraq.

At that date, 209,100 personnel had been trained, leaving a training backlog of over 90,000.[519] (The backlog could be greater, since not all of those trained are necessarily still serving as IPs.) The backlog has real-world implications—for example, a shortage of IPs, in August 2008, to help "hold" areas of Diyala province that had been cleared by Iraqi and coalition forces. As one senior U.S. official noted, "We've overwhelmed the system."[520]

According to MNSTC-I, the GoI intent is to catch up on the training backlog by July 2009. One approach has been to condense required training into a shorter period—the 240 hours of IP training usually take eight weeks but have been compressed into four weeks by lengthening the training day. In addition, recruits who already have a degree in another field are offered an accelerated process.[521]

In terms of IP capabilities, in September 2007, the Jones Commission concluded that the IPs were improving at the local level, particularly when the IPs were locally recruited from relatively ethnically homogenous neighborhoods.[522] In December 2007, General McCaffrey similarly observed that "many local units are now effectively providing security and intelligence penetration of their neighborhoods."[523]

In early 2008, a number of U.S. military commanders in Iraq described recent examples of specific operations planned and carried out in their areas of responsibility by Iraqi Police, stressing that these capabilities to plan and act independently—and successfully—had emerged relatively recently. Commanders also stressed the importance of the visible presence of the IPs at police stations and on patrol in local neighborhoods, and together with Iraqi Army and coalition forces at joint security stations, in helping provide population security.[524]

By early fall 2008, U.S. commanders noted that in general, the IPs were competent in basic skills—enough that the focus of embedded training and advisory efforts, and unit partnering, was shifting from basic policing skills to the professionalization of the force.[525] In Baghdad, the GoI and MND-B were in the process of handing over security responsibility, neighborhood by neighborhood, to the IPs. As one U.S. commander observed in August 2008, using common coalition parlance, the IPs are "Iraqi good enough."[526]

For their part, in early fall 2008, Iraqi Army commanders recognized the importance of the IPs as part of the total effort, but still had some doubts about their capabilities. As one IA commander observed, "Without coordination between the IA and the IPs, there would be no security. But," he added, "the soldiers are more effective than the police."[527]

One long-standing concern of practitioners and observers, still unresolved, is infiltration of the IPs. In September 2007, the Jones Commission noted that the IPs were "... incapable today of providing security at a level sufficient to protect Iraqi neighborhoods from insurgents and sectarian violence," in part because they were "compromised by militia and insurgent infiltration."[528] In June 2008, DOD stated that "militia and criminal intimidation and influences" were among the serious challenges still faced by the IPs.[529] In August 2008, U.S. military officials confirmed that "there's some terrorist and some nationalist infiltration" of the IPs.[530]

Iraqi National Police

The Iraqi National Police (NPs), unlike the IPs, are intended to be a national asset, not a regionally based one. While they initially focused on Baghdad, Interior Ministry is in the process of "regionalizing" the force, with the goal of establishing a presence in all provinces except those of the KRG, where they will provide backup for the IPs.[531] As of early 2009, the first two NP Divisions were based in Baghdad; the 3rd Division had established a presence in Salah ad Din with plans to expand to Diyala and Anbar; and the 4th Division had established a presence in Basra with plans to expand to Wasit, Maysan, and Dhi Qar.[532]

The Department of Defense reported in December 2008 that 18 of the 33 NP battalions were "capable of planning, executing, and sustaining operations with limited coalition support."[533] As of January 2009, there were 43,000 National Police assigned. Somewhat confusingly, 52,513 National Police had been trained—this number may include some who were removed from service or are no longer serving for other reasons.[534] DOD reports that the desired endstrength is approximately 60,000.[535]

Particularly in their early days, the NPs more consistently prompted concerns about competence, corruption, and sectarian bias, than any other Iraqi security force. In June 2007, out-going MNSTC-I Commander Lieutenant General Martin Dempsey testified to Congress that the NPs were "the single organization in Iraq with the most sectarian influence and sectarian problems."[536] In September 2007, the Jones Commission stated flatly: "The National Police have proven operationally ineffective. Sectarianism in its units undermines its ability to provide security; the force is not viable in its current form."[537]

Outside experts suggested several possible remedies. The Iraq Study Group recommended moving the NPs from the Interior Ministry to the Ministry of Defense, and giving them closer supervision.[538] The Jones Commission recommended disbanding the NPs altogether.[539]

The Iraqi leadership opted for a different approach. One step was replacing NP senior leaders. Between late 2006 and January 2008, both of the NP division commanders, all 9 brigade commanders, and about 18 of 28 battalion commanders were replaced.[540] The other major step was retraining—or "re-bluing"—both leaders and ranks, with the help of Italy's *Carabinieri*, under the rubric of the NATO Training Mission-Iraq. As of early 2009, the *Carabinieri* were gradually increasing their training and advisory support to the NPs, and continuing to support the NPs' professionalization efforts.

In early 2008, some U.S. commanders in Iraq confirmed that there had been serious problems with the NPs, and suggested that the leadership changes and re-education had so far produced mixed results. As one Brigade Commander noted, "The National Police have been terrible!"[541] One Division Commander praised the work of one NP brigade in solving problems in his area of responsibility, while noting that another NP brigade actually is the problem.[542] One coalition leader credits Iraqi National Police Commander Major General Hussein with recognizing the challenges the NPs faced and with making this remark: "The National Police has two enemies— the insurgency, and our own reputation."[543]

In August 2008, MNSTC-I noted that the re-bluing process had been accelerated by boosting capacity from 450 to 900 students at a time. MNSTC-I added that the new NP commander is a "tremendous officer."[544] U.S. commanders in Baghdad added that the NPs were being used very much like the Iraqi Army forces. One official added that the NPs were "pretty damned good!"[545]

Looking ahead, one future challenge for the Iraqi National Police is likely to be transitioning from an Army-like counter-insurgency role to a high-end policing function.

Department of Border Enforcement

The Department of Border Enforcement (DBE) faces the daunting task of protecting Iraq's 3,650 kilometers of land borders, some of it rugged and mountainous, against apparent infiltration by extremists from some neighbor countries, as well as controlling the usual flow of cross-border traffic.

As of October 31, 2008, the DBE had 40,328 assigned personnel, of 45,550 authorized, and of whom only 36,673 had been trained. They were organized into 13 brigades with 44 line battalions and 7 commando battalions.[546] The training gap—and the relatively low level of training in general—impinge on the DBE's effectiveness.[547] Given the ratio of distances to personnel, and the current capabilities of those personnel, the DBE—as DOD put it in December 2007—is "stretched thin."[548] The Jones Commission stated it more flatly in September 2007: "Iraq's borders are porous."[549] The numbers and capabilities of the DBE do not appear to have progressed substantially since that time.

The Iraqi Government's proposed way forward, over three years, includes constructing up to 712 border forts and annexes, to establish a line-of-sight perimeter, and increasing the use of biometric scan systems and personal information databases.[550]

Some U.S. officials complain that the MoI does very little to support the DBE and that, in the words of one U.S. commander, the DBE is "grossly under-funded." For example, in al Anbar province, instead of giving the DBE fuel, the MoI provided money to buy fuel. But at the long, remote border, the only fuel available for purchase was from the black market, which cost double the market price.[551]

Both coalition advisors and outside assessments have pointed out that the DBE continues to face additional challenges from corruption. In early 2008, coalition officials in Iraq agreed with the assessments by the Jones Commission that the DBE was infiltrated by outside interests, and that some members were apparently involved in cross-border smuggling.[552] In part to address such concerns, in September 2008, the Ports of Entry Directorate, previously subordinate to the DBE, was ordered to report directly to the MoI.

Oil Police

The Iraqi Oil Police (OP) is responsible for protection oil production infrastructure. Since January 2008, the MoI has paid OP salaries and held responsibility for sustainment, while the Ministry of Oil is responsible for developing and maintaining infrastructure; some reports suggest a need to further clarify these roles and responsibilities. DOD reported that as of October 2008, the OP included 29,411 assigned personnel, organized in nine battalions. Training is highly rudimentary—a three-week course—and according to DOD, the OP "lacks the basic equipment required to perform its mission."[553]

Ministry of the Interior

Both coalition advisors and outside assessments have consistently pointed to two serious shortcomings in the Ministry of Interior (MoI) itself: a lack of capacity and corruption.

Capacity challenges apparently plague most of the Ministry's activities. The Department of Defense reported in June 2008: "Coalition advisors continue to report steady but uneven improvement in the MoI's ability to perform key ministry functions, such as force management, personnel management, acquisition, training, logistics and sustainment, and the development and implementation of plans and policies."[554] By December 2008, DOD reported that the MoI's ability to plan had improved somewhat, but was still "not yet directly linked to resource allocation and program management."[555]

One particularly serious constraint, according to coalition officials, is that the Ministry of Interior lacks sufficient capacity to process the large and growing demand for personnel—to screen recruits, to train them, and to continue to account for them.[556] To address this shortcoming, the Ministry is expanding the capacity of its training base to include 12 new training centers and the expansion of 6 existing ones; and rapidly generating officers through a recall and training program for former army and police officers.[557] According to MNSTC-I, an additional pressure on the MoI training system was the absorption, in early 2008, of the "oil police," whose training to guard pipelines did not, in the words of one official, turn them into "LA cops."[558]

Corruption—and the perception of corruption—may be the even more difficult challenge for the MoI to eradicate. In December 2006, the Iraq Study Group concluded flatly that the MoI was corrupt. In September 2007, the Jones Commission assessed that "... sectarianism and corruption are pervasive in the MoI," and that the Ministry is "... widely regarded as being dysfunctional and sectarian."[559] In January 2008, one coalition advisor stated bluntly that the MoI is filled with "card-carrying gangsters."[560]

The MoI has apparently taken some steps to battle internal corruption. The Department of Defense reported that in 2007, the MoI had opened 6,652 investigations of ministry personnel. Of these, 6,159 were closed during 2007, including 1,112 that resulted in firings, 438 in disciplinary actions, and 23 in forced retirement.[561]

Ministry of Defense

In September 2007, the Jones Commission concluded that the Ministry of Defense (MoD) suffered from "bureaucratic inexperience, excessive layering, and over-centralization."[562] In December 2008, DOD noted some progress but observed that "significant challenges remain," and that "logistical and sustainment capability remain[ed] a major area of concern and...much effort must yet be directed to the sustainment and logistical support capability within the ISF at the operational and strategic levels."[563]

In early 2008, MNF-I officials suggested that compared to other Iraqi ministries, the MoD is a model of progress—it has not faced the magnitude of corruption endemic at the MoI, and with close advisory support from the coalition, it has made substantial progress in both management and strategic planning.[564]

One major future challenge for the Ministry of Defense is likely to be clarifying and rationalizing the chain of command. As the Jones Commission stated in September 2007: "Parallel lines of direct communication to military units have been established under the control of the Prime Minister. He is perceived by many as having created a second, and politically motivated, chain of command."[565] U.S. military officials confirmed this assessment in August 2008, and DOD noted in September 2008 that "MoD performance is hampered by ineffective coordination and unclear lines of authority, hampering unity of command."[566]

As of early fall 2008, Iraqi Army divisions reported to the Iraqi Ground Forces Command, which reported to the Joint Headquarters, which reported in turn to the MoD. However, some forces, from both the MoD and the MoI, fall under provincial Operations Commands, usually led by a General Officer from the Iraqi Army, which may report in practice directly to the office of the Prime Minister. Both ministries and uniformed operational headquarters, according to U.S. commanders in Iraq, are sometimes left out of the de facto chain of command.

Operations Commands are in theory a temporary measure, designed to closely integrate the counter-insurgency efforts by all of the ISF in a given geographical area. Commands have been established in the provinces of Baghdad, Basrah, Karbala, Anbar, Ninewah, Diyala, and (as an exception) in the city of Samarra.[567] Some U.S. and Iraqi commanders have suggested the possibility that Operations Commands might evolve into three-star Army Corps headquarters, perhaps with a geographic reach wider than a single province.[568] As of early fall 2008, no plans were in place for such a transition. Further, while the "Corps" concept might be appropriate to the current internal counter-insurgency fight, an externally focused Army would not ordinarily "own battle space" domestically.

Another challenge for the MoD to resolve, according to MNSTC-I officials, is centralized decision-making. As of August 2008, the vast majority of decisions were channeled personally to the Minister, which hinders efficient functioning. DOD reported in March 2009 that the "Defense Minister reviews almost all procurement and maintenance funding decisions and approves most equipment purchases, and that in some cases review by the Prime Minister is required."[569] A MNSTC-I official noted that the premise seems to be, "If you don't make a decision, you can't get in trouble."[570]

One further challenge, according to MNSTC-I officials, is the MoD's difficulty in identifying requirements, budgeting for them, and obligating and spending the required funds. In 2006 and 2007, GoI spending on the ISF exceeded spending by the Iraqi Security Forces Fund, and that trend is projected to continue. The MoD remains hampered, according to MNSTC-I, by the fact that their "direct contracting capability is not fully developed."[571]

A final challenge may simply be capacity. According to DOD, as of December 2008, about 40% of civilian positions within the MoD were not filled.[572]

IRAQI POPULATION: "RECONCILIATION"

A central tenet of counter-insurgency is reaching out to the local population and securing at least their acceptance, if not their active support.

In Iraq, a number of U.S. military commanders have pointed to changes in the attitudes and behavior of the Iraqi population as the most important difference between 2008 and earlier periods. In December 2007, for example, the out-going commander of Multi-National Division- Baghdad, Major General Joseph Fil, noted: "I attribute a great deal of the security progress to the willingness of the population to step forward and band together against terrorist and criminal militia."[573]

Coalition and Iraqi government efforts to reach out to the Iraqi population have increasingly fallen under the broad semantic rubric of "reconciliation." As of 2008, the term is very broadly used—from U.S. national strategy, to congressional legislation, to the names of Iraqi government structures and of offices and job titles in coalition headquarters.[574] The term is variously used, but in the broadest sense, it refers to a multi-lateral reconciliation among all sub-groups and members of Iraqi society, except the self-designated truly "irreconcilables" and those who may have disqualified themselves by some egregious action.

In practice, "reconciliation" in Iraq has taken a number of forms, several of which, discussed below, have played critical roles in shaping the security climate.

Coalition Outreach to the Disaffected

Early in OIF, coalition forces recognized the importance of reaching out to disaffected Iraqi communities, but coalition efforts were constrained by lack of expertise, limited resources, and— initially—policy decisions.

In 2003, some CPA and CJTF-7 leaders recognized the importance and the complexity of tribal dynamics in Iraq.[575] As coalition forces commanders on the ground throughout Iraq frequently engaged with local tribal leaders, it rapidly became apparent that the coalition lacked detailed expertise in tribal history and dynamics. The Iraqi Governing Council (IGC)—the first nationallevel advisory body, established by CPA in July 2003—included very little tribal representation.[576]

In summer 2003, coalition forces launched a concerted outreach effort to Sunni Arab communities in the restive "Sunni Triangle" in central and north-central Iraq. On August 7, 2003, CENTCOM Commander General John Abizaid convened community leaders from throughout the region to urge them to cease all tacit support for insurgents, in exchange for future assistance with reconstruction needs, political representation, and other concerns.[577] However, for most of the rest of that year, the very limited presence of coalition civilian experts in these provinces, and limited resources for reconstruction, made it difficult to fully implement the proposed "bargain."

By early 2004, CPA established an outreach office, to engage directly with both tribal leaders and leaders of other disaffected groups, including some religious extremists. Also in early 2004, U.S. national leadership crafted a series of "Sunni engagement strategies" that included "carrots" such as greater political representation, economic assistance, and detainee releases.

By 2005, coalition leaders in Iraq began to pursue more direct contacts with insurgents and their supporters—in coordination with, and often brokered by, Iraqi leaders. As a rule, those talks were reportedly based on a familiar theme—a cessation of violent action against Iraqis and the coalition, in exchange for benefits that might include amnesty for some detainees, and improved opportunities to participate politically or economically in Iraqi society.[578]

Some critics have suggested that "negotiating" with known or suspected perpetrators of violence is an ethically ambiguous practice that, moreover, is unlikely to succeed because it depends for its success on commitments by those who have violated the rule of law.

Coalition leaders confirm that they understand who these interlocutors are. In December 2007, MNF-I official Major General Paul Newton, a UK officer leading the outreach effort, commented,"Do we talk to people with blood on their hands? I certainly hope so. There is no point in us talking to people who haven't."[579] As an MNC-I senior official with considerable experience in Iraq described it in early 2008, "You reconcile with your enemy, not with your friend."[580]

In the view of some participants and observers, what may have distinguished the 2007 outreach from earlier efforts was a change in the perceptions of insurgents and would-be insurgents about their own prospects. As the MNC-I senior official added, "You can only reconcile with an enemy when he feels a sense of hopelessness."[581] As MNF-I officials described it in 2008, "At some point, fatigue sets in, and expediency brings them to the table."

By 2008, as described by senior MNF-I officials, the outreach effort included not only Sunni insurgents, the main focus, but also Shi'a extremists. The levers available to the coalition to offer included possible restoration of stipends, possible restoration of a post in the ISF, or agreements that the person agreeing to "reconcile" will not be killed. The GoI is "part of the management" of the reconciliation initiatives. One of the challenges to the effort, MNF-I officials note, is the possibility that some members of the Iraqi population will misinterpret the initiatives as signs of sectarian favoritism. Another challenge, officials report, is that coalition influence is simply diminishing—"Iraqis listen much less than in the past."[582]

Meanwhile, MND-North launched a similar but apparently separate reconciliation initiative, which started in the Sunni insurgent stronghold town of Hawija, in At Ta'amin province. The program's key targets were "economic insurgents"—those who were in it to make money, rather than ideologues. The program offers them "negotiated surrender," including being moved to a "no-target list," and participants must clear a Board that includes representatives of GoI civilian leadership, the ISF, and coalition forces. U.S. forces and PRT counterparts have used several funding sources to try to find civilian jobs for the program's "graduates." As of August 2008, the program had had over 2,100 participants across MND-North. MND-North officials have described participants as coming forward and saying effectively, "I don't want to fight anymore. I'm tired of running. I want to sleep in my own home at night."[583]

"Awakening" Movements

In the views of many practitioners and observers, "awakening" movements have powerfully reshaped the security climate as well as the political climate in many parts of Iraq. While they all have "ground-up" origins—and borrow from one another's experiences—they vary greatly in character, and in likely impact, by region.

Origins of the Awakening Movement in Al Anbar

The movements got their start in Al Anbar province. As described by Multi-National Force-West leaders, in the aftermath of regime removal, Al Anbar was a "perfect storm": The region was traditionally independent-minded, and relatively secular, but dependent on the central government for key resources. After the old regime collapsed, the province's big state-owned enterprises closed, state pensions were not being paid, De-Ba'athification policies meant lost jobs, and many Anbaris felt disenfranchised and left out of national-level politics.[584]

That context provided fertile ground for Al Qaeda affiliates to infiltrate the region with promises to "rescue" the population, but their actions proved to be absolutely brutal—including swift and violent punishment, or even death, for perceived infractions. One observer has called it a "campaign of murder and intimidation," including the murders of prominent local tribal leaders.[585]

The first rising in Al Anbar took place in 2005—a movement that became known as the "Desert Protectors." Members of local tribes in al Qaim and Haditha volunteered to begin working with some U.S. Special Operations Forces and later with the Marines.[586]

The movement that became known as the "awakening" developed later, in Al Anbar's capital Ramadi, drawing on the model of the Desert Protectors—including the premise of an alliance among several key tribes. The initial leading figure of the awakening was Sheikh Abdul Sattar Buzaigh al-Rishawi, of the Albu Risha tribe, who was killed on September 13, 2007, by a roadside bomb. In late 2006, he had spearheaded the signing of a manifesto denouncing Al Qaeda and pledging support to coalition forces. According to MNF-West, by January 2008, of the eleven sheikhs who initially stood up to challenge Al Qaeda, six were dead.[587] The movement, initially known as *Sahawa al Anbar* when it formed around a core from the Albu Risha tribe, changed its name to *Sahawa al Iraq* as more tribes joined the cause, and later to *Mutammar Sahwat al- Iraq*.[588]

According to MNF-West, leading sheikhs in the awakening movement describe their relationship with Al Qaeda as a "blood feud." The tribal leaders do not want coalition forces to stay forever— they simply want help killing Al Qaeda.[589]

Spread of the Awakening Movements to the North

During 2007, awakenings began to "spread" through the provinces of north-central Iraq—Ninewah, Salah ad Din, Kirkuk (At Ta'amin), and Diyala—drawing on the Al Anbar example. Several aspects of the northern "climate" may have encouraged some Sunni Arabs to selforganize to protect their interests.

As in Al Anbar, there was an Al Qaeda affiliate presence in the north-central provinces. In the wake of successful surge operations in Baghdad, Al Qaeda affiliates took up residence in several parts of the region, including Mosul and the upper Diyala River Valley.[590]

Sunni Arabs in northern provinces, like those in Al Anbar, already had some grounds for eeling politically disenfranchised. In Ninewah, for example, Sunni Arabs, who constitute about 75% of the province's population, generally did not vote in provincial elections and were thus underrepresented on the current Provincial Council.[591]

Across the north (and unique to the region), according to Multi-National Division-North leaders, de facto Kurdish expansion has extended across the Green Line that separates the Kurdistan Regional Government from the rest of Iraq, into parts of Mosul and oil-rich Kirkuk. In Kirkuk, in particular, many Kurds have taken up residence—or returned to live—in anticipation of a popular referendum that will decide Kirkuk's political future.[592] Coalition officials judge that some Sunni Arabs in the region find this dynamic threatening.[593]

Spread of the Awakening Movements to the South

Both security conditions on the ground, and direct exposure to "awakenings" elsewhere in Iraq, helped generate nascent "awakening" movements among some tribal leaders in largely Shi'apopulated southern Iraq. These incipient initiatives shared with their Sunni Arab counterparts their ground-up impetus, based on a desire for security and opportunity for their families, and a disinclination to be imposed on by outsiders.

The character of the southern movements, however, was distinctly different from those in northcentral Iraq, due to a quite different political and religious backdrop, and thus quite different "targets" of frustration.[594] The most prominent feature of politics in southern Iraq remains the power struggle between two major political groupings and the militias that back them: on one hand, the Islamic Supreme Council in Iraq (ISCI, formerly SCIRI) and its Badr militia; and on the other hand, the Office of the Martyr Sadr, led by Muqtada al-Sadr, and its militia, the *Jaish al- Mahdi* (JAM). Schisms in the *Jaish al-Mahdi*, in the wake of al-Sadr's declared ceasefire, produced violent splinter groups—"special groups"—apparently acting independently of al-Sadr but with reported ties to Iran.[595]

MNF-I leaders suggested that the southern "awakening" movements were motivated primarily by growing popular impatience with both of the leading contenders for political power in the south, and in particular, with their past or current Iranian connections. ISCI's Badr forces were trained in Iran, during the Iran-Iraq War. Muqtada al-Sadr has maintained personal ties with clerics in Iran, and JAM "special groups" reportedly enjoy Iranian training and support.[596]

Security Volunteers and "Sons of Iraq" (SoIs)

Military commanders in Iraq have credited the "Sons of Iraq" (SoIs)—originally known as "concerned local citizens"—with playing an essential and substantial role in the improvement of security in Iraq, beginning in late 2007.[597] One commander noted in August 2008 that the program was "a cost-effective way to buy security."[598] While terminology and specific characteristics varied geographically and over time, in general, SoIs were local residents who stepped forward, in some organized way, to help protect and defend their communities. In late 2008, the SoI program entered a major transition phase, when the Government of Iraq took the first steps toward assuming full responsibility, including the paying of salaries, for the program. As of spring 2009, the transition of responsibility had been completed, but the integration of former SoIs into permanent ISF or civilian employment had made little headway.

Composition of the "Sons of Iraq"
MNF-I noted that as of August, 2008, before the transition to Iraqi Government control began, there were 99,374 SoIs in Iraq altogether; 4,060 on 14 contracts in MNF-West's area, Al Anbar province; 29,177 on 275 contracts in MND-North's area, which includes the four provinces north and east of Baghdad; 28,754 on 182 contracts in MND-Baghdad's area; 35,381 on 267 contracts in MND-Center's area, which then included four provinces immediately south of Baghdad; 2,002 on 41 contracts in MND-Center South's area, which then included Qadisiyah province and has since been incorporated into MND-Center; and none in MND-Southeast's area, which included the four southernmost provinces.[599]

The majority of SoIs, but not all of them, were Sunni Arabs. The Department of Defense reported that as of March 2008, about 71,500 were Sunni and about 19,500 Shi'a.[600] As of January 2009, MNC-I estimated the mix at about 85% Sunni, 15% Shi'a.[601] Most groups of SoIs—who typically worked in the communities they live in—were relatively homogenous but some were mixed. For example, in January 2008, in the area of Multi-National Division-Center, a mixed region south of Baghdad, 60% of the SoI groups were Sunni Arab, 20% were Shi'a Arab, and 20% were mixed.[602]

U.S. commanders readily admitted that the SoIs include former insurgents. One Brigade Commander commented, "There's no doubt that some of these concerned citizens were at least tacitly participating in the insurgency before us," and one Division Commander stated more boldly: "80% of these guys are former insurgents."[603] Other commanders noted, in early 2008, that the SoIs included not only "reformed" insurgents, but also some infiltrators currently affiliated with extremist groups.[604]

ISF commanders, too, harbored no illusions about the backgrounds of many SoIs, and they shared with their U.S. counterparts a concern about current infiltration. In August 2008, Major General Oothman, the Commanding General of the 8th Iraqi Army Division, expressed concern that AQI could corrupt the SoIs. He noted that AQI had already infiltrated the SoIs and, he added, it could be the case that some SoIs may simply be "playing both sides."[605]

Origins of the "Sons of Iraq" Movement

The SoI movement was not the product of a carefully crafted strategy by the Government of Iraq or by coalition forces. Instead, like the "awakenings," it began from the ground up—in this case, as a series of *ad hoc*, neighborhood watch-like initiatives by Iraqis who self-organized and "deployed" to key locations in their own communities, to dissuade potential trouble-makers. The response by coalition forces to the dynamic was also initially *ad hoc*, as some coalition units provided volunteers in their areas with equipment, or payments in kind for information, or other forms of support. Frequently, coalition forces named their new partners—with heroic-sounding names like the "Ghazaliyah Guardians," or with NFL team names.

MNF-I leaders and commanders on the ground observed that SoIs initially came forward only after Al Qaeda affiliates and other threats were eliminated from an area. Some commanders also pointed out that SoIs volunteered to serve once a coalition forces presence had been established—they had to be convinced that coalition forces would actually remain in the area and not pull back to their FOBs.[606]

The "Sons of Iraq" System

After its piecemeal beginnings, the SoI system was loosely standardized by coalition forces, in coordination with Iraqi security forces counterparts.

Coalition forces paid the SoIs, with funding from the Commanders Emergency Response Program (CERP), based on 90-day renewable contracts. The money was paid to a single contractor, often a tribal sheikh or other community leader, who was then responsible for paying the SoIs' salaries and providing any uniforms, vehicles or other equipment that might be required. In practice, most SoIs earned about $300 per month, roughly equivalent to about two-thirds of the total income of a member of the Iraqi Police. The GoI reportedly agreed to continue to pay roughly the same salary as it assumed responsibility for the SoIs.[607]

SoI salaries varied somewhat by region. In August 2008, for example, Multi-National Division- Center noted that SoIs in their area each earned about $240 per month. In some cases, U.S. units established pay-for-performance systems. For example, in Kirkuk, SoI performance was reviewed daily. If they performed well, they received a bonus. If they did poorly—such as the SoI team that propped up a scarecrow at a checkpoint they were supposed to be manning—their collective contract was docked by $2,000.[608]

In many locations, U.S. division and brigade commanders on the ground reinforced the message that the SoIs "worked for" the ISF, while the coalition forces paid them. In other locations, the understanding on the ground was that the SoIs worked "with" the ISF.[609] In practice, however, SoIs were intended to fill the gaps—to "thicken the ranks"—where ISF presence was limited, so they were more likely to have regular interaction with coalition forces counterparts than with the ISF.[610]

Most SoIs were hired to man check points or to protect critical infrastructure, and to provide information about suspicious activity. In August 2008, for example, Multi-National Division- Center noted that the SoIs in its area maintained 2,159 check points, and had turned in 668 IEDs between June 2007 and August 2008.[611] MNF-I leaders and commanders on the ground stressed that SoI contributions have directly saved lives and equipment—as a rule, the level of IED attacks in a given area went down after an SoI group was established there.[612] Some commanders wryly admitted that part of the reason may be that some SoIs themselves were formerly IED emplacers.

One new development in 2008 was the formation of some groups of "Daughters of Iraq." Like the SoIs, they were security volunteers from local neighborhoods. Their job, after receiving training, was to work with the ISF to screen female Iraqis, to show respect for Iraqi culture and traditions.[613] In late 2008, DOD estimated that about one-third of suicide bombers were female.[614] As of March 2009, there were more than 600 "Daughters" working under coalition control in Anbar, Diyala, and parts of Salah ad Din provinces, and about 400 more working under Iraqi control through the Baghdad Operations Command; their incorporation is a separate process from that of the SoIs.[615] In addition, in preparation for the January 2009 provincial elections, the GoI successfully recruited hundreds more temporary "Daughters" to search females.

Security Volunteers in Al Anbar: Provincial Security Force

Multi-National Force-West leaders noted in the past that "'concerned local citizen' was not a term of art in Al Anbar province," where security volunteers were organized in several alternative ways.

In Al Anbar, early tribal offers to provide volunteers were channeled into the formation of "provincial security forces" (PSF)—a gateway step to joining the Iraqi security forces in a more permanent capacity. Members of the PSF, who received 80 hours of training from the Marines, formally became personnel of the Ministry of Interior, and the MoI pays their salaries.[616] Other local residents in Al Anbar self-organized into neighborhood watch-style organizations.[617]

Iraqi Government and Other Views of the "Sons of Iraq"

From its inception, the SoI movement raised some concerns among both Iraqis and some outside observers.

Some Iraqi Government officials, and representatives of official and unofficial groups in Iraq, who might otherwise have extraordinarily little in common, shared a concern that the SoIs could return to violence, form new militias, or otherwise pose a threat to the authority or influence they currently enjoy.[618]

Key Shi'a leaders of the Government of Iraq apparently had concerns about a potential ground-up challenge to their leadership, based on Shi'a tribal organizations, which could theoretically grow out of SoI groups in the south. Prime Minister Maliki named a very close associate, a Shi'a Arab, to head the Implementation and Follow-up Committee on National Reconciliation (IFCNR), the body responsible, among other matters, for facilitating the integration of SoIs into Iraqi government structures.[619] In turn, neither supporters of Muqtada al-Sadr nor members of the Islamic Supreme Council of Iraq—or the militias that support them—were apparently eager to face competition for influence in Shi'a-populated southern Iraq.

Meanwhile, a leading Sunni Arab political party, the Iraqi Islamic Party, reportedly viewed the SoIs and related awakening movements as potential organized competitors for support among Sunni Arab Iraqis. Some observers suggested that northern Kurds, in turn, might be reluctant to see the rise of more organized Sunni Arab constituencies, including armed potential fighters, in politically contested cities such as Kirkuk.

In December 2007, at a session of the Ministerial Committee on National Security (MCNS), Iraqi government and coalition leaders reached an agreement confirming the ground rules for the SoI program. Those rules included a cap on the total number of SoIs nationwide, of 103,000, as well as a complete prohibition against SoI recruitment and hiring in Multi-National Division-Southeast's area—Iraq's four southernmost, largely Shi'a-inhabited, provinces. The rules also stipulated, for example, that SoIs could not represent political parties, that SoI groups must reflect the demographic balance in their area, and that coalition forces could not arm the SoIs.[620]

Following the December MCNS session, key Iraqi leaders—including Prime Minister Maliki, his National Security Advisor Mowaffaq al-Rubbaie, and ISCI leader Abdul Aziz Hakim—all publicly expressed support for the SoI program.

Meanwhile, outside observers expressed concerns that the SoI movement might create an alternative—and a potential future challenge—to the national government's monopoly on the legitimate use of violence, by empowering new forces that may or may not support the central government in the future. "At worst," one observer commented, "it will perpetuate a fractured and fractious Iraq."[621]

"Sons of Iraq" Integration into Permanent Jobs

From the outset, the Government of Iraq (GoI) and coalition forces shared the view that the SoI program would be temporary. The "way forward" agreed to in December 2007 included, in principle, integrating some SoIs—roughly 20%—into the Iraqi security forces, and facilitating employment for the rest in the public or private sector. In either case, the plans included getting the SoIs off of the CERP payroll; the initial goal was July 2008.[622] As the GoI began to assume direct responsibility for the SoIs in late 2008, the basic goal of integration remained in force.

By any measure, the transition of SoIs into permanent jobs proceeded slowly. Accurately recording the data sometimes proved difficult, since the SoI population was never static—new members were being recruited as some old members were "transitioned." MNF-I noted that between December 2, 2007, and August 16, 2008, 5,189 SoIs transitioned to the Iraqi Police, 53 SoIs transitioned into other Iraqi security forces, and 2,515 SoIs transitioned into "non-security" jobs. During that time, an additional 3,547 SoIs quit, were killed in action, went missing, or were dismissed for disciplinary reasons. Previously, in 2007 before the December 2, 2007, MCNS decision, approximately 3,900 "concerned local citizens" were hired by the Iraqi Police.[623]

For most of the SoIs interested in joining the ISF, the top choice was the Iraqi Police, which would allow them to continue to serve in their local communities.[624] An application process was put in place for SoIs seeking to become IPs, but it was cumbersome. After the SoI declared his interest, local-level screenings were carried out by coalition forces, local civilian officials, local tribal sheikhs, and appropriate ISF representatives. The review process considered, among other issues, an applicant's background, proof of residency, and any special skills the applicant may have, as well as the area's demographic balance. Formal ISF requirements also included literacy, a physical fitness test, and a medical check. Those candidates who passed through these reviews were referred to the Implementation and Follow-up Committee on National Reconciliation (IFCNR), attached to the office of the Prime Minister, for approval. Candidates approved by IFCNR were forwarded to the Ministry of Interior for vetting, selection and—if successful—the issuing of hiring orders. Applications did not specifically state that a candidate is a SoI.[625] One major constraint on the incorporation of SoIs into the Iraqi Police was that the MoI's personnel and training systems were overloaded and could not easily absorb a large influx of new personnel. Another constraint was the reported continuing reluctance on the part of some MoI officials to bring SoIs on board.[626]

For those SoIs not incorporated into the ISF, the broad intent was to facilitate their transition into civilian jobs—ideally, jobs that are both sustainable and actually productive.[627] One major constraint was the absence of a thriving and diverse private sector, so most proposals and programs focused on potential state sector jobs.

In 2008, the Coalition worked with several Iraqi ministries to establish the Joint Technical Education and Reintegration Program (JTERP), which was launched in two pilot locations on March 23, 2008.[628] The program was designed to include vocational training, on-the-job training, and job placement, with priority to SoIs and recently released detainees.[629] In August 2008, U.S. commanders on the ground reported that little progress had been made—that the program, in the words of one commander, had "stalled."[630]

Another initiative in 2008, launched by MNC-I based on the recommendation of commanders on the ground, proposed the creation of "Civil Service Departments" (CSDs), as part of a new Civil Services Corps, modeled loosely on the New Deal-era Civilian Conservation Corps.[631] As planned, the CSDs would provide essential services such as electricity, sewage, and sports, to complement, not replace, those already provided by existing Iraqi government bodies. In early 2008, MNC-I launched a pilot CSD project in the Ar Rashid district of Baghdad, including 390 employees drawn in part from former SoIs, and in August 2008, a CSD with about 500 employees opened in Kirkuk.

MNC-I planned to provide some initial funding for the project with the goal of transferring full funding responsibility to the Iraqi government during calendar year 2009. The theory, explained one Brigade Commander, was "build it and they will come"—that is, once the new structure demonstrated its worth, the Iraqi government would fully embrace the initiative.[632] For its part, IFCNR expressed initial support, encouraging increasing both the size and number of the proposed CSDs, and reportedly agreeing to pay the salaries of CSD employees, while the coalition provided equipment and training costs.[633]

As of August 2008, however, MNC-I officials noted that progress on establishing the CSDs was very slow. One commander on the ground stated, "Frankly, we're not getting anywhere—there's no apparent way forward for the program."[634] By late summer 2008, MNC-I officials began to consider alternatives, including a "rapid employment initiative," a temporary measure that would put people back to work—for example, cleaning the streets—and provide them with some income.[635]

GoI Assumption of Responsibility for the SoIs

In September 2008, the Government of Iraq announced that it planned to assume responsibility for the Sons of Iraq as of October 2008, far ahead of the long-standing timeline. At a press conference that month, Minister of Defense Abd al-Qadir explained that the Sons of Iraq were "our sons, our citizens," so it was perfectly natural for the GoI to assume responsibility for them. He noted that the SoIs had contributed to security, and the GoI would be "loyal" to them. He added, however, that all Iraqi citizens were subject to the law, and so "the government might arrest or detain some elements" of the SoIs. In that case, he noted, Iraqi ministries would be responsible for protecting the detained SoIs from attack or harassment by elements of AQI or the former ruling Ba'ath Party.[636] U.S. civilian and military officials in Iraq initially expressed concerns about the precipitate GoI initiative, including the possibility that the GoI might use the assumption of responsibility to disband the SoIs without providing adequate follow-on employment.[637]

On October 1, 2008, the GoI assumed responsibility for the approximately 54,000 SoIs in Baghdad province. Reportedly, there were no immediate mass desertions of their posts by SoIs, or a higher level than usual of detentions of SoIs by Iraqi security forces.[638] In November 2008, the GoI, through the Baghdad Operations Command, paid monthly salaries to approximately 95% of those SoIs.[639] On January 1, 2009, the GoI assumed responsibility for SoIs in four more provinces—Diyala, Babil, Wasit, and Qadisiyah. The GoI assumed responsibility for SoIs in Anbar province on February 1, and for SoIs in Ninewah and Kirkuk Provinces on March 1, 2009. The final transition, of SoIs in Salah ad Din province, was scheduled for April 1, 2009.

As of mid-March 2009, according to MNC-I, there were 81,773 SoIs under GoI control, and approximately 10,000 SoIs remaining under coalition control.[640] The GoI's stated intent remained the integration of 20% of the former SoIs into jobs with the ISF. Since the GoI began to assume responsibility for the SoIs on October 1, 2008, approximately 5,000 SoIs had transitioned to permanent employment with the Iraqi police, and 500 to jobs with the Iraqi Army. For the rest of the SoIs, the GoI's stated intent remained to secure them civilian jobs, an effort spearheaded by IFCNR. Several GoI civilian ministries had indicated their readiness to create jobs for some former SoIs—including 10,000 positions at the Ministry of Education, and 3,000 positions at the Ministry of Health.[641]

In March 2009, Major General Michael Ferriter, MNC-I Deputy Commanding General, stated optimistically, "It'll take six to seven months to complete the job transition and I predict success." Meanwhile, a number of SoIs have reportedly expressed greater skepticism, voicing concerns about delays in the payment of salaries, the absence of prospects for permanent employment, and arrests of some former SoIs.[642]

Detainee Operations

By 2008, the broad "reconciliation" intent had extended to an additional subset of the Iraqi population—those who had been detained by coalition forces. Coalition detainee operations were adjusted substantially at the start of January 2009, as the new U.S.-Iraqi "SOFA" went into effect.

Accountability

By the beginning of 2008, coalition detainee operations had evolved markedly from the days of the formal occupation, when they were characterized by under-staffing, limited facilities, and— due to ongoing aggressive military operations—a large and quickly growing detainee population. In the early days, it was common to find local communities frustrated first by detentions they perceived to be groundless, and then by the difficulty of determining the location and status of those detained.[643]

One important, gradual change, according to coalition officials, was much better accountability, based on the introduction of biometrics, better information-sharing throughout the detention system, and simply better cultural familiarity with the multi-part names commonly used in the region.[644]

"COIN Inside the Wire" Detainee Program

A second major change, introduced by MNF-I beginning in late 2007, was a set of "COIN inside the wire" practices, designed to identify and separate the true "irreconcilables" from the rest of the detainees.[645]

These approaches were based partly on a better understanding of the detainee population, which apparently includes far more opportunists than ring-leaders—for example, under-employed young men who agree to emplace an IED in exchange for a one-time payment. The pervasiveness of "opportunism" as a motive seems to be corroborated by the low recidivism rate—about 9 out of 100, as of January 2008.[646]

According to coalition officials, in the past, the coalition had used its theater internment facilities simply to "warehouse" detainees. Those facilities effectively served as "jihadist universities" where detainees with extremist agendas could recruit and train followers.

As part of "COIN inside the wire," the coalition isolated the hard-core cases in higher-security compounds, removing their influence. Meanwhile, the coalition cultivated the majority of the detainee population by providing detainees with voluntary literacy programs, to the grammar school level, for illiterate detainees. Vocational training programs, including wood working, sewing and masonry, and opportunities to earn a small income during detention were introduced. These included a brick factory at Camp Bucca where detainees could earn money by making bricks, which were stamped with the inscription, in Arabic, "rebuilding the nation brick by brick." Imams visit the facilities to provide detainees, on a voluntary basis, with religious education. A family visitation program allowed about 1,600 visits per week.[647] According to a senior coalition official, "Now detainees themselves point out the trouble-makers."[648]

Detainee Releases

A third initiative was a series of detainee releases, an effort given additional impetus in 2008 by negotiations over the new security agreement, which was expected to require the transfer of detainees from U.S. to Iraqi custody.

TF-134 officials noted in August 2008 that for about 9% of detainees at that time, U.S. forces had "releasable evidence with legal sufficiency in Iraqi courts." Of concern to U.S. civilian and military officials are the members of the rest of the "legacy" population" of detainees, for whom no such evidence exists, but who might pose security risks to the Iraqi population or to U.S. forces in Iraq.[649]

To help streamline the problem—and to further the cause of reconciliation—MNF-I, through TF-134, launched an accelerated, targeted detainee release program. Releases were based on reviews by the MNF-I Review Committee. Detainees themselves were given the opportunity to present their side of the story, and good behavior during detention was taken into consideration. TF-134 noted in August 2008 that word had apparently got back to detainees that good behavior counted, and could accelerate the parole date.

In the past, some U.S. ground commanders had expressed concerns about the practical implications of the program, wondering in particular how jobs would be found for the released detainees, and what would restrain them from low-level, opportunistic criminality if fullemployment jobs were not found.[650] Partly to help allay such concerns, representatives of the "battle space owners" were included as participants in the board deliberations and decisions about releases.

The release program also made use of a guarantor system, in which tribal sheikhs and other local leaders could vouch for, and accept responsibility for, the future good conduct of detainees released back to their communities.[651] Release ceremonies were formal events, and former detainees swear an oath to Iraq.

During 2007, the detainee population grew from about 14,000 at the start of the year to a peak of 26,000 in November, due to surge operations and better incoming information from Iraqi sources. As of September 2008, there were about 19,000 detainees in coalition theater internment facilities,[652] and by November the number had dropped to about 15,800.[653]

In the event, the security agreement required U.S. forces to turn over custody of detainees to Iraqi authorities; those for whom no warrants were issued would be released "in a safe and orderly manner."[654] In January 2009, Iraqi and U.S. officials reached an agreement on a deliberate process by which the U.S. military would transfer 1,500 detainees per month to Iraqi authorities.[655] Some observers expect that some detainees held by U.S. forces may benefit, upon transfer to Iraqi custody, from the February 2008 Amnesty Law, which allowed the granting of amnesty to Iraqis accused or convicted of certain categories of crimes.

CIVIL/MILITARY PARTNERSHIP IN GOVERNANCE AND ECONOMICS

From the earliest days after major combat operations, civilian and military coalition leaders in Iraq recognized the central importance of the governance and economics "lines of operation"— indeed, military commanders have consistently viewed them as essential counterparts to security. The 2007 surge "theory of the case" adjusted the sequencing— improved security would now lay the groundwork for progress in governance and economics—but all three lines of operation remained essential to long-term success. The Iraqi government would have the lead role in governance and economics, but the coalition, including civilian and military personnel, would support their efforts.

The key tension over time has centered on the balance of civilian and military roles and responsibilities in these areas. While all practitioners agreed that civilian agencies are best placed, by training and experience, to lead the governance and economics lines of operation, civilian efforts have been hampered by the relatively limited resources of their agencies, and by delayed and limited staffing. Military forces, with far greater numbers of "boots on the ground," have sometimes stepped in to spearhead these efforts, and have consistently played at least a supporting role.

The 2007 surge included a revitalization of the civilian/military Provincial Reconstruction Team effort. At the same time, as security conditions on the ground improved, in 2007 and 2008, military units turned a greater share of their own attention to governance and economic activities. Current debates include future civilian and military roles in supporting Iraqi capacity-building, as the U.S. force presence in Iraq draws down. One critical limiting factor may be the diminishing appetite of Iraqi officials and practitioners to be "mentored," as the *de facto* exercise of Iraqi sovereignty expands.

Civil/Military Partnership in Iraq: Background

The idea to apply coordinated civilian and military capabilities at the provincial level in Iraq dates from before the start of the formal occupation. Throughout, that "coordination" has had two important aspects: coordination within civil/military teams assigned to the provinces, and coordination between those teams and their military unit counterparts.

Early military operational-level post-war plans called for provincial-level "Governorate Support Teams," led by State Department personnel and including military Civil Affairs officers and representatives of the U.S. Agency for International Development.[656]

Under the Coalition Provisional Authority, those plans began to be realized, with some delays and in slightly modified form. The State Department (and some coalition partner countries) provided Foreign Service Officers to serve as "Governorate Coordinators," who were eventually supported by small, civil/military staffs. In August 2003—before most provinces were staffed—CPA and CJTF-7 launched what became a regular series of regional meetings, bringing Division Commanders and CPA Coordinators from Iraq's provinces to Baghdad, to share concerns and lessons learned.[657]

At the end of the formal occupation—and thus the tenure of the CPA—the new U.S. Embassy established several Regional Embassy Offices to provide consular services, but the provincially based "GC" system was disestablished.

Provincial Reconstruction Teams

Provincial Reconstruction Teams (PRTs), per se, were established in Iraq in 2005, as provincially based offices led by State Department officials, with mixed civilian/military staffs. The term "PRT" was borrowed from Afghanistan, where PRTs, primarily military-staffed, take a wide variety of forms, depending in part on which coalition country leads them. As of 2008, the stated purpose of the PRTs in Iraq was as follows: "To assist Iraq's provincial and local governments' capacity to develop a transparent and sustained capability to govern, while supporting economic, political, and social development and respect for the rule of law."[658]

In 2007, as part of the surge, the PRT effort was expanded in scale, on the premise that increased security would create growing opportunities for meaningful economic and governance work at the provincial level. In June 2007, President Bush praised the effort, noting: "Much of the progress we are seeing is the result of the work of our Provincial Reconstruction Teams. These teams bring together military and civilian experts to help local Iraqi communities pursue reconciliation, strengthen moderates, and speed the transition to Iraqi self-reliance."[659]

PRTs are based on a Memorandum of Agreement between the Department of State and the Department of Defense, signed on February 22, 2007, and retroactively applicable to previously established PRTs. The Memorandum named PRTs "a joint DoS-DoD mission," which falls "under joint policy guidance from the Chief of Mission and the Commander of MNF-I." By mandate, the Department of State leads the PRTs, the PRTs report to the Office of Provincial Affairs (OPA) at the U.S. Embassy in Baghdad, and the Chief of Mission "provides political and economic guidance and direction to all PRTs." Brigade Combat Team commanders partnered with PRTs exercise authority only for "security and movement of personnel."[660]

As of January 2009, there were 28 PRT-like structures in Iraq, with about 800 total staff. These teams "cover" all of Iraq—but that coverage is uneven. The 28 teams included 14 full PRTs, 12 U.S.-led, one led by the UK (in Basra), and one led by Italy (in Dhi Qar); 10 smaller "embedded PRTs" (ePRTs) partnered with Brigade Combat Teams; and 4 non-self-sustaining "provincial support teams" which are based with a full PRT but cover another location—that is, personnel based in Irbil cover Sulaymaniyah and Dahuk in northern Iraq, and personnel based in Dhi Qar cover Muthanna and Maysan in southern Iraq.[661]

The size and composition of the various forms of PRTs varies substantially. The embedded PRTs may be as small as a four- or six-person core staff. In August 2008, for example, full PRTs sizes ranged from the streamlined staff of 16 in Najaf, to 53 in Mosul and about 70 in Kirkuk.[662] While PRTs typically work closely with U.S. military Civil Affairs teams, those CA are not typically counted as working "for" the PRTs. Human Terrain Teams (HTTs) may also work closely with— but not for—PRTs; HTTs include highly trained social scientists recruited to help maneuver u nits map the cultural environment.

In January 2008, the single largest group of PRT personnel was "locally engaged staff." Of the 798 personnel then on duty, 73 were State Department Foreign Service Officers, and 25 were USAID Foreign Service Officers. The U.S. Departments of Agriculture and Justice provided specific, critical expertise in small numbers—16 and 6, respectively. Contractors and Department of Defense personnel—civilian and military—filled many of the remaining slots.[663]

By August 2008, OPA noted that about "85% of the DoD civilians" who were sent in during the "surge" in 2007 to backfill vacant PRT positions, had been replaced by "Department of State hires"—either "3161's" or outside contractors.[664] Some of those hires provided highly specialized skills. For example, the ePRT that covering the part of Baghdad that includes the zoo included an epidemiologist. The PRT in Najaf, where a new commercial airport opened in 2008, included a retired Air Force pilot who had run a commercial airport in Arizona.[665]

Also in August 2008, in addition to military individual augmentees provided by DOD, some maneuver units on the ground in Iraq had contributed personnel directly to their partner PRTs, to help shore up their efforts. MND-Baghdad officials noted that they had provided 20 personnel to the Baghdad PRT. An MNF-West official noted that, as of October 15, 2008, MNF-West itself was "getting out of the civil-military operations business," and would instead contribute 30 or 40 Marines to work directly for the PRT. "The time is right," an MNF-West official noted, "to transition the whole effort" to the PRT.[666]

As of January 2009, the total number of PRT personnel was still about 800, of whom 453 were staffed or managed by the Department of State – including personnel from State, AID and other civilian agencies, and 3161's. The remaining PRT staff included locally engaged staff, bilingualbicultural advisors, and DOD personnel.[667]

Within PRTs, the civil/military balance of responsibilities varies by location. At the Baghdad PRT, for example, as of January 2008, members of the U.S. military had the lead responsibility for PRT operations, and for all infrastructure projects and half of the rule of law efforts (including police, detainees, and prisons). They shared responsibility with civilian counterparts for economics and governance initiatives.[668]

Coordination between PRTs and Military Units

Perhaps more important in terms of impact than civil/military coordination within PRTs, is civil/military coordination between PRTs and the military units they partner with. Those arrangements have varied greatly over time and by location.

Each ePRT is co-located and partnered with a Brigade Combat Team (BCT). Some ePRTs have their own transportation and force protection assets, and thus are able to operate independently. Others—including some of the smallest ePRTs in Baghdad—rely on their partner BCT to support their operations. In August 2008, the head of one particularly small ePRT noted that his usual practice is to accompany the BCT commander on his daily movements around the battle space.[669]

In August 2008, OPA confirmed that the ePRTs formally report up through their respective provincial PRTs to the Office of Provincial Affairs at the U.S. Embassy. The ePRTs have a "coordination" relationship with their partner BCTs. For example, members of one ePRT noted that when they write a cable, they show it to the BCT commander, not for "clearance" but simply or input. Anecdotal evidence suggests that in some cases, BCT commanders request information and point out areas where ePRTs could help. In August 2008, officials at one multi-national division noted that in practice, ePRT members "take direction from the BCT commander." Some ePRTs may thus function more like a BCT staff section than a partner organization.[670]

The much-larger full PRTs typically operate much more independently. There has been great variation in the type of military units PRTs are partnered with, which has ranged from a BCT that has responsibility for the same province, as in north central Iraq; to a single two-star headquarters, as in the partnership with MNF-West in Al Anbar province; to, in the case of the Baghdad PRT, two Division headquarters (MND-Baghdad, responsible for the city, and MNDCenter, responsible for other parts of the province).

U.S. military commanders on the ground typically praise their collaboration with the ePRTs. The staff of one BCT in Baghdad, pleased with their ePRT, reportedly praise them by saying, "You can't tell they're civilians!" U.S. military attitudes toward, and patterns of cooperation with, the full PRTs are more varied. In August 2008 in Kirkuk, leaders of the 1st brigade of 10th Mountain Division and its partner PRT unanimously underscored the closeness of their working relationship—their integrated organization and regular collaboration were evident in their descriptions of the shared challenges they faced and initiatives to meet those challenges. In another region in August 2008, a multi-national division official, asked about their relationship with PRT partners, replied with emphasis, "We like our *ePRTs*...."[671]

In general, military commanders in Iraq have stressed the need for far more of the PRTs' expertise and presence, particularly once the security climate began to improve. Some commanders have asked, "Where's the civilian surge?" while some officials at MNF-I put it more bluntly: "Get State out here!"[672]

Looking ahead, one division commander noted in August 2008, "This is a window of opportunity with the lowest attack rates ever. Embassy people should be out more every day now, like we are." Another senior commander on the ground suggested that "ePRTs could become the main effort," and that even as some BCTs redeploy, their partner ePRTs could remain to continue their work.[673]

Civilian officials, however, have sought to temper such expectations. OPA officials stressed in early 2008 that the current PRT presence *was* the civilian surge.[674] In August 2008, U.S. Embassy officials noted that the current PRT footprint would likely be the "high-water mark," and that— based on congressional direction—the Embassy had already begun a "PRT strategic drawdown plan." Some Embassy officials commented that in some locations, the PRT presence might already be too heavy and cumbersome—as one official observed, with 53 people in Mosul, "it's not clear there's a full day's work for everyone." Some suggested that for the future, as the number of civilian personnel diminishes, it would be helpful to target PRT efforts on particular areas of need, such as agriculture, public health, and local governance capacity.[675]

Some OPA and PRT officials, meanwhile, have expressed frustration with the military in Iraq for trying to do too much governance and economic work, instead of leaving those missions to far better qualified civilian experts. As one civilian official expressed in early 2008: "The military needs to start transitioning governance and economics to other agencies."[676] Apparently most military commanders would agree—many have noted that they would readily transition responsibilities whenever civilians are available to receive them. As one division commander noted in August 2008, "We don't have the right expertise."[677]

Many practitioners and outside observers have noted that institutional cultural differences help shape the PRT/military relationships. One civilian official in Iraq commented, only partly tongue in cheek, that it is a case of "sit back and reflect" versus "take that hill!"[678] For example, in 2007, one Division, frustrated by delays in the arrival of ePRTs, launched a campaign to "recruit" ePRT members from its own staff and subordinate units. Officials at OPA, at U.S. Embassy Baghdad, the office to which PRTs and ePRTs report, viewed that initiative as stepping on their prerogatives.[679]

Other practitioners stress that individual personalities play the key role. As one civilian official commented in early 2008: "It's mostly about personalities—it's not something you can just fix."[680]

Some civilian and military officials have suggested that more appropriately targeted training might better prepare civilians for PRT service, particularly those scheduled to work closely with military units. In 2008, some current civilian PRT members note that their pre-deployment visit to Ft. Bragg, and their counter-insurgency training at the Phoenix Academy at Camp Taji, Iraq, were invaluable, primarily for the exposure they provided to military culture and organization.[681] By 2009, predeployment training for new PRT members had expanded to include exercising with U.S. BCTs also preparing to deploy, at the National Training Center at Ft. Irwin, California, or the Joint Readiness Training Center at Ft. Polk, Louisiana.

Some civilian officials have expressed concern that as U.S. military forces in Iraq draw down, there might not be sufficient military resources to provide movement and force protection for PRTs. In August 2008, one division commander noted that if the security climate continued to improve, it would be possible to dedicate more military assets to directly supporting the PRTs— perhaps providing each one with a full Company.[682] By January 2009, some civilian and military officials speculated that as the overall U.S. effort in Iraq shifts from counterinsurgency to stability operations, the PRTs might assume the overall lead role for capacity-building, with U.S. military forces in support.

Military Role in Governance and Economics

While civilian and military officials generally agree that governance and economics-related tasks might in theory be better performed by civilian experts, as of early fall 2008, coalition forces in Iraq continued to play significant roles in those fields.

Governance

The Office of Provincial Affairs briefing materials state: "PRTs serve as the primary U.S. government interface between U.S., coalition partners, and provincial and local governments throughout all of Iraq's 18 provinces."[683] It might be more accurate to say that PRTs play the "lead" role in governance, rather than the "primary" one, given the sheer magnitude of ongoing interaction by coalition forces with Iraqi provincial and local officials.[684]

In Baghdad, for example, the full Baghdad PRT interacts with the Governor, the Mayor, and the Provincial Council Chair, while ePRTs are tasked to work with the district- and neighborhoodlevel councils. A small ePRT, with responsibility for a given district, might work closely with that district council, but due to personnel and resource constraints, the ePRT might have difficulty working equally closely and frequently with all of the subordinate neighborhood councils within that district.

Military units are likely to have far more frequent interactions with Iraqi officials. Battalion commanders meet regularly with neighborhood councils, Civil Affairs units and other military staff work continually with local officials on essential services and other public works projects, and Captains and their staffs at Joint Security Stations—and their ISF counterparts—meet often with local officials who use the JSSs as community meeting sites.[685]

In August 2008, for example, PRT and BCT officials described their division of labor: the BCT commander engages the provincial governor, battalion commanders engage the district councils, and company commanders engage sub-district councils and groups of local *mukhtars*. The PRT, in turn, focuses on the provincial government, helping tie it more closely into the national government. The PRT also mentors young military officers in governance work.[686]

A central and long-standing focus of coalition governance efforts is helping Iraqis achieve connectivity between the top-down national ministries and their appointed representatives for each province, on one hand, and the ground-up provincial and local governments chosen by local populations, on the other. Military commanders in every region have attested that provincial officials have no authority over—and little relationship with—the ministerially appointed representatives for their province.[687] In August 2008, one division commander explained, "Where the military can help is in building informal bridges among tribal councils, the Iraqi Security Forces, and local government—and it still needs a forcing function at the national level."[688]

As described by Colonel Tom James, commander of the 4th BCT of 3rd Infantry Division, stationed south of Baghdad in early 2008, "One of the things we really focused on is linkages, making sure that local governments are representative of the people, and they they're linked to higher governments so that we can process, prioritize, and resource the people that need things."[689]

Current governance efforts by coalition forces include fostering connectivity among the levels of government by mentoring Iraqi interlocutors at each level. For example, in one town south of Baghdad, community leaders were apparently frustrated because they felt disconnected from the deliberations of the nearest local council. The Army Captain leading the JSS in the city started bringing local community leaders together regularly, helping them to articulate and prioritize their concerns. Coalition forces then connected that informal body with the Iraqi officials formally chosen to represent that area. That mentoring was then backed up by higher levels of the Captain's chain of command, on their frequent visits.[690]

In one area of Baghdad, a Brigade Commander and representatives of his subordinate units regularly reviewed the membership of all the local councils, based on the units' frequent interactions with them, checking for vacancies, for the presence of "outsiders" from outside a given neighborhood, and for roughly accurate reflections of the demographic balance. Where local councils fell short, the units that regularly engaged them pointed out the concerns to them and urged improvement.[691]

In the views of many commanders, PRTs and ePRTs are simply not robust enough to conduct the governance mission comprehensively. As one Division staff member framed the issue, in early 2008, "The Division needs to help the PRTs help establish governance."[692]

Economics

Military commanders in Iraq confirm that for U.S. personnel, economic policy guidance is provided by the U.S. Embassy, and that PRTs have the lead role in the economic line of operation. As in the field of governance, since the earliest post-major combat days, the U.S. military has played a role in the economic reconstruction of Iraq.

The military role in economic reconstruction has typically focused on local-level initiatives. In 2008, one economic focus for the military was neighborhood economic revitalization—usually measured in terms of the number of small shops opened. The first shops to reopen in a neighborhood, as security improves, typically included fruit and vegetable stands, and shops selling convenience foods like bottles of soda. To facilitate that process, commanders sometimes sought a local Iraqi partner to serve as the primary contractor for reconstruction in a neighborhood, and to encourage other local entrepreneurs to come onboard.[693] By January 2008, in addition, military commanders, were tasked to keep an eye open for potential "medium-sized businesses" to support.[694]

Commanders have also been able to make available micro-grants, through a Department of Defense program, which allowed them to provide fledgling Iraqi businesses with start-up funds ranging from several hundred to several thousand dollars, to purchase equipment or raw materials. For example, in early 2008, a micro-grant enabled one man in Baghdad to buy power saws and raw wood to jumpstart his furniture-making business.[695]

In August 2008, one BCT commander noted, "We've had great success reopening small businesses!" But both civilian and military officials in Iraq note that the number of open shops may be a better gauge of the security climate in a community—how safe the local population feels—than of economic revitalization. Longer-term, sustainable development, civilian and military officials note, requires not just local shops but also production—which in turn requires sustainable and secure systems of supply and distribution, as well as a customer base. Civilian development experts in Iraq caution that this will simply take time.[696]

In August 2008, U.S. Embassy officials explained that imposing economic policy discipline in the regions—among PRTs as well as military units—is a challenge.[697] This may help explain what some called the "great poultry debate" of 2008. In mid-2008, as part of the search for sustainable economic activity, some military and PRT officials proposed supporting the development of domestic poultry and egg farming. Some argued that such a business required relatively low startup costs, and would provide both employment and income for local families. Officials at the U.S. Embassy, and some civilian and military practitioners in the field, countered that such efforts stood little chance of being profitable—it cost $2 to buy a chicken to eat from Brazil, while a domestic Iraqi chicken would cost much more than that, given the costs of importing feed and cooling the chickens and their eggs. One BCT commander noted, "poultry farming is a big deal for us," while a senior Embassy official countered, "There's no business plan."[698]

Meanwhile, military commanders have continued to make use of the Commanders Emergency Response Program (CERP), which provides brigade commanders with discretionary funding for a wide array of projects. As of mid-2008, the majority of CERP funding was being used to support essential services, and other sustained initiatives such as the Sons of Iraq program. Anecdotally, in some instances, CERP may have lost some of its initial flexibility—in the accounts of several BCT commanders, who earlier had been free to spend CERP funds at their own discretion, they had recently been required to seek approval from their Division headquarters to spend CERP money.

As of August 2008, there was no formal requirement for military units to coordinate CERP spending with Iraqi officials or with PRT or ePRT counterparts, and some OPA and PRT officials have raised concerns about insufficient civil/military coordination. Division, Brigade and Battalion Commanders have noted that most projects nominated for CERP support are initially put forward by local Iraqi officials and residents. Further, although it is not mandated, the military typically cross-walks proposed initiatives with the existing plans of local Iraqi councils.[699] In Kirkuk, BCT and PRT officials noted that they share all project information and coordinate with Iraqis "at stage one of any project." In Baghdad, one PRT and its ePRT partner noted that they coordinate on all projects and select the most expedient source of funding, and that they coordinate all projects with the appropriate Iraqi body—the right Ministry, district council, or neighborhood council.[700]

In 2008, some Members of Congress expressed frustration with the extensive use of CERP on projects either that might not be necessary, or that the Iraqis might be able to pay for themselves. Some civilian officials in Baghdad shared the concern about the use of CERP. Too-liberal use of CERP funding, some have argued, could counteract the broad policy goal of encouraging Iraqis to solve as many problems as possible by themselves. As an example, one official, pointing to a summer 2008 proposal by one division to spend $62 million on an electrification project, noted, "We're getting out of that kind of business." The big problem, one official observed in August 2008, is that "we're not giving Iraqis the freedom to fail." Some military commanders on the ground shared that concern—one noted in August 2008, "We've wasted a lot of CERP money in the past."[701] In September 10, 2008, testimony before the House Armed Services Committee, Under Secretary of Defense for Policy Eric Edelman noted that DOD was in the process of reviewing and refining the criteria for the use of CERP.[702]

Meanwhile, in 2008, some transitions in the use of CERP were underway, due in part to the GoI's introduction of Iraqi CERP (I-CERP)—GoI funds that U.S. forces may help Iraqi counterparts spend. Multi-National Force-West officials noted in August 2008 that they were "giving CERP money back," a conscious decision to help make the Iraqi system work. Instead of CERP, the Marines were spending I-CERP. MND-Baghdad officials suggested, meanwhile, that using ICERP might be "teaching the Iraqis bad habits," that is, that when civilian channels are not fast enough, the military takes charge.[703]

ASSESSING SECURITY TRENDS

Strategically based decision-making about the United States' next steps in Iraq and its future relations with that country requires a clear assessment of trends to date in security conditions, and a clear evaluation of the factors that produced those changes.

Security Situation by the Metrics

Multi-National Force-Iraq leaders use a series of quantitative metrics to track and describe both snapshots of the security situation and trajectories over time. The qualitative significance of the metrics is open to some interpretation, but overall, as of early 2009, the metrics suggested that security gains achieved in 2008 had been maintained.

Overall Attacks

The metric usually described first is "overall attacks"—including attacks against Iraqi infrastructure and government facilities; bombs found and exploded; small arms attacks including snipers, ambushes, and grenades; and mortar, rocket and surface-to-air attacks.

According to MNF-I, overall attacks grew from a low point in early 2004, when records begin, to a peak of over 1,500 weekly attacks in June and July 2007, just as the final surge units arrived in Iraq and Operation Phantom Thunder was launched. That gradual growth was punctuated by sharp upward spikes at key Iraqi political junctures, including the January 2005 elections and the October 2005 constitutional referendum, and, less sharply, during Ramadan each year. After July 2007, the overall level of attacks declined sharply, punctuated by a spike during Iraqi and coalition operations in Basra and Sadr City, in March 2008. By late 2008, the level of attacks had fallen to well under 200 per week – levels last witnessed at the beginning of 2004 – and those gains held through February 2009.[704]

Commanders on the ground point out that a low level of attacks in a given geographical area does not necessarily mean that no adversaries remain there. It could also indicate that a place—such as Arab Jabour south of Baghdad, in late 2007—was being used as a sanctuary.[705] In turn, a high level of attacks is generally expected, at least temporarily, during major operations in an area, as extremist groups attempt to push back.[706]

Iraqi Civilian Deaths

Another key metric tracked by MNF-I is the number of Iraqi civilian deaths due to the actions of extremists.[707] The number of monthly deaths peaked in late 2006—at just over 1,500 per month according to coalition data, and about 3,750 per month according to combined Iraqi and coalition data. MNF-I reports that beginning in July and August 2007, after all the "surge" forces had arrived in Iraq, the level of civilian deaths fell sharply and then continued to decline through January 2008, a decline of over 72%. Iraqi sources record a spike in civilian deaths in late March 2008, during the military operations in Basra and Sadr City. Coalition data, and combined Iraqi and coalition data, both indicate a continued reduction to between 200 and 300 by January 2009.[708]

Weapons Caches

A further metric regularly recorded and tracked is the number of weapons caches found and cleared. That number skyrocketed from 1,884 in 2004 (the first year of full, available records), to 6,957 in 2007, and 9,154 in 2008, with 503 caches found and cleared in January 2009.[709]

The cache numbers alone, however, tell an incomplete story, first of all because the size and contents of the caches are not indicated. In addition, there is no way to confirm the discovery success rate by comparing the number of caches found with the total number of weapons caches in Iraq at any given point. Larger numbers of found caches could indicate that the problem is growing—for example, that more weapons are coming into Iraq. Larger numbers could also simply reflect more aggressive—and more successful—operations, based on better information from Iraqi sources about cache locations.

High-Profile Attacks

MNF-I also tracks the category of "high profile attacks"—including explosions involving the use of car bombs, suicide car bombs, and individuals wearing suicide vests. In 2007, the monthly total reached a peak of about 130 in March before falling, unevenly, to about 40 in December 2007. MNF-I noted that erecting barriers and hardening sites, as well as kinetic operations against would-be perpetrators, had helped lower the total of vehicular attacks.[710] After a gradual rise during the first two months of 2008, high-profile attacks spiked in March, during military operations in Basra and Sadr City. By the end of January 2009, the number had fallen considerably, to well below 20.[711]

Improvised Explosive Devices (IEDs)

MNF-I tracks improvised explosive devices (IEDs) based on two metrics—the number of IED explosions, and the total number of IED incidents including explosions, IEDs found and disarmed, and IED hoaxes. The second metric can be viewed as a broader measure of adversary intent.

MNF-I reports that the number of IED explosions spiked in October 2006 during Ramadan; remained high until July 2007, just before the start of a series of surge-based Corps-level offensives; and fell sharply until October 2007. The number of total IED incidents followed a similar trajectory over that time period.[712] The incidence of IED explosions, relatively level at the beginning of 2008, spiked in late spring during the offensive operation in Basra and Sadr City, and again in late summer during operations in Diyala and Ninewah provinces. By December 2008 the level of IED explosions had fallen to levels last seen at the beginning of 2004, of less than 50 per month.[713]

IED use can also be evaluated qualitatively, as well as quantitatively. In late 2007, one of the deadliest forms of IEDs in use was the explosively formed penetrator (EFP), supplied as a rule from Iran. EFP use declined in late 2007 but experienced a brief upsurge in early 2008, before declining again through early 2009.[714] In November 2007, a new and very deadly threat appeared—improvised rocket-assisted mortars (IRAMs). Built from a rocket, a propane tank, and ball bearings, IRAMs are indiscriminate and powerful in their effects. In August 2008, MNC-I reported that 13 IRAM attacks had taken place altogether, most recently in July 2008.

By the end of 2007, less sophisticated forms of IEDs—such as command wire- and pressure plate-detonated devices—had become the most common, possibly indicating a degradation in the supply networks or ability to coordinate and operate of the adversary. In August 2008, the most recent IED "innovation" was the use of building-borne IEDs, that is, buildings wired to explode, and the use of female suicide bombers increased markedly.[715] Late 2008 saw the rise of "sticky IEDs"—small bombs attached magnetically to the undersides of vehicles, and set off by remote control or timer.[716] By early 2009, as security measures designed to prevent vehicle-borne attacks improved, the use of person-borne IEDs (PBIEDs) increased.[717]

Explaining the Security Gains

In 2008, as consensus grew that security gains had been achieved on the ground in Iraq, some debates developed concerning which factors, or combination of factors, had contributed, or contributed most, to those improvements. From a social science perspective, the results are "untestable" —the "experiment" cannot be repeated holding one or more variables constant.

MNF-I leaders and commanders on the ground attributed the improvements in the security situation not just to one or two key factors, but to a compendium of factors. Moreover, commanders noted, those factors were made particularly effective by their interaction effects— for example, coalition personnel with previous service in Iraq, making use of more sophisticated technologies.

The most fundamental factor may have been what former MNF-I Commanding General, General David Petraeus, has called a shift in the "intellectual construct" from an emphasis on transition— a quick hand-over to Iraqis—to a counter-insurgency (COIN) focus on achieving population security. Another key COIN component of that intellectual construct was recognizing the need to separate the irreconcilables from the reconcilables—as GEN Petraeus observed, "You're not going to kill your way out of an insurgency."[718]

Additional key factors frequently cited by commanders in Iraq include targeted operations by special operations forces; operations and much greater presence by conventional coalition forces; operations, presence, and greatly improved capabilities of Iraqi Security Forces; the rejection of extremists by the "awakening" movements; efforts by the Sons of Iraq and other security volunteers, and Muqtada al-Sadr's ceasefire and separation from the violent "special groups" wings of his organization.[719]

In addition, according to commanders, in recent years, far more intelligence assets became available in-country, and at lower levels of command, greatly improving commanders' ability to make decisions and respond in a timely way. New technologies—particularly rapidly fielded counter-IED equipment and approaches—helped coalition forces against the adversaries' deadliest weapons and saved lives.[720]

Not only did various components of force contribute to the fight, their efforts were far better integrated than they were several years ago, and that integration also helps explain security improvements to date. For example, commanders note that the air component increased the intelligence, surveillance and reconnaissance (ISR) assets available to ground commanders, to support and inform their operations. The greater ground forces presence, and the better information from Iraqis that it generated, in turn, made possible the more frequent and more effective use of air strikes.

Commanders on the ground have noted that the increasingly sophisticated technologies available to SOF have strengthened their efforts to kill or capture high-value targets. Commanders have stressed, however, that "you can't get Al Qaeda by just using SOF." MNF-I officials have noted that coalition forces tried the SOF-only approach in Ramadi for four years, but it ultimately proved insufficient. They add that SOF is most effective when it draws on conventional forces' intimate knowledge of local communities, based on the close contacts conventional forces have with ISF, SOIs, and local tribes. Then, following SOF actions, conventional forces play the essential role of "holding" the area, with a strong, visible presence.[721]

Finally, as many practitioners on the ground have pointed out, by the time of the surge, force leaders, staff, commanders, and troops in the field typically brought significant previous

Operation Iraqi Freedom: Strategies, Approaches, Results and Issues for Congress 249

Iraq experience to the mission. Most leaders and commanders have served at least one previous tour in Iraq, and their familiarity with Iraqi governing structures, basic laws, and customs, is markedly greater than the limited knowledge the first coalition teams brought to Iraq.[722] Leaders also point out that they have had time to absorb the lessons from their earlier tours, including absorbing the 2006 COIN manual that captured lessons from recent operational experience.[723]

Source: Map Resources. Adapted by CRS.

Figure 1. Map of Iraq

ADDITIONAL CRS REPORTS

For further information about Iraq-related issues, see CRS Report RL33110, *The Cost of Iraq, Afghanistan, and Other Global War on Terror Operations Since 9/11*, by Amy Belasco; CRS Report RL34064, *Iraq: Oil and Gas Legislation, Revenue Sharing, and U.S. Policy*, by Christopher M. Blanchard; CRS Report RL33834, *Defense Contracting in Iraq and Afghanistan: Issues and Options for Congress*, by Valerie Bailey Grasso; CRS Report R40011, *U.S.–Iraq Withdrawal/Status of Forces Agreement: Issues for Congressional Oversight*, by R. Chuck Mason; CRS Report RL31339, *Iraq: Post-Saddam Governance and Security*, by Kenneth Katzman; CRS Report RL31833, *Iraq: Reconstruction Assistance*, by Curt Tarnoff; and CRS Report RL34568, *U.S.-Iraq Strategic Framework and Status of Forces Agreement: Congressional Response*, by Matthew C. Weed.

Author Contact Information

Catherine Dale
Specialist in International Security
cdale@crs.loc.gov, 7-8983

End Notes

[1] Secretary of Defense Robert M. Gates, Statement for the Record, Senate Armed Services Committee, January 27, 2009, available at http://www.defenselink.mil/speeches/speech.aspx?speechid=1337.

[2] President Barack Obama, "Responsibly Ending the War in Iraq" remarks, Camp Lejeune, North Carolina, February 27, 2009, available at http://www.whitehouse.gov/the_press Ending-the-War-in-Iraq/.

[3] See David Ignatius, "A Farewell Warning on Iraq," *Washington Post*, January 18, 2009; and Secretary of Defense Robert M. Gates, Statement for the Record, Senate Armed Services Committee, January 27, 2009, available at http://www.defenselink.mil/speeches/speech.

[4] See "President Bush Address to the Nation, March 17, 2003," the televised speech that included a 48-hour ultimatum to Saddam Hussein and his sons, available at http://www.whitehouse.gov/news/releases/2003/03/20030317-7.html.

[5] See "Authorization for Use of Military Force Against Iraq Resolution of 2002," H.J.Res. 114, Section 3(a), signed into law on October 16, 2002, (P.L. 107-243). The Senate vote was 77-23, and the House vote 296-133.

[6] Rod Nordland, "No Victory Dances," interview with General David Petraeus, *Newsweek*, August 21, 2008. On September 16, 2008, GEN Petraeus relinquished command of MNF-I to Army General Raymond Odierno, a former Commanding General of Multi-National Corps-Iraq (MNC-I), the operational-level command under MNF-I whose area of responsibility includes all of Iraq. On October 31, 2008, GEN Petraeus assumed command of U.S. Central Command, to which MNF-I reports.

[7] In the United States, the Bush Administration carried out "consultations" with key Members of Congress on the operationally-focused draft agreement. The Administration's stated position was that the document was not a treaty and therefore did not require formal congressional approval.

[8] The formal title of the document is "Strategic Framework Agreement for a Relationship of Friendship and Cooperation between the United States of America and the Republic of Iraq," and it is available at the White House website, http://www.whitehouse.gov/infocus/iraq/SE_SFA.pdf. See also the "Declaration of Principles for a Long-Term Relationship of Cooperation and Friendship Between the Republic of Iraq and the United States of America," November 26, 2007, available at http://www.whitehouse.gov/news/releases/2007/11/20071126-11.html.

[9] The document, formally entitled, "Agreement Between the United States of America and the Republic of Iraq on the Withdrawal of United States Forces from Iraq and the Organization of their Activities during their Temporary Presence in Iraq," is available at http://www.whitehouse.gov/infocus/iraq/SE_SOFA.pdf. The

current UN resolution, UN Security Council Resolution 1790 (2007), December 18, 2007, is available at http://daccessdds.un.org/doc/UNDOC/ GEN/N07/650/72/PDF/N0765072.pdf?OpenElement.

[10] "SOFA," Article 24, para.1,2.

[11] "SOFA," Article 27, para.3. See also strategic framework agreement, Section 1, para.4.

[12] See "SOFA" Article 27, para 1: "In the event of any external or internal threat or aggression against Iraq that would violate its sovereignty, political independence, or territorial integrity, waters, airspace, its democratic system or its elected institutions, and upon request by the Government of Iraq, the Parties shall immediately initiate strategic deliberations and as may be mutually agreed, the United States shall take appropriate measures, including diplomatic, economic, or military measures, or any other measure, to deter such a threat."

[13] "SOFA," Article 4, para.2.

[14] "SOFA," Article 22.

[15] "SOFA," Article 12, para.1.

[16] The "SOFA" mandates the formation of a Joint Ministerial Committee tasked to address interpretation and implementation of the agreement. That body is tasked to appoint a Joint Military Operations Coordination Committee (JMOCC) to oversee military operations. It is also tasked to appoint a separate Joint Committee—which may in turn appoint Subcommittees—to oversee issues outside the competence of the JMOCC. See "SOFA" Article 23.

[17] President Barack Obama, "Responsibly Ending the War in Iraq" remarks, Camp Lejeune, North Carolina, February 27, 2009, available at http://www.whitehouse.gov/the_press Ending-the-War-in-Iraq/.

[18] The "2010" timeline is attributed to senior logistics official at U.S. Central Command Terry Moores, in Chelsea J. Carter, "Road Map out of Iraq Takes Shape," *Seattle Times,* March 2, 2009. Commandant of the Marine Corps General James Conway stated in a January 2009 speech, before President Obama's Afghanistan troop increase announcement: "My belief is that by the middle of the year, you'll see a significant number of Marines in Afghanistan. Those must of necessity come from Iraq." See Otto Kreisher, "Marine Commandant Expects Troop Surge in Afghanistan," *National Journal,* January 15, 2009.

[19] For the purposes of rough calculation, a BCT can be said to include about 3,500 Soldiers. In Iraq, BCT headquarters have sometimes had command of additional units, giving total BCT force sizes of up to 5,000.

[20] Anthony Shadid, "12,000 U.S. Troops to Leave Iraq," *Washington Post,* March 9, 2009.

[21] Emily S. Rueb, "Gates Defends Iraq Withdrawal Plan," *New York Times,* March 2, 2009

[22] Interviews with MNF-I officials, February, March 2009.

[23] MNF-I officials, Interviews, February 2009.

[24] Remarks by Secretary Gates on *Meet the Press*, cited in Sean Lengell, "Gates: Pullout Timeline Workable," *Washington Times,* March 2, 2009.

[25] See Elisabeth Bummiller and Thom Shanker, "Generals Propose a Timetable for Iraq," *The New York Times,* December 18, 2008; and Elisabeth Bummiller and Thom Shanker, "Military Planners, in Nod to Obama, are Preparing for a Faster Iraq Withdrawal," *The New York Times,* January 15, 2009.

[26] Peter Baker and Alissa J. Rubin, "Obama Seeks Accord with Military on Iraq," *Washington Post,* January 29, 2009. GEN Odierno added, "The longer we go, if we get through the elections, we get closer and closer to not being able to backslide."

[27] Andrew England and Demetri Sevastopulo, "US General Stresses Need for Time," *Financial Times,* February 17, 2009.

[28] See for example Kevin Benson, "Shift the Debate on Iraq from 'When' to 'How,'" *Atlanta Journal-Constitution,* August 12, 2007. Colonel Benson was the lead OIF planner for CFLCC.

[29] For example, several days before the January 31, 2009, provincial elections, Iraqi Prime Minister Nouri al Maliki told a political rally that he believed that the timeline for the withdrawal of U.S. troops from Iraq "will be brought forward," earlier than the deadline specified in the security agreement. See Robert H. Reid, "Iraqi Leader Predicts Faster U.S. Withdrawal," *Atlanta Journal-Constitution,* January 27, 2009.

[30] On February 17, 2009, President Obama announced approval of DOD requests to deploy approximately 17,000 additional U.S. troops to Afghanistan. Those troops were scheduled to include the 2nd Marine Expeditionary Brigade (MEB), from Camp Lejeune, NC, in late spring; the 5th Stryker Brigade, 2nd Infantry Division, from Ft. Lewis, WA, in mid-summer; and approximately 5,000 enablers. See President Barack Obama, "Statement by the President on Afghanistan," The White House, February 17, 2009, available at http://www.whitehouse.gov/the_press_office/Statement-by-the-President-on-Afghanistan/; and DOD News Releases, "DoD Announces Afghanistan Troop Deployment," February 17, 2009, available at http://www.defenselink.mil/releases/release.aspx?releaseid=12493. Two further troop increases had previously been approved: the deployment of 3rd Brigade Combat Team, 10th Mountain Division, which took place in January and February 2009; and the deployment of the combat aviation brigade of the 82nd Airborne Division, who began deploying in March 2009. On March 27, 2009, announcing the new U.S. Strategy for Afghanistan and Pakistan, President Obama stated that an additional 4,000 U.S. troops would deploy to Afghanistan to train and advise the Afghan National Security Forces.

[31] In a December 2007 assessment, retired General Barry McCaffrey advocated a reduction in the U.S. deployment to Iraq – down to 12 BCTs by January 2009 – due to stress on the force. He commented that "The Army is

starting to unravel," pointing to current recruiting campaigns that are bringing on board "those who should not be in uniform" due e.g. to drug use or criminality; to the loss of mid-career officers and NCOs; and to the "stretched and under-resourced" Reserve Component. See General Barry R. McCaffrey, "After Action Report, Visit Iraq and Kuwait 5-11 December 2007," December 18, 2007, submitted as a Statement for the Record for the HASC O&I Subcommittee hearing on January 16, 2008.

[32] Speaker Pelosi commented, "I don't know what the justification is for …a presence of 50,000 troops in Iraq." See Emily S. Rueb, "Gates Defends Iraq Withdrawal Plan," *New York Times,* March 2, 2009. When the White House provided a pre-briefing to Congressional leaders, ahead of the public announcement of the new policy, Majority Leader Reid noted, "I am happy to listen to the Secretary of Defense, the President, but when they talk about 50,000, that's a little higher number than I had anticipated." See Major Garrett, "Obama Sets 2010 Timetable for Iraq Withdrawal," *Fox News,* February 26, 2009.

[33] See Michael O'Hanlon and Kenneth M. Pollack, "Iraq's Year of Living Dangerously," *New York Times*, February 26, 2009.

[34] In a recent interview, the Special Representative of the U.N. Secretary-General for Iraq, Staffan de Mistura, asked about his biggest worry for the future of Iraq, stated: "If I had to choose which one keep me awake at night, it is the disputed areas, because tension between Arabs and Kurds." See Monte Morin and Tina Susman, "16 Killed in Suicide Attack in Northern Iraq," *Los Angeles Times,* February 6, 2009.

[35] Interviews with MNF-I officials and subordinate commanders, and with the Governor of at Ta'amin province (of which Kirkuk is the capital), August 2008. U.S. commanders describe a summer 2008 visit to Kirkuk by the Iraqi Minister of Defense, who was reportedly surprised to discover, in contrast to information he had received, that there were not "two Kurdish *pesh merga* divisions" in Kirkuk.

[36] Department of Defense, "Measuring Stability and Security in Iraq," December 2008, p.1.

[37] Interviews with MNF-I officials and subordinate commanders, August and October 2008, and February 2009.

[38] See Ned Parker and Caesar Ahmed, "Sons of Iraq Movement Suffers Another Blow," *Los Angeles Times,* March 30, 2009; and Rod Nordland, "Rebellious Sunni Council Disarmed After Clashes, Officials in Baghdad Say," *New York Times,* March 30, 2009.

[39] Interviews with U.S. civilian and military officials in Baghdad, Najaf, Diwaniyah, Basra; with UK officials in Basra; and with Iraqi officials in Najaf, Diwaniyah, Basra, 2008 and 2009.

[40] Interviews with MNF-I officials, August and September 2008, and February 2009, and "Security Incidents" slides, Multi-National Forces-Iraq, January 31, 2009.

[41] Anne Gearan, "U.S. General Says No Further Withdrawals Planned," *Washington Post,* March 9, 2009.

[42] Associated Press, "Al Qaida Stronghold of Mosul is proving a Security Nightmare," *Arizona Daily Star,* March 10, 2009.

[43] Interviews with MNF-I officials and subordinate commanders, August 2008.

[44] Interviews with commanders serving under MNF-I, August 2008. As of December 2008, 13 of Iraq's 18 provinces had transitioned to PIC. PIC provinces and their dates of designation included Muthanna, July 2006; Dhi Qar, September 2006; An Najaf, December 2006; Maysan, April 2007; Irbil, Sulaymaniyah and Dahuk, May 2007; Karbala, October 2007; Basrah, December 2007; Qadisiyah, July 2008; Anbar, September 2008; Babil, October 2008; Wasit, October 2008.

[45] See Sudarsan Raghavan, "U.S. Takes Control of Basra Base," *Washington Post,"* April 1, 2009.

[46] See "MND-C, MND-SE Operating Areas Combine to Create MND-South," MNF-I press release, April 1, 2009, available at http://www.mnf-iraq.com/index.php?option=com_content&task=view&id=25981&Itemid=128.

[47] Interviews with U.S. civilian and military officials, Baghdad, August 2008.

[48] President Barack Obama, "Responsibly Ending the War in Iraq" remarks, Camp Lejeune, North Carolina, February 27, 2009, available at http://www.whitehouse.gov/the_press Ending-the-War-in-Iraq/.

[49] President Barack Obama, "Responsibly Ending the War in Iraq" remarks, Camp Lejeune, North Carolina, February 27, 2009, available at http://www.whitehouse.gov/the_press Ending-the-War-in-Iraq/.

[50] Secretary of Defense Robert M. Gates, Statement for the Record, Senate Armed Services Committee, January 27, 2009, available at http://www.defenselink.mil/speeches/speech.aspx?speechid=1337. On September 10, 2008, in testimony before the House Armed Services Committee, he stated that "… we should expect to be involved in Iraq for many years to come, although in changing and increasingly limited ways." See Robert M. Gates, Statement before the House Armed Services Committee, September 10, 2008.

[51] Interviews with U.S. civilian and military officials, Baghdad, August 2008, and with Iraqi civilian and military officials, August 2008.

[52] Anthony Shadid, "U.S. Downed Iranian Drone Over Iraq," *Washington Post,* March 17, 2009.

[53] Interviews with MNF-I and MNC-I officials, August 2008. Furthermore, it is conceivable that the planned increase in U.S. troop presence in Afghanistan, across Iran's eastern border, may magnify the sense of uneasiness of some Iranian leaders.

[54] See Secretary of Defense Robert Gates, U.S. Global Leadership Campaign, Washington DC, July 15, 2008, available at http://www.defenselink.mil/speeches/speech.aspx?speechid=1262.

[55] John Nagl, *Institutionalizing Adaptation: It's Time for an Army Advisor Corps*, Center for a New American Security, Washington, DC, June 2007.

[56] Charmingly but surely unintentionally, the word "beso" means "kiss" in Spanish.
[57] Kris Osborn, "New U.S. Army Unit Adds Stability-Ops Troops," *Defense News,* March 10, 2009.
[58] See Department of Defense, *National Defense Strategy*, June 2008, available at http://www.defenselink.mil/news/2008%20national%20defense%20strategy.pdf; and Department of Defense, *Quadrennial Roles and Missions Review Report*, January 2009, available at http://www.defenselink.mil/news/Jan2009/QRMFinalReport_v26Jan.pdf
[59] For an overview of the interagency reform debates, see CRS Report RL34455, *Organizing the U.S. Government for National Security: Overview of the Interagency Reform Debates*, by Catherine Dale, Nina M. Serafino, and Pat Towell. On the role of DOD in foreign assistance activities, including security forces training and reconstruction activities, see CRS Report RL34639, *The Department of Defense Role in Foreign Assistance: Background, Major Issues, and Options for Congress*, by Nina M. Serafino et al. On the capabilities of U.S. government civilian agencies, see CRS Report RL32862, *Peacekeeping/Stabilization and Conflict Transitions: Background and Congressional Action on the Civilian Response/Reserve Corps and other Civilian Stabilization and Reconstruction Capabilities*, by Nina M. Serafino and Martin A. Weiss.
[60] President Obama's Presidential Policy Directive-1 (PPD-1), which describes the organization of the national security system and replaced the George W. Bush Administration's National Security Presidential Directive-1 (NSPD-1), includes several measures that apparently aim at instilling greater rigor. For example, the National Security Advisor is specifically instructed to carry out key support functions for the sessions of the National Security Council (NSC) "in a timely manner." In turn, in supporting the sessions of the NSC Deputies Committee, the Deputy National Security Advisor is tasked to ensure that all papers for discussion "fully analyze the issues, fairly and adequately set out the facts, consider a full range of views and options, and satisfactorily assess the prospects, risks, and implications of each." See Presidential Policy Directive-1, "Organization of the National Security System," February 13, 2009, available at http://www.fas.org/irp/offdocs/ppd/ppd-1.pdf.
[61] The war in Afghanistan has raised a similar set of concerns, but it has offered a different set of empirical models for consideration. In Afghanistan, U.S. Provincial Reconstruction Teams (PRTs) are almost exclusively military organizations, led by an Air Force or Navy officer and reporting up a military chain of command. U.S. Government civilian agencies – particularly the Department of State, the U.S. Agency for International Development, and the U.S. Department of Agriculture – have deployed experts to serve in key positions with both PRTs, and Division- and Brigade-sized task forces, but until 2009, the number of civilian experts was small. See CRS Report R40156, *War in Afghanistan: Strategy, Military Operations, and Issues for Congress*, by Catherine Dale.
[62] The Subcommittee on Oversight and Investigations of the House Armed Services Committee hosted a series of hearings about PRTs in Iraq and Afghanistan, and the potential implications for future U.S. inter-agency coordination and organization. See House Armed Services Committee, Subcommittee on Oversight and Investigation, "Agency Stovepipes vs. Strategic Agility: Lessons We Need to Learn from Provincial Reconstruction Teams in Iraq and Afghanistan, April 2008, available at http://armedservices.house.gov/pdfs/Reports/PRT_Report.pdf. The Army's Center for Army Lessons Learned, at Fort Leavenworth, Kansas, has conducted interviews with PRT participants and published initial observations. See "PRT Playbook: Tactics, Techniques and Procedures," Center for Army Lessons Learned, No. 07-34, September 2007. See also Rusty Barber and Sam Parker, "Evaluating Iraq's Provincial Reconstruction Teams While Drawdown Looms: a USIP Trip Report," United States Institute of Peace, December 2008.
[63] Colonel Dominic J. Caraccilo, who led a brigade in the Mahmudiyah area south of Baghdad, quoted in Larry Kaplow, "The Last Day of the War," *Newsweek*, January 12, 2009. See also "Marine Commander Says Iraq Pullout in 16 Months 'Doable'," National Journal, February 24, 2009, based on an interview with Marine Major General John Kelly at the completion of his tour as Multi-National Force-West Commanding General, who stressed that leaving too slowly could keep the ISF from taking control.
[64] Interviews with MNFI officials, January and February 2009.
[65] Interviews with MNC-I, MNSTC-I, and MNF-I subordinate commands including MNF-W, August 2008.
[66] Interviews with MNF-I and MNC-I officials, and subordinate commands, August 2008. In the view of many experts, one issue shaping the quality of the transition teams has been individual incentive to serve on such teams, based on the degree to which promotion boards favorably regard such service. Some DOD officials note that the incentives, based on personnel rules, are improving, while some practitioners note anecdotally that training missions tend not to be as highly regarded as more traditional combat assignments.
[67] Interviews with MNC-I officials, and subordinate commanders, August 2008.
[68] Interviews with MNF-I and MNSTC-I officials, August 2008. For example, some argue, a U.S. Army Colonel simply has not held high enough leadership positions within his own Department of Defense to be an appropriate advisor to an Iraqi Minister.
[69] For example, in December 2008, Major General Mark Hertling, then-Commanding General of Multi-National Division-North, noted that most U.S. forces in his area had already moved outside cities, with some exceptions, for example the city of Mosul, "where they have combat outposts throughout the city because there is still a significant fight against al Qaeda in that city." See Major General Mark Hertling, DOD News

Briefing, December 8, 2008. See also Ernesto Londono, "U.S. Prepares to Hand Over Baghdad Base," *Washington Post*, December 25, 2008. For specific examples of FOB closures, see Richard Tomkins, "U.S. Starts to Leave Key Iraq Bases," *Washington Times,* February 23, 2009.

[70] Sudarsan Raghavan and Qais Mizher, "Troops Will Remain in Iraqi Cities After June, Odierno Says," *Washington Post*, December 14, 2008; and Elisabeth Bumiller and Thom Shanker, "Generals Propose a Timetable for Iraq," *New York Times*, December 18, 2008.

[71] Brigadier General Fred Rudesheim, MNC-I Operational Update, March 15, 2009, transcript available at http://www.mnf-iraq.com/index.php?option=com_content&task=view&id=25810&Itemid=131.

[72] Jane Arraf, "U.S. General: American Forces May Not Leave Key Iraqi Cities," *Christian Science Monitor,* March 27, 2009.

[73] Interview with MNF-I official, February 2009; and MNF-I, slide "U.S. and Iraqi Security Agreement," February 2009. Broad oversight is provided by the Joint Ministerial Committee (JMC), co-chaired by the Iraqi Prime Minister, and the U.S. Ambassador and MNF-I Commanding General. Underneath that body, the Joint Military Operations Coordination Committee (JMOCC), co-chaired by the Iraqi Minister of Defense and the MNF-I Commanding General, includes sub-sections, under U.S.-Iraqi co-chairmanship: Temporary Committee for Iraqi Handover; Military Operations, Training and Logistical Support; Vehicle, Vessel and Aircraft Movement; Transfer of Security Responsibility to the Provinces. Also underneath the JMC, the Joint Committee, co-chaired by the Iraqi Minister of the Interior and the US Ambassador and MNF-I Commander, includes sub-sections, under U.S.-Iraqi co-chairmanship: Detainee Affairs, Agreed Upon Facilities and Areas, Claims, Point of Entry, Imports and Exports, Jurisdiction, Frequency Management, and Surveillance and Control of Airspace.

[74] GEN Raymond Odierno, letter dated December 4 2008, available at https://www.mnf-iraq.com/images Gs_Messages/cg_letter_on_the_security_agreement.pdf.

[75] Interview with MNF-I official, February 2009, Washington DC.

[76] Interviews with MNC-I officials, August 2008. The counterinsurgency guidance issued by GEN Odierno on September 16, 2008, had already emphasized that as the ISF stand up, coalition forces will increasingly "enable from overwatch." See "Multi-National Force-Iraq Commander's Counterinsurgency Guidance," September 16, 2008, available at http://www.mnf-iraq.com-odierno_coin_guidance.pdf.

[77] See Colonel Butch Kievenaar, Commander, 2nd Brigade Combat Team, 4th Infantry Division, DOD News Briefing, January 5, 2009, available at http://www.defenselink.mil/transcripts transcript/aspx? trancriptid=4335.

[78] "SOFA," Article 9, para.4-5.

[79] Interviews with MNF-I officials and subordinate commanders, August 2008.

[80] Interviews with MNC-I and subordinate commands, August 2008.

[81] "No detention or arrest may be carried out by the United States Forces (except with respect to detention or arrest of members of the United States Forces and of the civilian component) except through an Iraqi decision issued in accordance with Iraqi law and pursuant to Article 4." If U.S. forces do detain Iraqis, "such persons much be handed over to competent Iraqi authorities within 24 hours." "SOFA," Article 22, para.1-2.

[82] "SOFA," Article 22, para.4.

[83] MNF-I press release, November 30, 2008.

[84] Interviews with MNF-I officials and subordinate commanders, August 2008.

[85] Interview, MNF-I official, February 2009.

[86] Interview, MNF-I official, February 2009; and see Tom A. Peter, "U.S. to Hand Its Captives to Iraqi Courts," *Christian Science Monitor*, January 29, 2009.

[87] See Rod Nordland, "With Local Control, New Troubles in Iraq," *New York Times*, March 16, 2008. The article cites the released detainees' tribal leader, Salah Rasheed al-Goud, as saying that local police from the town of Haditha, in Anbar province, hunted the men down, handcuffed them, and shot them.

[88] Anthony Shadid, "In Iraq, Chaos Feared as U.S. Closes Prison," *Washington Post*, March 22, 2009.

[89] Interviews with Multi-National Division commanders, August 2008. As one noted, "What you see is the U.S. military, but we don't have the expertise."

[90] Interviews with MNC-I officials, August 2008.

[91] Interviews with U.S. military officials and PRT members, August 2008.

[92] Interviews with Multi-National Division commanders and subordinate commanders, August 2008.

[93] Interview with Multi-National Division commander, August 2008.

[94] Interviews with the Governor of Najaf, the Governor of Basra, August 2008.

[95] Interview with the Office of Provincial Affairs (OPA), U.S. Embassy, August 2008. When PRT leaders were asked how many subject matter experts they would like to receive, they reportedly requested a total of 170.

[96] Interviews with U.S. Embassy and Department of State officials, August and December 2008, and January 2009.

[97] See transcript, Secretary of Defense Robert M. Gates, House Armed Services Committee, hearing on Defense Department Priorities, Washington, DC, January 27, 2009.

[98] Interviews with U.S. civilian and military officials at the Najaf FOB.

[99] Communications with U.S. military officials in Baghdad, and U.S. civilian officials in Washington, DC, January 2009.
[100] Department of Defense, *U.S.CENTCOM Contractor Census Report,* Q1 2009.
[101] See Gordon Lubold, "A Drawdown of Contractors in Iraq," *Christian Science Monitor*, March 4, 2009; and Karen DeYoung, "U.S. Moves to Replace Contractors in Iraq," *Washington Post*, March 17, 2009.
[102] See Article 12, paragraph 2, "Agreement Between the United States of America and the Republic of Iraq on the Withdrawal of United States Forces from Iraq and the Organization of their Activities during their Temporary Presence in Iraq," available at http://www.whitehouse.gov/infocus/iraq/SE_SOFA.pdf.
[103] Karen DeYoung, "U.S. Moves to Replace Contractors in Iraq," *Washington Post*, March 17, 2009.
[104] See Julian E. Barnes, "In Iraq Withdrawal, Equipment poses a Key Logistical Challenge," *Los Angeles Times*, March 16, 2009. The author interviewed U.S. Army Major General Kenneth Dowd, Director of Logistics J-4, CENTCOM J4, who explained that equipment stockpiled in the region "…will be primarily the big gear, stuff like MRAPs, tanks…so we don't have to move and lift all this heavy stuff."
[105] On options available to the Congress, their constitutionality, and their possible impact, see CRS Report RL33837, *Congressional Authority to Limit U.S. Military Operations in Iraq*, by Jennifer K. Elsea, Michael John Garcia, and Thomas J. Nicola. For examples of tools available to Congress in general for shaping U.S. military operations, see CRS Report RL33803, *Congressional Restrictions on U.S. Military Operations in Vietnam, Cambodia, Laos, Somalia, and Kosovo: Funding and Non-Funding Approaches*, by Amy Belasco
[106] *Duncan Hunter National Defense Authorization Act for Fiscal Year 2009*, P.L. 110-417, October 14, 2008, §1211. This section repeated language from the FY2008 NDAA.
[107] *Supplemental Appropriations Act, 2008*, P.L. 110-252, June 30, 2008, §1402(e).
[108] See *U.S. Troop Readiness, Veterans' Care, Katrina Recovery, and Iraq Accountability Appropriations Act of 2007*, P.L. 110-28, May 25, 2007, §1314(b)(1)(A), which lists the 18 benchmarks. In §1314(c)(1), the Act specified that no funding appropriated for Iraq might be obligated or expended unless and until the President certified that Iraqi is making progress on each of the benchmarks.
[109] *Supplemental Appropriations Act, 2008*, P.L. 110-252, June 30, 2008, §9204. DOD submitted its first report pursuant to this requirement, entitled "Measuring Stability and Security in Iraq," in January 2009 (dated December 2008). DOD had previously submitted to Congress reports with this title, also known as "9010 reports," pursuant to a requirement in the *Department of Defense Appropriations Act 2007*, P.L. 109-289 §9010, as amended.
[110] Overall, some 300,000 sorties were flown. In 2002 for example, Iraqi forces fired on coalition aircraft 500 times, prompting 90 coalition air strikes against Iraqi targets. See Suzann Chapman, "The War Before the War," *Air Force Magazine,* February 2004. Chapman cites Air Force General John Jumper as noting in March 2003 that between June 2002 and March 2003, the U.S. Air Force flew about 4,000 sorties against Iraq's air defense system, surface-to-air missiles, and command and control.
[111] See the December 1, 1997, issue of the *Weekly Standard*, with a series of articles, under the heading "Saddam Must Go," including "Overthrow Him," by Zalmay Khalilzad and Paul Wolfowitz.
[112] The Iraq Liberation Act, P.L. 105-338, October 31, 1998, authorized support to "Iraqi democratic opposition organizations" and included provisions concerning how to identify such organizations.
[113] *The National Security Strategy of the United States of America*, September 2002, p.15, available at http://www.whitehouse.gov/nsc/nss/pdf.
[114] Chapter VII of the Charter of the United Nations authorizes the U.N. Security Council to "determine the existence of any threat to the peace, breach of the peace, or act of aggression" (Article 39), and should the Council consider other specified measures inadequate, to "take such action by air, sea, or land forces as may be necessary to maintain or restore international peace and security" (Article 42), see Charter of the United Nations, available at http://www.un.org/ aboutun/charter/.
[115] President Bush's Address to the United Nations General Assembly, September 12, 2002, New York, NY, available at the White House website http://www.whitehouse.gov/news/releases/2002/09/20020912-1.html.
[116] China, France, Russian Federation, United Kingdom, United States. Each of the 15 Council members has one vote. Procedural matters are made by an affirmative vote of at least 9 of the 15. Substantive matters require nine votes, including concurring votes from the 5 permanent members. See http://www.un. org/sc/members.asp.
[117] United Nations Security Council Resolution 1441, 8 November 2002, paragraphs 1, 2, 4, and 13.
[118] President Bush Address to the Nation, March 17, 2003, available at http://www.whitehouse. gov/news/releases/2003/ 03/20030317-7.html.
[119] Clausewitz made the point more forcefully: "No one starts a war, or rather, no one in his senses ought to do so, without first being clear in his mind what he intends to achieve by that war and how he intends to conduct it." Carl von Clausewitz, *On War*, Michael Howard and Peter Paret, eds., Princeton NJ: Princeton University Press, 1976.
[120] President Bush Address to the Nation, March 17, 2003, available at http://www.whitehouse. gov/news/releases/2003/ 03/200   30317-7.html.
[121] Ibid.

[122] Information from CENTCOM, CFLCC and V Corps planners, 2002 and 2003. From July 2002 to July 2004, the author served as the Political Advisor (POLAD) to the Commanding General (CG) of U.S. Army V Corps. That service included deploying with V Corps in early 2003 to Kuwait and then Iraq. In Iraq, the author served as POLAD to the CG of the Combined Joint Task Force-7 (CJTF-7), and then the Multi-National Force-Iraq (MNF-I).

[123] *National Strategy for Victory in Iraq*, November 30, 2005, available at http://www.whitehouse.gov/infocus/iraq/iraq_national_strategy_20051130.pdf.

[124] "Highlights of the Iraq Strategy Review" slides, National Security Council, January 2007, available at http://www.whitehouse.gov/nsc/iraq/2007/iraq-strategy011007.pdf.

[125] Department of Defense, "Measuring Stability and Security in Iraq," December 2008, submitted in accordance with §9204, Department of Defense Supplemental Appropriations Act 2008, P.L.110-252.

[126] Department of Defense, "Measuring Stability and Security in Iraq," March 2009, submitted in accordance with §9204, Department of Defense Supplemental Appropriations Act 2008, P.L.110-252, and also with §1508(c) of the Department of Defense Authorization Act for 2009, P.L. 110-417, p.iii.

[127] Information from CENTCOM, CFLCC and V Corps planners, 2002, 2003, and 2008.

[128] Interviews with planners who participated in the process, 2002 and 2003. Bob Woodward cites Secretary Rumsfeld as saying, at a December 4, 2001, planning session, "I'm not sure that that much force is needed, given what we've learned coming out of Afghanistan." Bob Woodward, Plan of Attack, New York: Simon and Schuster, 2004.

[129] Conversations with Office of the Secretary of Defense officials, 2005 and 2006.

[130] *The National Security Strategy of the United States of America*, September 2002, p.29, available at http://www.whitehouse.gov/nsc/nss/pdf.

[131] The "Powell Doctrine," generally acknowledged as the basis for the first Gulf War, was a collection of ideas, not a written document. Other key elements included force should only be used as a last resort, when there is a clear threat; there must be strong public support for the use of force; there must be a clear exit strategy. The Powell Doctrine derived in part from the Weinberger Doctrine, named after former Secretary of Defense Caspar Weinberger, Powell's one-time boss, which had been based on some Vietnam "lessons learned."

[132] Interviews with planners, 2002 and 2003. See also Bob Woodward, *Plan of Attack*, New York: Simon and Schuster, 2004.

[133] Information from CENTCOM and CFLCC planners, and Office of the Secretary of Defense officials, 2002 and 2003.

[134] Interviews with planners, 2002 and 2003. See also Michael R. Gordon and General Bernard E. Trainor, *Cobra II: The Inside Story and the Invasion and Occupation of Iraq*, New York: Vintage Books, 2006; and Bob Woodward, Plan of Attack, New York: Simon and Schuster, 2004.

[135] Interviews with planners and slide review, 2002 and 2003. See "Top Secret Polo Step" collection, "Compartmented Planning Effort, 15 August 2002" CENTCOM brief, obtained through the Freedom of Information Act and posted by the National Security Archive, The George Washington University, available at http://www.gwu.edu/~nsarchiv/ NSAEBB/NSAEBB214/index.htm.

[136] Gordon and Trainor note that this issue was debated at the March 2002 CENTCOM Component Commanders Conference. Michael R. Gordon and General Bernard E. Trainor, *Cobra II: The Inside Story and the Invasion and Occupation of Iraq*, New York: Vintage Books, 2006.

[137] Information from planners, 2002, 2003, and 2008.

[138] Interviews with planners and slide review, 2002 and 2003. See "Top Secret Polo Step" collection, "Compartmented Planning Effort, 15 August 2002" CENTCOM brief, obtained through the Freedom of Information Act and posted by the National Security Archive, The George Washington University, available at http://www.gwu.edu/~nsarchiv/ NSAEBB/NSAEBB214/index.htm. See also Michael R. Gordon and General Bernard E. Trainor, *Cobra II: The Inside Story and the Invasion and Occupation of Iraq*, New York: Vintage Books, 2006.

[139] "Hybrid" simply referred descriptively to the plan—it was not the formal name of a plan—although some senior leaders later seemed to use "Hybrid" as a proper noun.

[140] Interviews with planners and slide review, 2002, 2003 and 2008; "Compartmented Planning Effort"; and Gordon and Trainor, *Cobra II*.

[141] Information from V Corps leaders and staff, 2003.

[142] William S. Wallace, Interview, Frontline, Public Broadcasting System, February 26, 2004, available at http://www.pbs.org/wgbh/pages/frontline/shows/invasion/interviews/Wallace.html. He quickly added, "But I was comfortable with the degree of training of those forces that were available to us."

[143] See Robin Wright and Tom Ricks, "Bremer Criticizes Troop Levels," *Washington Post*, October 5, 2004. Ambassador Bremer's remarks were quoted from a nominally off-the-record talk he gave at DePauw University on September 17, 2004.

[144] Information from CENTCOM, CFLCC, V Corps, and Division Commanders, 2003, 2004 and 2008, and from Office of the Secretary of Defense officials, 2003 and 2004.

[145] Interviews with event organizers, 2002 and 2003. See Michael Howard, "Conference Delegates Vie for Political Role in New Iraq," *The Guardian*, December 16, 2002; and Judith Miller, "Ending Conference, Iraqi Dissidents Insist on Self-Government," *The New York Times*, March 3, 2003.

[146] Information from Department of State and Office of the Secretary of Defense officials, 2002 and 2003.

[147] Interviews with State officials responsible for the project, 2002 and 2003, and participation in some project sessions.

[148] Information from CFLCC planners, 2003 and 2008.

[149] Ahmed Chalabi, leader of the Iraqi opposition umbrella group Iraqi National Congress, was one key figure with whom OSD maintained contact, and some practitioners and observers have maintained that OSD sought primarily to "crown Chalabi." However, according to OSD officials, the "theory of the case," that is, introducing a new Iraqi leadership as soon as possible, was more important part of the argument than individual personalities. Information from the Office of the Secretary of Defense, Joint Staff, and Department of State officials, 2002 and 2003.

[150] Tommy Franks, *American Soldier*, New York: Regan Books, 2004, p.393. Franks reports that the remarks were made at a 5 August 2002 session of the National Security Council.

[151] Interviews with officials from the NSC, State Department, Office of the Secretary of Defense, and the Joint Staff, 2002 and 2003.

[152] Information from NSC staff, and Department of State and Office of the Secretary of Defense officials, 2003 and 2008. In testimony before the Senate Foreign Relations Committee, on February 11, 2003, then-Under Secretary of Defense for Policy Doug Feith, who favored "putting Iraqis in charge," describing the possible post-Saddam political process, named the key elements of the "mega-brief," including the Iraqi Consultative Council, the judicial council, the drafting of a constitution followed by a referendum, and early local elections. See Douglas J. Feith, *War and Decision: Inside the Pentagon at the Dawn of the War on Terrorism*. New York: Harper, 2008, p.369.

[153] During the spring of 2003, while combat operations commenced and U.S. commanders on the ground were wholly occupied with the fight, inter-agency wrangling concerning post-Saddam governance apparently continued. Former Under Secretary of Defense Doug Feith writes that in March 2003, his office, OSD (Policy), drafted a concept that called for the early appointment of an Iraqi Interim Authority (IIA) that would share leadership responsibilities with the coalition—that is, it would be less than an interim government, but more than a merely consultative body. Feith writes that the IIA concept was approved by President Bush at a session of the National Security Council on March 10, 2003. (See Douglas J. Feith, *War and Decision: Inside the Pentagon at the Dawn of the War on Terrorism*. New York: Harper, 2008, p.408.) During his brief tenure in Iraq, with a view to identifying Iraqis to play interim roles, Jay Garner, leader of the Organization for Reconstruction and Humanitarian Assistance (ORHA) hosted two "big-tent" meetings of Iraqi expats and community leaders, on April 15, 2003, in Nasariyah, and on April 28, 2003, in Baghdad. In early May 2003, just before President Bush announced that a new Coalition Provisional Authority, led by Ambassador L. Paul "Jerry" Bremer would supersede ORHA, Garner stated publicly that a "nucleus" of a "temporary" Iraqi leadership would emerge by later that month. After his arrival, Bremer slowed the process and, in July 2003, created the Iraqi Governing Council—an interim body like both the ICC and IIA concepts, with relatively little authority. Bremer has argued that at the time of his own appointment to head CPA in early May, the President's direction to him was not to hurry, but to "take the time necessary to create a stable political environment." See L. Paul Bremer III, "Facts for Feith: CPA History," *National Review Online*, March 19, 2008. It is possible that despite some broad presidential direction, key senior practitioners failed to reach a single, shared understanding of the role that an interim Iraqi body would play and the authority it would exercise.

[154] Information from CENTCOM planners, 2003 and 2006.

[155] Tommy Franks, *American Soldier*, New York: Regan Books, 2004.

[156] "Compartmented Planning Effort, 15 August 2002" brief, part of "Top Secret Polo Step" collection, obtained through the Freedom of Information Act and posted by the National Security Archive, The George Washington University, available at http://www.gwu.edu/~nsarchiv/NSAEBB/NSAEBB214/Tab%20I.pdf.

[157] Tommy Franks, *American Soldier*, New York: Regan Books, 2004.

[158] Interviews with officials from the Office of the Secretary of Defense, the Joint Staff, the Department of State, and the NSC staff, 2002 and 2003.

[159] Interviews with TFIV leaders and members, and with CFLCC staff, 2003. See also Michael R. Gordon and General Bernard E. Trainor, *Cobra II: The Inside Story and the Invasion and Occupation of Iraq*, New York: Vintage Books, 2006.

[160] They included Lieutenant General Ron Adams, Lieutenant General Jerry Bates, Major General Bruce Moore, and Brigadier General Buck Walters. The initial leadership team also included one senior leader from the Department of State, Ambassador Barbara Bodine, a noted Arabist and regional expert.

[161] Information from ORHA senior leaders, and CENTCOM and CFLCC staff, 2003.

[162] The U.S. Coast Guard, the only military service that reports to the Department of Homeland Security rather than the Department of Defense, contributed personnel to conduct maritime-interception operations and to conduct coastal patrols.

[163] See Bob Woodward, *Plan of Attack*, New York: Simon and Schuster, 2004, pp.208-212; Michael R. Gordon and General Bernard E. Trainor, *Cobra II: The Inside Story and the Invasion and Occupation of Iraq*, New York: Vintage Books, 2006, pp.156-157, 188-189, 388; and "Top Secret Polo Step" collection, "Compartmented Planning Effort, 15 August 2002" CENTCOM brief, obtained through the Freedom of Information Act and posted by the National Security Archive, The George Washington University, available at http://www.gwu.edu/~nsarchiv/NSAEBB/NSAEBB214/ index.htm.

[164] Information from CENTCOM, CFLCC and V Corps planners, 2003. See also Andrew Krepinevich, "Operation Iraqi Freedom: A First-Blush Assessment," Center for Strategic and Budgetary Assessments, 2003.

[165] Andrew Krepinevich, "Operation Iraqi Freedom: A First-Blush Assessment," Center for Strategic and Budgetary Assessments, 2003.

[166] Some discrepancies in contemporary press coverage and later accounts are due to the eight-hour time difference between Washington D.C., where President Bush issued the 48-hour ultimatum on the evening of March 17; and Baghdad, where that ultimatum expired in the early morning of March 20. The timeline of operations, described here, is based on the time in Baghdad.

[167] Information from V Corps leaders and staff, 2003. The basic facts of the case, during the initial days of OIF, were extremely well-documented by the international press. For one clear account, see Romesh Ratnesar, "Awestruck," *Time*, March 23, 2003. See also Michael R. Gordon and General Bernard E. Trainor, *Cobra II: The Inside Story and the Invasion and Occupation of Iraq*, New York: Vintage Books, 2006.

[168] For an in-depth description from the tactical level of the Army's role in OIF through major combat operations, commissioned by the Army and written by participants, see Gregory Fontenot, E.J. Degen, and David Tohn, *On Point: The United States Army in Operation Iraqi Freedom*, Annapolis, MD: Naval Institute Press, 2005.

[169] Interviews with participants, 2003. See also PBS Frontline, "Interview: Lt.Gen. James Conway," February 26, 2004, at http://www.pbs.org/wgbh/pages/frontline/shows/invasion/interviews/conway.html#marines.

[170] PBS Frontline, "Interview: COL David Perkins," February 26, 2004, at http://www.pbs.org/wgbh/pages/ frontline/ shows/invasion/interviews/perkins.html#thunder.

[171] See Press Conference with Major General David Petraeus, May 13, 2003, at http://www.defenselink.mil/ transcripts transcript.aspx?transcriptid=2601. For an account from the perspective of a battalion commander in the 101st Airborne Division, see Christopher Hughes, *War on Two Fronts: An Infantry Commander's War in Iraq and the Pentagon*, Drexel Hill, PA: Casemate, 2007.

[172] Rick Atkinson, "General: A Longer War Likely," *Washington Post*, March 28, 2003. Asked whether this suggested the likelihood of a much longer war than forecast, LTG Wallace replied, "It's beginning to look that way." Asked later that day for his reaction to these comments, Secretary Rumsfeld noted, "Well, I didn't read the article—I saw the headline." See DOD Press Briefing with Secretary Rumsfeld, March 28, 2003, available at http://www.defenselink.mil/ transcripts/transcript.aspx?transcriptid=2180s].

[173] Information from V Corps staff, 2003.

[174] Information from Office of the Secretary of Defense officials, and CFLCC and CJTF-7 officials, 2003.

[175] Information from CENTCOM and V Corps officials, 2003. Curiously, Chalabi and the fighters, apparently viewing themselves as a stronger incarnation of the Taszar training program, adopted the name "Free Iraqi Forces." To distinguish them from the Taszar-trained Iraqis, the Department of Defense called them the "Free Iraqi Fighting Force."

[176] See Michael Gordon and Bernard Trainor, "Dash to Baghdad left top U.S. Generals Divided," *The New York Times*, March 13, 2006.

[177] "Looters ransack Baghdad museum," *BBC News*, April 12, 2003. See also John Burns, "A Nation at War: The Iraqis, Looting and a Suicide Attack as Chaos Grows in Baghdad," *The New York Times*, April 11, 2003. Secretary of Defense Donald Rumsfeld described the dynamic as "untidiness," and a manifestation of "pent-up feelings that may result from decades of repression" directed against the old regime. See Department of Defense News Briefing, Secretary of Defense Donald Rumsfeld, April 11, 2003, available at http://www.defenselink.mil/transcripts transcript.aspx?transcriptid=2367.

[178] See an assessment by an OIF participant: Colonel Mark Klingelhoefer, "Captured Enemy Ammunition in Operation Iraqi Freedom and its Strategic Importance in Post-Conflict Operations," U.S. Army War College, March 18, 2005, available at http://www.strategicstudiesinstitute.army.mil/pdffiles/ksil72.pdf.

[179] See John Burns, "A Nation at War: The Iraqis, Looting and a Suicide Attack as Chaos Grows in Baghdad," *The New York Times*, April 11, 2003, who quotes a Marine on guard in Baghdad as saying, "we just don't have enough troops."

[180] Information from Department of State, Office of the Secretary of Defense and CENTCOM officials, and participant observation, 2003.

[181] "President Bush Announces Major Combat Operations in Iraq Have Ended," May 1, 2003, at http://www.whitehouse.gov/news/releases/2003/05/20030501-15.html.

[182] United Nations Security Council Resolution 1483 (2003), 22 May 2003, Preambular Section.

[183] United Nations Security Council Resolution 1511 (2003), 16 October 2003.
[184] United Nations Security Council Resolution 1546 (2004), 8 June 2004 (letters). Subsequently, the U.N. mandate was extended annually.
[185] Ibid., para. 9.
[186] Ibid., para. 10.
[187] The ceremony marking the establishment (Full Operational Capability) of the Multi-National Force-Iraq, in May 2004, included a parade of representatives of each coalition partner country. An Iraqi General participated in the parade like all the other coalition members—and then brought the house down when, unscripted, he kissed the Iraqi flag.
[188] United Nations Security Council Resolution 1546 (2004), 8 June 2004 (letters).
[189] Coalition Provisional Authority Order 17 (revised), "Status of the Coalition Provisional Authority, MNF-Iraq, Certain Missions and Personnel in Iraq," available at http://www.iraqcoalition.org/regulations 20040627_CPAORD_17_Status_of_Coalition_Rev__with_Annex_A.pdf.
[190] UN Security Council Resolution 1790 (2007), December 18, 2007, available at http://daccessdds.un.org/doc/UNDOC/GEN/N07/650/72/PDF/N0765072.pdf?OpenElement.
[191] See "Agreement between the United States of America and the Republic of Iraq on the Withdrawal of United States Forces from Iraq and the Organization of their Activities during their Temporary Presence in Iraq."
[192] For an account of the year of formal occupation from one of the key protagonists, see L. Paul Bremer III with Malcolm McConnell, *My Year in Iraq: The Struggle to Build a Future of Hope*, New York: Simon & Schuster, 2006. For an account of that year by a journalist who spent considerable time at CPA headquarters, see Rajiv Chandrasekaran, *Imperial Life in the Emerald City*, New York: Vintage Books, 2006. For a hard-hitting critique of both civilian and military mistakes during the occupation, see Thomas E. Ricks, *Fiasco: The American Military Adventure in Iraq*, New York: The Penguin Press, 2006.
[193] Information from CFLCC and V Corps staff, 2003.
[194] The previous day, June 14, The V Corps Commanding General who led V Corps during OIF major combat, LTG Wallace, handed command of the Corps to LTG Sanchez. LTG Sanchez had come to Iraq several weeks earlier as the Commanding General of 1st Armored Division. The few CFLCC staff still remaining in Baghdad redeployed to Kuwait.
[195] The phrase, borrowed from field artillery, does not necessarily translate smoothly into bureaucratic relationships. CPA tended to assume that the military command in Iraq simply worked for CPA. In May 2003, at his first meeting with the V Corps Commander, discussing whether their organizations would retain separate headquarters, Ambassador Bremer pointed his finger at the General's chest and said, "It is my commander's intent that you co-locate with me." Participant observation, 2003.
[196] The 2004 split of CJTF-7 into a higher, four-star HQ, and a lower, three-star HQ, was strongly recommended, in order to give the commanders time to focus full-time on two very large portfolios—strategic work with U.S. and Iraqi leadership, and supervising operations throughout Iraq. As of January 2008, MNF-I and MNC-I staff were reportedly beginning to plan a re-merger of the two headquarters, perhaps to take effect at the following Corps rotation, to avoid apparent duplication of effort by some staff sections.
[197] Joint Staff information paper, "Boots on the Ground," February 1, 2009.
[198] Department of Defense News Transcript, MG Buford C. Blount III from Baghdad, May 15, 2003, available at http://www.defenselink.mil/transcripts/transcript.aspx?transcriptid=2608.
[199] Department of Defense News Briefing with Secretary Gates and General Pace from the Pentagon, April 11, 2007, available at http://www.defenselink.mil/transcripts/transcript.aspx?transcriptid=3928. Secretary Gates clarified that the current expectation was that "not more than 15 months" would generally mean "15 months."
[200] Department of Defense Press Release, "DoD Announces Changes to Reserve Component Force Management Policy," January 11, 2007, available at http://www.defenselink.mil/releases/release.aspx?releaseid=10389. The policy is based on unit rotations; individuals who transfer between units may find themselves out of synch with the rotation policy goals. See for example John Vandiver, "Families want answers about deployments and dwell time," *Stars and Stripes*, May 11, 2007.
[201] White House, "Fact Sheet: The Way Forward in Iraq," April 10, 2008, available at http://www.whitehouse.gov/news/releases/2008/04/20080410-4.html.
[202] For more detailed information about past foreign contributions to Iraq, including coalition forces, see CRS Report RL32105, *Iraq: Foreign Contributions to Stabilization and Reconstruction*, by Christopher M. Blanchard and Catherine Dale.
[203] See "Australia withdraws troops from Iraq," Reuters, June 1, 2008; and "Australia ends combat operations in Iraq," CNN, June 2, 2008; and interviews with MNF-I officials, August 2008.
[204] Michael Evans, "British Forces to Start Leaving Iraq in March: Down to 400 by Summer," *London Times*, December 10, 2008.
[205] See "Iraq Signs Foreign Troops Deals," *BBC News*, December 31, 2009.
[206] See "350 Romanian Soldiers Stay in Iraq to Help Country's Reconstruction," *Bucharest Herald*, January 26, 2009.

[207] See "Iraq Signs Foreign Troops Deals," *BBC News,* December 31, 2009; "El Salvador to Withdraw Troops From Iraq," *Voice of America News*, December 24, 2009; "Estonia's 34 Troops Withdrawn from Iraq," *CNN*, January 22, 2009.
[208] See NATO Training Mission-Iraq website, at http://www.afsouth.nato.int/JFCN_Missions/NTMI/Factsheets/NTMI_part.htm
[209] Department of Defense, "Measuring Stability and Security in Iraq," December 2008.
[210] Based on accounts from detainees and others, MNF-I leaders assess that underemployment, more often than unemployment, is a prime motivation for those recruited to place an IED in return for a one-time cash payment.
[211] Interviews with MNF-I and MNC-I officials, January 2008.
[212] Interviews with MNF-I and MNC-I officials and subordinate commanders, January 2008.
[213] Department of Defense, "Measuring Stability and Security in Iraq," March 2009, p.7.
[214] Interviews with MNF-I, MNC-I, and MND-North officials, January 2008.
[215] Interviews with MNC-I and subordinate commanders, August 2008.
[216] Interviews with MNC-I and MNF-W commanders and other officials, August 2008.
[217] Department of Defense, "Measuring Stability and Security in Iraq," December 2008.
[218] Department of Defense, "Measuring Stability and Security in Iraq," December 2008.
[219] See Heath Druzin, "Commander Assesses Iraq Challenges," *Mideast Stars and Stripes*, January 19, 2009.
[220] Marc Santora, "G.I.s Attacked by Iraqis in Uniforms," *New York Times,* February 25, 2009.
[221] DOD, "Measuring Stability and Security in Iraq," March 2009, p.22.
[222] Interviews with U.S. civilian and military officials, August 2008. See for example Nicholas Spangler and Mohammed al Dulaimy, "Al-Sadr would back Iraqi government for a price," *Arizona Daily Star*, July 31, 2008.
[223] See Sabrina Tavernise, "A Shiite Militia in Baghdad sees its power wane," *New York Times*, July 27, 2008.
[224] Interviews with MNF-I officials, Baghdad, January and August 2008. During the February 2008 state visit to Baghdad by Iranian President Mahmoud Ahmadinejad, Iranian and Iraqi officials reportedly signed an agreement on the renovation of border posts along their shared land and maritime borders. See "Iran, Iraq Emphasize Need for Renovation of Border Posts," Tehran IRNA agency in English, February 20 2008.
[225] In its March 2009 report, DOD stated, "Iran continues to pose a significant challenge to Iraq's long-term stability and political independence…it continues to host, train, fund, arm and guide militant groups that seek to bleed the U.S. in Iraq." See Department of Defense, "Measuring Stability and Security in Iraq," March 2009, p.v and 6.
[226] Interviews with MNF-I subordinate command officials, January 2008.
[227] Interviews with MNC-I and subordinate command officials, August 2008.
[228] Interviews with MNF-I and MNC-I officials, and subordinate commanders, and with Iraqi commanders, August 2008. See also "US: Quds, Hezbollah training hit squads in Iran," *Associated Press*, August 16, 2008. The author, citing a "senior U.S. military intelligence officer in Iraq," writes that Iraqis are being trained in Iran in reconnaissance, the use of small arms and improvised explosive devices, assassination techniques, and terrorist cell operations and communications.
[229] Sinan Salaheddin, "Iraqi Official Seeks War Shift from Fighting to Intelligence," *Philadelphia Inquirer*, March 15, 2009.
[230] Interviews with MNF-I officials, January 2008. See also Joseph Felter and Brian Fishman, "Iranian Strategy in Iraq: Politics and 'Other Means,'" Combating Terrorism Center at West Point, Occasional Paper Series, October 13, 2008.
[231] See for example, "Shiite Politics in Iraq: the Role of the Supreme Council," International Crisis Group, November 15, 2007, available at http://www.crisisgroup.org/home/index.cfm?id=5158. This view is shared by some key strategists at MNF-I, interviews, January and August 2008.
[232] See International Crisis Group, "Iraq's Provincial Elections: The Stakes," Middle East Report No.82, January 27, 2009, pp.25-26; and Matthew Duss and Peter Juul, "The Fractured Shi'a of Iraq: Understanding the Tensions Within Iraq's Majority," Center for American Progress, January 2009.
[233] Interviews with MNF-I subordinate officials, and PRT officials, 2008. By late 2008, the role of these councils had expanded beyond southern Iraq.
[234] President Talabani stated that he would request a ruling from the Federal Supreme Court on the question of the councils' constitutionality. See Alissa J. Rubin, "Clash in Iraq over a plan for councils intensifies," *New York Times*, Dec 4, 2008.
[235] Interviews with U.S. Embassy officials, August 2008.
[236] Interviews with the Governor of Basra, and with U.S. and UK military and civilian officials in Basra, August 2008. See also International Crisis Group, "Iraq's Provincial Elections: The Stakes," Middle East Report No.82, January 27, 2009, p.8.
[237] Interviews with Governors of Najaf, Basra; and Iraqi commanders in Diwaniyah and Basra, August 2008.

[238] See press accounts including Ellen Knickmeyer and K.I. Ibrahim, "Bombing Shatters Mosque in Iraq," *Washington Post*, February 23, 2006; and Robert F. Worth, "Muslim Clerics Call for an End to Iraqi Rioting," *The New York Times*, February 25, 2006.

[239] To be clear, as human rights groups stress, displacement is not a "solution." As a rule, in most situations, people are far more vulnerable in displacement than they are in their homes.

[240] Department of Defense, "Measuring Stability and Security in Iraq," December 2008.

[241] Department of Defense, "Measuring Stability and Security in Iraq," March 2009, p.8.

[242] Interviews with Iraqi officials responsible for resettlement in parts of Baghdad, August 2008. For example, in some Baghdad neighborhoods, Shi'a extremists from the *Jaish al-Mahdi* reportedly forced affluent Sunni Arabs to flee their homes, and then offered those "empty" homes, for a very nominal rent, to much less affluent Shi'a Arabs.

[243] Information from CJTF-7, MNF-I, DOD, and Iraqi officials, 2003 and 2004.

[244] "Turkey Extends Right to Attack," *New York Times*, October 9, 2008.

[245] See for example "Turkish jets in fresh Iraq strike," *BBC America*, December 26, 2007.

[246] See Alissa J. Rubin and Sabrina Tavernise, "Turkish Troops Enter Iraq in Pursuit of Kurdish Militants," *The New York Times*, February 23, 2008; Lolita Baldor, "Gates: Turkey Raid Won't Solve Problems," *Washington Post*, February 23, 2008; Yochi Dreazen, "U.S. Knew of Turkey's Plan to Hit PKK, Didn't Object," *Wall Street Journal*, February 26, 2008.

[247] See "Turkey strikes PKK headquarters in Kandil," *Turkish Daily News*, July 28, 2008.

[248] See Department of Defense, "Measuring Stability and Security in Iraq," March 2009, p.7.

[249] See "Iraq: Kurdish Rebels Reject Calls to Stop Fighting," Associated Press, March 24, 2009; "Turkish President Discusses Border Tensions in Baghdad," Voice of America News, March 24, 2009.

[250] Michael Isikoff and Mark Hosenball, "Terror Watch: Shades of Gray," *Newsweek*, October 17, 2007.

[251] Interviews with MNF-I and MNC-I officials, August 2008. Early indications of GoI intent were reportedly causing anxiety for members of the MeK.

[252] Multi-National Force-Iraq press conference, Mr. Abdul Qadr al-Mufriji, Minister of Defense, and LTG Frank Helmick, Commanding General, Multi-National Security Transition Command-Iraq, September 10, 2008.

[253] See Rod Nordland, "With Local Control, New Troubles in Iraq," *New York Times*, March 16, 2009.

[254] Scott Peterson, "Iran Pushes Iraq to Close MKO Camp," *Christian Science Monitor*, March 2, 2009.

[255] Carl von Clausewitz, *On War*, Michael Howard and Peter Paret, eds., Princeton NJ: Princeton University Press, 1976, p.88.

[256] See BBC, "US faces Iraq guerrilla war," July 16, 2003, available at http://news.bbc.co.uk/2/hi/middle_east/3072899.stm.

[257] Department of Defense News Briefing with Secretary Rumsfeld and General Myers, June 30, 2003, available at http://www.defenselink.mil/transcripts/transcript.aspx?transcriptid=2767. When a reporter read the DOD definition of guerrilla war—"military and paramilitary operations conducted in enemy-held or hostile territory by irregular, predominantly indigenous forces"—and asked whether that described the situation in Iraq, Secretary Rumsfeld replied, "It really doesn't."

[258] Ricardo S. Sanchez, *Wiser in Battle: A Soldier's Story*, New York: Harper, 2008, pp.231-232.

[259] Information from that officer and senior CJTF-7 staff, 2003 and 2004.

[260] News Briefing with Secretary of Defense Donald Rumsfeld and General Peter Pace, November 29, 2005, DOD website, available at http://www.defenselink.mil/transcripts/transcript.aspx?transcriptid=1492.

[261] Neither CPA nor CJTF-7 was responsible for the search for possible weapons of mass destruction. That mission was assigned to the Iraq Survey Group, which reported jointly to the Central Intelligence Agency (CIA) and DOD's Defense Intelligence Agency (DIA), and which carried out its work from June 2003 to September 2004. The group's final Report, "Comprehensive Report of the Special Advisor to the DCI on Iraq's WMD," and commonly known as the Duelfer Report, was published on September 30, 2004, and is available at https://www.cia.gov/library/reports/generalreports- 1/iraq_wmd_2004/index.html.

[262] Information from CJTF-7 leaders, and participant observation, 2003 and 2004.

[263] Major General Peter W. Chiarelli and Major Patrick Michaelis, "Winning the Peace: The Requirement for Full-Spectrum Operations," *Military Review*, July-August 2005, available at http://usacac.army.mil/CAC/milreview/ download/English/JulAug05/chiarelli.pdf. The authors characterized the lines of operation as "combat operations, train and employ security forces, essential services, promote governance, and economic pluralism." Echoing the views of CJTF-7 leaders, the authors added, "Further, those who viewed the attainment of security solely as a function of military action alone were mistaken."

[264] In January 2004, when abuse allegations were brought forward, CJTF-7 issued a press release noting that the command had ordered an inquiry into alleged detainee abuses. Abu Ghraib events prompted a number of investigations and reports. For one account of events and the policies that shaped them, see the Final Report of the Independent Panel to Review DoD Detention Operations, chaired by former Secretary of Defense James Schlesinger, and commissioned by then-Secretary of Defense Donald Rumsfeld "to provide independent professional advice on detainee abuses, what caused them, and what actions should be taken to preclude their repetition," available in book form, Department of Defense, *The Schlesinger Report: An Investigation of Abu*

Ghraib, New York: Cosimo Reports, November 15, 2005. For a detailed, critical account of Abu Ghraib events and their antecedents and impact, see Seymour Hersch, *Chain of Command: The Road from 9/11 to Abu Ghraib,* New York: Harper Perennial, 2005.

[265] Information from CJTF-7 and Division leaders, 2003 and 2004.

[266] Information from CJTF-7, 1AD, and 101st leaders, and participant observation, 2003 and 2004.

[267] Ricardo S. Sanchez, *Wiser in Battle: A Soldier's Story,* New York: Harper, 2008, p.232.

[268] These efforts continued an initiative to help form district and neighborhood advisory councils in Baghdad, launched by ORHA but discontinued by CPA.

[269] For a detailed account of the military operations, and the political and military events that led up to them, see Bing West, *No True Glory: A Frontline Account of the Battle for Fallujah,* New York: Bantam Books, 2005.

[270] Al Anbar province, in western Iraq, covers about one-third of Iraq's territory but is relatively lightly populated.

[271] IMEF headquarters and the 1st Marine Division returned to Iraq in spring 2004, after a short stay at home after major combat operations.

[272] The Iraq Governing Council (IGC) was a critical part of the U.S. strategy for transitioning responsibility and authority to Iraqi leaders. The plans, articulated in the Transitional Administrative Law approved in March 2004, called for the IGC to relinquish its advisory role to a new, appointed Iraqi Interim Government, to which CPA, in turn, would return full governing authority by June 30, 2004. An IGC collapse, it was considered, could disrupt or delay the plans.

[273] Information from CPA and CJTF-7 officials, and participant observation, 2004.

[274] Information from CJTF-7 and IMEF leaders, 2004. See also Bing West, *No True Glory: A Frontline Account of the Battle for Fallujah,* New York: Bantam Books, 2005.

[275] Bing West, *No True Glory: A Frontline Account of the Battle for Fallujah,* New York: Bantam Books, 2005.

[276] See for example Richard Beeston, "At home in the rubble: siege city reborn as giant gated community," *The Times Online,* May 19, 2005.

[277] A Commander's Action—or Initiatives—Group, is small group of smart thinkers, hand-selected by the commander to serve as his personal, in-house "think-tank."

[278] His book *Dereliction of Duty: Johnson, McNamara, the Joint Chiefs of Staff, and the Lies that led to Vietnam* (published by Harper Perennial, 1998) is widely read in U.S. military educational programs and elsewhere.

[279] Department of Defense Press Briefing, H.R. McMaster, September 13, 2005, available at http://www.defenselink.mil/transcripts/transcript.aspx?transcriptid=2106.

[280] See Thomas E. Ricks, "The Lessons of Counterinsurgency," *Washington Post,* February 16, 2006; "The Insurgency: Interview with COL H.R. McMaster," *Frontline,* PBS, February 21, 2006, available at http://www.pbs.org/wgbh/pages/ frontline/insurgency/interviews/mcmaster/html; and George Packer, "Letter from Iraq: The Lesson of Tal Afar," *The New Yorker,* April 10, 2006.

[281] Information from CENTCOM and CJTF-7 leaders, 2004.

[282] Department of Defense Press Briefing, H.R. McMaster, September 13, 2005, available at http://www.defenselink.mil/transcripts/transcript.aspx?transcriptid=2106.

[283] *Ibid.*

[284] David Ignatius wrote in the *Washington Post* that in 2005, a number of key Iraq decision-makers and practitioners, including COL McMasters' former boss at CENTCOM General Abizaid, were reading Lewis Sorley's book, *A Better War: The Unexamined Victories and the Final Tragedy of America's Last Years in Vietnam* (New York: Harcourt, 1999), which favorably describes General Abrams' "clear and hold" approach. See David Ignatius, "A Better Strategy for Iraq," *Washington Post,* November 4, 2005.

[285] Secretary Condoleezza Rice, Opening Remarks before the Senate Foreign Relations Committee, October 19, 2005, available at http://www.state.gov/secretary/rm/2005/55303.htm. To be clear, "strategy" refers in general to a set of "ways and means," linked with the "ends" they are intended to achieve. "Clear, hold, build" referred to a new set of approaches—of "ways and means"—but the Administration's broad stated goals had not changed.

[286] He said, "Our strategy is to clear, hold, and build. We're working to clear areas from terrorist control, to hold those areas securely, and to build lasting, democratic Iraqi institutions through an increasingly inclusive political process." See "President commemorates Veterans Day, Discusses War on Terror," November 11, 2005, Tobyhanna, Pennsylvania, available at http://www.whitehouse.gov/ news/releases/ 2005/11/print /20051111-1.html.

[287] The Strategy describes the security mandate to "clear, hold, build" this way: "Clear areas of enemy control by remaining on the offensive, killing and capturing enemy fighters and denying them safe haven; hold areas freed from enemy influence by ensuring that they remain under the control of the Iraqi government with an adequate Iraqi security force presence; and build Iraqi Security Forces and the capacity of local institutions to deliver services, advance the rule of law, and nurture civil society." See *National Strategy for Victory in Iraq,* November 30, 2005, p. 2, available at White House website, http://www.whitehouse.gov/ infocus/ iraq/iraq_national_strategy_20051130.pdf.

[288] Ibid., pp. 1-2.

[289] White House Fact Sheet: "Strategy for Victory—Clear, Hold, Build," March 20, 2006.

[290] Operations Update with Major General William B. Caldwell, Multi-National Forces-Iraq, July 24, 2006, available at http://www.mnf-iraq.com/index.php?option=com_content&task=view&id=1201&Itemid=131.

[291] MNF-I spokesman MG Caldwell attributed that phrase to Iraqi Prime Minister Nuri al-Maliki, see Operations Update with Major General William B. Caldwell, Multi-National Forces-Iraq, July 20, 2006, available at http://www.mnf-iraq.com/index.php?option=com_content&task=view&id=1027&Itemid=30.

[292] Operations Update with Major General William B. Caldwell, Multi-National Forces-Iraq, July 20, 2006, available at http://www.mnf-iraq.com/index.php?option=com_content&task=view&id=1027&Itemid=30.

[293] Press Conference of the President, the Rose Garden, June 14, 2006, available at http://www.whitehouse.gov/news/releases/2006/06/20060614.html.

[294] Operations Update with Major General William B. Caldwell, Multi-National Forces-Iraq, July 20, 2006, available at http://www.mnf-iraq.com/index.php?option=com_content&task=view&id=1027&Itemid=30.

[295] Press Briefing by Major General William B. Caldwell, Multi-National Force-Iraq, October 19, 2006, available at http://www.mnf-iraq.com/index.php?option=com_content&task=view&id=6585&Itemid=131.

[296] Operations Update with Major General William B. Caldwell, Multi-National Forces-Iraq, July 20, 2006, available at http://www.mnf-iraq.com/index.php?option=com_content&task=view&id=1027&Itemid=30.

[297] Press Briefing by Major General William B. Caldwell, Multi-National Force-Iraq, October 19, 2006, available at http://www.mnf-iraq.com/index.php?option=com_content&task=view&id=6585&Itemid=131.

[298] For a detailed account of theory and practice under the New Way Forward strategy, see Linda Robinson, *Tell Me How This Ends: General David Petraeus and the Search for a Way Out of Iraq*, New York: PublicAffairs, 2008.

[299] See "Fact Sheet: The New Way Forward in Iraq," January 10, 2007, available at http://www.whitehouse.gov/news/releases/2007/01/print/20070110-3.html.

[300] "Highlights of the Iraq Strategy Review," National Security Council, January 2007, available at http://www.whitehouse.gov/nsc/iraq/2007/iraq-strategy011007.pdf.

[301] President's Address to the Nation, January 10, 2007, available at White House website, http://www.whitehouse.gov/news/releases/2007/01/print/20070110-7.html.

[302] Conversations with ORHA, CPA and CJTF-7 staff, 2003 and 2004.

[303] Press Briefing by GEN David Petraeus, March 8, 2007, available at http://www.mnf-iraq.com/index.php?option=com_content&task=view&id=10475&Itemid=131.

[304] He added, "I think you have to have governance and security before you can have a viable economics plan." See "Remarks by General James T. Conway, Commandant of the Marine Corps," Center for a New American Security, October 15, 2007.

[305] Remarks by General James Jones, Meeting of the Atlantic Council of the United States, Washington, D.C., September 12, 2007. General Jones led the Independent Commission on the Security Forces of Iraq, required by U.S. Troop Readiness, Veterans' Care, Katrina Recovery, and Iraq Accountability Appropriations Act of 2007, Public Law 110-28, Section 1314. The Report is available at http://www.csis.org/media csis/pubs/isf.pdf, and discussed below.

[306] President's Address to the Nation, January 10, 2007, available at White House website, http://www.whitehouse.gov/news/releases/2007/01/print/20070110-7.html.

[307] See "Fact Sheet: Helping Iraq Achieve Economic and Political Stabilization," January 8, 2008, available at http://www.whitehouse.gov/news/releases/2008/01/20080108-4.html.

[308] A famous quote by T.E. Lawrence—"Lawrence of Arabia"—appears frequently in briefings and on office walls, of coalition forces in Iraq: "Do not try to do too much with your own hands. Better the Arabs do it tolerably than that you do it perfectly. It is their war, and you are there to help them, not to win it for them." The quote, although still popular, more closely reflects an emphasis on "transition" than on "population security."

[309] Conversations with Division Commanders, January 2008.

[310] Mission statement of one Multi-National Division, January 2008.

[311] Ray Odierno, "In Defense of Baghdad's Walls," *Los Angeles Times*, April 25, 2007.

[312] Dave Kilcullen, "The Urban Tourniquet—Gated Communities in Baghdad," April 27, 2007, at *Small Wars Journal*, http://www.smallwarsjournal.com/blog/2007/04/the-urban-tourniquet-gated-com/. Dr. Kilcullen has served at MNF-I in Baghdad as an advisor to GEN Petraeus.

[313] See for example Karin Brulliard, "'Gated Communities' for the War-Ravaged," *Washington Post*, April 23, 2007. See also Tim Kilbride, "Coalition Positioned to Break Iraq's Cycle of Violence," *American Forces Press Service*, May 25, 2007, available at http://www.defenselink.mil/news/newsarticle.aspx?id=46184).

[314] Information from Division and Brigade Commanders, January 2008.

[315] Interview, January 2008, Baghdad. MG Simmons brought to bear considerable comparative perspective. He held the post of III Corps DCG for over four and a half years, and thus also served as MNC-I DCG on the Corps' first tour in Iraq as the nucleus of MNC-I, from 2004 to 2005.

[316] Conversation with MNF-West leaders, January 2008.

[317] David Petraeus, Interview with Charles Gibson, *World News*, ABC, July 28, 2008. 318

[318] Press Briefing by GEN David Petraeus, March 8, 2007, available at http://www.mnf-iraq.com/index.php?option= com_content&task =view&id=10475&Itemid=131.

[319] Interviews with MNF-I subordinate commanders, January 2008.
[320] President's Address to the Nation, January 10, 2007, available at White House website, http://www.whitehouse.gov/ news/releases/2007/01/print/20070110-7.html.
[321] Press Briefing by General David Petraeus, March 8, 2007, available at http://www.mnf-iraq.com/ index.php?option=com_content&task=view&id=10475&Itemid=131.
[322] Adam Brookes, "Bush Iraq plan likely to cost dear," *BBC news*, January 11, 2007, available at http://news.bbc.co.uk/2/hi/americas/6250657.stm.
[323] President's Address to the Nation, January 10, 2007, available at White House website, http://www.whitehouse.gov/ news/releases/2007/01/print/20070110-7.html.
[324] "Baghdad" is the name of both the capital city and the province where it is located.
[325] See Department of Defense Press Briefing with Lieutenant General Odierno, May 31, 2007, available at http://www.defenselink.mil/transcripts/transcript.aspx?transcriptid=3973.
[326] See Department of Defense press briefing, Major General Joseph Fil, February 16, 2007, available at http://www.defenselink.mil/transcripts/transcript.aspx?transcriptid=3891.
[327] Information from Division Commanders and staff, January 2008.
[328] Information from MNC-I and Division officials, January 2008. See also Kimberly Kagan, "The Real Surge: Preparing for Operation Phantom Thunder," *Iraq Report*, The Institute for the Study of War and The Weekly Standard, February 14, 2007-June 15, 2007, available at http://www.understandingwar .org/IraqReport/ IraqReport05.pdf.
[329] Information fr om MND-Baghdad, January 2008.
[330] Retired Army Major General Scales provides a clear description of the early stages of these operations, based on a visit to Iraq in Robert H. Scales MG (ret), "Petraeus's Iraq," *Wall Street Journal*, November 21, 2007.
[331] Information from MND-North, January 2008.
[332] See Department of Defense News Briefing, Major General Mark Hertling, January 22, 2008, available at http://www.defenselink.mil/transcripts.
[333] See Department of Defense News Briefing, Maj.Gen. Walter Gaskin, December 10, 2007, http://www. defenselink.mil/transcripts.
[334] Interviews with MNC-I and MND-North officials, January and August 2008.
[335] Interviews with MNC-I and MND-N officials, August 2008. See also Solomon Moore, "In Mosul, New Test of Rebuilt Iraqi Army," *New York Times*, March 20, 2008; Moore reports that at one point, the demands of the surge in Baghdad left only 750 U.S. Soldiers in Mosul, and 2,000 in Ninewah altogether.
[336] See for example "Iraq to Go After Al-Qaeda in Mosul," Associated Press, *Washington Post*, January 25, 2008.
[337] Interviews with MND-N officials, August 2008. See Department of Defense, "Measuring Stability and Security in Iraq," June 2008, p.20.
[338] Information from MNF-I subordinate commanders, October 2008.
[339] Interviews with MNC-I officials and subordinate commanders, August 2008. The Corps-level operation in this region is called Operation DAN (Defeat Al-Qaeda in the North).
[340] Interview with MNF-I subordinate commander, August 2008.
[341] See Multi-National Force-Iraq press conference, Major General Mohammed al-Askari, Iraqi Ministry of Defense Spokesman, and Brigadier General David Perkins, MNF-I Spokesman, July 30, 2008.
[342] Interviews with MNF-I and MNC-I officials, and subordinate commanders, August 2008.
[343] See Multi-National Force-Iraq press conference, Major General Mohammed al-Askari, Iraqi Ministry of Defense Spokesman, and Brigadier General David Perkins, MNF-I Spokesman, July 30, 2008.
[344] See Multi-National Force-Iraq press conference, Major General Mohammed al-Askari, Iraqi Ministry of Defense Spokesman, and Brigadier General David Perkins, MNF-I Spokesman, July 30, 2008.
[345] Interviews with MNC-I officials and subordinate commanders, August 2008.
[346] Maliki stated publicly that the operation was going after "criminals, terrorist forces, and outlaws." See Alexandra Zavis, "Iraqi Shiites Clash in Basra," *Los Angeles Times*, March 26, 2008.
[347] Quoted by Alexandra Zavis, "Iraqi Shiites Clash in Basra," *Los Angeles Times*, March 26, 2008. See also "Iraq: Al- Basrah Clashes Could Prove Ominous," Radio Free Europe/ Radio Liberty, March 26, 2008; Sholnn Freeman and Sudarsan Raghavan, "Intense Fighting Erupts in Iraq," *Washington Post*, March 26, 2008; Michael Kamber and James Glanz, "Iraqi and U.S. Forces Battle Shiite Militia," *The New York Times*, March 26, 2008.
[348] Interviews with MNC-I subordinate commanders, and with Commanding General of the Basra Operations Command, Major General Mohammed Hameidi, August 2008.
[349] Interviews with MND-SE officials, August 2008.
[350] Interviews with UK military official, August 2008.
[351] Interviews with UK and Iraqi officials, Basra, August 2008.
[352] Interviews with UK military officials, Basra, August 2008.
[353] Interview with UK military official, Basra, August 2008.
[354] See "U.S. Forces Drawn Deeper Into Iraq Crackdown," *Reuters*, March 28, 2008.
[355] Interview with MNC-I official, August 2008.

[356] Interviews with MNC-I officials, August 2008. See also MNF-I Press Conference, Major General Kevin Bergner, March 26, 2008. In August 2008, reports emerged that UK ground forces did not enter the city during the heavy fighting, due to the prior accommodation with Moqtada al-Sadr, which provided that UK combat forces could not enter Basra without permission from the UK Minister of Defence. See Deborah Haynes and Michael Evans, "Secret Deal Kept British Army Out Of Battle for Basra," *London Times*, August 5, 2008.

[357] See Stephen Farrell and Qais Mizher, "Iraq Dismisses 1,300 After Basra Offensive," *New York Times*, April 14, 2008.

[358] Interview with MND-SE officials, August 2008. The officials noted that the situation in Basra, post-operations, was "a lot like Cairo."

[359] Interview with Iraqi Army commander, August 2008.

[360] Interview with senior U.S. commander, August 2008.

[361] Interviews with MNF-I and MNC-I officials, August 2008. See also Department of Defense, "Measuring Stability and Security in Iraq," June 2008, p.22.

[362] See Howard Lafranchi, "Hasty truce with Moqtada al-Sadr tests his sway in Baghdad stronghold," *Christian Science Monitor*, May 12, 2008. See also "Text of Sadr Ceasefire Agreement," posted by the Institute for the Study of War, translated by Nathaniel Rabkin, available at http://www.understandingwar.org/text-sadr-cease-fire-agreement.

[363] Interviews with MNF-I and MNC-I officials, August 2008. See Sabrina Tavernise, " A Shiite Militia in Baghdad Sees its Power Wane," *New York Times*, July 27, 2008.

[364] Interviews with MNC-I officials, August 2008. See also Department of Defense News Briefing, Colonel Charlie Flynn (USA), 1st Brigade, 82nd Airborne Division, June 26, 2008.

[365] Interviews with Task Force-134 officials, Baghdad, January 2008.

[366] Interviews with LTG Odierno, and MNC-I staff, January 2008.

[367] Interview with Division Commander, January 2008.

[368] At the Office of the Secretary of Defense, the Joint IED Defeat Organization, led since December 2007 by Lieutenant General Tom Metz, is mandated to facilitate the rapid development, production and fielding of new technologies and approaches.

[369] Interviews with MNC-I officials, August 2008.

[370] As one official observed, "It's like R&D," interview with MNC-I official, August 2008.

[371] Interviews with MNC-I officials, August 2008.

[372] Interviews with MNF-I and MNC-I officials, January and August 2008.

[373] Interviews with MNF-I and MNC-I officials, January and August 2008.

[374] Indeed, the ground Services themselves may tend to view counter-insurgency primarily as a ground forces effort. In his provocative monograph, "Shortchanging the Joint Fight?," Air Force Major General Charles Dunlap noted that the new Army and Marine Corps COIN doctrine, FM 3-24, devotes only a 5-page appendix to the role of air power in COIN, and argued for a "genuinely joint approach" that takes account of "the full potential of today's airpower capabilities." See Maj. Gen. Charles Dunlap, "Shortchanging the Joint Fight? An Airman's Assessment of FM 3-24 and the Case for Developing Truly Joint COIN Doctrine," Air University monograph, December 2007, available at http://aupress.maxwell.af.mil/121007dunlap.pdf.

[375] For a discussion of air operations in support of OIF and Operation Enduring Freedom in Afghanistan, including the widespread use of Unmanned Aerial Vehicles, see Mark Benjamin, "Killing 'Bubba' from the Skies," Slate.com, February 15, 2008, available at http://www.salon.com/news/feature/2008/02/15/air_war/.

[376] Anthony H. Cordesman, "US Airpower in Iraq and Afghanistan: 2004-2007," Center for Strategic and International Studies, December 13, 2007.

[377] MNF-I press briefing, Major General Dave Edgington, MNF-I Air Component Coordination Element Director, November 4, 2007, available at http://www.mnf-iraq.com/ index.php?option=com_content &task= view&id=15033&Itemid=128.

[378] "2004-2007 Combined Forces Air Component Commander Airpower Statistics," U.S. CENTAF Combined Air and Space Operations Center, January 3, 2008.

[379] Interview with Maj. Gen. Edgington, Baghdad, January 2008.

[380] See "The Insurgency: Can it be Defeated?" Interview with Kalev Sepp, *PBS Frontline*, February 21, 2006, available at http://www/pbs.org/wgbh.pages/frontline/insurgency/can/. Other observers question the use of kinetic air power
simply on the grounds that any risk of inadvertent civilian loss of life is unacceptable.

[381] Interviews with MNF-I and MNC-I leaders, January 2008.

[382] Anthony H. Cordesman, "US Airpower in Iraq and Afghanistan: 2004-2007," Center for Strategic and International Studies, December 13, 2007.

[383] Interviews with MNF-I and MNC-I officials, August 2008.

[384] Interviews with MNF-I and MNC-I officials, and subordinate commanders, August 2008.

[385] Information from CFLCC and V Corps planners, 2002 and 2003. See also Michael R. Gordon and General Bernard E. Trainor, *Cobra II: The Inside Story of the Invasion and Occupation of Iraq*, New York: Vintage Books, 2006.)

[386] See CPA Order 2, "Dissolution of Entities," available at http://www.iraqcoalition.org/regulations 20030823_CPAORD_2_Dissolution_of_Entities_with_Annex_A.pdf. Note that the date of the Order is given incorrectly on the CPA website table of contents, but is correctly printed on the Order itself.

[387] Previously the "Badr Brigade," subsequently the "Badr Organization."

[388] Regarding funding for the Iraqi civilian law enforcement system, Ambassador Bremer writes that CPA began with $25 million from the State Department to assess the Iraqi criminal justice system, and Ambassador Bremer allocated an additional $120 million from Iraqi government funds for training and equipping Iraqi police. See Ambassador L. Paul Bremer III, *My Year in Iraq: The Struggle to Build a Future of Hope*, New York: Simon and Schuster, 2006.

[389] Personal communications from CPA officials, 2003. Also, in his Iraq memoir, Ambassador Bremer minces no words. He quotes Doug Brand, the U.K. Constable who replaced Kerik, as saying, "The Army is sweeping up halfeducated men off the streets, running them through a three-week training course, arming them, and then calling them police. It's a scandal, pure and simple." See Ambassador L. Paul Bremer III, *My Year in Iraq: The Struggle to Build a Future of Hope*, New York: Simon and Schuster, 2006, page 183.

[390] In his memoir, Ambassador Bremer recalls an October 2003 meeting with CJTF-7 Commander LTG Sanchez, when he instructed CJTF-7 to stop recruiting police. The incident underscored the difficult position in the chain of command of CJTF-7 (see above), which was in direct support of CPA, but still reported to CENTCOM—which had instructed CJTF-7 to recruit and train police. Communications from CJTF-7 officials, 2003, and Ambassador L. Paul Bremer III, *My Year in Iraq: The Struggle to Build a Future of Hope*, New York: Simon and Schuster, 2006.

[391] Coalition Provisional Authority Order 22, "Creation of a New Iraqi Army," 18 August 2003, available at http://www.iraqcoalition.org/regulations/20030818_CPAORD_22_Creation_of_a_New_Iraqi_Army.pdf.

[392] See Ambassador L. Paul Bremer III, *My Year in Iraq: The Struggle to Build a Future of Hope*, New York: Simon and Schuster, 2006.

[393] See Coalition Provisional Authority Order 28, "Establishment of the Iraqi Civil Defense Corps," 3 September 2003, available at http://www.iraqcoalition.org/regulations 20030903_CPAORD_28_Est_ of_the_Iraqi_ Civil_Defense_Corps.pdf.

[394] Conversations with CPA and CJTF-7 leaders, 2003 and 2004. In his memoir, Ambassador Bremer describes a September 2003 meeting at which GEN Abizaid and LTG Sanchez proposed that CJTF-7 take over the police training mission. He observes in his memoir: "I didn't like it.... Although our soldiers were the best combat troops in the world, they had been trained and equipped for fast-moving operations where they killed the enemy, not for community policing and criminal investigations." See Ambassador L. Paul Bremer III, *My Year in Iraq: The Struggle to Build a Future of Hope*, New York: Simon and Schuster, 2006, pp.168-169.

[395] See National Security Presidential Directive 36, "United States Government Operations in Iraq," May 11, 2004, available at Federation of American Scientists website, http://www.fas.org/irp/offdocs/nspd/nspd051104.pdf.

[396] The first MNSTC-I Commanding General was then-LTG David Petraeus. In May 2004, CJTF-7 split into a higher, four-star headquarters, MNF-I, and a lower, three-star headquarters, MNC-I, (see above).

[397] Interviews with MNSTC-I officials, August 2008. See http://www.afsouth.nato.int/JFCN_Missions/NTM-I/NTMI. htm.

[398] See for example LTG Martin Dempsey, Statement before the House Armed Services Subcommittee on Oversight and Investigations, June 12, 2007, available at HASC website, http://armedservices. house.gov/pdfs/OI061207/ Dempsey_Testimony061207.pdf. The US Agency for International Development, and the U.S. Embassy's Iraq Transition Assistance Office, share responsibility for facilitating the development of all other Iraqi Ministries.

[399] See Major General Carter F. Ham, "Transition Team's Role in Iraq," *Military Training Technology*, Vol.12, Issue 1, April 10, 2007, available at http://www.military-training-technology.com/article.cfm?DocID=1972. In December 2006, the Iraq Study Group had recommended sharply enhancing the embedding program—down to the company level in the Iraqi Army—and "paying" for this increase in embedded troops with reductions in the number of troops assigned to combat brigades. See *The Iraq Study Group Report*, James A. Baker, III, and Lee H. Hamilton, Co-Chairs, December 6, 2006, Recommendation 44, p. 51, available at http://www.usip. org/isg/iraq_study_group_report/report/1206/ iraq_study_group_ report.pdf.

[400] In his memoir, Ambassador Bremer provides a clear example of the early focus of ISF training on transition, citing verbatim a memorandum from Secretary Rumsfeld to himself and General Abizaid: "Our goal should be to ramp up the Iraqi numbers, try to get some additional international forces and find ways to put less stress on our forces, enabling us to reduce the U.S. role. The faster the Iraqi forces grow, the lower the percentage will be of U.S. forces out of the total forces." Ambassador L. Paul Bremer III, *My Year in Iraq: The Struggle to Build a Future of Hope*, New York: Simon and Schuster, 2006, pp. 162.

[401] Conversations from MNF-I, MNC-I, and MNSTC-I officials, Baghdad, January 2008.

[402] U.S. Central Command Press Release, "Iraq Assistance Group Supports the Feature Performance," May 17, 2007, available at http://www2.centcom.mil/sites Iraq%20Assistance%20Group%20Supports%20the%20 Feature%20Performance.aspx. The IAG has been led since June 2008 by Brigadier General Keith Walker, Assistant Deputy Commander (Operations) for the 1st Infantry Division.

[403] Interviews with IAG officials, January 2008.
[404] Interviews with MNF-I, MNSTC-I, and MNC-I officials, August 2008, March 2009.
[405] See Major General Carter Ham, "Transition Team's Role in Iraq," *Military Training Technology*, Vol.12, Issue 1, April 10, 2007, available at http://www.military-training-technology.com/article.cfm?DocID=1972. Then-MG Ham wrote this piece while serving as the Commanding General, 1st Infantry Division, which was assigned responsibility for preparing transition teams to serve in Iraq and Afghanistan. LTG Ham now serves as the Joint Staff Director for Operations (J3).
[406] Ibid.
[407] Interviews with MNC-I officials and subordinate commanders, August 2008.
[408] Interviews with MNF-I, MNSTC-I, and MNC-I officials, and subordinate commanders, August 2008.
[409] See Department of Defense, "Measuring Stability and Security in Iraq," September 2008, p.42.
[410] See for example the Report of the Independent Commission on the Security Forces of Iraq, September 6, 2007, p.18, available at http://www.csis.org/media/csis/pubs/isf.pdf. The Commission noted: "U.S. military officers rather than senior civilian law enforcement personnel lead the Coalition training effort for the Iraqi Police Service; this arrangement has inadvertently marginalized civilian police advisors and limited the overall effectiveness of the training and advisory effort." "... The number of civilian international police advisors is insufficient." DOD apparently agrees— and refers to the low level of funding for, and availability of, IPAs.
[411] Interviews with MNSTC-I officials, August 2008.
[412] Interviews with MNF-W officials, January and August 2008.
[413] Interviews with MNSTC-I officials, and MNF-I subordinate commanders, August 2008.
[414] Department of Defense, "Measuring Stability and Security in Iraq," September 2008, p.51.
[415] IAG and other officials note that it would be difficult to streamline the teams any further, given their small size and the array of expertise they include.
[416] Interviews with MNF-W officials, January and August 2008. The Marines argue that this approach to training helps explain the success to date of the "two best Iraqi Army divisions"—the 1st and the 7th, which were established in Anbar province.
[417] Interviews with MNC-I officials and subordinate commanders, August 2008.
[418] Interviews with MNC-I subordinate commanders, August 2008. MNF-W noted that as early as February or March 2008, based on the improved capabilities of the Iraqi Army, they wanted to "de-MiTT," that is, withdraw their teams, from the battalion and brigade level. One commander said, "It's time to take the training wheels off of everything Iraqi, to get them off of the driveway and on to the street."
[419] For example, MNF-W, led by the Marines, had previously assigned Colonels to lead teams embedded with Iraqi divisions, but dropped the seniority to Lieutenant Colonel.
[420] Conversation with training official, January 2008.
[421] See Corporal Margaret Hughes, "USMC Forms MCTAG, Consolidates Reconnaissance Training," *Marine Corps News*, November 14, 2007, available at http://www.marines.mil/marinelink/mcn2000.nsf/ad983156332a819185256cb600677af3/2e2ee9165ebacf9a85257395006859a2?OpenDocument.
[422] Interview with MNF-W official, August 2008.
[423] The balance varies both by area and over time—for example, in January 2008, in MND-Center, a much higher percentage of training teams had been "taken out of hide." In August, in its area of responsibility, MND-B had 83 transition teams, of which 53 were external and 30 were internal.
[424] Interviews with MNF-I officials, January 2008. The "Iraq" training debate has helped fuel a larger, on-going debate about sourcing the full array of future training requirements. Most provocatively, Army Lieutenant Colonel John Nagl has proposed that the Army create a permanent, standing Advisor Corps, of 20,000 combat advisors, to develop the security forces of international partners. The three-star-led Corps would be responsible for doctrine, training, and employment, and would be prepared to deploy as needed. See John A. Nagl, "Institutionalizing Adaptation: It's Time for a Permanent Army Advisor Corps," The Future of the U.S. Military Series, Center for a New American Security, CNAS website http://www.cnas.org/en/cms/?145.
[425] Interviews with MNF-I officials and subordinate commanders, August 2008.
[426] Interview with MNC-I subordinate commander, August 2008.
[427] Department of Defense Press Briefing, Colonel Mike Kershaw, Pentagon, October 5, 2007, available at http://www.defenselink.mil/transcripts/transcript.aspx?transcriptid=4053.
[428] Interviews with MNC-I officials and subordinate commanders, August 2008. For a description of a unit partnership with the Iraqi Army, see Department of Defense News Briefing, Colonel Tom James, February 22, 2008. COL James' brigade, the 4th BCT of the 3rd Infantry Division, in northern Babil province under MND-Center, established a robust partnership with the 8th Iraqi Army Division, with regular leadership contacts at brigade and division level, in addition to the work of the embedded MiTT teams.
[429] Interviews with 1st BCT/10th Mountain officials, August 2008.
[430] Colonel Burt Thompson, DOD News Briefing, January 12, 2009, available at http://www.defenselink.mil/transcripts.
[431] Interviews with 2nd BCT/101st Airborne Division officials, August 2008.

[432] For example, in August 2008, MND-North noted that it would be useful to extend unit partnering to forces from the Department of Border Enforcement, but that operational requirements—including ongoing combat operations in Diyala and Ninewah provinces—had so far made that difficult.

[433] Interview with U.S. commander under MNF-I, August 2008.

[434] In its March 2009 Report, *Measuring Stability and Security in Iraq*, p.43, DOD reported that as of January 2009, the MoD was authorized approximately 203,000 personnel, and had almost 221,000 assigned. DOD added: "DoD previously reported on the number of Iraqi Security Forces personnel authorized and assigned by the Ministries of Defense and Interior and trained with the assistance of Coalition forces. With the expiration of the mandate of UNSCR 1790, the data is now included in the classified annex because specific military personnel strength for a sovereign nation is considered sensitive," see p.59.

[435] The chart does not include Ministry staff. The chart also does not reflect the Facilities Protection Service (FPS), an armed, uniformed service with about 100,000 members that provides critical infrastructure protection for ministries and other government organizations. An anticipated FPS Reform Law is expected to direct the consolidation of the FPS under the Interior Ministry, but according to MNSTC-I, the consolidation process was incomplete as of August 2008.

[436] Interviews with MNSTC-I officials, August 2008. In its December 2008 report, DOD reported that the ISF was projected to grow to between 609,000 and 646,000 by 2010, see Department of Defense, "Measuring Stability and Security in Iraq," December 2008, p.31.

[437] See *The Report of the Independent Commission on the Security Forces of Iraq*, September 6, 2007, available at http://www.csis.org/media/csis/pubs/isf.pdf. The Report was required by the U.S. Troop Readiness, Veterans' Care, Katrina Recovery, and Iraq Accountability Appropriations Act of 2007, Public Law 110-28. Section 1314(e)(2)(A) mandated DOD to commission an "independent private sector entity" to assess three things: (i) the readiness of the ISF to assume responsibility for maintaining the territorial integrity of Iraq, denying international terrorists a safe haven, and bringing greater security to Iraq's 18 provinces in the next 12 to 18 months, and bringing an end to sectarian violence to achieve national reconciliation; (ii) the training, equipping, command control and intelligence capabilities, and logistics capacity of the ISF; and (iii) the likelihood that, given the ISF's record of preparedness to date, following years of training and equipping by U.S. forces, the continued support of U.S. troops would contribute to the readiness of the ISF to fulfill the missions outlined in clause (i).

[438] Ibid, p. 12.

[439] General Barry R. McCaffrey, USA (ret), "Visit to Iraq and Kuwait, 5-11 December 2007, After Action Report," December 18, 2007.

[440] Communication from an MNC-I leader, January 2008.

[441] Communication from an MNC-I leader, January 2008.

[442] Interviews with MNC-I officials, and subordinate commanders, August 2008.

[443] Department of Defense, "Measuring Stability and Security in Iraq," June 2008.

[444] Interview with MNC-I official, August 2008.

[445] Department of Defense, "Measuring Stability and Security in Iraq," March 2009, p.v.

[446] Andrew England and Demetri Sevastopulo, "U.S. General Stresses Need for Time," *Financial Times*, February 17, 2009.

[447] Interviews with MNC-I officials, August 2008.

[448] Interview with Iraqi Army Division Commander, August 2008.

[449] Minister of Defense Abd al-Qadir, Multi-National Force-Iraq press conference, September 10, 2008.

[450] Interviews with MNF-I and MNSTC-I officials, August 2008.

[451] Department of Defense, "Measuring Stability and Security in Iraq," March 2009, p.33.

[452] As a rule, the operations commands cover a single province. An exception is the Samarra Operations Command, responsible only for the city of Samarra in Salah ad Din province, which was created in the wake of the Golden Mosque bombing.

[453] In August 2008, MNF-W officials noted that in al Anbar province, both the Governor and members of the Provincial Council were frustrated by their loss of direct influence, after the Anbar Operations Command was established. MND-N reported similar tensions with northern province Governors. Also in August 2008—after the seemingly successful operations in March of that year—the Governor of Basra expressed frustration that security control had been taken away from provincial officials. Interviews, August 2008.

[454] Interviews with MNC-I officials and subordinate commanders, August 2008. In August 2008, MND-N, for example, noted that in practice, the Ninewah Operations Command definitely commanded Iraqi Army forces in the province, but that its relationship with MoI forces was "less clear." In Baghdad, since the establishment of the Baghdad Operations Command, which formally has command over Interior Ministry forces in Baghdad, U.S. commanders have reported tensions between the BOC and the MoI. In general, the MoI has its own chain of command, from Provincial Directors of Police up to the MoI's National Command Center.

[455] Interviews with MND-B officials, August 2008.

[456] Interviews with Iraqi Army commanders, August 2008.

[457] Minister of Defense Abd al-Qadir, Multi-National Force-Iraq press conference, September 10, 2008.

[458] Department of Defense, "Measuring Stability and Security in Iraq," December 2008, p.43.
[459] Interviews with MNSTC-I officials, August 2008.
[460] Department of Defense, "Measuring Stability and Security in Iraq," December 2008.
[461] Conversations with coalition advisors, January 2008. See CRS Report RS22093, *The Iraqi Security Forces: The Challenge of Sectarian and Ethnic Influences*, by Jeremy M. Sharp.
[462] Interview with Iraqi provincial Governor, August 2008.
[463] "ISF Combat Battalion Operational Readiness Assessment" slide, Multi-National Corps-Iraq, December 20, 2009.
[464] Department of Defense, "Measuring Stability and Security in Iraq," March 2009, p.34.
[465] Department of Defense, "Measuring Stability and Security in Iraq," March 2009, p.47.
[466] See James A. Baker, III, and Lee H. Hamilton, Co-Chairs, *The Iraq Study Group Report,* December 6, 2006, p.12, available at http://www.usip.org/isg/iraq_study_group_report/report/1206/iraq_study_group_report.pdf.
[467] *The Report of the Independent Commission on the Security Forces of Iraq*, September 6, 2007, p. 14, available at http://www.csis.org/media/csis/pubs/isf.pdf.
[468] Department of Defense News Briefing, Major General Joseph Fil, December 17, 2007, available at http://www.defenselink.mil/transcripts/transcript.aspx?transcriptid=4107.
[469] Department of Defense News Briefing, Major General Mark Hertling, January 22, 2008, available at http://www.defenselink.mil/transcripts/transcript.aspx?transcriptid=4124.
[470] See Press Briefing, Lieutenant General Ray Odierno, January 17, 2008, available at http://www.defenselink.mil/transcripts/transcript.aspx?transcriptid=4122.
[471] Conversations with MNF-I leaders, January 2008.
[472] Interviews with MNF-I and MNC-I officials, and subordinate commanders, August 2008.
[473] Interview with MNF-W, August, 2008.
[474] Department of Defense, "Measuring Stability and Security in Iraq," March 2009, p.33.
[475] Colonel Todd McCaffrey, DOD News Briefing, January 26, 2009, available at http://www.defenselink.mil/transcripts transcript.aspx?transcriptid=4344.
[476] Concerning the consistency of the challenges, see Department of Defense Press Briefing, Colonel H.R. McMaster, September 13, 2005, available at http://www.defenselink.mil/transcripts/transcript.aspx?transcriptid=2106. COL McMaster, describing his partnership with Iraq Army units in Tal Afar in September 2005, commented that the Iraqi army needed "... the ability to command and control operations over wide areas ... greater logistical capabilities ... more experienced and effective leadership...."
[477] James A. Baker, III, and Lee H. Hamilton, Co-Chairs, *The Iraq Study Group Report,* December 6, 2006, available at http://www.usip.org/isg/iraq_study_group_report/report/1206/ iraq_study_group_report.pdf.
[478] Report of the Independent Commission on the Security Forces of Iraq, September 6, 2007, p.14 and p.9, available at http://www.csis.org/media/csis/pubs/isf.pdf.
[479] Mark Kimmitt, Testimony to the House Armed Services Committee, January 17, 2007.
[480] Department of Defense, "Measuring Stability and Security in Iraq," June 2008, p.51.
[481] Interview with MND-N, August 2008.
[482] Interview with MG Oothman, August 2008.
[483] Interview with MND-B officials, August 2008.
[484] Virtually every famous military commander in history has made note of the crucial role of logistics—some of them quite memorably. Alexander the Great is credited with observing, "My logisticians are a humorous lot—they know that if my campaign fails, they are the first ones I will slay."
[485] James A. Baker, III, and Lee H. Hamilton, Co-Chairs, *The Iraq Study Group Report,* December 6, 2006, available at http://www.usip.org/isg/iraq_study_group_report/report/1206/iraq_study_group_ report.pdf.
[486] Report of the Independent Commission on the Security Forces of Iraq, September 6, 2007, p.14 and p.13, available at http://www.csis.org/media/csis/pubs/isf.pdf.
[487] Lieutenant General James Dubik, testimony before the House Armed Services Committee, Washington, D.C., January 17, 2008.
[488] Department of Defense, "Measuring Stability and Security in Iraq," June 2008, p.51.
[489] Department of Defense, "Measuring Stability and Security in Iraq," March 2009, p.36.
[490] Andrew England and Demetri Sevastopulo, "U.S. General Stresses Need for Time," *Financial Times*, February 17, 2009.
[491] See DOD News Briefing, LTG Austin, June 23, 2008, http://www.defenselink.mil/transcripts transcript.aspx?transcriptid=4248.
[492] Interview with MG Oothman, August 2008. MG Oothman tells a story about the consequences of the lack of military hospitals: During military operations in al Kut, against Shi'a extremist militias, a young Army Lieutenant was wounded in the fight. He was sent to the local community hospital in al Kut. But the loyalties of that hospital staff were apparently not with the national government. They picked up the Lieutenant and put him on the floor, without treating him, so that they could tend to a wounded militia member. The Lieutenant died.

[493] Andrew England and Demetri Sevastopulo, "U.S. General Stresses Need for Time," *Financial Times*, February 17, 2009.
[494] Department of Defense, "Measuring Stability and Security in Iraq," December 2008, p.31.
[495] Interviews with MNSTC-I officials, August 2008.
[496] Interviews with MNSTC-I, August 2008. See Department of Defense, "Measuring Stability and Security in Iraq," March 2009, p.60.
[497] Report of the Independent Commission on the Security Forces of Iraq, September 6, 2007, p.9,15, available at http://www.csis.org/media/csis/pubs/isf.pdf.
[498] Interviews with MNSTC-I officials, August 2008.
[499] Department of Defense, "Measuring Stability and Security in Iraq," March 2009, p.50.
[500] Interviews with MNSTC-I officials, August 2008.
[501] Department of Defense, "Measuring Stability and Security in Iraq," March 2009, p.34, 51.
[502] Department of Defense, "Measuring Stability and Security in Iraq," June 2008, pp.56-7.
[503] Brig. Gen. Robert R. Allardice, Council on Foreign Relations, interview by Greg Bruno, February 5, 2008, audio tape available at http://www.cfr.org/publication/15421/allardice.html?breadcrumb=%2Fregion%2F405%2Firaq.
[504] Interview with MNF-I official, August 2008. The initial interest expressed by Iraqi MoD officials in F-16's, in summer 2008, seemed to reflect this perspective.
[505] Interviews with MNSTC-I officials, August 2008.
[506] Department of Defense, "Measuring Stability and Security in Iraq," March 2009, p.53.
[507] Department of Defense, "Measuring Stability and Security in Iraq," September 2008, p.54.
[508] Department of Defense, "Measuring Stability and Security in Iraq," December 2008, p.33. DOD reported that those figures still pertained as of February 2009, see Department of Defense, "Measuring Stability and Security in Iraq," March 2009, p.34.
[509] Interviews with MNSTC-I officials, August 2008.
[510] "Iraq, Kuwait on Joint Patrols," *Washington Post*, December 3, 2008.
[511] Interviews with MNSTC-I officials, August 2008.
[512] Department of Defense, "Measuring Stability and Security in Iraq," December 2008, p.31.
[513] Interviews with MNSTC-I officials, August 2008, and Department of Defense, "Measuring Stability and Security in Iraq," March 2009, p.54.
[514] Communications from MNC-I leaders and Division Commanders, January 2008.
[515] See for example Monte Morin, "Turning Iraqi Recruits into Commandos," *Stars and Stripes*, March 14, 2006.
[516] Report of the Independent Commission on the Security Forces of Iraq, September 6, 2007, p.16, available at http://www.csis.org/media/csis/pubs/isf.pdf.
[517] Interview with MNSTC-I official, August 2008.
[518] Interviews with MNSTC-I officials, August 2008.
[519] Department of Defense, "Measuring Stability and Security in Iraq," December 2008, p.31.
[520] Interview with MNSTC-I officials, August 2008.
[521] Interviews with MNSTC-I officials, August 2008.
[522] Report of the Independent Commission on the Security Forces of Iraq, September 6, 2007, p.9, available at http://www.csis.org/media/csis/pubs/isf.pdf.
[523] General Barry R. McCaffrey, USA (ret), "Visit to Iraq and Kuwait, 5-11 December 2007, After Action Report," December 18, 2007.
[524] Information from U.S. commanders, January 2008. In one example, the local IP commander briefed the multinational division commander in detail on the IPs' plans for the upcoming Ashura holiday. The plans included some coalition ISR assets—requested at the initiate of the IPs.
[525] Interviews with MNF-I, MNC-I, and MNSTC-I officials, and subordinate commanders, August 2008.
[526] Interview with MNC-I subordinate commander, August 2008.
[527] Interview with Iraqi division commander, August 2008.
[528] Report of the Independent Commission on the Security Forces of Iraq, September 6, 2007, p.18,10, available at http://www.csis.org/media/csis/pubs/isf.pdf.
[529] Department of Defense, "Measuring Stability and Security in Iraq," June 2008.
[530] Interview with MNC-I subordinate commander, August 2008.
[531] Information from MNSTC-I officials, January and August 2008.
[532] Department of Defense, "Measuring Stability and Security in Iraq," March 2009, p.41.
[533] Department of Defense, "Measuring Stability and Security in Iraq," December 2008, p.33.
[534] Department of Defense, "Measuring Stability and Security in Iraq," December 2008, p.31.
[535] Department of Defense, "Measuring Stability and Security in Iraq," March 2009.
[536] Lieutenant General Martin Dempsey, testimony to the House Armed Services Committee, Subcommittee on Oversight and Investigations, June 12, 2007, audio transcript available at http://www.house.gov/hasc/hearing_information.shtml.

[537] Report of the Independent Commission on the Security Forces of Iraq, September 6, 2007, p.20, available at http://www.csis.org/media/csis/pubs/isf.pdf.
[538] See James A. Baker, III, and Lee H. Hamilton, Co-Chairs, *The Iraq Study Group Report,* December 6, 2006, available at http://www.usip.org/isg/iraq_study_group_report/report/1206/iraq_study_group_ report.pdf.
[539] See Report of the Independent Commission on the Security Forces of Iraq, September 6, 2007, p.20, available at http://www.csis.org/media/csis/pubs/isf.pdf.
[540] Lieutenant General James Dubik, testimony before the House Armed Services Committee, Washington, D.C., January 17, 2008. LTG Dubik pointed out that "ten out of nine" brigade commanders were replaced, since two changes were made to one brigade's command.
[541] Information from Brigade Commander, Baghdad, January 2008.
[542] Information from Division Commander, January 2008.
[543] Information from MNF-I staff, January 2008.
[544] Interviews with MNSTC-I officials, August 2008.
[545] Interviews with MND-B officials, August 2008.
[546] Department of Defense, "Measuring Stability and Security in Iraq," December 2008, p.31, 40.
[547] Information from coalition advisors, January 2008.
[548] Department of Defense, "Measuring Stability and Security in Iraq," December 2007.
[549] Report of the Independent Commission on the Security Forces of Iraq, September 6, 2007, p.20, available at http://www.csis.org/media/csis/pubs/isf.pdf.
[550] Department of Defense, "Measuring Stability and Security in Iraq," September 2008, p.45.
[551] Interviews with MNC-I officials, subordinate commanders, August 2008.
[552] Information from MNF-I officials, January 2008, and Report of the Independent Commission on the Security Forces of Iraq, September 6, 2007, p.20, available at http://www.csis.org/media/csis/pubs/isf.pdf.
[553] Department of Defense, "Measuring Stability and Security in Iraq," December 2008, p.41.
[554] Department of Defense, "Measuring Stability and Security in Iraq," June 2008, p.40.
[555] Department of Defense, "Measuring Stability and Security in Iraq," December 2008, p.36.
[556] Interviews with coalition advisors, January and August 2008.
[557] Department of Defense, "Measuring Stability and Security in Iraq," September 2008, p.41.
[558] Interview with MNSTC-I official, August 2008.
[559] See James A. Baker, III, and Lee H. Hamilton, Co-Chairs, *The Iraq Study Group Report,* December 6, 2006, available at http://www.usip.org/isg/iraq_study_group_report/report/1206/iraq_study_group_report.pdf, and Report of the Independent Commission on the Security Forces of Iraq, September 6, 2007, p.17, available at http://www.csis.org/ media/csis/pubs/isf.pdf.
[560] Comment by coalition advisor, January 2008.
[561] Department of Defense, "Measuring Stability and Security in Iraq," March 2008. Through August 2008, DOD reported, the MoI Directorate of Internal Affairs opened 4,318 cases. Of these, it closed 4,198 cases, from which 377 employees were fired, and 297 were disciplined, see DOD, "Measuring Stability and Security in Iraq," September 2008, p.42.
[562] Report of the Independent Commission on the Security Forces of Iraq, September 6, 2007, pp.9,12, available at http://www.csis.org/media/csis/pubs/isf.pdf.
[563] Department of Defense, "Measuring Stability and Security in Iraq," December 2008, p.34.
[564] Conversations with MNF-I officials, January 2008.
[565] Conversations with MNF-I officials, January 2008, and Report of the Independent Commission on the Security Forces of Iraq, September 6, 2007, pp.13, available at http://www.csis.org/media/csis/pubs/isf.pdf.
[566] Interviews with MNF-I and MNSTC-I officials, and subordinate commanders, August 2008, and Department of Defense, "Measuring Stability and Security in Iraq," September 2008, p.47.
[567] Interviews with MNF-I officials and subordinate commanders, August 2008.
[568] Interviews with U.S. and Iraqi military officials, August 2008. The commander of the Basra Operations Command mused that the BaOC might evolve into a Corps headquarters for the adjoining provinces of Muthanna and Maysan as well as Basra but noted that this was just an idea.
[569] Department of Defense, "Measuring Stability and Security in Iraq," March 2009, p.33.
[570] Interviews with MNSTC-I officials, August 2008.
[571] Interviews with MNSTC-I officials, August 2008.
[572] Department of Defense, "Measuring Stability and Security in Iraq," December 2008, p.45.
[573] Department of Defense News Briefing, Major General Joseph Fil, Pentagon, December 17, 2007, available at http://www.defenselink.mil/transcripts. His comments echoed H.R. McMaster's assessment of the role of local population in 3ACR's successful COIN operations in Tal Afar in 2005.
[574] At the national level in Iraq, the key agency is the Implementation and Follow-up Committee for National Reconciliation (IFCNR), appointed by Prime Minister Maliki.
[575] For information about Iraqi tribes, see CRS Report RS22626, *Iraq: Tribal Structure, Social, and Political Activities,* by Hussein D. Hassan.

[576] Some members of CPA admitted that gaining a complete understanding of tribal dynamics and capturing them adequately in the IGC, in a very short time frame, was simply too complex, and the risks of error too great. Conversations with CPA officials, 2003.
[577] See Ricardo S. Sanchez, *Wiser in Battle: A Soldier's Story*, New York: Harper, 2008, see pp.238-9. Sanchez describes joining Abizaid to meet with tribal leaders and other community leaders, province by province.
[578] See for example Rory Carroll, "US in talks with Iraqi insurgents," *The Guardian*, June 10, 2005; Ned Parker and Tom Baldwin, "Peace deal offers Iraq insurgents an amnesty," *The Times*, June 23, 2006; and Colin Freeman, "British general to talk to Iraqi insurgents," *Telegraph*, December 11, 2007.
[579] See Colin Freeman, "British general to talk to Iraqi insurgents," *Telegraph*, December 11, 2007.
[580] Communication from MNC-I official, January 2008.
[581] Communication from MNC-I official, January 2008.
[582] Interviews with MNF-I officials, August 2008.
[583] Interviews with MND-N and subordinate unit officials, August 2008. See also Multi-National Force-Iraq press conference transcript, Major General Mark Hertling, Commanding General, Multi-National Division-North, July 27, 2008.
[584] Information from MNF-West leadership, January 2008. Information from coalition officials, and Al Anbar provincial and community leaders, 2003 and 2004.
[585] Bill Roggio, "Anbar Rising," Long War Journal, May 11, 2007, available at http://www.longwarjournal.org/archives/2007/05/anbar_rising.php. See also Mario Loyola, "Return of the Sheik," *National Review*, October 8, 2007.
[586] Information from MNF-West staff, 2007.
[587] Information from MNF-West leadership, January 2008.
[588] See William S. McCallister, "Iraqi Islamic Party, Kurds, and the Tribal Awakening," January 18, 2008, unpublished paper.
[589] Information from MNF-West leadership, January 2008.
[590] Information from MNF-I, MNC-I, and MND-North officials, January 2008.
[591] Information from MNF-I and MND-North officials, January 2008.
[592] Interviews with Multi-National Division-North officials, January and August 2008, and interviews with U.S. Embassy officials, August 2008.
[593] Interviews with MNF-I and MNC-I officials, and subordinate commanders, January and August 2008.
[594] For additional and slightly different views about the differences among awakening movements, see Mohammed Fadhil, "Why Southern Iraq Won't Awaken Like Anbar," November 7, 2007, available at http://pajamasmedia.com/ 2007/11/post_252.php.
[595] Interviews with MNF-I and MNC-I officials, January and August 2008.
[596] Interviews with MNF-I and MNC-I officials, January and August 2008. MNF-I notes that before regime change, 70% of the members of the Ba'ath Party were Shi'a.
[597] Interviews with MNF-I and MNC-I officials, and subordinate commanders, January and August 2008.
[598] Interview with U.S. brigade commander, August 2008.
[599] Information from MNF-I staff, August 2008.
[600] Department of Defense, "Measuring Security and Stability in Iraq," March 2008.
[601] LTC Jeffrey Kulmayer, Multi-National Corps-Iraq, DOD Bloggers Roundtable, January 8, 2009.
[602] Interviews with MND-C officials, January 2008.
[603] Department of Defense press briefing with Colonel Mike Kershaw, Pentagon, October 5, 2007, available at http://www.defenselink.mil/transcripts/transcript.aspx?transcriptid=4053; and conversation with a Division Commander, January 2008.
[604] Department of Defense News Briefing, Major General Mark Hertling, January 22, 2008, available at http://www.defenselink.mil/transcripts/transcript.aspx?transcriptid=4124.
[605] Interview with MG Oothman, August 2008.
[606] Information from MNF-I and MNC-I leaders, and division commanders, January 2008. See also Department of Defense News Briefing with Major General Walter Gaskin, Commanding General, MND-W, IIMEF, December 10, 2007, http://www.defenselink.mil/transcripts/transcript.aspx?transcriptid=4103, where Maj. Gen. Gaskin noted that coalition forces' elimination of Al Qaeda plays a role in prompting local Iraqis to serve.
[607] Interviews with MNC-I officials, January, August and September 2008.
[608] Interviews with U.S. forces in Kirkuk, August 2008.
[609] U.S. military officials in Kirkuk, for example, noted that the SoIs in the area certainly did not work for the ISF. Moreover, periodic tensions had arisen between the local ISF, whose leadership is primarily Kurdish, and the largely Sunni Arab SoIs. Interviews, August 2008.
[610] Participant observation, and interviews with division and brigade commanders, January 2008.
[611] Interviews with MND-C officials, August 2008.
[612] Conversations with MNF-I, MND-Baghdad, MND-Center and MND-North leaders, January and August 2008. See also Department of Defense Press Briefing with COL Mike Kershaw, October 5, 2007, available at

http://www.defenselink.mil/transcripts/transcript.aspx?transcriptid=4053. COL Kershaw notes that in his battle space, SOIs had established their own check points and secured those roads. He adds that, since the SOIs began working, IED attacks were down, and the SOIs had turned in, or given information about, "over 85 terrorists."

[613] See Multi-National Force-Iraq press conference transcript, Brigadier General David Perkins, MNF-I Spokesman and MG Mohammed al Askari, MoD Spokesman, July 30, 2008.

[614] Department of Defense, "Measuring Stability and Security in Iraq," December 2008, p.18.

[615] LTC Jeffrey Kulmayer, Multi-National Corps-Iraq, DOD Bloggers Roundtable, January 8, 2009; and DOD, "Measuring Stability and Security in Iraq," March 2009, p.21.

[616] Information from MNF-West staff, 2007.

[617] See Department of Defense News Briefing, Major General Walter Gaskin, December 10, 2007, available at http://www.defenselink.mil/transcripts/transcript.aspx?transcriptid=4103.

[618] Assessments by MNF-I and MNC-I leaders and staff, January 2008. See also William S. McCallister, "Iraqi Islamic Party, Kurds, and the Tribal Awakening," January 18, 2008, unpublished paper.

[619] Information from MNF-I and MNC-I leaders and staff, including some who have worked personally with IFCNR, January 2008.

[620] Information from MNF-I and MNC-I staff, January 2008.

[621] Anthony Bubalo, "Lawrence of Arabia is out of place in Iraq," *Financial Times*, November 11, 2007. See also, for example, Interview with Toby Dodge, Foreign Policy Online, September 2007, available at http://www.foreignpolicy.com/story/cms.php?story_id=3982.

[622] Information from MNF-I and MNC-I staff, January 2008.

[623] Interviews with MNF-I officials, August 2008.

[624] In June 2008, somewhat unusually, a brigade in Multi-National Division-Center reported that it was going through a "recruiting drive" to get SoIs to join the Iraqi Army, and had met with some success. See Department of Defense News Briefing, Colonel Terry Ferrell, 2nd Brigade, 3rd Infantry Division, June 19, 2008, available at http://www.defenselink.mil/transcripts/transcript.aspx?transcriptid=4247.

[625] Information from MNF-I, MNC-I, and commanders, January 2008.

[626] Interviews with MNF-I, MNC-I, and MNSTC-I officials, August 2008.

[627] The U.S. Agency for International Development, for example, runs a Community Stabilization Program, which typically pays relatively low salaries—approximately $90 per month—in exchange for tasks such as garbage collection. For SOIs' transition into the civilian world, the goal is to find, where possible, more directly productive employment.

[628] The two pilots are located in Tikrit and Mahmudiyah. The second phase is scheduled to include two larger pilots, in Kirkuk and Fallujah. Information from MNF-I, March 2008.

[629] See Department of Defense, "Measuring Stability and Security in Iraq," March 2008; and information from MNF-I, January and March 2008.

[630] Interviews with MNC-I officials and subordinate commanders, August 2008.

[631] Information about the CSD initiative, including the Jihad pilot, from MNC-I officials, January 2008.

[632] Interview with Brigade Commander, January 2008.

[633] Information from MNF-I and MNC-I, March 2008.

[634] Interviews with MNC-I officials, and MND-B official, August 2008.

[635] Interviews with MNC-I officials, August 2008.

[636] See Multi-National Force-Iraq press conference transcript, Minister of Defense Abd al-Qadir, September 10, 2008. One can imagine that not all Sons of Iraq would necessarily find the Minister's words reassuring.

[637] Interviews with U.S. Embassy officials, and MNF-I and MNC-I officials, and with subordinate commanders, August 2008.

[638] Information from MNC-I officials, October 2008.

[639] Department of Defense, "Measuring Stability and Security in Iraq," December 2008, p.iv.

[640] Multi-National Corps Iraq press release, "Sons of Iraq Transfer Nears Completion," March 11, 2009.

[641] Tim Cocks, "U.S. Hands Almost All Sunni Guards to Iraqi Control," Reuters, March 21, 2009.

[642] Rod Nordland and Alissa J. Rubin, "Sunni Fighters Say Iraq Didn't Keep Job Promises," *New York Times*, March 24, 2009.

[643] Information from CPA and CJTF-7 officials, 2003 and 2004.

[644] Information from MNF-I officials, January 2008.

[645] Information from MNF-I officials, January 2008.

[646] Over 78% of those detained by coalition forces are interned based on suspicion of some IED-related activity. The recidivism rate is based on numerical data. The under-employment assessment is based on accounts from detainees. Information from Task Force-134, Baghdad, January 2008.

[647] Information from MNF-I officials, January and April 2008, and see Donna Miles, "Anti-Insurgency Tactics Succeeding in Iraqi Detention Facilities," American Forces Press Service, March 12, 2008.

[648] Information from Task Force-134, Baghdad, January 2008.

[649] Interviews with U.S. Embassy officials, MNF-I and MNC-I officials, and TF-134, August 2008.

[650] Conversations with ground commanders, January 2008. One commander, asked for his views about the process, simply exclaimed, "Don't go there!"
[651] The use of a "guarantor system" for targeted detainee releases was initially applied in Iraq in 2004, Information from CJTF-7, 2004.
[652] Information from Task Force-134, Baghdad, January 2008, and from MNF-I, March and August 2008. See also Multi-National Force-Iraq Press Release 080908, "433 Detainees Released by Coalition Forces During Ramadan," September 8, 2008.
[653] MNF-I press release, November 30, 2008.
[654] "SOFA," Article 22, para.4.
[655] Interview with MNF-I official, February 2009.
[656] Information from CFLCC and V Corps planners, 2003.
[657] Information from CPA and CJTF-7 staff, and participant observation, 2003.
[658] Information from the Office of Provincial Affairs, U.S. Embassy Baghdad, January 2008.
[659] Cited in "Iraq PRTs" brochure, U.S. Agency for International Development, September 2007.
[660] "Memorandum of Agreement," dated February 22, 2007, signed by Deputy Secretary of State Negroponte and Deputy Secretary of Defense England.
[661] Interviews with MNC-I and Department of State officials, January 2009. As of January 2009, the ePRTs included 6 in Baghdad, 3 in Anbar, 1 in Diyala. In August 2008, MND-Center officials noted their intent, as U.S. forces established more of a presence in southern Iraq, to push a full PRT out to Maysan province, to co-locate with a U.S. battalion, to replace the Dhi Qar-based PST.
[662] Interviews with OPA and PRT officials, August 2008.
[663] Interviews with OPA officials, January and August 2008.
[664] Interviews with OPA officials, August 2008.
[665] Interviews with Baghdad ePRT and Najaf PRT officials, August 2008.
[666] Interviews with MND-Baghdad officials and MNF-West official, August 2008.
[667] Department of State, "PRT" slides, January 30, 2009.
[668] Information from Office of Provincial Affairs, January 2008.
[669] Interviews with ePRT officials, January and August 2008.
[670] Interviews with MND, BCT and PRT officials, January and August 2008.
[671] Interviews with BCT and PRT officials, Kirkuk, and with a multi-national division official, August 2008.
[672] Interviews with Division and BCT Commanders, and MNF-I officials, January 2008. It has been a common practice, throughout OIF, for military commanders to use "State" as a somewhat misleading shorthand to refer to civilian expertise from multiple agencies.
[673] Interviews with multi-national division commanders, August 2008.
[674] Interview with OPA, January 2008.
[675] Interviews with U.S. Embassy officials, August 2008. The U.S. Regional Embassy Office in Basra raised similar concerns—its 200 members, based at the Basra airport, rarely leave the office compound, Interviews with U.S. Embassy and REO officials, August 2008.
[676] Interview with PRT member, January 2008.
[677] Interviews with Division and Brigade Commanders, January 2008.
[678] Interview with OPA official, January 2008.
[679] Interviews with Division staff, and with OPA and PRT officials, January 2008.
[680] Interview with PRT official, January 2008.
[681] Interviews with PRT officials, January and August 2008.
[682] Interview with multi-national division commander, August 2008.
[683] "Provincial Reconstruction Teams" brief, Office of Provincial Affairs, January 2008.
[684] Coalition military "governance" efforts in 2008 are very similar to those in 2003. In 2003, faced with a very limited civilian presence, commanders "leaned forward" and worked with Iraqis to form provincial and local councils, to help Iraqis articulate, prioritize, and represent their concerns.
[685] Interviews with BCT commanders, BN commanders, CA personnel, and PRT officials, January and August 2008.
[686] Interviews with BCT and PRT officials, Kirkuk, August 2008.
[687] Interviews with commanders and staff in MNF-West, MND-North, MND-Baghdad, and MND-Center, January and August 2008. The problems were in part legacies of the centrally controlled old regime, including Iraq's 1969 Law of Governorates, based on a "strong center" model, which named specific authorities that provincial governments could exercise—for example, "consulting on ministerial regional appointments," and "promoting sanitation and public health."
[688] Interview with multi-national division commander, August 2008.
[689] See Department of Defense News Briefing, Colonel Tom James, February 22, 2008.
[690] Interviews with Division, Brigade, Battalion and Company Commanders, and participant observation, January 2008.
[691] Conversations with Brigade staff, January 2008.

[692] Conversation with Division staff, January 2008.
[693] In January 2008, coalition forces in the Ar Rashid district of southwest Baghdad were working closely with Iraqi cardiac surgeon and local resident, Dr. Moyad, on the revitalization of the 60th Street market area. Dr. Moyad had already successfully facilitated revitalization of another nearby market area.
[694] In the midst of a discussion with subordinates about possible medium-sized business opportunities in their area, one Brigade Commander sensibly interrupted, "Somebody tell me what a medium-sized business is!" Some civilian officials question the role of the military in developing medium-sized businesses.
[695] Conversations with brigade and battalion commanders, January 2008.
[696] Interviews with MNF-I, BCT and PRT officials, January and August 2008. The head of one ePRT stated bluntly, "There's no manufacturing."
[697] Interviews with U.S. Embassy officials, August 2008. One official noted: "It's hard enough to keep the Embassy on the same page, on economic policy, but it's really hard to impose that on PRTs...and then the Divisions!"
[698] Interviews with U.S. Embassy officials, BCT officials, PRT officials, August 2008. One can imagine that market forces may eventually resolved this "great debate."
[699] Interviews with Brigade and Battalion Commanders, January and August 2008. For example, residents of one town approached coalition forces at a JSS with a request for an ambulance. Checking with the local council, the unit found there were no immediate plans to meet that need, so the unit sought CERP funding to support the request. On the other hand, when the same local residents sought funding to renovate local schools, the unit discovered that the responsible Iraqi council had already formulated—though not yet implemented—prioritized school renovation plans, so the coalition unit did not seek CERP support for the schools.
[700] Interviews with BCT and PRT officials, August 2008.
[701] Interviews with U.S. Embassy, military, OPA and PRT officials, January and August 2008.
[702] Under Secretary of Defense for Policy Eric Edelman, testimony before the House Armed Services Committee, September 10, 2008.
[703] Interviews with MNF-W and MND-B officials, August 2008.
[704] Multi-National Force-Iraq summary slides, "Security Incidents," provided by MNF-I, January 31, 2009.
[705] Observation from MND-C, January 2008.
[706] MNF-I and MNC-I observations, January and August 2008.
[707] MNF-I tracks Iraqi civilian deaths by compiling coalition forces' reports of "significant acts"; by reviewing Iraqi reports from the Coalition Intelligence Operations Center which may be unverified; and then by checking where possible for redundancies. Reporting depends on coverage on accounts received by coalition or Iraqi personnel—and may not be comprehensive.
[708] Multi-National Force-Iraq summary slides, "Civilian Deaths," provided by MNF-I, January 31, 2009.
[709] Multi-National Force-Iraq summary slides, "Caches Found and Cleared," provided by MNF-I, January 31, 2009.
[710] Interviews with MNF-I and MNC-I officials, January 2008.
[711] Multi-National Force-Iraq summary slides, "High Profile Attacks (Explosions)," provided by MNF-I, January 31, 2009.
[712] Information from MNF-I and MNC-I staff, January 2008.
[713] Multi-National Force-Iraq summary slides, "IED Explosions Incidence," provided by MNF-I, January 31, 2009.
[714] Department of Defense, "Measuring Stability and Security in Iraq," December 2008, p.21.
[715] Interviews with MNC-I officials, January and August 2008. See also Thom Shanker, "New Lessons for the Army on Iraq Duty," *New York Times,* February 19, 2009.
[716] "Sticky IEDs" were initially used primarily to target Iraqi officials. In late November 2008, one was placed on the vehicle belong to National Public Radio journalists. See Ernest Londono, "Use of Sticky IEDs Rising in Iraq," *Washington Post,* Oct 9, 2008, and "NPR Journalist Narrowly Escapes Iraq Car Bomb," *Reuters,* December 1, 2008.
[717] Department of Defense, "Measuring Stability and Security in Iraq," March 2009, p.22.
[718] See Rob Norland, "No Victory Dances," interview with General David Petraeus, *Newsweek,* August 21, 2008. See also Linda Robinson, *Tell Me How This Ends: General David Petraeus and the Search for a Way Out of Iraq,* New York: PublicAffairs, 2008. Also, personal communications from GEN Petraeus, 2008.
[719] Interviews with MNF-I leaders, MNC-I leaders, and Division Commanders, January and August 2008.
[720] Interviews with MNF-I and MNC-I officials, and Division and Brigade Commanders, January and August 2008.
[721] Conversations with MNF-I leaders and staff, January 2008.
[722] Participant observation 2003 and 2004, and conversations with coalition leaders, staff, and commanders, 2008.
[723] FM 3-24, *Counterinsurgency,* December 2006, available at http://usacac.army.mil/CAC/Repository/Materials/COIN-FM3-24.pdf.

Chapter Sources

The following chapters have been previously published:

Chapter 1 – This is an edited, excerpted and augmented edition of a United States Congressional Research Service publication, Report Order Code RS21968, dated February 26, 2009.

Chapter 2 – This is an edited, excerpted and augmented edition of a United States Government Accountability Office (GAO), Report to Congressional Committees. Publication GAO-09-294SP, dated March 2009.

Chapter 3 – This is an edited, excerpted and augmented edition of a Report to Congress in accordance with the Department of Defense Supplemental Appropriations Act 2008 (Section 9204, Public Law 110-252), dated March, 2009.

Chapter 4 - This is an edited, excerpted and augmented edition of a United States Congressional Research Service publication, Report Order Code RL34387, dated April 2, 2009.

INDEX

9

9/11, 250, 262

A

absorption, 225
accidental, 194, 205
accidents, 30
accommodation, xi, 70, 201, 265
accountability, 29, 121, 126, 127, 133, 178, 236
accounting, 46, 86, 112, 121
accreditation, 130
accuracy, 107
achievement, 4, 22, 75, 163
adaptability, 183
adaptation, 188
adjudication, 160
adjustment, 152
administration, 7, 22, 23, 24, 25, 31, 32, 35, 37, 42, 49, 52, 55, 58, 65, 76, 78, 79, 95, 116, 118, 125, 170, 171
administrative, 41, 42, 139
advisory body, 2, 227
aerospace, 128
affiliates, 149, 182, 183, 192, 199, 200, 201, 228, 229, 231
Afghanistan, 28, 30, 36, 68, 86, 136, 145, 147, 152, 153, 154, 162, 163, 167, 170, 205, 212, 238, 250, 251, 252, 253, 256, 265, 267
Africa, 68
age, 6, 129
agent, 29, 209
aggression, 251, 255
agricultural, 78, 89, 90
agriculture, 90, 161, 241
aid, 57, 123, 149, 152, 184, 189, 261

air, xii, 63, 72, 93, 108, 118, 128, 129, 131, 144, 157, 158, 159, 162, 167, 168, 173, 174, 175, 176, 187, 192, 201, 202, 203, 204, 205, 209, 215, 219, 220, 221, 246, 248, 255, 265
Air Force, 29, 93, 107, 108, 128, 136, 159, 173, 187, 205, 210, 211, 213, 219, 220, 221, 240, 253, 255, 265
air traffic, 93, 129, 219
Aircraft, 112, 254
airports, 118
Al Qaeda, xii, 5, 71, 74, 99, 135, 149, 182, 192, 199, 200, 201, 228, 229, 231, 248, 272
Albania, xiii, 72
Allah, 221
allies, xii, 4, 6, 71, 83, 166, 176
alternative, 145, 148, 168, 232, 233
ambassadors, xiv, 73, 80
ambulance, 275
amendments, 3, 9, 11, 23, 27
Anbar Province, xiii, 72, 95, 100, 105
antagonistic, 190
antecedents, 164, 262
antibody, 190
ants, 152
anxiety, 261
appendix, ix, x, 19, 63, 66, 265
appetite, 150, 151, 155, 238
application, 58, 59, 107, 143, 188, 189, 191, 193, 234
appropriations, 35, 46, 48, 61, 68
Arabia, 2, 80, 85, 152, 263, 273
Arabian Gulf, 130
Arabs, 2, 5, 8, 101, 102, 143, 148, 149, 160, 182, 184, 191, 192, 193, 229, 230, 252, 261, 263
argument, 257
Arizona, 240, 252, 260
armed conflict, 8
armed forces, 201, 218
Armed Forces, 152, 163

Armenia, xiii, 72
Army Corps of Engineers, ix, 19, 37, 38, 58, 92, 190
arrest, 27, 159, 235, 254
articulation, 165
Asia, 21
assassination, 260
assault, 127, 220
assertiveness, 150, 200
assessment, 4, 27, 32, 40, 117, 124, 127, 139, 163, 205, 215, 217, 219, 225, 245, 251, 258, 271, 273
assessment procedures, 124
assets, 29, 34, 107, 108, 111, 126, 133, 153, 159, 162, 173, 201, 203, 205, 207, 211, 219, 220, 221, 240, 242, 248, 270
assignment, 167, 178
assumptions, 28, 34, 170, 180
Atlantic, 263
ATM, 87
attacks, ix, xi, 19, 22, 58, 63, 71, 80, 94, 96, 97, 98, 99, 100, 101, 103, 105, 144, 164, 165, 166, 168, 173, 174, 181, 182, 183, 186, 187, 197, 202, 205, 232, 246, 247, 273
attitudes, 226, 241
auditing, ix, 19, 58
Australia, xii, 44, 56, 72, 76, 150, 172, 181, 259
authority, x, 2, 3, 23, 25, 27, 38, 39, 51, 69, 74, 75, 76, 77, 83, 93, 109, 120, 121, 122, 124, 131, 159, 170, 176, 177, 178, 179, 206, 207, 225, 232, 239, 243, 257, 262
automaticity, 165
automation, 109, 121
autonomy, 113, 124
availability, 27, 29, 34, 92, 127, 155, 198, 205, 267
aviation, 131, 196, 251
awareness, 93, 122, 209
Azerbaijan, xiii, 72

B

back, 6, 34, 98, 130, 133, 155, 160, 164, 176, 191, 193, 195, 200, 201, 204, 207, 230, 231, 235, 237, 241, 245, 246, 260
background information, 59
Bahrain, xiv, 73, 80
bail, 77
Balkans, 34
banking, 84, 87, 93
banks, 46, 84, 87
Barack Obama, 250, 251, 252
barriers, 197, 247
behavior, 75, 175, 176, 226, 237
benchmarks, 4, 163, 255
benefits, 82, 180, 186, 227

bias, 160, 223
bilateral relations, vii, x, xv, 69, 141, 142, 143, 188
biometric, 87, 121, 126, 197, 224
birth, 193
black market, 224
blackouts, 91
blame, 8
blocks, 193
blog, 263
blood, 227, 229
boats, 130, 220
bomb, 107, 229
border security, 81, 82
Bosnia, xiii, 32, 72
breakdown, 89, 133
budget deficit, ix, xiii, 19, 47, 72
budget surplus, ix, 19, 46, 47, 61
budgetary resources, 46, 48
building blocks, 206
buildings, 119, 130, 175, 192, 247
Bulgaria, xiii, 72, 182
Bush Administration, vii, 1, 4, 5, 12, 143, 164, 165, 189, 250, 253
bypass, 75

C

cache, 246
Cambodia, 255
campaigns, 81, 101, 173, 252
Canada, 56
candidates, 6, 7, 12, 77, 102, 132, 133, 171, 234
capacity building, 78
capital expenditure, 113
capital goods, 50
cargo, 112, 174, 203, 220
CAS, 157, 159, 204
case study, 60
catalyst, 156, 201
cease-fire, 63, 102, 265
cell, 161, 260
Census, 75, 255
CENTCOM, 162, 166, 167, 168, 171, 172, 173, 178, 187, 189, 193, 204, 207, 208, 227, 255, 256, 257, 258, 262, 266
Central Bank, xiii, 46, 61, 67, 73, 87, 117, 135
Central Intelligence Agency, 261
certification, 115, 118
chain of command, 29, 122, 178, 198, 205, 221, 225, 226, 243, 253, 266, 268
channels, 245
Chief Justice, 79
Chief of Staff, 123, 124, 135

Index

children, 50
Chile, 56
China, 85, 89, 255
cholera, 50, 93
Christians, 9, 101
CIA, 167, 168, 172, 173, 176, 261
citizens, xi, 49, 71, 86, 94, 102, 107, 161, 164, 166, 188, 192, 195, 197, 230, 231, 233, 235
citizenship, 187
civil law, 3, 33
civil servant, xiii, 72, 179
civil society, 262
class size, 128
classes, 111
classical, 189, 193
classrooms, 127
clinics, 92, 116
close relationships, 157
closure, 80
CNN, 259, 260
Coalition Provisional Authority, 2, 3, 25, 37, 59, 61, 76, 169, 177, 178, 179, 189, 206, 238, 257, 259, 266
coalitions, xi, 2, 3, 7, 70
Coast Guard, 93, 258
coercion, 193
Cold War, 167
collaboration, 116, 156, 158, 195, 241
collateral damage, 103
colleges, 119
collisions, 93
commerce, 151, 196
commercial bank, 46
Committee on Appropriations, 20, 21
Committee on Armed Services, 20
Committee on Homeland Security, 20
Committee on Oversight and Government Reform, 21
communication, 93, 126, 174, 178, 183, 225
communities, 4, 49, 109, 159, 160, 175, 189, 190, 194, 196, 197, 227, 230, 231, 234, 236, 237, 239, 248
community, xiv, 43, 55, 57, 61, 73, 75, 83, 96, 98, 107, 109, 115, 116, 148, 166, 176, 190, 192, 197, 205, 227, 231, 243, 244, 257, 262, 266, 269, 272
community relations, 109
compensation, 45
competence, 77, 130, 218, 223, 251
competition, vii, 1, 5, 105, 149, 233
competitor, xii, 71
complement, 156, 234
complexity, 227
compliance, 80, 93, 118, 121, 164, 165, 187

components, 97, 116, 123, 145, 180, 196, 248
composition, 40, 209, 211, 239
compounds, 120, 133, 236
comprehension, 84
concentration, 200
concrete, 197
conditioning, 48
confessions, 26
conflict, 4, 8, 49, 108, 151, 165, 217, 221
confrontation, 103
confusion, 29, 98, 174, 215
Congress, 10, 17, 18, 34, 35, 48, 56, 69, 129, 141, 142, 143, 147, 152, 154, 161, 163, 164, 166, 183, 187, 218, 223, 245, 250, 253, 255, 257, 277
connective tissue, 160
connectivity, 114, 171, 243
consensus, 122, 248
consolidation, 41, 119, 146, 148, 214, 268
Constitution, 2, 53, 75, 77, 101, 251
constraints, 107, 113, 125, 130, 144, 159, 209, 242
construction, 37, 68, 87, 88, 90, 92, 111, 113, 124, 127, 131
consulting, 61, 274
consumer goods, 184
contamination, 92
contingency, 24, 31, 33, 37, 42, 153
continuity, 180
contractors, xv, 25, 26, 27, 29, 31, 32, 33, 41, 59, 68, 87, 141, 142, 161, 162, 177, 179, 180, 191, 239
contracts, 26, 31, 32, 59, 78, 84, 87, 88, 89, 92, 113, 119, 120, 121, 210, 230, 231
conversion, 87
cooling, 244
COP, 198
COR, 3, 5, 6, 11, 14
corruption, 75, 80, 116, 118, 122, 223, 224, 225
cost-effective, 230
costs, 32, 34, 35, 36, 40, 41, 42, 46, 48, 60, 93, 112, 119, 121, 162, 234, 244
Council of Ministers, 52, 76, 135
counterintelligence, 133
counter-terror, x, xi, xv, 70, 71, 76, 132, 141, 142, 145, 151
courts, xiv, 3, 52, 73, 79, 122, 159, 237
covering, 179, 239
CPA, 2, 3, 25, 26, 119, 169, 178, 179, 187, 189, 190, 191, 192, 206, 207, 210, 227, 238, 257, 259, 261, 262, 263, 266, 272, 273, 274
CRC, 11, 77, 135
credibility, 192
credit, 87, 90
creditor nation, 68
creditors, 43, 44, 61, 85

crimes, xiv, 26, 52, 73, 79, 80, 237
criminal activity, 81
criminal justice, xiv, 73, 79, 266
criminality, 186, 237, 252
criminals, 167, 184, 189, 201, 202, 264
critical infrastructure, 87, 119, 232, 268
criticism, 169
cross-border, 184, 187, 224
crown, 257
CRS, vii, 1, 14, 249, 250, 253, 255, 259, 269, 271
crude oil, 46, 47, 61, 67, 87, 88, 89
cultural differences, 241
culture, 144, 216, 232, 242
currency, 170
curriculum, 79, 110, 115, 116, 130, 211, 212
curriculum development, 115
cycles, 125, 139, 203
Czech Republic, xiii, 72

D

data collection, 116
database, 31, 121
DCI, 261
deaths, 96, 105, 246, 275
debates, 75, 148, 154, 155, 164, 167, 169, 170, 171, 191, 192, 212, 238, 248, 253
debt, xiii, 43, 44, 61, 73, 83, 85
decentralization, xi, 70
decision makers, 34, 35, 109, 120
decision-making process, 119, 154
decisions, 13, 31, 34, 35, 56, 109, 119, 129, 144, 151, 152, 153, 155, 162, 169, 176, 180, 181, 182, 203, 212, 215, 217, 226, 227, 237, 248
defense, 2, 25, 34, 35, 48, 63, 68, 79, 109, 112, 120, 145, 167, 182, 220, 255
Defense Authorization Act, x, 69, 139, 163, 255, 256
Defense Cooperation Agreement, 29
deficit, xiii, 73, 107
definition, 261
degradation, 247
degrading, 33
delivery, xi, xv, 51, 71, 74, 112, 114, 123, 129, 130, 133, 188
demobilization, 12
democracy, xi, 2, 6, 70
Democracy Fund, 61
Democratic Party, 147
demographics, 86
Denmark, xiii, 72, 182
Department of Agriculture, 90, 138, 253
Department of Defense, v, viii, x, 17, 23, 25, 28, 34, 53, 60, 68, 69, 87, 138, 139, 153, 166, 169, 170,
171, 172, 179, 181, 183, 184, 187, 203, 210, 213, 214, 223, 224, 225, 230, 239, 244, 252, 253, 255, 256, 258, 259, 260, 261, 262, 264, 265, 267, 268, 269, 270, 271, 272, 273, 274, 275, 277
Department of Homeland Security, 62, 258
Department of Justice, 135
Department of State, viii, 18, 23, 26, 28, 38, 40, 44, 52, 53, 55, 68, 161, 163, 171, 186, 210, 213, 239, 240, 253, 254, 257, 258, 274
deposits, 3, 46, 61, 87
desert, 173, 174, 193, 200, 201
destruction, 109, 192
detachment, xiii, 72
detainees, x, 12, 25, 26, 52, 70, 79, 86, 122, 132, 145, 159, 160, 227, 234, 236, 237, 240, 254, 260, 273
detention, x, 69, 75, 77, 79, 122, 132, 148, 159, 236, 237, 254
discipline, 155, 244
discretionary, 190, 244
diseases, 50, 93
displaced persons, xi, 57, 70, 82, 86, 102
displacement, 186, 261
disposition, 29, 30, 81, 122, 162, 187
disputes, xv, 3, 4, 11, 74, 94
dissatisfaction, 83
distribution, xi, 11, 22, 50, 70, 77, 83, 88, 91, 92, 108, 111, 114, 118, 122, 123, 124, 126, 154, 185, 244
dividends, 114
division, 5, 75, 103, 108, 111, 117, 124, 127, 153, 171, 174, 178, 197, 199, 201, 211, 212, 215, 216, 217, 218, 223, 232, 240, 241, 242, 243, 245, 267, 270, 272, 274
division of labor, 153, 178, 216, 243
Doha, 178
dominance, 5
donors, 44, 80
download, 261
draft, ix, 2, 3, 5, 19, 29, 48, 62, 79, 170, 250
drinking, 50, 92
drinking water, 50, 92
drought, 84, 89, 91
drug trafficking, 116
drug use, 252
due process, 26
duplication, 259
durability, xiv, 4, 74
duration, 177, 178, 211
duties, 171

E

echoing, 210, 218
economic activity, 244
economic assistance, 227
economic development, ix, xiv, xv, 19, 43, 47, 74, 83, 85, 86, 93, 141, 142, 143
economic growth, ix, 19, 83
economic policy, 243, 244, 275
economic reform, 44
economic resources, 185
economic stability, 86
Economic Support Fund, 4, 61
economics, 144, 237, 238, 240, 241, 242, 263
Education, 85, 126, 133, 137, 234
educational institutions, 110, 208
educational programs, 262
egg, 196, 244
Egypt, xiv, 73, 80
El Salvador, xiii, 72, 182, 260
election, vii, 1, 2, 3, 5, 6, 7, 8, 9, 10, 12, 15, 23, 65, 114
election law, 5, 12
electoral process, 94
electrical power, 192
electricity, viii, xiv, 17, 22, 38, 45, 49, 50, 51, 61, 68, 73, 83, 90, 91, 92, 127, 138, 171, 234
electronic banking, 87
emergency response, 107
employees, 25, 26, 27, 33, 37, 41, 68, 116, 118, 119, 121, 139, 162, 234, 271
employment, xiii, 56, 72, 73, 75, 82, 86, 89, 95, 148, 183, 203, 230, 233, 234, 235, 244, 267, 273
empowered, 170
energy, 3, 51, 81, 144, 186, 212
engagement, viii, xv, 18, 85, 128, 142, 143, 158, 193, 227
England, 251, 268, 269, 270, 274
English Language, 111, 129, 135
English language proficiency, 110, 116
enrollment, 110
enthusiasm, 6
entrepreneurs, 244
entrepreneurship, 86
environment, xi, xiv, 32, 40, 63, 70, 71, 73, 74, 77, 86, 92, 93, 96, 99, 100, 109, 144, 158, 186, 239, 257
estimating, 34, 55, 60, 61
Estonia, xiii, 72, 182, 260
ethics, 115, 116, 118, 127
ethnic groups, xi, 70
Europe, 56, 264
European Union, 116

evacuation, 38, 39, 107, 124, 209
evening, 258
exchange rate, xiii, 73
exclusion, 5
execution, xii, 48, 71, 72, 78, 83, 84, 107, 108, 109, 112, 113, 120, 121, 147, 154, 163, 216
exercise, xiv, 26, 33, 40, 73, 150, 162, 163, 168, 171, 176, 184, 215, 238, 239, 257, 274
expenditures, 46, 47, 50, 61, 84, 85, 113, 119, 121
expertise, 124, 130, 156, 160, 161, 180, 191, 203, 210, 218, 227, 239, 241, 254, 267, 274
explosions, 247
explosives, 202
exports, 49, 67, 84, 87, 88
exposure, 100, 229, 242
expulsion, 188
extremism, xi, 71

F

F-16, 112, 270
facilitators, 81, 97
failure, 8, 31, 165
family, 3, 98, 122, 202, 205, 236
farming, 90, 244
farming techniques, 90
fears, xi, 5, 70, 95, 160
Fedayeen, 173, 174
federal government, 53, 54
Federal Reserve Bank, 46
federalism, 77, 185
feedback, 120
feelings, 258
females, 232
fighters, xii, 5, 7, 71, 81, 97, 100, 108, 143, 173, 174, 175, 182, 183, 192, 201, 204, 206, 233, 258, 262
finance, 43, 44, 46, 68, 131
financial resources, 80
financial system, 87
financing, 78, 89
fingerprinting, 197
fire, xii, 63, 72, 102, 127, 128, 173, 174, 215, 265
fire fighting, 128
fires, 211, 219
fish, 183
fitness, 234
flexibility, x, 70, 244
flight, 128, 175
flow, xii, 28, 29, 71, 123, 168, 175, 183, 184, 198, 199, 201, 224
fluctuations, 149
focusing, 87, 211
food production, 89

foreign assistance, 39, 41, 48, 253
foreign direct investment, 86
foreign exchange, 47
foreign investment, 51, 86, 93
Foreign Military Sales, 47, 112, 135
foreign policy, 40
Foreign Relations Committee, 194, 257, 262
fragility, 198
free market economy, 86
freedom, 94, 99, 101, 102, 183, 202, 203, 245
Freedom of Information Act, 256, 257, 258
friction, 8, 109
frustration, 190, 207, 229, 241, 245, 268
fuel, 88, 91, 92, 114, 118, 123, 127, 138, 190, 205, 218, 224, 267
full capacity, 92
funding, 34, 35, 36, 44, 57, 60, 62, 78, 85, 107, 111, 113, 117, 118, 119, 120, 127, 131, 132, 163, 184, 207, 226, 228, 231, 234, 244, 245, 255, 266, 267, 275
funds, xiii, 35, 39, 44, 47, 49, 50, 56, 61, 73, 84, 87, 112, 113, 120, 124, 160, 190, 226, 244, 245, 266
furniture, 244
fusion, 131, 132, 201

G

gangs, 201
garbage, 273
gas, 3, 53, 78, 83, 88, 89, 91, 92
gas turbine, 91, 92
gauge, 214, 244
GDP, 83, 84, 85, 89, 136
General Electric, 92, 136
general intelligence, 122
generation, xiv, 50, 73, 83, 90, 91, 92, 107, 108, 109, 112, 117, 118, 123, 125, 127, 129, 132, 218
generators, 92, 123, 127
Geneva, 62
Georgia, xiii, 72, 181
Germany, 152, 168
get-out-the-vote, 185
global economy, vii, x, 69, 81, 166
Global War on Terror, viii, 17, 34, 60, 68, 250
goals, viii, x, 17, 18, 40, 61, 69, 75, 98, 113, 122, 165, 181, 182, 186, 259, 262
goods and services, 47, 120, 185
Government Accountability Office (GAO), viii, 4, 17, 277
government policy, 163
government revenues, 67
governors, 6, 76, 78
grants, 43, 44, 76, 244

gravity, 7, 100, 198, 200
greed, 98
grids, 171
gross domestic product, 46
Gross Domestic Product, 136
grounding, 220
group cooperation, 98
groups, xi, xii, 25, 62, 70, 71, 74, 76, 81, 94, 95, 98, 100, 101, 102, 103, 105, 152, 167, 170, 184, 185, 186, 197, 199, 200, 205, 226, 227, 230, 231, 232, 233, 243, 246, 248, 260, 261
growth, ix, xiii, 19, 58, 72, 80, 83, 85, 86, 93, 105, 107, 108, 113, 119, 127, 128, 129, 130, 138, 139, 149, 155, 217, 246
guerrilla, 189, 261
guidance, 28, 32, 58, 59, 87, 114, 130, 145, 151, 153, 167, 170, 171, 187, 192, 197, 199, 239, 243, 254
guidelines, 26, 121
Gulf War, 164, 165, 167, 168, 171, 256
GWOT, 34, 35, 36, 60

H

handedness, 7
hands, 165, 211, 227, 263
harassment, 235
hardening, 91, 247
harm, 160, 184
hazardous materials, 35
healing, 4
health, 50, 55, 68, 93, 112, 114, 116, 124, 144, 180
health services, 93, 116
healthcare, xiv, 73, 90, 92, 116
hearing, 79, 122, 163, 252, 254, 270
height, vii, xv, 8, 13, 141, 142, 197, 200
helicopters, 216, 219
Hezbollah, xii, 71, 94, 137, 149, 184, 260
high-level, 68
highways, 119
hips, 109
hiring, 41, 108, 109, 114, 116, 117, 119, 120, 121, 122, 125, 132, 203, 233, 234
Homeland Security, 20, 62, 258
homeowners, 82
homogenous, 103, 222, 230
hopelessness, 228
hospital, 269
hospitality, 86
hospitals, 39, 92, 119, 219, 269
host, xii, 26, 55, 56, 71, 86, 153, 154, 155, 156, 161, 162, 195, 260
hostage, 174
hostile acts, 165

House, 20, 21, 147, 152, 161, 163, 178, 245, 250, 252, 253, 254, 266, 269, 270, 271, 275
housing, 31, 34, 38, 39, 57, 68, 82
HPA, 97, 136
hub, 37, 183
human, 26, 82, 92, 105, 115, 116, 117, 121, 132, 261
human capital, 82
human rights, 26, 115, 116, 132, 261
human security, 105
humanitarian, 38, 39, 55, 62, 109, 123, 164, 177, 178, 190, 203
humorous, 269
Hungary, 175, 182
hydrocarbon, xi, 52, 54, 70, 77
hydrocarbons, 3, 78
hydroelectric power, 91

I

ICC, 170, 257
ice, 107
id, 23, 165, 190, 196, 207, 225, 252, 254, 260, 263, 264, 265, 273
identification, 121, 126, 197, 205
identity, 8
IDP, 82, 136
IDPs, 82, 186
IEDs, 182, 203, 204, 205, 232, 247, 275
illusions, 231
images, 17, 254
IMF, 44, 46, 61, 83, 85, 136
immunity, 26, 45
implementation, x, xi, xiv, 4, 25, 33, 34, 41, 51, 59, 62, 69, 70, 74, 76, 77, 78, 79, 82, 109, 112, 120, 122, 123, 126, 145, 154, 163, 185, 188, 224, 251
imports, 91
Improvised Explosive Devices (IEDs), 247
INA, 2
incentive, 253
incentives, 56, 124, 253
incidence, 247
Incidents, 252, 275
income, 98, 231, 235, 236, 244
incumbents, 6, 185
independence, xii, 5, 71, 208, 251, 260
indication, xv, 141, 142
indicators, 182
indigenous, 212, 261
industry, 86, 87, 89, 90
ineffectiveness, 118
Infiltration, 172
inflammatory, 148
inflation, xiii, 73, 85, 138

inflationary pressures, xiii, 73
information sharing, 114, 126
information technology, 41, 144
Information Technology, 83, 111, 135
infrastructure, xi, xii, xiii, xv, 38, 44, 49, 51, 71, 72, 74, 83, 87, 89, 90, 93, 107, 108, 109, 116, 117, 118, 119, 120, 121, 122, 124, 127, 128, 129, 131, 166, 167, 171, 183, 190, 221, 224, 232, 240, 246, 268
inherited, 49, 179
inhibitors, 123
initial state, 208
innovation, 203, 247
insight, 59, 171
inspections, 122, 132, 165
Inspector General, 32, 80, 110, 122, 136
inspectors, 164
instability, xiv, 74, 98, 99
Institute of Peace, 253
institutions, 62, 83, 110, 154, 157, 169, 175, 194, 208, 216, 251, 262
instruction, 80, 111, 115, 116, 120, 126, 129, 149
instructors, 107, 108, 111, 119, 127
instruments, 68
integration, 75, 81, 95, 123, 125, 143, 148, 153, 154, 160, 161, 221, 230, 233, 235, 248
integrity, 138, 166, 251, 268
intelligence, xii, 72, 82, 97, 107, 108, 110, 115, 116, 131, 132, 151, 153, 166, 167, 172, 181, 201, 203, 209, 210, 211, 215, 217, 218, 219, 221, 222, 248, 260, 268
Intelligence Community, 110, 136
intelligence gathering, 108, 217
intentions, 174, 187
interaction, 158, 232, 242, 248
interaction effects, 248
interactions, 242, 243
interdependence, 194
interface, 112, 121, 242
interference, 13, 81, 198
internally displaced person, xi, 57, 70, 82
international investment, 86
international law, 25, 176
International Military Education and Training, 133
International Monetary Fund, xiv, 44, 61, 67, 73, 83, 136
International Reconstruction Fund Facility for Iraq, 44
international standards, 26
interoperability, 216
interpersonal relations, 98
interpersonal relationships, 98
interview, 250, 252, 253, 265, 270, 275

interviews, ix, 19, 58, 133, 253, 256, 258, 259, 260, 262, 272
intimidation, xi, xiv, 70, 73, 79, 101, 183, 193, 222, 228
inventories, 126
Investigations, 80, 253, 266, 270
investigative, 116
investment, viii, ix, 18, 19, 44, 46, 47, 48, 49, 50, 51, 78, 81, 83, 84, 86, 87, 91, 93
investors, 81, 86, 87
IP, 103, 105, 117, 119, 136, 222, 270
Iran, vii, xi, xii, 1, 5, 7, 44, 70, 71, 75, 81, 97, 100, 102, 103, 152, 164, 173, 181, 184, 185, 187, 188, 189, 199, 206, 230, 247, 252, 260, 261
Iraq Study Group, 217, 218, 223, 225, 266, 269, 271
Iraq War, 230
irrigation, 89
Islam, 3, 172, 186
Islamic, xii, 2, 3, 7, 8, 10, 71, 102, 136, 182, 185, 199, 201, 206, 230, 233, 272, 273
Islamic law, 3
isolation, 108
Italy, 44, 62, 130, 152, 174, 182, 208, 223, 239

J

Japan, xiii, 44, 72, 152
jihadist, 100, 236
job creation, 93
jobs, xiii, 11, 13, 72, 86, 87, 90, 148, 162, 212, 228, 233, 234, 235, 237
joining, 232, 234, 272
Joint Chiefs, 163, 167, 189, 262
joint ventures, 87
Jordan, xiv, 55, 56, 62, 73, 80
Jordanian, 55, 62
journalists, 275
JSS, 198, 243, 275
judge, 229
judges, xiv, 3, 73, 79, 122
judgment, 188, 205
judiciary, 79
jurisdiction, 25, 26, 27, 33, 68, 76, 145, 154, 162
justice, xiv, 73, 76, 79, 122, 266
justification, 252
juvenile detention facilities, 79
juvenile justice, 79

K

Katrina, 163, 255, 263, 268
Kazakhstan, xiii, 72
kidnapping, 52

killing, 189, 190, 200, 229, 262
King, 139, 219
Korea, xiii, 72, 181
Kosovo, 32, 34, 255
Kurdish, vii, 1, 3, 5, 8, 9, 10, 75, 101, 103, 118, 132, 133, 148, 152, 164, 172, 174, 175, 186, 193, 229, 252, 261, 272
Kurdistan Workers Party (PKK), 186
Kurds, 2, 3, 4, 5, 8, 11, 75, 101, 102, 148, 149, 164, 169, 175, 176, 193, 200, 206, 229, 233, 252, 272, 273
Kuwait, xiv, 28, 29, 45, 59, 73, 80, 162, 168, 171, 172, 173, 174, 175, 178, 211, 221, 252, 256, 259, 268, 270

L

labor, 86, 171, 182
lack of opportunities, 183
land, 113, 118, 144, 174, 200, 224, 255, 260
language, 58, 59, 110, 115, 116, 144, 148, 165, 166, 176, 177, 194, 196, 255
Laos, 255
large-scale, 100, 183, 187, 192, 212
Latvia, xiii, 72
law enforcement, 108, 144, 160, 171, 186, 206, 207, 210, 266, 267
laws, vii, 1, 4, 11, 12, 22, 33, 52, 53, 54, 62, 77, 84, 107, 113, 249
layering, 225
leadership abilities, 218
learning, 188, 193
Lebanon, xiv, 73, 80
legal protection, 27
legal systems, 75
legislation, viii, x, 3, 4, 12, 18, 22, 52, 53, 54, 62, 69, 75, 76, 77, 78, 83, 177, 226
legislative calendar, 75
letters of credit, 47, 84
liberal, 245
licenses, 86
liens, 45
life-cycle, 125
lift, 131, 193, 202, 203, 255
likelihood, 205, 258, 268
limitations, 58, 59, 60, 120
linguistic, 32
links, 40
literacy, 95, 234, 236
Lithuania, xiii, 72, 182
living conditions, 122
loans, 43, 44
local community, 116, 190, 243, 269

local government, 101, 105, 190, 239, 242, 243
location, 40, 146, 161, 173, 178, 193, 236, 239, 240
locus, 184
logistics, xii, xiii, 37, 72, 107, 108, 109, 111, 114, 119, 122, 123, 130, 131, 146, 156, 157, 173, 181, 201, 211, 215, 217, 218, 219, 224, 251, 268, 269
London, 169, 179, 259, 265
long distance, 173
Los Angeles, 252, 255, 263, 264
losses, 45, 99, 102, 165
Louisiana, 242
low-level, 98, 100, 102, 152, 237
LTA, 139
LTC, 272, 273

M

M1, 125
Macedonia, xiii, 72
mainstream, 8, 9
maintenance, xiv, 31, 34, 48, 50, 73, 88, 91, 92, 108, 109, 111, 112, 114, 119, 123, 125, 127, 128, 129, 134, 176, 177, 216, 218, 219, 226
males, 183
management, vii, xv, 31, 32, 35, 37, 53, 78, 88, 89, 95, 109, 112, 113, 114, 115, 116, 121, 123, 125, 126, 127, 141, 142, 157, 210, 224, 225, 228
mandates, 76, 110, 150, 155, 177, 251
manpower, 125, 127
mantle, 178
manufacturing, 120, 275
mapping, 162, 203
Marine Corps, 145, 196, 204, 211, 214, 251, 263, 265, 267
Marines, 130, 145, 156, 173, 174, 192, 201, 210, 220, 229, 232, 240, 245, 251, 267
maritime, 130, 181, 220, 258, 260
market, xiii, 72, 86, 95, 103, 107, 224, 275
masonry, 236
material resources, 117
mbpd, 49, 88, 89, 137
measures, vii, x, 25, 58, 69, 82, 97, 99, 122, 163, 164, 176, 177, 195, 197, 247, 251, 253, 255
media, viii, 12, 17, 81, 100, 263, 267, 268, 269, 270, 271
mediation, 75
mediators, 8
medical expertise, 211
medicine, 128
Mediterranean, 175
MEF, 173, 174
membership, 243
men, 115, 183, 236, 254, 266

mentor, 124, 146, 155, 158, 197, 208, 209, 210
mentoring, 39, 78, 109, 152, 157, 190, 208, 209, 243
metric, 58, 160, 246, 247
mid-career, 129, 252
Middle East, 15, 21, 128, 192, 260
militant, xii, 71, 74, 97, 100, 102, 260
militias, vii, 1, 8, 12, 13, 52, 53, 63, 94, 105, 149, 183, 185, 201, 203, 206, 230, 232, 233, 269
million barrels per day, xiii, 49, 72, 88
Ministry of Education, 235
Ministry of Oil, 49, 88, 137, 224
minorities, 5, 12, 101, 133
minority, 10, 14, 96, 148, 200
miscommunication, 189
misleading, 77, 274
missiles, 129, 165, 168, 173, 255
missions, xiii, 60, 72, 76, 81, 86, 94, 108, 111, 114, 117, 121, 128, 155, 157, 158, 172, 176, 182, 208, 220, 241, 253, 268
misunderstanding, 189
MND, 157, 199, 201, 202, 217, 218, 222, 228, 230, 240, 241, 245, 252, 260, 264, 265, 267, 268, 269, 271, 272, 273, 274, 275
mobility, 112, 204, 205, 219
modalities, 154, 177
models, 253
moderates, 239
modernization, 112, 120, 215, 216
modules, 126
Moldova, xiii, 72
momentum, 174
money, 51, 81, 98, 160, 224, 228, 231, 236, 244, 245
Mongolia, xiii, 72
monopoly, 233
morale, 130
moratorium, 185
morning, 258
MOS, 133
motion, 5, 6, 205
motivation, 98, 260
mountains, 103
movement, 7, 8, 38, 94, 97, 98, 99, 101, 102, 114, 161, 183, 184, 192, 193, 202, 203, 229, 231, 232, 233, 239, 242
multi-ethnic, 148
murder, 52, 96, 228
Muslim, 261

N

naming, 80, 157
nation, xiv, 3, 44, 74, 86, 110, 139, 153, 154, 155, 156, 195, 196, 198, 205, 236, 268

National Defense Authorization Act, 163, 255
national interests, xv, 142, 143, 151
National Public Radio, 275
National Security Council, 171, 253, 256, 257, 263
National Security Strategy, 165, 167, 255, 256
National Strategy, 166, 194, 195, 196, 256, 262
nationalism, xii, 7, 71, 98
NATO, xiii, 72, 76, 110, 126, 137, 182, 208, 223, 260
natural, 88, 205, 235
natural gas, 88
Navy, 107, 108, 130, 136, 173, 205, 210, 211, 213, 220, 221, 253
Near East, 60
neglect, 49, 91
negotiating, 84, 92, 227
negotiation, xii, 71
Netherlands, 182
network, 93, 111, 114, 121, 182, 183, 184, 200, 203
New Way Forward, viii, 17, 18, 47, 52, 65, 143, 188, 195, 196, 197, 208, 263
New York, 46, 206, 251, 252, 254, 255, 256, 257, 258, 259, 260, 261, 262, 263, 264, 265, 266, 272, 273, 275
New York Times, 251, 252, 254, 257, 258, 260, 261, 264, 265, 273, 275
New Zealand, 182
NFL, 231
NGOs, 62
nongovernmental, 62, 63
non-violent, 105
normal, 93, 193, 202, 210
NPR, 275
NRC, 121, 137
NSC, 253, 257
nucleus, 171, 179, 181, 257, 263

O

obligate, 107, 113
obligations, 35, 60, 165, 176
observations, 253, 275
occupational, 211
Office of Management and Budget, 40, 60, 68
Offices of Congressional Relations and Public Affairs, x, 19
offshore, 109, 220
off-the-shelf, 203
OIF, xv, 141, 142, 143, 144, 145, 150, 153, 154, 160, 161, 164, 166, 167, 169, 170, 171, 172, 173, 174, 179, 180, 181, 187, 188, 189, 193, 204, 205, 227, 251, 258, 259, 265, 274

oil, viii, xii, xiii, 3, 11, 17, 22, 38, 45, 46, 47, 49, 51, 53, 54, 61, 67, 68, 72, 77, 78, 81, 83, 84, 85, 87, 88, 89, 93, 107, 109, 118, 119, 131, 148, 163, 165, 173, 220, 224, 225, 229
oil production, xiii, 49, 72, 87, 118, 224
oil revenues, 3, 22, 45, 53, 83, 148
Oman, 80
on-the-job training, 120, 133, 234
Operation Enduring Freedom, 68, 265
Operation Iraqi Freedom, v, vii, viii, xv, 7, 17, 34, 35, 60, 68, 96, 141, 142, 160, 164, 165, 204, 258
Operators, 132
opportunism, 236
opposition, xi, 5, 70, 97, 147, 164, 175, 176, 183, 187, 255, 257
organic, 111, 122, 146, 207
organized crime, 116
orientation, 211
oversight, viii, xv, 17, 31, 32, 33, 35, 76, 78, 119, 142, 143, 154, 163, 214, 254
ownership, 87, 107, 112

P

Pakistan, 251
paramilitary, 173, 261
parole, 77, 237
participant observation, 258, 261, 262, 274
partnership, xii, 71, 106, 108, 120, 131, 143, 144, 151, 152, 156, 157, 166, 177, 178, 194, 200, 204, 209, 210, 212, 213, 215, 221, 240, 267, 269
partnerships, 90, 115, 158, 161, 190, 213
payroll, 5, 58, 93, 131, 213, 214, 233
Pennsylvania, 262
pensions, 11, 87, 228
Pentagon, 171, 172, 189, 257, 258, 259, 267, 271, 272
perception, 102, 103, 105, 181, 215, 225
performance indicator, x, 69, 163
periodic, 96, 102, 110, 272
permit, 87
personal communication, 275
personal control, 98
petroleum, 123
petroleum products, 123
PFC, 174
photographs, 160
physical fitness, 234
physical therapist, 124
physicians, xiv, 73, 92, 116, 124
pilots, 128, 129, 219, 220, 273
pipelines, 89, 118, 156, 225
plague, 103, 224

plants, 50, 88, 90, 92, 127
platforms, 109
play, 38, 41, 98, 101, 150, 169, 242, 248, 257
pluralism, 261
plurality, 8
Poland, xiii, 72, 172, 181, 182
police, xiii, 13, 22, 39, 72, 110, 113, 114, 115, 116, 117, 119, 125, 130, 139, 160, 183, 190, 195, 198, 199, 201, 202, 206, 207, 209, 210, 212, 214, 216, 221, 222, 225, 235, 240, 254, 266, 267
policy makers, 110, 151, 154, 165
political enemies, 11
political leaders, 82, 83, 151, 184, 185, 192
political parties, xi, 6, 70, 75, 148, 185, 233
political power, 185, 230
political stability, 163
politicians, 77
politics, 4, 5, 6, 7, 182, 196, 228, 229
polling, 6, 10, 93, 94, 138
poor, 7, 32, 51, 79, 88, 92, 98, 107
porous, 183, 200, 224
portfolios, 259
ports, 118, 130
posture, 28, 83, 123, 139, 190, 197, 201, 215
poultry, 244
power, vii, xi, xii, xiv, 1, 2, 3, 4, 5, 7, 50, 54, 68, 70, 71, 74, 75, 86, 88, 89, 91, 92, 98, 127, 149, 151, 166, 167, 170, 182, 184, 185, 187, 192, 204, 205, 216, 230, 244, 260, 265
power generation, 50
power plant, 88, 92, 184
powers, 3, 11, 12, 52, 53, 76, 131, 176
PPD, 253
pragmatic, 182
precedents, 188
predictability, 181
preference, 170
preparedness, 268
presidency, 8, 53
president, 2, 3
President Bush, viii, 2, 17, 65, 143, 144, 165, 166, 167, 170, 171, 173, 176, 178, 180, 181, 192, 194, 196, 198, 207, 239, 250, 255, 257, 258
presidential elections, 164
presidential veto, 5
press, x, 11, 12, 13, 14, 19, 174, 180, 187, 188, 189, 197, 204, 215, 216, 235, 250, 251, 252, 254, 258, 261, 264, 265, 268, 272, 273, 274
pressure, 5, 23, 81, 98, 100, 101, 181, 202, 225, 247
price changes, 93
prices, xii, xiii, 47, 72, 83, 84, 85, 87, 88, 120, 131, 138
primacy, 103

printing, 124
prisons, 79, 240
private, xiii, 26, 32, 49, 72, 75, 82, 83, 85, 86, 87, 89, 93, 161, 175, 233, 234, 268
private investment, 49, 86, 87
private sector, xiii, 72, 83, 85, 86, 233, 234, 268
production, xiii, xiv, 45, 49, 51, 61, 72, 73, 87, 88, 89, 90, 100, 118, 203, 218, 244, 265
productivity, 49
professionalism, 105, 108, 110, 119, 126
professionalization, 110, 115, 210, 222, 223
pro-Iranian, vii, 1, 81
propaganda, 101
propane, 203, 247
property, iv, xi, 29, 30, 35, 70, 82, 111, 192
prosthetics, 124
protection, x, xv, 14, 17, 27, 70, 76, 79, 91, 119, 141, 142, 145, 159, 161, 186, 197, 224, 240, 242, 268
protocols, 110, 118
Provincial Reconstruction Team, xiv, 37, 41, 73, 78, 135, 137, 146, 150, 154, 155, 197, 238, 239, 253, 274
Provincial Reconstruction Team (PRT), 78
provocation, 103, 168
proxy, 81, 152, 184
PRT, 37, 41, 78, 137, 161, 228, 238, 239, 240, 241, 242, 243, 244, 253, 254, 260, 274, 275
PST, 274
PTT, 210
public, vii, 41, 50, 56, 58, 61, 67, 68, 75, 78, 80, 84, 94, 95, 99, 109, 116, 149, 154, 165, 173, 187, 188, 194, 203, 233, 241, 242, 252, 256, 274
public administration, 78
public enterprises, 61, 67
public health, 241, 274
public sector, 84
public service, 41, 56, 203
public support, 99, 256
public works projects, 242
punishment, 228
purchasing power, 86

Q

Qatar, xiv, 73, 80
quality control, 115
quality of life, 105

R

R&D, 265
RAC, 117, 137
radar, 168

radio, 126
rail, 93
Ramadan, 63, 246, 247, 274
range, xiv, 38, 40, 73, 114, 127, 165, 166, 182, 215, 253
rat, 225
raw materials, 244
reading, 262
real estate, 107
recall, 206, 225
recidivism, 236, 273
recidivism rate, 236, 273
recognition, 107
reconcile, 121, 227, 228
reconciliation, viii, xi, xiii, 4, 5, 17, 22, 52, 53, 54, 70, 72, 75, 90, 105, 143, 147, 164, 196, 201, 226, 227, 228, 236, 237, 239, 268
reconstruction, viii, ix, 14, 17, 19, 31, 38, 43, 44, 45, 46, 48, 49, 51, 58, 61, 68, 78, 81, 85, 108, 130, 154, 160, 164, 177, 178, 181, 190, 206, 217, 227, 243, 244, 253
recovery, 42, 102
recruiting, 117, 207, 216, 219, 252, 266, 273
redundancy, 89, 146
refineries, 118
refining, 88, 89, 245
reflection, 156, 204
reforms, 80, 84
refuge, 183, 199
refugee admission, 62
refugee camps, 56, 57
refugees, xi, 55, 56, 57, 62, 70, 81, 82, 103
regional, vii, x, xii, xiv, 2, 3, 11, 69, 71, 73, 78, 80, 103, 110, 111, 132, 133, 134, 151, 160, 166, 177, 190, 196, 238, 257, 274
Registry, 86
regression, 75
regular, 9, 82, 166, 175, 179, 220, 232, 238, 241, 267
regulations, 121, 259, 266
regulatory framework, 93
rehabilitate, 89
rehabilitation, 81, 130
rehearsing, 168
rejection, xi, 71, 143, 248
relationship, x, xiv, xv, 69, 73, 74, 75, 90, 110, 142, 143, 150, 152, 155, 157, 177, 178, 179, 188, 196, 229, 240, 241, 243, 268
relationships, xiv, 73, 76, 81, 87, 98, 109, 146, 157, 161, 167, 172, 178, 184, 191, 198, 203, 204, 241, 259
reliability, 35, 58, 60, 83, 90
rent, 261
repair, 34, 35, 81, 88, 93, 111, 123, 124, 125, 131

repatriation, 55
repression, 258
reputation, 202, 223
reserves, 46, 47, 148
resettlement, 56, 57, 62, 148, 186, 261
resistance, 94, 98, 100, 131, 164, 173, 174, 184, 199, 202, 203
resolution, xi, xv, 45, 54, 70, 74, 177, 251
resource allocation, 113, 225
resources, viii, ix, xi, xiv, 11, 18, 19, 32, 39, 46, 47, 48, 50, 52, 53, 70, 74, 75, 80, 101, 107, 117, 122, 128, 149, 153, 154, 161, 163, 169, 172, 176, 182, 183, 185, 191, 206, 216, 227, 228, 238, 242
responsibilities, viii, 18, 29, 32, 33, 110, 117, 118, 153, 154, 155, 160, 169, 170, 171, 176, 181, 197, 208, 209, 224, 238, 240, 241, 257
responsiveness, 116
restitution, xi, 70, 82, 186
restructuring, 61, 84, 87
retail, 87, 118
retaliation, 160
retirement, 121, 129, 225
returns, 82, 106
revenue, 11, 49, 67, 68, 77, 84, 93
rhetoric, 147, 211
risk, vii, xiv, 1, 30, 41, 50, 73, 147, 148, 153, 155, 265
risks, 41, 50, 68, 205, 237, 253, 272
Robert Gates, xv, 141, 142, 146, 153, 163, 181, 252
rolling, 85
Romania, xii, 44, 72, 76, 150, 182
rotations, 92, 163, 259
rule of law, vii, x, xiv, 7, 69, 73, 79, 116, 131, 169, 182, 227, 239, 240, 262
rural areas, 102, 183, 200, 201
Russian, 181, 255

S

sabotage, 118
Saddam Hussein, xv, 2, 8, 43, 44, 45, 141, 143, 165, 166, 173, 175, 176, 250
safe drinking water, 50, 92
safeguard, 41, 116
safety, 93, 185
salaries, 47, 84, 111, 113, 148, 224, 230, 231, 232, 234, 235, 273
salary, 124, 231
sales, 46, 47, 111, 209, 216
sanctions, 49, 164
sand, 174
sanitation, 39, 274
Saudi Arabia, 2, 80, 85, 152

Index

SBA, 85, 138
scandal, 266
scheduling, 109, 128, 220
school, 39, 119, 126, 146, 147, 155, 236, 275
scores, 11, 148, 198
search, 25, 190, 194, 220, 232, 244, 261
Secretary of Defense, xv, 141, 142, 146, 153, 163, 167, 170, 171, 175, 178, 181, 203, 207, 218, 245, 250, 252, 254, 256, 257, 258, 261, 265, 274, 275
Secretary of State, 68, 177, 194, 274
Secretary-General, 252
secular, 7, 77
secure communication, 132
Security Council, 25, 45, 59, 68, 74, 138, 143, 165, 171, 176, 177, 251, 253, 255, 256, 257, 258, 259, 263
security services, 31
segregation, 186
semantic, 226
Senate, 20, 147, 152, 163, 194, 250, 252, 257, 262
Senate Foreign Relations Committee, 194, 257, 262
sensors, 205
separation, 248
September 11, 165
sequencing, 173, 237
series, viii, x, 2, 4, 17, 69, 89, 116, 147, 169, 170, 180, 183, 184, 186, 187, 191, 192, 195, 198, 199, 200, 205, 227, 231, 237, 238, 245, 247, 253, 255
sewage, xiv, 50, 73, 92, 127, 234
Shahid, 6, 9
shape, 151, 152, 153, 162, 163, 164, 181, 185, 189, 241
shaping, 162, 227, 253, 255
shares, 209
Sharia, 98
sharing, 11, 41, 54, 79, 110, 114, 126, 151, 155, 203, 236
Shiite, 2, 3, 6, 8, 10, 13, 143, 148, 149, 160, 164, 180, 184, 186, 260, 264, 265
Shiites, 2, 3, 7, 8, 12, 13, 264
shipping, 92
shock, 173, 174, 190
shoot, 127, 149, 164, 211
short supply, 156
shortage, xiv, 47, 50, 73, 109, 116, 124, 128, 129, 133, 222
shortages, 30
short-term, 165, 166
shunts, 12
Siemens, 92
sign, 85
signaling, xv, 74
signals, 221

signs, 190, 228
sites, 37, 81, 86, 106, 111, 119, 168, 172, 173, 209, 243, 247, 266
skeleton, 172, 206
skilled labor, 171
skills, 92, 95, 116, 125, 126, 139, 149, 151, 156, 157, 159, 162, 208, 210, 211, 222, 234, 239
sleep, 228
Slovenia, 182
smuggling, 118, 184, 224
social development, 239
social infrastructure, 55
social services, 184
social structure, 191
software, 121
Somalia, 255
South Korea, 150, 152
sovereignty, xv, 2, 74, 144, 150, 177, 179, 187, 238, 251
specialization, 110
spectrum, 35, 92, 112, 128, 153, 156, 220
speech, xv, 64, 141, 142, 145, 166, 194, 250, 251, 252
speed, 93, 239
sponsor, vii, x, 69, 166, 169
sporadic, 102
sports, 234
stability, vii, x, xii, xiv, xv, 1, 25, 27, 69, 71, 73, 74, 86, 94, 95, 102, 104, 141, 142, 146, 149, 151, 153, 163, 167, 176, 177, 242, 260
stabilization, viii, 17, 46, 68, 146
stabilize, 31, 43, 54
staff development, 129
staffing, 40, 41, 60, 82, 92, 161, 179, 236, 238
stages, 80, 159, 187, 213, 219, 220, 264
stakeholders, 77
standard of living, 94
standardization, 156
standards, ix, 19, 26, 58, 115, 130, 165, 211
State Department, 64, 169, 170, 206, 238, 239, 257, 266
state-owned, 84, 87, 228
state-owned banks, 84, 87
state-owned enterprises, 228
statistics, 127, 133
steady state, 36, 133
stock, 111, 123
storage, 97, 114, 127, 131
storms, 174
strain, 130, 147
strategic planning, 45, 48, 62, 116, 206, 207, 225
streams, 44

strength, 4, 5, 7, 81, 101, 107, 117, 119, 123, 127, 129, 133, 139, 151, 182, 190, 197, 268
stress, 147, 151, 180, 181, 204, 215, 242, 251, 261, 266
stretching, 164
strikes, 167, 187, 192, 202, 204, 248, 255, 261
students, 110, 115, 116, 127, 128, 129, 187, 223
success rate, 246
suffering, 98, 102
suicide, 63, 96, 97, 99, 101, 193, 197, 232, 247
suicide bombers, 96, 97, 99, 193, 232, 247
summer, 5, 80, 107, 168, 179, 182, 184, 192, 210, 227, 234, 245, 247, 251, 252, 270
Sunni, xi, xii, 2, 3, 5, 6, 7, 8, 9, 10, 13, 52, 70, 71, 75, 76, 94, 98, 100, 101, 102, 132, 133, 143, 148, 149, 160, 180, 182, 185, 186, 191, 192, 193, 199, 200, 216, 227, 228, 229, 230, 233, 252, 261, 272, 273
supervision, 39, 182, 207, 223
supervisors, 59
supplemental, 4, 35, 83, 84, 113, 121
supply, xiv, 26, 29, 49, 73, 83, 88, 90, 92, 94, 111, 114, 125, 128, 174, 199, 218, 244, 247
Supreme Court, 260
surface-to-air missiles, 255
Surgeon General, 124
surgical, 183
surplus, ix, 19, 46, 47, 67
surprise, 168, 174
surveillance, xii, 72, 107, 159, 181, 215, 219, 248
suspects, 109
sustainability, 49
sustainable development, 244
Switzerland, 62
symbols, 12
synchronization, 126, 167
Syria, xiv, 55, 56, 62, 73, 80, 81, 183, 193

T

tactics, 63, 68, 101, 183, 189, 192, 202, 203, 212
TAL, 2, 3
tankers, 118
tanks, 125, 174, 216, 255
target identification, 205
targets, 79, 102, 153, 159, 164, 167, 172, 198, 199, 204, 205, 228, 229, 248, 255
task force, 80, 123, 180, 201, 203, 253
taxes, 46, 61, 67
teaching, 111, 245
team members, 211
technical assistance, 44, 78, 84, 157
technicians, 50, 88, 124

Tehran, xii, 71, 81, 184, 187, 188, 260
telecommunications, 90
temperature, 199
tenants, 106
tension, xv, 8, 74, 83, 101, 102, 238, 252
tenure, 191, 238, 257
term plans, xiii, 72
terminals, 87
territorial, 109, 166, 251, 268
territory, xii, 71, 152, 175, 176, 187, 195, 261, 262
terrorism, vii, x, xv, 35, 69, 70, 76, 103, 132, 141, 142, 145, 151, 165, 166, 182, 186, 221
terrorist, xii, 71, 100, 103, 109, 139, 151, 166, 184, 222, 226, 260, 262, 264
terrorist groups, 103
terrorists, xv, 12, 78, 104, 141, 143, 151, 165, 167, 189, 197, 198, 268, 273
testimony, 161, 194, 218, 245, 252, 257, 269, 270, 271, 275
thinking, 170, 196, 218
threat, xii, 25, 26, 49, 71, 81, 102, 103, 123, 139, 143, 145, 152, 160, 182, 203, 232, 247, 251, 255, 256
threatened, 8, 192
threatened violence, 8
threatening, 229
threats, 13, 27, 105, 144, 160, 166, 167, 216, 220, 231
threshold, 3, 6, 11
time consuming, 29, 113
time frame, x, 69, 75, 169, 178, 272
timetable, ix, 5, 18, 22, 23, 24, 25, 28, 146
timing, 173, 192
tissue, 160
title, 250, 255
tolerance, 81
Tonga, xiii, 72
top-down, 243
total expenditures, 47, 61
total revenue, 47
tourism, 86
tourist, 86
tourniquet, 263
tracking, 113, 123
traction, 189
trade, 34, 35, 81, 82, 95, 151, 165, 193
traffic, 93, 108, 116, 129, 184, 219, 221, 224
trainees, 126, 132
training programs, 51, 75, 127, 129, 207, 236
trajectory, 182, 247
trans, 91, 138
transcript, 254, 258, 259, 261, 262, 264, 267, 269, 270, 272, 273

transcripts, 254, 258, 259, 261, 262, 264, 267, 269, 271, 272, 273
transfer, x, 26, 35, 52, 69, 74, 75, 76, 87, 95, 113, 119, 145, 159, 160, 177, 179, 237, 259
transformation, 151, 167
Transitional Administrative Law, 2, 262
transitions, 41, 147, 149, 151, 158, 245
translation, 9
transmission, 50, 91, 111
transparency, 35, 122
transparent, 35, 201, 239
transport, 126, 216, 219
transportation, xiv, 29, 34, 73, 81, 90, 111, 114, 125, 138, 162, 177, 203, 240
transportation infrastructure, 90
reasury, ix, 19, 44, 48, 50, 58, 60, 61, 66, 67, 79, 85, 87
treaties, 118
trial, 52, 79, 122, 153
tribal, 2, 5, 7, 8, 95, 100, 132, 149, 185, 191, 227, 228, 229, 231, 232, 234, 237, 243, 254, 272
tribes, 8, 100, 229, 248, 271
troop surge, 4, 13, 143
trucks, 118
trust, xii, 44, 72, 103, 105, 109, 158
trust fund, 44
Tunisia, 80
turbulent, 212
Turkey, xiv, 10, 73, 80, 82, 103, 148, 168, 174, 182, 186, 187, 261
turnout, 77
turnover, 129

U

U.N. Security Council, 165, 177, 255
U.S. Agency for International Development, ix, 19, 39, 50, 58, 78, 138, 238, 253, 273, 274
U.S. Department of Agriculture, 90, 138, 253
U.S. Department of Agriculture (USDA), 90
U.S. Treasury, 85
UAE, 80, 85, 87, 138
Ukraine, xiii, 72, 182
UN, 25, 26, 44, 45, 55, 57, 59, 61, 62, 63, 68, 74, 77, 78, 80, 82, 123, 138, 150, 177, 182, 251, 259
uncertainty, 165
unclassified, 58, 60, 64, 166
underemployment, 83, 86, 98, 260
unemployment, 83, 86, 98, 260
UNHCR, 55, 56, 62, 82, 138
uniform, 252
United Arab Emirates, xiv, 73, 80, 138

United Kingdom, xii, 44, 72, 76, 150, 164, 169, 172, 176, 179, 181, 182, 255
United Nations, xi, 2, 25, 44, 50, 53, 54, 55, 56, 59, 62, 63, 70, 82, 138, 143, 144, 164, 165, 176, 177, 182, 186, 255, 258, 259
United Nations High Commissioner for Refugees, 56, 62, 138, 186
universities, 90, 236
Unmanned Aerial Vehicles, 265
updating, 62
urban areas, 118, 157, 158, 173, 174, 183, 186
USAID, ix, 19, 39, 58, 62, 78, 84, 90, 138, 239
USDA, 90, 138

V

vacancies, 4, 243
validation, 121
values, 115
variables, 248
variation, 153, 156, 240
vehicles, 47, 111, 114, 123, 133, 174, 194, 203, 231, 247
vessels, 131, 220
veterans, 5, 121
Vice President, ix, 19, 81
Vietnam, 193, 194, 255, 256, 262
violence, vii, viii, ix, xi, xiv, 1, 4, 6, 8, 13, 17, 19, 22, 47, 58, 63, 70, 71, 74, 75, 86, 93, 95, 96, 98, 100, 101, 102, 105, 107, 114, 143, 148, 149, 160, 182, 183, 184, 185, 186, 195, 196, 198, 199, 201, 222, 227, 232, 233, 268
violent, xii, xiv, 6, 8, 25, 63, 71, 73, 100, 105, 182, 183, 227, 228, 230, 248
violent crime, xiv, 73
visas, 56
visible, 147, 170, 173, 190, 194, 212, 222, 248
vision, xiv, xv, 74, 113, 142, 167, 221
vocational, 79, 95, 234
vocational training, 95, 234
voice, 102, 149, 183
voicing, 235
Volunteers, 230, 232
voter turnout, 77
voters, 2, 3, 6, 7, 10, 77, 96
voting, 6, 12
vulnerability, 93

W

wage payments, 113
wages, 84, 119
Wall Street Journal, 261, 264

war, vii, viii, xv, 18, 22, 24, 35, 40, 141, 142, 145, 147, 154, 162, 163, 164, 165, 166, 167, 168, 169, 170, 171, 172, 174, 175, 178, 179, 180, 187, 188, 189, 190, 206, 214, 238, 253, 255, 258, 261, 263, 265
War on Terror, viii, 17, 34, 60, 68, 250, 257, 262
warehousing, 111, 127
warfare, 153
warrants, 25, 27, 77, 159, 160, 237
Washington Post, 250, 251, 252, 254, 255, 256, 258, 261, 262, 263, 264, 270, 275
water, viii, xiv, 17, 22, 39, 49, 50, 51, 61, 68, 73, 89, 90, 92, 118, 188, 241
watershed, xv, 141, 142
waterways, 50
weakness, 84, 113, 121
weapons, xv, 25, 79, 97, 109, 118, 121, 125, 126, 127, 128, 133, 141, 143, 164, 176, 177, 187, 194, 195, 200, 202, 203, 204, 205, 246, 248, 261
weapons of mass destruction, xv, 141, 143, 164, 261
weapons of mass destruction (WMD), 164
websites, 100
wells, 173
White House, 166, 178, 194, 196, 197, 250, 251, 252, 255, 259, 262, 263, 264

wholesale, 5
winning, 2, 8, 15, 104
winter, 78
withdrawal, x, 5, 69, 76, 144, 145, 146, 147, 155, 157, 181, 251
WMD, 164, 165, 166, 168, 172, 261
women, 3, 4, 6, 12, 79, 96, 115
wood, 236, 244
workers, 6, 93
Workers Party, 186
workforce, 33, 40
working groups, 170
workload, 32, 40, 41
World Bank, 44, 50, 84, 87
World Food Program, 62
worry, 252

Y

Yemen, 80
yield, 121, 191
young men, 236